The Case for Eyewitness Identification Reform

WILLIAM COLLINS

ABA
AMERICAN BAR ASSOCIATION
Criminal Justice Section

Cover design by Jill Tedhams/ABA Design

Printed in the United States of America.

28 27 26 25 24   5 4 3 2 1

Library of Congress Cataloging-in-Publication Data

Names: Collins, William (Writer on eyewitness identification), author.
Title: The case for eyewitness identification reform / William Collins.
Description: Chicago : American Bar Association, 2024. | Includes bibliographical references. | Summary: "This book is divided into seven chapters. The first four concern the status quo with respect to eyewitness identification procedures and the laws response to them. Chapter 1 lays out the existing eyewitness identification practices used in most jurisdictions; Chapter 2 sets forth the law governing eyewitness identification admissibility, as embodied primarily by U.S. Supreme Court's decision in Manson, 432 U.S. 98; Chapter 3 examines how judges tend to instruct juries with respect to the reliability of eyewitness identification evidence, focusing on the D.C. Circuit's opinion United States v. Telfaire, 469 F.2d 552 (D.C. Cir. 1972) (per curiam); and Chapter 4 examines the circumstances under which experts are permitted to testify regarding the reliability of eyewitness identification evidence"-- Provided by publisher.
Identifiers: LCCN 2024017675 (print) | LCCN 2024017676 (ebook) | ISBN 9781639055203 (hardcover) | ISBN 9781639055210 (ebook)
Subjects: LCSH: Eyewitness identification--United States. | Admissible evidence--United States. | Expert evidence--United States. | United States. Supreme Court. | Law reform--United States. | Perception. | Memory.
Classification: LCC KF9672 .C65 2024 (print) | LCC KF9672 (ebook) | DDC 347.73/66--dc23/eng/20240512
LC record available at https://lccn.loc.gov/2024017675
LC ebook record available at https://lccn.loc.gov/2024017676

To Emily Voshell, whose expertise in this area (and many others) predates and outstrips my own. Without your help and encouragement, I never could have written this book.

To the late Richard K. Gilbert, Esq., whose enthusiasm for improving jury instructions related to eyewitness identification helped to inspire this book.

To my colleagues in the appellate division who likewise inspired and encouraged me.

Contents

Introduction: (Why) Do Eyewitness Identifications Still Matter?

If you are reading this book, then you are probably already at least somewhat aware of the special problems that eyewitness identifications present for the criminal legal system and those who have the misfortune to find themselves at its mercy. You may be aware that such identifications have a well-deserved reputation for being one of the least reliable, most persuasive forms of evidence known to man.[1] You may also be aware that, as of the writing of this book, they have contributed to more than 12,000 years of wrongful incarceration suffered by nearly one thousand people since 1989.[2] You may be even further aware that, at least at one time not too long ago, mistaken identifications were "responsible for more wrongful convictions than all other causes combined"[3] and that this problem affects Black Americans much more than whites.[4]

Despite all of this, there is much reason to think that, when it comes to the scourge of misidentification-related false convictions, the worst may be behind us. Because DNA testing has become so widely available and is so

1. Innocence Staff, *How Eyewitness Misidentification Can Send Innocent People to Prison*, Innocence Project (Apr. 14, 2020), https://innocenceproject.org/how-eyewitness-misidentification-can-send-innocent-people-to-prison/.

2. *Exonerations in the United States Map*, Nat'l Registry Exonerations, https://www.law.umich.edu/special/exoneration/Pages/Exonerations-in-the-United-States-Map.aspx.

3. *2019 Report of the United States Court of Appeals for the Third Circuit Task Force on Eyewitness Identifications*, 92 Temp. L. Rev. 1, 10-11 (2019).

4. *See, e.g.*, Margaret Bull Kovera, *The Role of Suspect Development Practices in Eyewitness Identification Accuracy and Racial Disparities in Wrongful Conviction*, 17 Soc. Issues Pol'y Rev. 125 (2024), https://doi.org/10.1111/sipr.12102; Samuel R. Gross et al., Race and Wrongful Convictions in the United States 2022, at iii (2022), https://www.law.umich.edu/special/exoneration/Documents/Race%20Report%20Preview.pdf.

"effective at identifying a person who left testable biological evidence at a particular location," the National Registry of Exonerations estimates "that for the last 14 years, all (or nearly all) innocent rape suspects in the United States who might benefit from DNA testing were never convicted because the DNA evidence cleared them before trial."[5] Meanwhile, mistaken identifications do not figure as prominently in other types of wrongful convictions.[6] Other wrongful convictions have been prevented thanks to the availability of surveillance and location data that cell phones and wireless carriers routinely gather and store.[7] Meanwhile, over the course of the past decade and a half, judges and policymakers in many jurisdictions have adopted best practice reforms in a number of areas designed to reduce the likelihood of wrongful conviction due to mistaken identification. All of this suggests that the scope of the eyewitness identification problem is diminishing.

So, are we in the clear? Should those who have thus far devoted their careers to understanding and exposing the power of suggestion in the context of eyewitness identification declare victory and refocus their attention on other worthy causes, like reining in our rapidly expanding surveillance state? Should those responsible for training America's public defenders remove eyewitness identification from their curricula? Should I have devoted my precious time away from work to researching and writing this book? Should you devote any of your precious time to reading it?

You alone know the answer to the last question. But my answer to the first two is emphatically "no." It would be a mistake to think that society will be rid of the special reliability problems associated with eyewitness identification any time soon. For one thing, not every crime will happen on a camera or involve the transfer of DNA. For another, there may be times when other methods help only to narrow down a suspect but do not resolve the question of identity in a manner that prosecutors find sufficiently convincing. Surveillance may not capture facial features in fine enough detail. Although DNA testing is even more sensitive than it used to be, mixtures can be difficult to interpret. In such cases, authorities will turn to eyewitness identification for confirmation if possible. And for as long as show-ups and photo arrays do not require a suspect's consent or judicial preauthorization, police may prefer them to those methods that may require one or the other.

5. Gross et al., *supra* note 4, at iii at 25–26.
6. *Id.*
7. *See, e.g.*, Joseph Goldstein, *Jailing the Wrong Man: Mug Shot Searches Persist in New York, Despite Serious Risks*, N.Y. Times, Jan. 5, 2019, https://www.nytimes.com/2019/01/05/nyregion/nypd-mug-shots-false-identification.html.

Most importantly, for all the well-publicized fallibility of eyewitness identification evidence, prosecutors and police still have good reason to think that jurors find them uniquely persuasive. As a preeminent scholar in the field once wrote, "there is almost nothing more convincing than a live human being who takes the stand, points a finger at the defendant, and says 'That's the one!'"[8] This observation has been confirmed by research published as recently as 2020—when an eyewitness expresses certainty about an identification on the witness stand, mock jurors have a hard time setting that certainty aside to consider other salient factors, even when the eyewitness was not sure about the identification during their first encounter with the mock defendant.[9] For as long as this remains true, police will have a strong incentive to pursue eyewitness identifications, no matter how unreliable they are.

Creating meaningful safeguards against the risk of wrongful arrest, prosecution, and conviction due to mistaken identification is a more pressing moral obligation than ever because we have a better understanding of the factors that lead to mistaken identification than we ever have, and even a single preventable wrongful conviction is one too many. Moreover, the risks of mistaken identification are not equally born by all members of society. "Black people are 13.6 percent of the American population but 53 percent of the 3,200 exonerations listed in the National Registry of Exonerations. Judging from exonerations, innocent Black Americans are seven times more likely than white Americans to be falsely convicted of serious crimes."[10] As discussed more throughout the course of this book, being mistakenly identified as the perpetrator of a crime can have life altering consequences—such as the loss of liberty or employment and the almost inevitable trauma from being arrested—even when that false identification does not ultimately lead to a wrongful conviction.

This book is divided into seven chapters. The first four concern the status quo with respect to eyewitness identification procedures and the law's response to them. Chapter 1 lays out the existing eyewitness identification practices used in most jurisdictions; Chapter 2 sets forth the law governing eyewitness identification admissibility, as embodied primarily by the U.S. Supreme Court's decision in *Manson v. Brathwaite*, 432 U.S. 98 (1977); Chapter 3 examines how judges tend to instruct juries with respect to the

---

8. *Watkins v. Sowders*, 449 U.S. 341, 352 (1981) (Brennan, J., dissenting) (emphasis in original omitted) (quoting Elizabeth F. Loftus, Eyewitness Testimony 19 (1979)).

9. Brandon L. Garrett et al., *Factoring the Role of Eyewitness Evidence in the Courtroom*, 17 J. Empirical L. Stud. 556, 557 (2020), https://doi.org/10.1111/jels.12259.

10. Gross et al., *supra* note 4, at iii.

reliability of eyewitness identification evidence, focusing on the D.C. Circuit's opinion *United States v. Telfaire*, 469 F.2d 552 (D.C. Cir. 1972) (per curiam); and Chapter 4 examines the circumstances under which experts are permitted to testify regarding the reliability of eyewitness identification evidence.

In each of these first four chapters, the book addresses three questions: (1) where are we (or what is the current state of law and/or practice); (2) how did we get here (or what circumstances led to this particular state of affairs); and (3) what's wrong with the status quo (or why is the current system in need of reform)? The second question is critical but sometimes overlooked in discussions about eyewitness identification reform, which tend to focus (correctly, in my view) on the considerable progress that psychologists have made toward understanding the vagaries of perception and memory over the past fifty years, since the key cases in this area were decided. The findings of this research are a necessary point of departure in any discussion about the merits of key eyewitness identification precedent, as it reveals just how much we have learned about eyewitness reliability since these landmark cases were decided. Even so, it is only by placing the current police practices and the legal regimes that have enabled them into the proper sociohistorical context that we might understand and overcome institutional and cultural barriers to change.[11]

Chapter 5 summarizes recent research on memory and perception, insofar as it relates to eyewitness identification. Chapter 6 sets forth the system and estimator variables. Chapter 7 makes the case for a three-pronged approach to reform; that is, barring identification evidence that is either (1) obtained by suggestive means, taking into account all system variables, or (2) whose probative value does not substantially outweigh its prejudice when taking into account both system and estimator variables, and further (3) instructing juries to consider both system and estimator variables, insofar as they are implicated by the evidence, noting the recent efforts of states across the country to implement such changes. Embracing these recommendations will not only reduce the number of wrongful convictions. By effectively deterring suggestive police practice, it should reduce the number of lesser intrusions upon the liberty and property of the innocent, such as investigative detentions and arrests.

---

11. *See, e.g.*, Oona A. Hathaway, *Path Dependence in the Law: The Course and Pattern of Legal Change in a Common Law System*, 86 Iowa L. Rev. 101 (2003).

1

Police Identification Procedures

The vast majority of identifications that play any role in securing a criminal conviction or guilty plea arise out of an identification procedure that a law enforcement officer has arranged. So how do police obtain identifications? What techniques do police rely on to generate them? The following chapter attempts to answer this question, by providing an overview of the most commonly used procedures.

Before delving into specifics, a note about what it means for an eyewitness to identify someone, when the police are involved. To identify is to assert that two (temporally disparate) things are in fact (different instantiations of) the same thing.[1] An eyewitness identification is, in turn, any assertion of identity that is based on someone's powers of personal observation. ("Person A is the same person I saw robbing the convenience store.") Recognition is the feeling we get when we perceive something (we think) we have perceived before. Whether that feeling is strong or weak will depend, largely

1. *See, e.g.*, Wigmore, Science of Judicial Proof, § 250, at 532–34 (1937). This "diachronic" definition of identification applies in most legal settings, but there are others. *See, e.g.*, *Identity Over Time*, Stanford Encyclopedia of Philosophy (Oct. 6, 2016), https://plato.stanford.edu/entries/identity-time/.

but not exclusively, on factors outside of the police's control: namely, the strength of a person's recollection and how well they perceived the person they are trying to identify in the first place. However, strength of recognition is not the sole determinant of a person's willingness to identify. Rather, as discussed further in Chapter 5, that willingness also depends on how badly people want to avoid accusing or exonerating someone incorrectly.

As a practical matter, identification procedures do not just reveal when one person recognizes another; they reveal when a person's willingness to identify exceeds any reservations they may have about doing so, and they may induce that willingness in a manner that is unmoored from the strength of recognition. To paraphrase Glanville Williams, "the danger" of even the least suggestive lineup "is that the witness expects to find the guilty person present, and therefore points out the man who he thinks is most like the one he remembers."[2] Herein lies the problem: although the legal system depends on identification procedures to generate proof of genuine recognition, it may not be clear how poorly they perform in this regard until better evidence (DNA, typically) emerges to contradict the results. In this way they are not unlike police interrogation techniques. As, "[i]n an important sense," both identifications and confessions are the byproduct of a person's "interaction [with a] police investigator," they fall into a small category of evidence that police "generate" rather than "obtain."[3]

In attempting to understand these procedures, it is important to consider the historical context for their development. In this regard, eyewitness identification procedures have much in common with interrogation techniques. Both developed in response to "the rise of cities and the creation of organized police departments" during the late 1800s.[4] Before this time, both interrogation and identification were largely "public affair[s]," administered by magistrates in open court.[5] Just as the "increase in crime" led police to develop new methods of extracting confessions in private,[6] so too did it spark the development of extrajudicial identification procedures to appease the public's growing desire for carceral responses to crime. Moreover, just as

---

2. Glanville Williams, Proof of Guilt 96 (1957).

3. Sandra Guerra Thompson, *Judicial Gatekeeping of Police-Generated Witness Testimony*, 102 J. Crim. L. & Criminology 329, 331 (2012).

4. James L. Trainum, How the Police Generate False Confessions: An Inside Look at the Interrogation Room 11 (2016).

5. *Id.*

6. *Id.*

the increased perception of insecurity served to diminish "long held skepticism" toward the interrogation methods that police innovated,[7] so too did it help to expand novel identification procedures, even in the absence of studies tending to prove their validity.

Regarding the identification procedures and protocols that modern police officers favor, there has not been much empirical research. This section relies heavily on a survey of more than 600 law enforcement agencies across the country conducted by the Police Executive Research Forum (PERF) in 2010 and 2011.[8] This survey has its limitations, chief among them that the data gathered are now more than ten years old. More recent data are needed to gauge how much our rapidly increasing surveillance and facial recognition capacity have changed the landscape of eyewitness identification evidence and whether recent calls for more accountable policing following the killings of unarmed Black women and men have forced tighter internal regulation in the area of eyewitness identification. In the absence of more recent data, however, the 2010 survey provides a certain degree of insight into how training and policy concerning police identifications have evolved over the years and the direction in which they are trending currently. In this regard, it is worth noting that, at least as of 2010, most policing agencies in the country left the administration of identification procedures to the discretion of individual officers and their immediate supervisors in the chain of command—77 percent of agencies lacked any formal written policy for show-ups and 64 percent reported no written policy for lineups or photo arrays.[9]

The ensuing discussion distinguishes between those police identification procedures, such as lineups, photo-arrays, and show-ups, that are designed to probe whether (and generate proof that) an eyewitness recognizes the target of an investigation, and those, such as mugshot searches, sketches, composites, and field views, that are designed to help narrow the universe of potential suspects to one or more people whom they could investigate further (while also generating evidence of identity that could be admissible

7. *Id.*

8. Police Exec. Rsch. F., A National Survey of Eyewitness Identification Procedures in Law Enforcement Agencies (2013), [hereinafter PERF Survey], https://www.policeforum.org/assets/docs/Free_Online_Documents/Eyewitness_Identification/a%20national%20survey%20of%20eyewitness%20identification%20procedures%20in%20law%20enforcement%20agencies%202013.pdf.

9. *Id.* at 29.

in court). Although many resources have been devoted to understanding what tends to make lineups and other "recognition" procedures more or less fair, suggestive, or reliable, "narrowing" procedures warrant at least as much scrutiny, as they are frequently used to narrow down the identity of a suspect who is then placed in a lineup and "have the potential to introduce biases of the sort that blind lineup procedures are designed to avoid."[10]

I. When Police Already Have a Suspect in Mind . . .

A. Live Lineups

In a live lineup, the target of an investigation is presented to the accused in person, alongside one or more other "fillers" or "foils" who either resemble the suspect or fit the description of the perpetrator that the witness has provided.[11] Such confrontations almost always take place inside of a police station. To protect the eyewitness's identity, the eyewitness usually views the lineup from behind a one-way mirror.[12] Live lineups are most often conducted with five fillers,[13] who may be instructed to sit or stand.[14]

Among Western law enforcement agencies, use of the live lineup dates back to the nineteenth century. The earliest recorded lineup or "identity parade," as it is known in the United Kingdom, was convened in 1821 to uncover the identity of the British soldiers responsible for killing two civilians at Cumberland Gate during Queen Caroline's funeral procession.[15] As explained further in Table 1.1, this parade was a high-profile failure that yielded no criminal charges. Nevertheless, from this inauspicious start, the identity parade eventually spread throughout "those countries in which the English system of prosecution is followed."[16]

---

10. NAT'L RSCH. COUNCIL OF THE NAT'L ACADS., IDENTIFYING THE CULPRIT: ASSESSING EYEWITNESS IDENTIFICATION 29 (2014) [hereinafter NAT'L RSCH. COUNCIL].

11. *Id.* at 25; PERF SURVEY, *supra* note 8, at 104.

12. NAT'L RSCH. COUNCIL, *supra* note 10, at 25.

13. PERF Survey, *supra* note 8, at 104.

14. NAT'L RSCH. COUNCIL, *supra* note 10, at 25.

15. EDWARD HIGGS, IDENTIFYING THE ENGLISH: A HISTORY OF PERSONAL IDENTIFICATION 1500 TO THE PRESENT 128 (2017).

16. P. DEVLIN, REPORT TO THE SECRETARY OF STATE FOR THE HOME DEPARTMENT OF THE DEPARTMENTAL COMMITTEE ON EVIDENCE OF IDENTIFICATION IN CRIMINAL CASES ¶ 1.10, at 3 (1976) [hereinafter DEVLIN REPORT].

The First "Identity Parade"

In addition to being politically charged, the identity parade to identify the Cumberland Gate shooters was marred by poor viewing conditions and interference from the barracks where it took place. Before her death, Queen Caroline had been an icon of the radical reform movement that swept Britain's working class after the Napoleonic wars. Public support for her only intensified after King George IV sought to annul their marriage, on the eve of his ascension to the throne in 1820. Upon her death, mere weeks after George's coronation, authorities planned a funeral procession via an unpublicized route, for fear that the traditional path through London's city center would start a riot. In retaliation for this perceived slight, the Queen's supporters erected barricades along the procession route and threw rocks at the guards who tried to remove them. The guards, in turn, opened fire, killing two.

The funeral procession of Queen Caroline Augut [sic], 14 1821 at Cumberland Gate, Hyde Park. [England: Pub. Augut by T Dolby, 299 Strand]. Photograph. https://www.loc.gov/item/2006689143/.

During the subsequent inquest, the Grand Jury petitioned to have the entire troop paraded, in uniform and on horseback, before those eyewitnesses who professed some ability to identify the perpetrators. The request was approved by the presiding magistrate and the Secretary of State. However, when the eyewitnesses arrived at the barracks for the parade, some were turned away, and those permitted to enter were subjected to prolonged detention before the parade went forward. When the parade finally began, each witness was permitted a single, hurried inspection of the many guards presented, and multiple witnesses complained of poor viewing conditions. In the end, only one witness made an identification. Even so, the grand jury returned a verdict of "murder by an officer to the jury unknown" and the matter concluded without charges.

By all accounts, the catalyst for the spread of the identity parade was "judicial criticism of cruder methods of identification such as a direct confrontation between the witness and the suspect," that is, the show-up.[17] Notably, although the identity parade used to investigate the Cumberland Gate shootings occurred in 1821, London's Metropolitan Police Department did not include the identity parade in its operations manual until 1860, upon "some remarks of the Assistant Judge of the Middlesex Session."[18]

Despite having remained a familiar trope of police procedurals until very recently,[19] live lineups are now fairly uncommon in the United States, having been supplanted by photographic lineups. Indeed, although lineups were a regular feature of shows like *Law and Order* in the 1990s, they were on the decline even then. A nationwide survey of police departments published in 1993 found that the average officer had conducted more than four times as many photographic lineups as live lineups in the preceding year (thirty-nine photographic lineups to nine live lineups).[20] By 2010, live lineups were the most infrequently used identification procedure in the United States, with only about one-fifth of U.S. law enforcement agencies (21 percent) reporting

17. *Id.*

18. *Id.* ¶ 5.29, at 112.

19. In the cold open to an episode of the TV sitcom *Brooklyn Nine-Nine* that originally aired in 2018, the protagonist leads a lineup in a rendition of the song "I Want It That Way" by the Backstreet Boys. *See Brooklyn Nine-Nine: DFW* (Fox television broadcast Apr. 12, 2018); *see also* Brooklyn Nine-Nine, *I Want It That Way*, YouTube (Oct. 11, 2018), https://youtu.be/HlBYdiXdUa8?si=BUe6BIAn-UtL5Uiu.

20. Michael S. Wolgalter et al., *How Police Officers Construct Lineups: A National Survey*, 37 Proc. Hum. Factors & Ergonomics Soc'y 37th Ann. Meeting 640, 641 (1993), https://www.academia.edu/download/64901312/62_Wogalter_Malpass_Burger_1993_.pdf.

any live lineup in the preceding twelve months.[21] Among those agencies, the average number of lineups conducted was just two.[22] The vast majority of departments (84 percent) had no formal policy concerning live lineup composition or administration and "[f]ewer than 10 percent" of agencies administered any training on how to conduct them.[23]

The live lineup's decline is consistent with its relative lack of convenience and utility from a law enforcement perspective.[24] Live lineups require the suspect's physical presence, and thus have almost no value as a means of securing an arrest warrant.[25] Finding live fillers takes longer than retrieving filler photographs from a computer database.[26] Indeed, finding enough live fillers who fit the suspect's description may be impossible in smaller jurisdictions.[27] As will be discussed further in Chapter 2, conducting a live lineup may require judicial pre-authorization, whereas conducting a photographic lineup does not. Moreover, a live lineup may trigger a person's right to have counsel present depending on when it is conducted.[28] Police may not welcome defense counsel's presence, if they wish to conceal a witness's identity or if, as most defense lawyers believe, they wish to avoid exposing their methods to counsel's scrutiny.[29] Finally, as noted above, photographic lineups give police greater flexibility both as to lineup location and the concealment of distinguishing facial features that might otherwise stand out.

As will be discussed further in the context of photographic lineups, live lineups may be presented **simultaneously** (all at once) or **sequentially** (one-at-a-time) by administrators who are **nonblind, blind,** or **blinded.** Whereas truly blind administrators are blind to the identity of the identification target (i.e., the person suspected of committing the crime under investigation), and thus incapable of providing cues about that person's identity, blinded administrators know the target's identity but take precautions to

---

21. PERF SURVEY, *supra* note 8, at 48.

22. *Id.*

23. *Id.* at ix–x, 57.

24. NAT'L RSCH. COUNCIL, *supra* note 10, at 25.

25. *Id.* at 26 n.17.

26. *Id.* at 25.

27. *Id.* at 25; *see also, e.g.*, *Neil v. Biggers*, 409 U.S. 188, 195 (1972) ("In an effort to construct a suitable lineup, the police checked the city jail and the city juvenile home. Finding no one at either place fitting respondent's unusual physical description, they conducted a showup instead.").

28. *United States v. Wade*, 388 U.S. 218 (1967); *Gilbert v. California*, 388 U.S. 263 (1967).

29. *See, e.g.*, NAT'L RSCH. COUNCIL, *supra* note 10, at 25 (noting that counsel's presence makes live lineups "less attractive" to police and prosecutors).

avoid learning where that person is located in the lineup. As of 2010, most live lineups were presented simultaneously by a nonblind administrator.[30] Likewise, live lineups may be preceded by a variety of **preliminary instructions** and subject to a variety of **documentation** practices. Live lineups are more likely to be accompanied by formal written instructions and audiovisual documentation than photographic lineups,[31] but less likely to be constrained by a formal written policy or accompanied by a witness's confidence statement.[32]

B. Photographic Lineups

The photographic lineup or photospread is the identification procedure most commonly used by law enforcement agencies in the United States.[33] In a photographic lineup, an eyewitness is given the opportunity to identify a known suspect's photograph from among the photographs of other "fillers" or "foils" who either resemble the suspect or fit the description of the perpetrator that the witness has provided.[34] Over the years, researchers have examined how the location, composition, presentation, and documentation of a lineup can affect its fairness and reliability. The findings of their research have been incorporated into police practice only selectively.

1. Location

There is general consensus that lineups should be administered somewhere that "avoids exposing the witness to information or evidence that could influence the witness's identification, including information about the case, the progress of the investigation, or the suspect."[35] A witness should not overhear a detective discussing the status of the case or see a suspect's face on a wanted poster or a BOLO ("Be on the Lookout") flier before viewing a lineup.[36]

One potential advantage of photographic lineups over the live, in-person alternative is that photographic lineups can theoretically be reviewed in a

---

30. PERF Survey, *supra* note 8, at 63.

31. *Id.* at 52, 54.

32. *Id.* at 53–54.

33. Nat'l Rsch. Council, *supra* note 10, at 23; PERF Survey, *supra* note 8, at 104 at 48, 58.

34. PERF Survey, *supra* note 8, at 104; Nat'l Rsch. Council, *supra* note 10, at 23.

35. Memorandum from Sally Yates, Deputy Attorney General, to Heads of Department Law Enforcement Components, All Department Prosecutors 1 (Jan. 6, 2017), https://www.justice.gov/file/923201/download [hereinafter Yates Memo].

36. *See id.* at 1.

variety of locations, unlike live lineups, which are difficult, if not impossible, to conduct outside of a police station.[37] A detective may offer to present a photographic lineup to a witness in his or her home or workplace, if going to the station is not convenient. However, the need to document the results of the lineup in a particular way, for instance, by video recording it (see the following discussion), may impede this flexibility.

2. *Composition*

Whether a lineup is live or photographic, lineup composition "is a matter of great importance."[38] Lineup composition encompasses a variety of issues that might affect a lineup's reliability, including the number of fillers in the lineup, the selection of those fillers, and the formatting.

a. Number of Fillers

The majority practice in the United States, which has been endorsed by the U.S. Department of Justice (DOJ),[39] is to use at least five filler photographs in each lineup.[40] Nevertheless, at last check, only about 70 percent of jurisdictions mandate the use of a specific number of fillers, and among those jurisdictions that had no policy in place, the number of fillers used ranged from one to eleven.

b. Filler Selection

For the lineup to serve as a meaningful test of the witness's recognition of the suspect, fillers must be unknown and unfamiliar to the witness and selected based on how well they approximate any description that the witness provided earlier in the investigation.[41] Psychologists have developed various methods of testing whether a lineup has been fairly constructed. These methods involve using mock witnesses to assess whether the lineup participants are sufficiently similar to each other and/or any verbal description that the eyewitness has provided to serve as a true test of the eyewitness's

---

37. *See, e.g.*, *Stovall v. Denno*, 388 U.S. 293, 302 (1967).

38. Elizabeth F. Loftus, Eyewitness Testimony 144 (2d ed. 1996).

39. Yates Memo, *supra* note 35, at 2; U.S. Dep't of Just., Off. Just. Programs, Eyewitness Evidence: A Guide for Law Enforcement 9 (1999), https://www.ojp.gov/pdffiles1/nij/178240.pdf.

40. PERF Survey, *supra* note 8, at 58.

41. Nat'l Rsch. Council, *supra* note 10, at 23.

recollection of the perpetrator.[42] These measures are discussed in Chapter 6 on **system variables.**

For the past few decades, the task of selecting fillers for photographic lineups has been greatly simplified by the use of computer systems with access to image databases.[43] These computer systems retrieve filler photographs based on user-selected criteria that may include gender, race, hair length and color, facial hair, height, skin tone, and other distinguishing features. These computer systems further allow officers to reject fillers, when the officer determines that they are suggestive or otherwise inappropriate. In these circumstances, the system generates an alternate photograph for the officer to use in the lineup.

Finally, these computer systems allow officers to conceal and alter the distinguishing marks on a person's face to create a consistent appearance across suspect and fillers.[44] The DOJ recommends that alteration or concealment be used to address any "scar, tattoo, or mole, or distinctive clothing that would make [a suspect] stand out in a photo array."[45] However, as of 2010, fewer than 10 percent of U.S. law enforcement agencies had an official policy regarding such alterations.[46]

c. Photo Formatting

An area of concern specific to photographic lineup composition involves the consistency of formatting across photographs of the suspect and fillers. Variations in "size, background, format, and color" of the photograph and extraneous written information may hint at the source of the photograph—in particular, that it was taken at the time of an arrest—thereby biasing the witness's selection.[47] The DOJ recommends that photographs be "numbered or labeled in a manner that does not disclose any person's identity or the source of the photograph."[48] Computerized filler selection systems may help to ensure that photographs adhere to these basic guidelines.[49] Even so, in a recent survey, "only a small percentage [of agencies]

---

42. Jungwon Lee et al., *Validity of Mock-Witness Measures for Assessing Lineup Fairness*, 28 Psych., Crime, & L. 215 (2021), https://www.researchgate.net/publication/350459067_Validity_of_mock-witness_measures_for_assessing_lineup_fairness.
43. Nat'l Rsch. Council, *supra* note 10, at 23; U.S. Dep't of Just., *supra* note 39, at 9.
44. PERF Survey, *supra* note 8, at 57.
45. Yates Memo, *supra* note 35.
46. PERF Survey, *supra* note 8, at 57.
47. Yates Memo, *supra* note 35, at 2.
48. *Id.*
49. PERF Survey, *supra* note 8, at 75.

(12.1%)" reported "using computers for this purpose"[50] and less than half (42.1 percent) reported training their personnel that "administrators must ensure that no information regarding prior arrests is visible to witness on photos."[51]

3. *Presentation*

Police departments have developed a variety of methods for presenting photographic lineups to eyewitnesses. By far, the most common procedures involve printed photographs that the witness can examine.[52] However, a small but growing number of departments now arrange for lineups to be viewed on computer terminals or laptop computers.[53]

a. Preliminary Instructions

Because "[i]t is important that eyewitnesses understand how a lineup works and what is expected of them," "[t]he vast majority of agencies provide some type of general instructions to witnesses prior to an eyewitness identification procedure, and also require either a verbal or written acknowledgment from witnesses indicating that they understood the instructions provided."[54] Common instructions include:

- That the perpetrator may or may not be present in the lineup;
- That the witness need not make any identification;
- That the investigation will continue regardless of whether the witness makes an identification; and
- That the perpetrator's appearance may have changed since the incident.[55]

Although some agencies have elected to provide these instructions in writing and further to request written acknowledgment of the eyewitness understanding before the lineup begins,[56] as of 2010, the majority of agencies appeared to trust an exclusively oral methodology: only 40 percent provided written instructions and only 27.6 percent requested written acknowledgment of eyewitness understanding.[57]

---

50. *Id.* at 85.
51. *Id.* at 81.
52. *Id.* at 60–61.
53. *Id.*
54. PERF Survey, *supra* note 8, at 81–82; *see also* Yates Memo, *supra* note 35, at 3–4.
55. PERF Survey, *supra* note 8, at 52–53.
56. Yates Memo, *supra* note 35, at 3–4; U.S. Dep't of Just., *supra* note 39, at 33.
57. PERF Survey, *supra* note 8, at 52.

b. Simultaneous v. Sequential Administration

Photographic lineups may be viewed **simultaneously** or **sequentially**. When viewed simultaneously, they are typically presented in a two-by-three matrix, resulting in a photospread or -array, commonly referred to as a "six pack."[58] Most departments either print the six pack onto a single piece of paper or tape the separate photographs into a sleeve or a folder with precut holes or windows.[59]

If the lineup is sequential, the photographs may be handed to the witness one at a time in separate folders to prevent the lineup administrator from knowing when the witness is examining the suspect's photograph. In this kind of "blinded" sequential lineup, two folders containing only white paper may be inserted into the back of the lineup to prevent the witness from knowing that the array ends after the sixth photo.[60] This kind of "backloading" is done to alleviate any pressure the witness might feel to identify as the end of the array approaches.

The rules for conducting simultaneous photographic lineups are fairly straightforward. After receiving and reviewing the photo-array, the eyewitness tells the administrator whether he or she recognizes someone as the perpetrator or identification target. If the witness provides ambiguous feedback ("I think it's number 4."), the administrator may seek clarification ("What do you mean by that?").[61] If the witness makes a selection, the administrator documents the selection and, in most jurisdictions, makes some effort to ascertain and record the witness's level of confidence in their selection.[62]

On the other hand, authorities seem to have different ideas about what constitutes a sequential lineup. To most psychologists, sequential lineups require not only that witnesses view them one photograph at a time, but also that witnesses indicate whether or not they recognize the person in the photograph in front of them before being allowed to proceed to the next photograph.[63] However, the DOJ has emphasized that a witness should be advised that they may view the entire lineup before making a selection and

---

58. Nat'l Rsch. Council, *supra* note 10, at 23.
59. PERF Survey, *supra* note 8, at 60–61; Nat'l Rsch. Council, *supra* note 10, at 23.
60. Nat'l Rsch. Council, *supra* note 10, at 27.
61. Yates Memo, *supra* note 35, § 8.3 at 5.
62. PERF Survey, *supra* note 8, at 53–54.
63. *See, e.g.*, PERF Survey, *supra* note 8, at 118; Beth Schuster, *Police Lineups: Making Eyewitness Identification More Reliable*, Oct. 1, 2007, https://nij.ojp.gov/topics/articles/police-lineups-making-eyewitness-identification-more-reliable (accessed Aug. 12, 2022); Nat'l Rsch. Council, *supra* note 10, at 23 (noting that in a sequential lineup, "[o]fficers . . . display the photographs one at a time to the witness and ask whether she or he recognizes each one.").

that the lineup will continue even if they select someone before it ends.[64] The main difference between the DOJ's version of sequential and the psychological community's is that, in the DOJ's version, failure to identify someone cannot be construed as a nonidentification until the witness has seen the entire lineup enough times to satisfy their subjective decision-making criteria. On the other hand, the stricter version of "sequential" encourages witnesses to immediately exclude people they do not recognize, at least preliminarily, in order to move on to the next photograph.

Over the last few decades, scholars and legal professionals have studied and debated whether some form of sequential lineup produces more accurate, reliable identification decisions, and is therefore preferable to simultaneous lineups. This topic will be discussed in Chapter 6 on **system variables.**

c. Double-Blind/"Blinded" Administration

Another source of potential bias in photographic lineups involves the administrator's knowledge of the suspect and where he or she is located in the lineup. As detailed more in Chapter 6, "[l]aw enforcement officers . . . showing a witness a lineup or photo array may provide subtle cues that [can] impact an eyewitness's memory of the perpetrator without the officer even being aware of how his or her interaction with the witness is affecting the witness's memory."[65] Thus, "[t]he [lineup] administrator must avoid any words, sounds, expressions, actions or behaviors that suggest who the suspect is" and "ensure that he or she does not suggest to the witness—even unintentionally—which photograph contains the image of the suspect."[66]

To neutralize the risk of administrator influence, authorities recommend that lineups be presented by an administrator with no connection to the case and no knowledge of what the suspect looks like.[67] Such lineup procedures are considered "double blind" because neither the investigator nor the witness is aware of who is a suspect or a filler.[68] Where double-blind administration is not feasible (for instance, because a smaller department cannot spare the manpower), the authorities recommend that administrators "blind"

64. Yates Memo, *supra* note 35, § 6.3.9 at 3. Thus, if the witness wants to see a specific person's photograph again, the entire lineup should be presented again.

65. *2019 Report of the United States Court of Appeals for the Third Circuit Task Force on Eyewitness Identifications*, 92 Temp. L. Rev. 1, 25 (2019) [hereinafter *2019 Third Circuit Task Force Report*].

66. Yates Memo, *supra* note 35, §§ 5.1, 8.1 at 2, 5.

67. *Id.* § 5.1 at 2; Nat'l Rsch. Council, *supra* note 10, at 106.

68. Schuster, *supra* note 63.

themselves to the suspect's location in the lineup.[69] For simultaneous lineups, this kind of "blinded" administration can be accomplished by using a computer to randomize the order of the lineup and a physical barrier, like a wall or a screen, to block the administrator's view of the lineup.[70] Alternatively, administrators may utilize blinded sequential presentation, whereby lineup photographs are placed into separate folders, shuffled, and handed to the witness one at a time.[71] In this technique, the administrator's view of each photograph is blocked by the folder that contains it.

Despite how many authorities recommend blind administration, and despite how easy it is to blind an administrator, there appear to be a substantial number of law enforcement agencies that do not require blind administration. The most common objections to true double-blind administration involves the perceived benefit of having photo-arrays administered by those with whom eyewitnesses already have some rapport, so that these officers can put eyewitnesses at ease before the arrays are presented, and the additional manpower required for officers to serve as blind administrators.[72] As of 2010, most agencies had no official policy in this regard, and the clear majority practice was to forgo any form of blind administration.[73]

4. *Documentation*

Because lineup procedures can exert such a powerful influence on the reliability of the identification, thorough documentation of the identification process is a matter of great importance. Almost all U.S. law enforcement agencies require or encourage some kind of documentation when an identification procedure results in a positive identification.[74] However, documentation methods for these procedures vary widely across departments.

For some departments, documentation may be limited to the unstructured reporting by the administrator. Other departments require preparation of specialized reports.[75] The precise information included in these reports may vary, but it appears that most request a witness's **confidence**

---

69. Yates Memo, *supra* note 35, § 5.2 at 3.

70. *Id.* § 5.3 at 3.

71. *Id.* § 5.3 at 3; Nat'l Rsch. Council, *supra* note 10, at 27.

72. Nancy K. Steblay, Double-Blind Sequential Police Lineup Procedures: Toward an Integrated Laboratory & Field Practice Perspective 25 (2004), https://www.ojp.gov/pdffiles1/nij/grants/246939.pdf.

73. PERF Survey, *supra* note 8, at x.

74. *Id.* at 54–55.

75. *Id.* at 54, 88.

statement, that is, a verbatim self-report of how confident the witness is in the identification.[76] Other information sought by the report may include the names of those present during the procedure, the amount of time it took the witness to make an identification, the witness's emotional response to the person identified, and the number of times the witness viewed the lineup if it was sequential.[77] In addition, it is common to have witnesses document their own selections by signing and dating the photograph they have selected.[78] Finally, as of 2010, a small minority of departments had also begun video- and audio recording lineup administration.[79]

Documentation of nonidentifications is even more inconsistent among U.S. law enforcement agencies than documentation of positive identifications. Although a majority of U.S. law enforcement agencies (63 percent) required documentation of nonidentifications, that percentage was still less than the number that require or encourage documentation of identifications.[80] An even smaller percentage reported that they documented confidence statements related to those nonidentifications.

C. Video-Recorded Lineups

Although photographic lineups are unquestionably more convenient than their live counterparts, it has long been theorized that live lineups facilitate stronger recognition by allowing eyewitnesses to see more of a person's body, as well as any speech or mannerisms that might elicit recognition of the perpetrator.[81] The theory that live lineups provide a better identification opportunity than photographic lineups is called the "live superiority" hypothesis. Although it has found little support in experimental settings,[82] it nevertheless inspired some police departments to develop the capacity to administer video-recorded lineups, where participants are filmed from

---

76. *Id.* at 54–55; *see also id.* at 103 (defining confidence statement).

77. Yates Memo, *supra* note 35, § 9.3 at 6.

78. *Id.* § 9.2 at 6.

79. PERF Survey, *supra* note 8, at 54; Yates Memo, *supra* note 35, § 9.1.1 at 5.

80. PERF Survey, *supra* note 8, at 54–55.

81. Michael S. Wolgalter et al., *A National Survey of U.S. Police on Preparation and Conduct of Identification Lineups*, 10 Psychol. Crime & L. 69, 78 (2004); *see, e.g.*, Eva Rubínová et al., *Live Presentation for Eyewitness Identification Is Not Superior to Photo or Video Presentation*, 10 J. Appl. Rsch. Memory Cog. 167 (2021), https://www.sciencedirect.com/science/article/pii/S221136812030070X; Ryan J. Fitzgerald et al., *Eyewitness Identification: Live, Photo, and Video Lineups*, 24 Psychol. Crime & L. 307 (2018).

82. Rubínová et al., *supra* note 81; Fitzgerald et al., *supra* note 81.

various angles and distances, thereby preserving the "fidelity of live lineups" and allowing police to edit out "biasing behaviors."[83]

The idea for maintaining a database of such video-recorded likenesses has been attributed to John Henry Wigmore.[84] In Wigmore's version, the database would consist of "100 talking films of men from various occupations, races, etc.," with each person "photographed in a number of stock movements, with and without hat and coat, and . . . read[ing] aloud a standard passage."[85] Each of these videos would last at least two minutes.[86] When the police desired to administer a lineup, the eyewitness would view a film of the suspect alongside 24 different fillers prepared in the same manner, ranking their degree of certainty in any identification rendered according to a three-tiered scale.[87] At the turn of the twenty-first century, researchers predicted that the widespread availability of high quality, low cost video-recording technology might make this kind of video lineup "commonplace."[88] However, this future has yet to materialize in the United States.

The United Kingdom is a different story. There, photo-arrays never took hold, and video-recorded lineups are the predominant form of identification procedure used by law enforcement, having largely supplanted the live lineup early in the past 20 years.[89] In 2003, the West Yorkshire Police pioneered a system for creating video lineups called Video Identification Parade Electronic Recording or "VIPER" for short.[90] VIPER allows the police to assemble lineups from prerecorded videos of fillers.[91] As with the live lineups that the United Kingdom has favored historically, fillers are generally compensated for their appearances, and the system's integrity depends on the willingness of large numbers of people to contribute their likeness to VIPER's database. The resulting lineups can be viewed in an "identification suite" or even burned onto a DVD for home viewing (assuming the

83. Wolgalter et al., *supra* note 81, at 78.

84. *United States v. Wade*, 388 U.S. 218, 239 n.30 (1967) (citing Wigmore, The Science of Judicial Proof 541 (3d ed. 1937)).

85. *Id.*

86. 3 Wigmore, Evidence § 786a, at 210 (Chadbourn rev. 1970).

87. *Id.*

88. Wolgalter et al., *supra* note 81, at 78.

89. Ruth Horry et al., *Video Identification of Suspects: A Discussion of Current Practice and Policy in the United Kingdom*, 7 Policing 307, 308 (2013), https://doi.org/10.1093/police/pat008.

90. Betsy Reed, *Don't Round Up the Usual Suspects: The End of the ID Parade*, Guardian (UK), Aug. 23, 2015, https://www.theguardian.com/uk-news/shortcuts/2015/aug/23/dont-round-up-the-usual-suspects-the-end-of-the-id-parade.

91. *Id.*

witness still has access to a DVD player) and are much cheaper to administer than their live counterparts.[92] Following several pilot programs in cities and townships across the United Kingdom, authorities rolled VIPER out nationally.

VIPER lineups are sequential, consisting of a series of fifteen-second video clips, showing the head and shoulders of one individual,[93] rather than the two-minute-long clips that Wigmore envisioned. In each fifteen-second clip, the subject looks directly at the camera before turning to show their profile. By law, lineups must include at least eight fillers in addition to the suspect, and eyewitnesses must see the entire lineup twice before making a decision. However, eyewitnesses can view the clips as many times as they wish. If an individual is selected, the eyewitness is shown that particular video clip again to confirm the identification.

D. Show-Ups

In a show-up, police show one or more suspects to an eyewitness without any fillers.[94] It would seem that for most of human history, show-ups were the only method that police and prosecutors used to generate and ascertain an eyewitness's willingness to identify the target of an investigation. Although it would be impossible to pinpoint when the first show-up took place, a notable early example involved a woman accused of plotting against King Louis XIV of France, during the "Affair of the Poisons," between 1677 and 1682. During this "Affair," police arrested hundreds on suspicion of poisoning and black magic, resulting in at least thirty-four executions.[95] As the investigation progressed, it swept up members of the royal court, including the king's former mistress, Claude de Vin des Oeillets, who was accused of organizing a satanic ritual ("black mass") to control the king.[96] When confronted with this accusation, Mlle des Oeillets asked to be brought before her accusers—a defrocked priest, a mystic, and the daughter of a fortune-teller, all of whom had been jailed already in connection with the Affair—insisting that none would even recognize her.[97] This gambit backfired, as

---

92. *Id.*

93. Horry et al., *supra* note 89, at 308.

94. NAT'L RSCH. COUNCIL, *supra* note 10, at 27–28.

95. ANNE SOMERSET, THE AFFAIR OF THE POISONS 306 (2004), https://archive.org/details/affairofpoisonsm00some_0/page/n9/mode/2up.

96. *Id.* at 270, 272.

97. *Id.* at 279–80.

Claude de Vin des Oeillets by Pierre Minard, Circle of Pierre Mignard – Portrait of a Lady in a white silk dress.

all three witnesses identified her without hesitation.[98] Nevertheless, Mlle des Oeillets was spared the judgment of the "Chamber Ardente" ("Burning Chamber"), after persuading investigators that her accusers must have

98. *Id.*

been mistaken.[99] Although historians continue to debate her involvement in various conspiracies, there is some consensus that this show-up was a farce, given the inherently suggestive circumstances under which it took place (i.e., in the basement of an actual dungeon) and given her accusers' obvious motive to identify whomever was put before them, in the hopes of avoiding or forestalling their own executions.[100]

Show-ups are the second most common identification procedure in the United States.[101] They typically occur when a suspect has been apprehended close in time and place to the offense under investigation. To facilitate the show-up, police may transport the witness to the suspect or vice versa.[102] Because the Fourth Amendment restricts the police's ability to inflict warrantless detention on those they are investigating, show-ups tend to occur within two hours of when the offense occurred[103] or within ninety minutes of when the suspect was detained.[104]

For more than half a century, courts and experts have agreed that show-ups are inherently suggestive and pose a greater risk of irreparable misidentification than either kind of lineup because eyewitnesses cannot help knowing that the person before them is a suspect in the crime they witnessed.[105] The show-up's suggestiveness may be exacerbated by the methods used to subdue the suspect, for instance, where the suspect appears in handcuffs, is surrounded by police, is held in the back of a police car, or has sustained injuries during their encounter with the police.[106] All of these factors serve as further indicia of guilt that can influence the eyewitness consciously or subconsciously to make an identification. And yet, despite these widely acknowledged and publicized risks, the show-up remains one of

99. *Id.* at 307. In this regard, Mlle des Oeillets may have benefited from the fact that the king remained fond of her and that another of his mistresses had hired a lawyer to discredit the investigation, having been named in it herself. *See id.* at 286.

100. *Id.* at 280.

101. PERF Survey, *supra* note 8, at 48.

102. *Id.* at 58.

103. Nat'l Rsch. Council, *supra* note 10, at 27–28; PERF Survey, *supra* note 8, at 58 ("Of the respondents that conduct show-ups, 37.1 percent recommend a time frame limit after the crime beyond which a show-up should not be conducted. The mean amount of time to conduct a show-up is 2.3 hours, and the median is one hour.").

104. *See, e.g., United States v. Place*, 462 U.S. 696 (1983) ("[A]lthough we decline to adopt any outside time limitation for a permissible Terry stop, we have never approved a seizure of the person for the prolonged 90-minute period involved here and cannot do so on the facts presented by this case."); Wayne R. LaFave, 4 Search & Seizure § 9.2(f), n.276 (6th ed.) (collecting cases).

105. *2019 Third Circuit Task Force Report*, *supra* note 65, at 42 n. 202 (collecting cases).

106. *Id.* at 45.

the country's most common forms of identification due to the appreciation, among judges and policymakers alike, for its capacity to "promptly clear [at least some] innocent suspects," while allowing police to focus their resources productively according to the eyewitness's feedback during the show-up.[107]

Show-ups are especially problematic because they cannot be administered blindly. At best, the police can bring in an officer to do the show-up who is unfamiliar with the witness, the suspect, and the nature of the witness's accusations. However, police tend resist this sort of blinding protocol for a few reasons. First, they argue that the time constraints inherent in a show-up may render blind administration infeasible.[108] A truly "blind" administrator would need to be insulated not just from any initial report, but also any subsequent radio transmission about the investigation. Such a person may be exceedingly difficult to find in short order. Second, some have argued that there are rapport-building and information-sharing advantages to having the show-up run by the officer who received the initial complaint.[109] Third, police tend to be skeptical of the benefit of bringing in an unfamiliar officer because, ultimately, such blinding does not prevent the officer or witness from knowing that the person in the show-up is a suspect; it only prevents the officer from knowing why the person in the show-up is a suspect.

Apart from "blind" administration, most of what police can do to mitigate the suggestiveness of a show-up involves (1) minimizing the use of suggestive cues, such as handcuffing; (2) assuring the witness that the person shown may not be the perpetrator and that the investigation will continue even without an identification; (3) preventing any feedback that might reinforce the impression that the show-up would not be happening unless the police thought—and had good reason to think—they had their perpetrator; and (4) precisely documenting the show-up in its entirety, including any uncertainty the witness may have regarding their identification.[110] And yet,

---

107. Nat'l Rsch. Council, *supra* note 10, at 28; *2019 Third Circuit Task Force Report*, *supra* note 65, at 43 & n.203; *see, e.g.*, *Simmons v. United States*, 390 U.S. 377, 384 (1968) (approving the use of a suggestive photographic "show-up" procedure because "[d]espite the hazards of [the procedure], [it] ha[d] been used widely and effectively in criminal law enforcement . . . [to] spar[e] innocent suspects the ignominy of arrest by allowing eyewitnesses to exonerate them through scrutiny of photographs").

108. *See* Nat'l Rsch. Council, *supra* note 10, at 28 ("[T]he nature of a showup does not lend itself to the use of a blinded procedure. A showup is designed to promptly clear innocent suspects, thereby sparing them from a prolonged period of detention as the investigation continues. Delaying the showup to locate an uninvolved officer may defeat that purpose.").

109. Steblay, *supra* note 72, at 25.

110. *2019 Third Circuit Task Force Report*, *supra* note 65, at 43–46.

for as much as the reliability of a show-up appears to depend on precise administration, instruction, feedback, and documentation, show-ups do not appear to be any more tightly regulated than other identification procedures. Rather, in most respects, regulation appears to be looser.

Unlike the eyewitness viewing a lineup, who is likely to receive a standardized set of written or verbal instructions from a detective, as of 2010, a witness viewing a show-up was more likely to receive informal verbal instructions about how the show-up will proceed.[111] Those instructions were just as likely to state that the perpetrator may or may not be present, but much less likely to state that the investigation will continue even if the witness is not able to identify the suspect.[112] Those instructions were more likely to come from a patrol officer,[113] which is unsurprising given the role that patrol officers take in the initial response to a criminal complaint as compared to detectives. If a show-up ends in a positive identification, it is equally likely to be accompanied by documentation of a witness's confidence statement.[114] Although recent increases in the use of body-worn cameras has made video- and audio recording more widely available in the context of show-ups,[115] it is not clear what percentage of departments mandate the use of body-worn cameras during this type of citizen encounter. Moreover, survey data indicate that police are more likely to exempt show-ups from their normal prohibition on including the same suspect in multiple identification procedures viewed by the same witness.[116]

The need for operational flexibility is often cited as a justification for the lax manner in which police departments tend to regulate show-ups. Authorities claim that certain safety issues inherent in the pursuit and apprehension of a suspect make it difficult to adhere to specific protocol in administering

111. PERF SURVEY, *supra* note 8, at 51.

112. *Id.* at 53.

113. *Id.* at 51.

114. *Id.* at 54.

115. *Id.* at 54–55.

116. *Id.* at 87. As the Supreme Court has recognized, including the same suspect in multiple procedures viewed by the same witness is highly suggestive because it communicates to the witness, repeatedly: "*This* is the [suspect]." *Foster v. California*, 394 U.S. 440, 443 (1969). For this reason, "the vast majority" of U.S. law enforcement agencies (90.4 percent) surveyed in 2010 reported that they "rarely or never allow the same eyewitness to view the same suspect in more than one identification procedure." PERF SURVEY, *supra* note 8, at 87. However, show-up identifications were the most common exception to this rule, with departments permitting their officers to conduct "a show-up followed by a photo lineup" more often than any other combination of procedures. *Id.*

a show-up.[117] Thus, perhaps the most we can do to regulate show-ups is to encourage police to use them sparingly. This book will return to the debate over how strongly show-ups should be regulated and/or discouraged in Chapter 6.

E. Confirmatory Photo Displays

When police have developed a suspect, but do not have that person in custody, they may also show an eyewitness one or more photos of the suspect without any fillers to see if the witness recognizes the suspect. These photos may depict the suspect alone, as in a mugshot, or in a group of people, as in a personal snapshot taken from the suspect's phone or social media account. Precisely how often the police use single-suspect photo displays is unknown, but the most recent survey data suggest that it is not done routinely.[118] Showing photos of a single suspect to an eyewitness is considered "both highly suggestive and unnecessarily so because – in the absence of extraordinary circumstances – the police can easily put together a photo array."[119] Nevertheless, this procedure has been tolerated under exigent circumstances, for instance, when police need confirmation of a suspect's identity in order to respond to an ongoing threat to public safety.[120]

Police may also use single-suspect photo displays to confirm the identity of someone with whom a witness is (allegedly) familiar.[121] Although such confirmatory displays are considered less suggestive and more reliable because of the witness's familiarity with the identification target, familiarity exists on a spectrum,[122] and the circumstances underlying the witness's familiarity may bias them toward identification. Someone who caught only a fleeting glimpse of the person who stole their car may be more likely to blame the person they saw peering into car windows on a previous occasion.

---

117. Nat'l Rsch. Council, *supra* note 10, at 28.

118. Nat'l Rsch. Council, *supra* note 10, at 28 (describing the practice as "occasion[al]"); PERF Survey, *supra* note 8, at 50 (noting identification procedures used by departments across the country; omitting single-suspect photo displays).

119. Randy Hertz et al., The Trial Manual for Defense Attorneys in Juvenile Delinquency Cases 1059 (2023 ed.), https://www.defendyouthrights.org/wp-content/uploads/Chap-25-ID-Suppression-Motions.pdf.

120. *Simmons v. United States*, 390 U.S. 377 (1968).

121. Nat'l Rsch. Council, *supra* note 10, at 28. Fans of *The Wire* will recall when Andre Royo's character "Bubbles" helped Detective Kima Greggs identify members of the Barksdale crew by arranging to have them photographed in various hats, enabling Greggs to debrief Bubbles about each crew member using the photos as points of reference. *The Wire: The Detail* (HBO June 9, 2002).

122. *Parker v. United States*, 249 A.3d 388, 402 (D.C. 2021).

Moreover, complications arise in complex, fast-moving, stressful situations when the witness must remember not only who was present but also who engaged in a criminal act and who was a bystander. These topics will be discussed under the rubric of **transference** in the coming chapters.

II. When Police Want to Develop a Suspect

A. Mugshot Searches

In a mugshot search, a witness peruses the routine booking photos of "known offenders" to see whether the perpetrator of the witnessed crime is among them.[123] This kind of search is almost as old as photography itself. Indeed, "[s]ome of the very earliest photographs from the late 1830s are of alleged and/or convicted criminals, and law enforcement officials used photographs of criminals in Belgium as early as the 1840s to track down wrong-doers."[124] In 1857, eighteen years after Louis-Jacques-Mandé Daguerre revealed the daguerreotype method of capturing images at the French Academy of Sciences in Paris,[125] an NYPD sergeant named Lefferts began "collecting daguerreotype portraits of [alleged] pickpockets, burglars and other criminals" to display on a wall at the Headquarters of the Detective Police.[126] Lefferts's "Rogue's Gallery of the Detective Police" quickly amassed hundreds of portraits.[127] Its purpose was to shame "hardened" and "incorrigible" "offenders," while enabling eyewitnesses to identify the perpetrators of recent crimes from among those depicted.[128] Less than a month into operation, it had led to several arrests and convinced "three or four" of those who had been "unenviably distinguished" as "thieves" to "quit[] New York for parts unknown."[129] The concept of the rogue's gallery eventually gave way to printed volumes of routine booking photos ("mug books"), but not before becoming an attraction unto itself.[130]

---

123. *Id.* at 104.

124. David R. Papke, *A History of the Mugshot*, Marquette U. L. Sch. Faculty Blog, https://law.marquette.edu/facultyblog/2013/10/a-history-of-the-mug-shot/.

125. *See The Daguerrotype Medium*, Libr. Cong., https://www.loc.gov/collections/daguerreotypes/articles-and-essays/the-daguerreotype-medium/.

126. Joseph Goldstein, *Jailing the Wrong Man: Mug Shot Searches Persist in New York, Despite Serious Risks*, N.Y. Times (Jan. 5, 2019), https://www.nytimes.com/2019/01/05/nyregion/nypd-mug-shots-false-identification.html.

127. *Id.*

128. *Dageurrotype Gallery of Criminals at the Detective Police Office*, N.Y. Times, 1, Dec. 5, 1857, https://timesmachine.nytimes.com/timesmachine/1857/12/05/78514460.pdf.

129. *The Rogue's Portrait Gallery*, N.Y. Times, 2, June 7, 1858, https://timesmachine.nytimes.com/timesmachine/1858/06/07/78536641.pdf.

130. Goldstein, *supra* note 126.

George Grantham Bain Collection (Library of Congress).

One hundred fifty years later, mugshot searches remain one method by which some police departments approach "difficult-to-solve crimes," when "other evidence is scarce."[131] By a 2010 estimate, they were embraced by more than a quarter of the law enforcement agencies in the country, including 44 percent of those with five hundred or more sworn officers.[132] Although physical mug books still exist, mugshot searches are done mostly by computer now.[133] For instance, the NYPD uses a program called Photo-Manager.[134] In such programs, "[d]etectives enter a description of the perpetrator into [the] database, which then spits out dozens or even hundreds of matching photos," which "[t]he witness scrolls through, in hopes of recognizing the culprit."[135] Mug books, likewise, tend to be sorted by gender, race, and age to enable witnesses to quickly narrow the universe of possible suspects.[136]

1. *Criticisms*

Mugshot searches have long been criticized as highly suggestive because they encourage witnesses to make a comparative judgment regarding which mugshot most resembles their memory of the perpetrator, when there may be no reason to believe that the persons depicted were in the area and the witness's memory of the perpetrator may be too weak to enable

131. *Id.*
132. PERF Survey, *supra* note 8, at 67.
133. *Id.*; *2019 Third Circuit Task Force Report*, *supra* note 65, at 67.
134. Goldstein, *supra* note 126.
135. *Id.*
136. PERF Survey, *supra* note 8, at 67.

recognition.[137] Open-ended searches are considered especially suggestive because combing through a seemingly endless stream of mugshot photos has the potential to wear a witness down into selecting anyone who "reminds them of the culprit."[138] Those who defend the mugshot search insist that, notwithstanding the bias inherent in the mugshot search, it can be a sound method of generating leads in cases that are otherwise devoid of any.[139] They believe that mistaken identifications can be ferreted out by placing the suspect in a lineup for confirmation of identification, after the witness has indicated recognition in the mugshot search. However, anecdotes suggest that by the time the witness has selected someone's mugshot, it may be too late to correct that selection with an unbiased lineup; the witness may be irreparably convinced that the person in the mugshot is responsible for the crime they witnessed.[140]

The Toll of Faulty Mugshot Searches

On January 5, 2019, the New York Times reported on the NYPD's routine use of mugshot searches to investigate crimes where the alleged perpetrator was someone unfamiliar to the eyewitness, highlighting three cases where this practice led to the prolonged incarceration of Black men who were apparently innocent of the crimes charged.[141]

- Police arrested a father of eight named St. Clair Steward in connection with a 2018 shooting, after the victim identified him during a mugshot search. Mr. Steward's face had been the thirty-first one presented to the victim during the mugshot review. Thereafter, the victim identified Mr. Steward as the shooter during a live lineup. Mr. Steward was charged with attempted murder and jailed for two months, before DNA testing apparently excluded him as a possible suspect and the case was dismissed.

(continued)

137. Goldstein, *supra* note 126.
138. *Id.*
139. *Id.*
140. *Id.*
141. *Id.*

The Toll of Faulty Mugshot Searches *(continued)*

- Derrick Penn was likewise jailed for three different armed robberies in 2014 based on the results of a mugshot search. The victim of one of the robberies had identified him after reviewing more than three hundred photographs. Later, all three victims selected him from among the fillers in a live lineup. The prosecution dismissed his case after location data from his cell phone suggested that he had been miles away from the location of all three robberies. By then he had missed his daughter's kindergarten graduation.
- A Brooklyn plumber, who had been arrested for threatening another man with a gun over a parking spot, was similarly released after cellphone location data suggested that he had been nowhere near the scene of the incident. The victim in that case had selected the plumber's picture during a mugshot search after reviewing 849 other photographs and had maintained confidence in his identification throughout the proceedings leading up to the case's dismissal.

In all three cases, eyewitnesses were asked to perform lengthy, open-ended mugshot searches, despite their lack of familiarity with the perpetrators, and had little trouble confirming their choice of suspect, even after they were presented with that person in a lineup containing fillers. The significance of these circumstances is explored in upcoming chapters.

Mugshot searches also raise serious privacy concerns for those included in the database, whose prior contact with the criminal legal system would be exposed if their mugshot were to be seen by anyone familiar with their face. These privacy concerns have taken on all new dimensions in the era of commercial internet criminal history research. Now "[i]t is possible to round up mug shots from public records and post them regardless of whether the pictured individuals have been prosecuted and/or convicted" and there are "[o]ver 80 profit-seeking mug-shot sites" that people can peruse.[142]

Some recommend that mugshot searches be limited to certain kinds of crimes and that they be administered in such a way as to conceal the criminal history of the individuals depicted. Given that mugshot searches are

142. Papke, *A History of the Mugshot, supra* note 124.

most suggestive when the witness is tasked with perusing a daunting number of mugshots, some departments have enacted policies to limit the number of mugshots a witness may be asked to view. However, at last check, the vast majority had no formal written policy concerning how to conduct a mugshot search and had imposed no limit on the number of mugshots that a witness could view.[143]

2. *Yearbooks and Gang Databases*

Mugshot databases are not the only photo-compilation that police departments use to develop suspects. If they believe a perpetrator is affiliated with an institution that maintains its own proprietary photo-compilation, they are likely to look there first.[144] Thus, police may ask a witness to review a yearbook, if the perpetrator might attend or work in a school, or an employee database, if the perpetrator might work at a particular company.[145]

Likewise, many jurisdictions maintain databases of known and suspected gang members that they use when they suspect a crime is gang-related.[146] These databases differ from mugshot databases in that they may contain photos from a wide array of sources, not just routine booking photos, and because in some jurisdictions their use and maintenance are regulated by statute.[147] By contrast, laws regulating mugshots disclosure have been slow to develop, which has led to the proliferation of online mugshot purveyors and online reputation management services alike.[148]

Finally, some departments have adapted the gang-database model to networks of people that do not identify as gangs or participate in organized gang activity. Examples include residents of a particular neighborhood, apartment complex, or public housing unit. With the help of social media, policing districts and precincts can compile photos of people with suspected

---

143. PERF SURVEY, *supra* note 8, at 67.

144. NAT'L RSCH. COUNCIL, *supra* note 10, at 28.

145. *Id.* at 28–29.

146. *2019 Third Circuit Task Force Report*, *supra* note 65, at 67.

147. *See* 34 U.S.C. § 41507; ARIZ. REV. STAT. § 13-3115; CAL. PEN. CODE § 186.34; COLO. REV. STAT. § 24-33.5-415.3; FLA. STAT. § 874.09; GA. CODE ANN. § 16-15-11; 20 ILL. COMP. STAT. § 2605/2605-305; IND. CODE § 5-14-3-4; MINN. STAT. § 299C.091; NEV. REV. STAT. ANN. § 480.535; N.C. GEN. STAT. § 14-50.27A; N.D. CENT. CODE § 27-20-53; S.C. CODE ANN. § 16-8-320; TENN. CODE ANN. § 38-6-102; TEX. CODE CRIM. PROC. ART. 61.02, ET SEQ.; VA. CODE ANN. § 52-8.6; WASH. REV. CODE § 43.43.762; W. VA. CODE § 15A-12-5.

148. *See, e.g.*, *Mug Shots and Booking Photo Websites*, NAT'L CONF. STATE LEGIS. (AUG. 8, 2022) https://www.ncsl.org/research/telecommunications-and-information-technology/mug-shots-and-booking-photo-websites.aspx.

ties to certain areas or individuals and show them to witnesses when they suspect a crime implicates a particular location, network, or affiliation. The use and maintenance of such databases is generally unregulated.

B. Police Sketches and Composite Images

If police obtain the image of an unidentified suspect, they may publicize or circulate it through various channels to generate leads as to the suspect's identity. Departments disseminate these images by hanging wanted posters and "Be on the Lookout" fliers in high-traffic public spaces, such as post offices, bus shelters, and public transit stations.[149] In addition, these images are almost always disseminated internally, through the supervisory chain of command and/or electronic distribution lists dedicated to persons of interest.[150] They are often forwarded to other law enforcement agencies as well.[151] They may be sent to news media for broadcast and publication.[152] Increasingly, they are posted on departmental websites and social media accounts.[153]

Images disseminated by police tend to come from surveillance footage, composite images, police sketches, or some combination of the three. For these purposes, "police sketches" are those drawn by a human sketch artist based on eyewitness input.[154] "Composite images" are those constructed using a computer program or its analog equivalent. The most recent available data suggests that police sketch artists retain a small role in rendering the images of suspects and persons of interest in the United States, although some departments use a computer program, such as Identi-Kit, which boasts the ability to create billions of faces out of thousands of different feature options.[155] Some small number of departments may still use the analog forerunners to these computer programs: transparent, acetate printouts of facial features (eyes, noses, mouths, etc.) that can be laid on top of each other to create a true "composite."[156]

---

149. PERF Survey, *supra* note 8, at 66.
150. *Id.*
151. *Id.*
152. *Id.*
153. IACP Law Enforcement Policy Center, Social Media: Concepts and Issues Paper (May 2019), https://www.theiacp.org/sites/default/files/2019-05/Social%20Media%20Paper%20-%202019.pdf.
154. PERF Survey, *supra* note 8, at 66.
155. *Id.*
156. *Id.*

1. *Sketches, Illustrations, and Artist's Renderings*

Forensic illustrations have a long history in the criminal legal systems of Europe and the United States, dating back to the earliest courtroom sketches of the 1600s.[157] Although wanted notices and broadside proclamations offering reward for the capture of fugitives have been around for almost as long, the idea of putting the wanted individual's likeness on such a notice or proclamation does not appear to have emerged until the late 1800s, when developments in printing and photography enabled the publication of actual photographs of the wanted individuals. Before then, these notices and proclamations tended either to omit the likeness of the wanted person altogether or, as with many fugitive slave notices, to feature a stock image.[158]

The earliest documented attempts to use forensic illustration to bring about an arrest involved suspects whose identities were already known to the investigating authorities. In these cases, the sketch's preparation was frequently guided by a reference photograph or the description of someone who was familiar with the suspect before they (allegedly) committed the crime under investigation.[159] For instance, in 1881, publication of Percy Lefroy Mapleton's sketch in the *Telegraph* led to his capture in connection with a murder on the Brighton Railway.[160] Scotland Yard deployed a similar tactic to pursue Dr. Harvey Crippen, after he was accused of murdering his wife and burying her dismembered body in the cellar of their London residence.[161] When Dr. Crippen fled the country with his mistress, authorities tried to expedite his capture by publishing an artist's rendering of what he might look like disguised in a beard. Dr. Crippen was eventually identified on a steamer bound for New York, after the ship's captain noticed that the "son" traveling with Dr. Crippen was really a grown woman (his mistress) in disguise.

---

157. Elena Martinique, *What Do Courtroom Sketch Artists Do?*, WIDEWALLS (Oct. 20, 2019), https://www.widewalls.ch/magazine/courtroom-sketch-artists.

158. *See, e.g.*, RACHEL HALL, WANTED: THE OUTLAW IN AMERICAN VISUAL CULTURE 42 (2009).

159. KAREN T. TAYLOR, FORENSIC ART AND ILLUSTRATION 12–13 (2000).

160. *See, e.g.* ADAM WOOD, THE TRIAL OF PERCY LEFROY MAPLETON (2019); *Trial of Percy Lefroy Mapleton*, IND. UNIV. PRESS, https://iupress.org/9781911273608/trial-of-percy-lefroy-mapleton/.

161. TAYLOR, *supra* note 159, at 15–16.

Sketch of Mapleton published in the *Telegraph.* Public Domain, https://commons.wikimedia.org/w/index.php?curid=3584831.

Although these high-profile cases helped legitimize the sketch as a viable tool for facilitating fugitive capture, they did little to foreshadow the prominent role that sketches would come to play in generating leads about suspects whose identities were unknown to the police. In such lead-generating cases, the artist cannot rely on a photographic reference or a description from someone who knew the suspect well, as they often can when police know the identity of the person they are pursuing, and therefore must rely exclusively on the descriptions of those who encountered the suspect during the alleged crime under investigation. The idea of using a hand-drawn sketch to generate leads under these constraints does not appear to have arisen until 1920, when a bomb went off on Wall Street, killing forty and injuring hundreds more outside of the JP Morgan building.[162] The bomb had been delivered in a horse-drawn cart, and after locating a nearby blacksmith who had shod the foot of a horse carrying a suspicious load on the day in question, authorities commissioned a portrait of the cart's driver based on the blacksmith's description. Although the ensuing investigation led to no arrests or convictions (most believe the bombing was the work of one or more anarchists who managed to avoid capture by fleeing back to Italy), the incident lent credibility to the sketch as a means of generating leads regarding an unknown suspect's identity and whereabouts.[163] Over the last century, authorities have used sketches to attempt to identify a number of high-profile suspects—from the Lindbergh baby's kidnapper, to "D.B. Cooper," the hijacker of Northwest Orient Flight 305, to the "Hillside Strangler," to the "Zodiac Killer," the "Son of Sam," the "Unabomber," and the perpetrator of the 1995 Oklahoma City bombing—with varying degrees of success.[164]

---

162. *Id.* at 17–18.

163. Caroline M. Wilkinson, *A Review of Forensic Art*, 5 Rsch. & Reps. Forensic Med. Sci. 17, 18 (2015), http://dx.doi.org/10.2147/RRFMS.S60767.

164. *See generally* Taylor, *supra* note 159, at 17–42.

FBI Sketch of "D.B. Cooper," the Hijacker of Northwest Orient Flight 305. https://www.britannica.com/biography/D-B-Cooper#/media/1/2081799/219515.

Forensic illustration achieved the peak of its cultural relevance in the 1980s and 1990s, with the formation of the International Association for Identification or "IAI," a professional organization dedicated to creating professional standards for how sketches should be prepared, and the foundation of various training programs for forensic artists, including a course sponsored by the Federal Bureau of Investigation (FBI).[165] Around the same time, sketches were regularly featured on TV programs like "America's Most Wanted."[166] However, the final episode of "America's Most Wanted" aired in 2011, and forensic illustration has been considered "a dying art" for an even longer period of time.[167] As of 2005, American law enforcement agencies only employed nineteen full-time professional sketch artists, and the work of generating images of a suspect had largely shifted to mechanical and computer-based composite systems.[168]

Despite the high-profile nature of the work done by forensic illustrators, and the existence of professional organizations like the IAI, there has never

165. *Id.* at 32.
166. *Id.* at 35; Hall, *supra* note 158, at 110.
167. Graham M. Davies & Tim Valentine, *Facial Composites: Forensic Utility and Psychological Research*, in 2 Handbook of Eyewitness Psychology (Michael P. Toglia et al., eds 2007).
168. *Id.*

been a great deal of consensus regarding the appropriate method for preparing a sketch.[169] While a number of experienced artists have written books and articles expounding on their own methodologies, their views tend to differ on basic issues, such as whether it is appropriate to consult photographic reference material, to use caricature to emphasize distinctive features, or to attempt to capture a characteristic facial expression.[170] Notably, although "[m]ost [American] artists work directly with the witness, . . . FBI operatives are taught to work at a distance from a description provided by a field officer."[171] Indeed, the FBI pioneered this practice in the 1960s.[172] Forensic artists in the United Kingdom likewise have tended to prepare sketches with little to no direct input from witnesses, instead relying on descriptive input from the notes of investigators.[173] Some attribute the decline of the forensic art profession in the United States to the need for sketch artists to serve as both artist and interviewer.[174]

2. *Mechanical and Computerized Composites*

As detailed more fully later on, composite "kits" were developed in the 1950s to streamline the process of generating a suspect's image from an eyewitness's verbal description. At that time, although sketches were considered a reliable mechanism for generating leads about a suspect's identity and location, a decent sketch could take hours to complete, during which time any promising lead might grow cold. Moreover, while sketch artists had yet to herald the impending death of their profession, they were nevertheless in short supply relative to the number of cases where police might think to use their services. The only alternative to having an artist produce a drawing was to have a witness search through mug books ad nauseam until they recognized a face, which could be equally time consuming.[175] Thus, police began looking into ways to allow eyewitnesses to reconstruct faces that did not require a professional forensic artist. Although the attempt to develop this technology did not begin until the 1950s, the principles underlying it date back much further, to the turn of the twentieth century.

169. *Id.*
170. *Id.*
171. *Id.*
172. Taylor, *supra* note 159, at 22–23.
173. *Id.* at 33.
174. Davies & Valentine, *supra* note 167.
175. As already noted, the results of such searches can be very unreliable.

a. Toward a "Scientific" Understanding of the Face

Modern composite image technology owes its existence to a low-level clerk in the Paris Police Department named Alphonse Bertillon, who, in the late 1800s, was inspired to create a system for classifying facial features by a particularly tedious task. Bertillon had been assigned to hand-copy the biometric information that his colleagues recorded about each person they had arrested.[176] Through this process, Bertillon came to suspect that poor data-collection practices were hindering his department's ability to identify those who had previously been arrested or convicted of a different crime.[177] (Then, as now, lawmakers and law-enforcers were keenly interested in documenting and punishing recidivism.) Thus, and inspired by the field of evolutionary biology, Bertillon spent years creating and refining a complex taxonomy of specific, identifying facial features ("anthropometry" or "Bertillonage") and further devised a method for recording this information on an identification card ("portrait parle" or "speaking portrait"), that also contained the person's mugshot.[178] Bertillon's final contribution was to organize this information into physical databases that police could query using information about a person's features.[179] Before his death in 1914, "Bertillonage" was embraced by law enforcement agencies all over the world, with Bertillon personally overseeing a division of the Paris police force dedicated to its implementation.[180] However, his methods ultimately proved unsustainable, as departments struggled to measure and document the physical attributes of their detainees in the meticulous manner he prescribed.[181] Departments eventually abandoned "Bertillonage" for a technique they regarded as more efficient and reliable: fingerprint comparison.

176. Jessica Helfand, *Alphonse Bertillon and the Troubling Pursuit of Human Metrics*, MIT Press Reader (May 5, 2021), https://thereader.mitpress.mit.edu/the-troubling-pursuit-of-human-metrics.

177. *Id.*

178. *Id.*

179. *Id.*

180. *Id.*

181. *Id.*

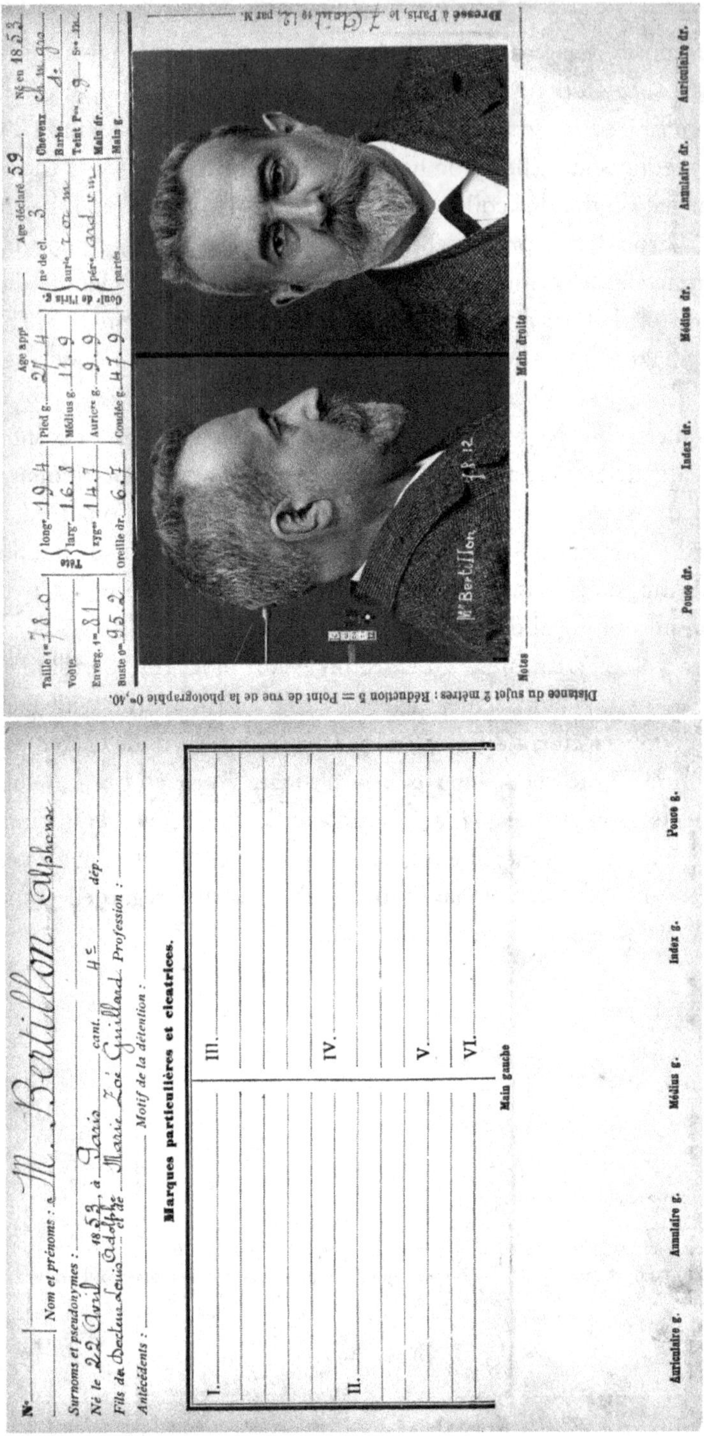

"Portrait Parle" of Alphonse Bertillon, https://en.wikipedia.org/wiki/File:Bertillon,_Alphonse,_fiche_anthropom%C3%A9trique_recto-verso.jpg

The "West Brothers" Incident

By the time of Bertillon's death in 1914, his methods were already well on their way to becoming obsolete, as law enforcement officials increasingly put their trust in fingerprinting.[182] A significant moment in this transition occurred in 1903, when Bertillonage proved unable to distinguish two men admitted to the U.S. Penitentiary at Leavenworth, Kansas, at different times. After taking the anthropometric measurements of a newly admitted prisoner named "Will West," officials concluded that he had already been admitted under the name "William West." Although the new Mr. West denied any previous admission to the prison (presumably, to avoid a charge of escape or classification as a recidivist) officials determined that his measurements were indistinguishable from those of William West. In the end, the prison only accepted that the two Wests were different people after examining the two men's distinctive fingerprint records and consulting the prison's own records, which revealed that the old Mr. West was still serving his sentence of life imprisonment. In the aftermath of this incident, American law enforcement concluded that fingerprints were more likely to be unique to a single person and therefore, more valuable as a means of identification than the painstaking measurements that Bertillon advocated. By the time Bertillon's defenders had a chance to weigh in, insisting that there must have been some mistake in how his methods were applied, it was already too late.[183] The damage to Bertillonage's reputation had already been done. Bertillon's writing suggests that he remained skeptical of the forensic potential of fingerprinting until his esteemed associate Francis Galton—the English polymath and eugenicist, *see infra*—estimated that the likelihood of two people sharing identical fingerprints was 1 in 64 trillion.[184] The irony is that Galton's conjecture about the rarity of fingerprints has never been substantiated by scientific research.[185]

182. Stewart Van Cleve, *The Bertillon System, Science and Crime in the Global Information Age*, HISTORYAPOLIS PROJECT (Apr. 23, 2014), http://historyapolis.com/blog/2014/04/23/the-bertillon-system-science-and-crime-in-the-global-information-age.

183. HENRY T.F. RHODES, ALPHONSE BERTILLON: FATHER OF SCIENTIFIC DETECTION (1956), https://catalog.hathitrust.org/Record/001273933.

184. *See* 3A KARL PEARSON, LIFE, LETTERS, AND LABOURS OF FRANCIS GALTON 144–45 (1930), https://galton.org/cgi-bin/searchImages/galton/search/pearson/vol3a/pages/vol3a_0165.htm; *The Chance of Identical Fingerprints: 1 in 64 trillion*, SCI. AM. (Aug. 6, 2020), https://www.scientificamerican.com/article/the-chance-of-identical-fingerprints-1-in-64-trillion.

185. *See, e.g.*, Clive Thompson, *The Myth of Fingerprints*, SMITHSONIAN (Apr. 26, 2019), https://www.smithsonianmag.com/science-nature/myth-fingerprints-180971640/.

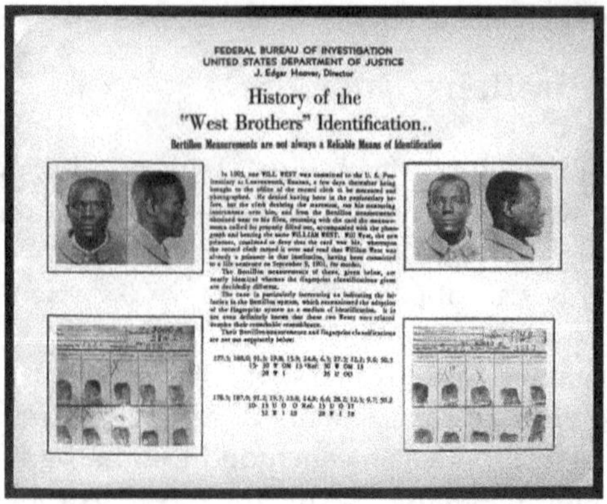

History of the "West Brothers" Identification. Photo from the Collection of the National Law Enforcement Museum, Washington, D.C. (1960).

Even so, Bertillon's legacy lives on in the mugshot and the composite techniques he inspired. First, although, as discussed above, law enforcement use of mugshots predates Bertillon's work by several years, he is credited with innovating the modern convention of photographing every person's full face and profile and creating an ideal lighting setup for such photography.[186] Before Bertillon, police photographed their detainees in a variety of ways, making systematic comparison impossible or at best, unreliable.[187] Under Bertillon, the Paris Police adopted a standard practice of capturing every person's full face and profile under the same favorable lighting conditions.[188] This was no small feat in Bertillon's time, as it involved identifying ideal exposure time, as well as lighting and camera placement. Bertillon's parameters and practice quickly spread to other departments and continue today.

Second, and more generally, Bertillon pioneered the feature-based, "scientific" understanding of the human face, which continues to inform modern composite technology. Whereas for all of human history, people had relied on inscrutable, holistic assessments of appearance to determine questions of identity (in the absence of distinguishing marks), Bertillon believed that true facial recognition could (best) be achieved by the correct classification of

---

186. Rhodes, *supra* note 183, at 103.
187. *Id.*
188. *Id.*

individual features according to their size, shape, and displacement.[189] Like the pioneers of statistics whose work inspired Bertillon, he believed that it was possible to index a person's physical traits (say, the distance between a person's eyes) against some population average that could be estimated using a sufficiently large number of observations.[190] To this end, Bertillon poured over mugshots and took as many measurements of the incarcerated as he could.[191] His efforts culminated in a diagram of the different kinds of features and hairstyles that he believed his fellow officers might encounter, what he called his *Tableau Synoptique Des Traits Physionomiques*. Bertillon believed that by studying this diagram, police could become more proficient in capturing anthropometric data about those they arrested, while also improving their ability to recognize suspects they had never seen before, based on description alone.[192]

Although Bertillon's "Tableau" of features could have easily served as a template for creating composite imagery, the idea of reconstructing a person's likeness from component parts did not gain traction as a forensic discipline until the mid-twentieth century, well after Bertillon had died and his methods had fallen into disuse. Before then, the sole source of innovation in the field of composite technology was Francis Galton—founder of the eugenics movement, which favored restricting procreation to those with hereditary traits that they considered desirable—and a proponent of physiognomy, the belief that physical traits (especially facial features) were indicative of moral character and the propensity to commit crime.[193] In the late 1870s, around the same time that Bertillon began measuring noses and chins, Galton began experimenting with composite imagery by exposing photographic negatives of different human faces on the same light-sensitive material.[194]

---

189. *Id.* at 105.

190. Helfand, *supra* note 176.

191. *Id.*

192. *Id.*

193. Colin Getty Tredoux et al., *Construction of Facial Composites from Eyewitness Memory*, *in* BIOMEDICAL VISUALISATION: ADVANCES IN EXPERIMENTAL MEDICINE AND BIOLOGY at 155 (2023); Dr. Kris Belden-Adams, *Alphonse Bertillon, Mugshot and Record of Francis Galton*, SMARTHISTORY (Feb. 28, 2023), https://smarthistory.org/alphonse-bertillon-mugshot-and-record-of-francis-galton.

194. Belden-Adams, *supra* note 193; Tredoux et al., *supra* note 193, at 154; *see also Galton and Composite Photography*, U. COLL. LONDON *https://www.ucl.ac.uk/culture/galton-collection/galton-and-composite-photography*.

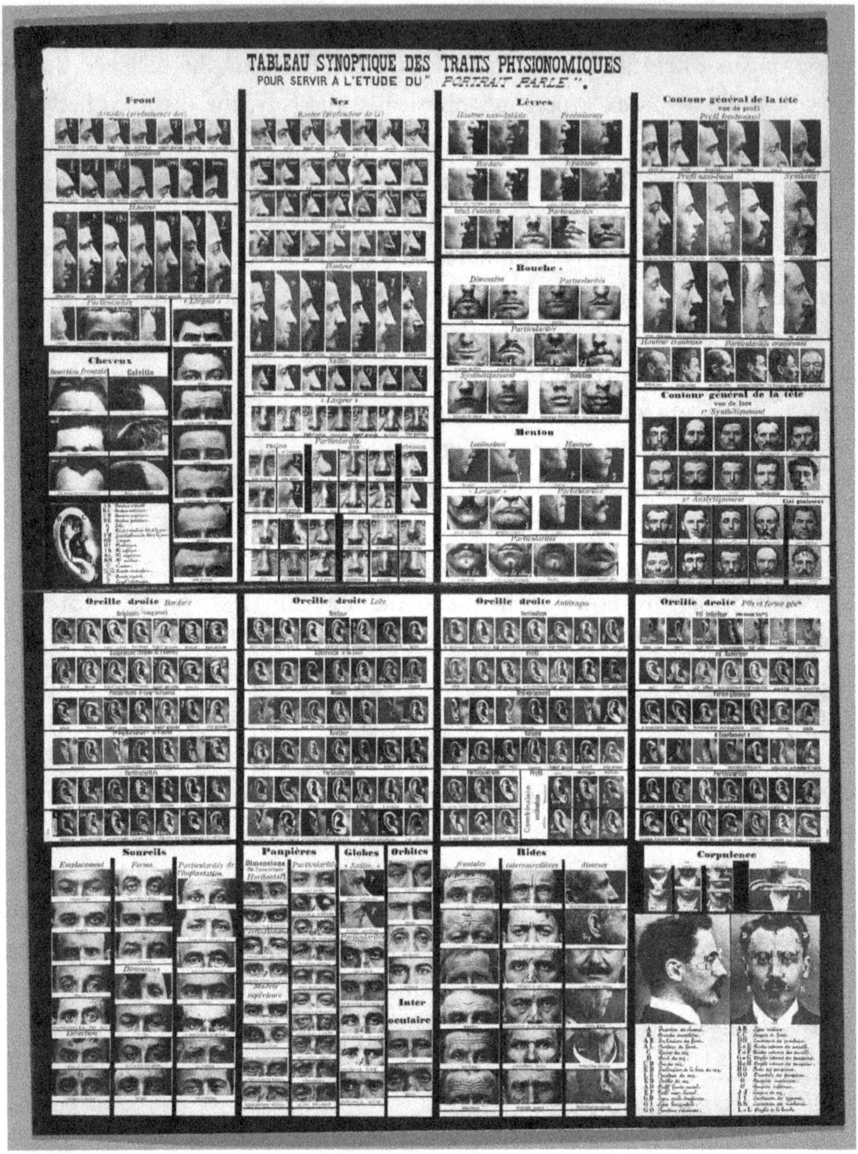

Bertillon's *Tableau Synoptique Des Traits Physionomiques* ("Synoptic Table of Physionomic Traits"). Courtesy of the Metropolitan Museum of Art, New York.

Galton's Composites of Criminal Types. Source: David Green, "Veins of Resemblance: Photography and Eugenics," *Oxford Art Journal* 7, no. 2 (1985): 3–16.

However, Galton's goal was not to facilitate the apprehension of suspects by creating an image consistent with an eyewitness description. Indeed, his methods would have been impractical for that purpose. Rather, his goal was to create a visual profile of what he thought the prototypical criminal would look like.[195] Thereafter, he applied his composite techniques to other types he considered undesirable—the mentally ill, those suffering from tuberculosis, and the "Jews."[196] Galton went on to use his composite techniques to create "transformers"—a series of images capturing a gradual transition from one image into another.[197] By varying the amount of time each photographic negative was exposed to light-sensitive material, Galton could give different "weights" to each image in the composite, thereby making one image stand out more or less than the other(s).[198] Although Galton's techniques were undeniably sophisticated, in some ways foreshadowing the technology currently used in facial reconstruction and

195. Belden-Adams, *supra* note 193; Tredoux et al., *supra* note 193, at 154.

196. *Composite Portraits of Criminal Types* (1877), MET, https://www.metmuseum.org/art/collection/search/301897.

197. Tredoux et al., *supra* note 193, at 154.

198. *Id.*

recognition software, his composites failed to make an impression on the law enforcement community, and his view that physiognomy could predict criminality (or any other behavior) was eventually dismissed as bigoted and unscientific.[199]

Bertillon, Galton, and Physiognomy

Bertillon's attempts to classify facial features coincided with the widespread popularity of biologically deterministic theories of crime—for instance, phrenology, Cesare Lombroso's theory that differences in the topology of the skull could explain differences in intelligence and disposition.[200] Although Bertillon was openly skeptical of such theories,[201] his work drew no shortage of interest from those who subscribed to them. Notably, Francis Galton was an avid supporter of Bertillon's measurements to identify those arrested by the police—so much so that he was initially skeptical of his contemporaries' interest in using fingerprints for the same purpose.[202] Galton and Bertillon corresponded regarding their shared interest in anthropometry,[203] and Galton eventually sat for a mugshot "portrait" in Bertillon's Paris studio. *See* the image reproduced here of Galton's mugshot. Bertillon's skepticism notwithstanding, his work arguably helped to create the circumstances where biological determinism could thrive, insofar as the mugshot that he innovated continues to shape public perception of what "criminals" tend to look like. For an in-depth discussion of this topic, see Helfand, note 176, and Belden-Adams, note 193.

199. *Id.* at 154–55.

200. Helfand, *supra* note 176.

201. James McArdle, *February 14: Photofit*, ON THIS DATE IN PHOTOGRAPHY (Feb. 13, 2018), https://onthisdateinphotography.com/2018/02/13/february-13-photofit; Belden-Adams, *supra* note 193.

202. NEW YORK STATE DIVISION OF CRIMINAL JUSTICE SERVICES, ORIGINS OF THE NEW YORK STATE BUREAU OF IDENTIFICATION (1997), https://www.criminaljustice.ny.gov/ojis/history/fp_sys.htm. When Galton did become interested in fingerprints, his interest had less to do with using fingerprints as an aid to identification, and more to do with using them "as an aid in determining heredity and racial background." *Id.*

203. 3A PEARSON, *supra* note 184, at 143.

Bertillon, Galton, and Physiognomy *(continued)*

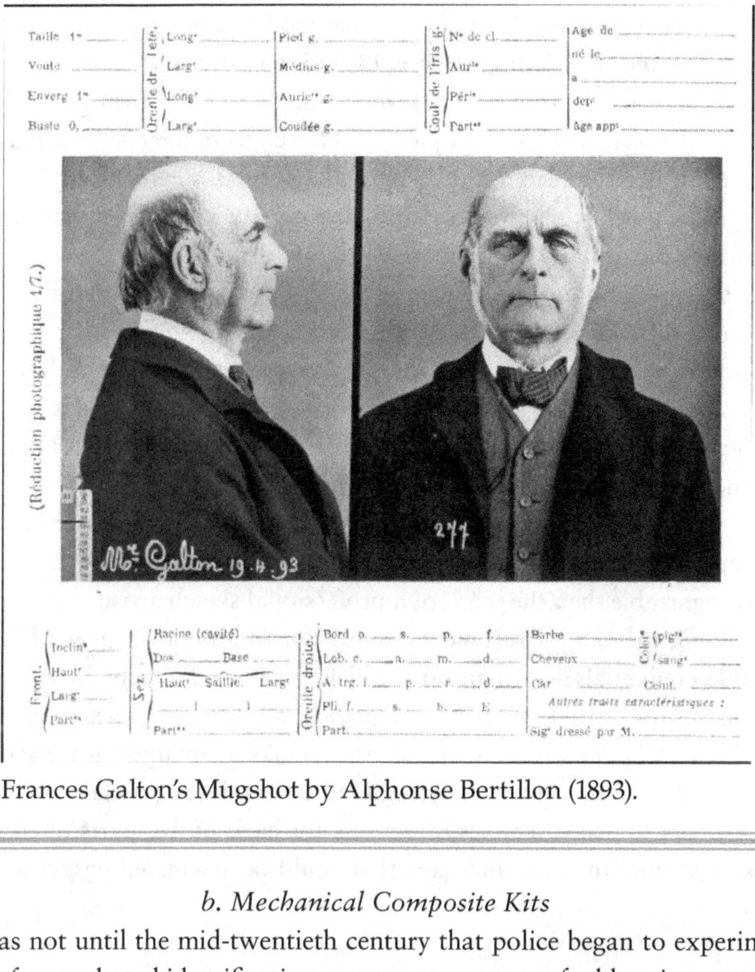

Frances Galton's Mugshot by Alphonse Bertillon (1893).

b. Mechanical Composite Kits

It was not until the mid-twentieth century that police began to experiment with feature-based identification systems as a means of addressing concerns about the cost and availability of professional sketch artists.[204] In the 1940s and '50s, after experimenting with Bertillon's idea of mugshot books that could be searched using information about a person's facial features, Hugh McDonald, a detective in the Identification Bureau of the Los Angeles Police Department, developed the original Identi-Kit, consisting of several hundred acetate sheets with line drawings of different facial features that could

204. *See, e.g.*, W.R. Hopper, *Photo-FIT—The Penry Facial Identification Technique*, 13 J. Forensic Sci. Soc. 77, 77 (1973), https://doi.org/10.1016/S0015-7368(73)70772-6.

be combined manually by a trained "operator" to form a composite based on an eyewitness description.[205] Around the same time, a Royal Canadian Mounted Police corporal named Reg Abbott developed a system to allow eyewitnesses to create a three-dimensional model of the suspect's face using plaster.[206] After completing a series of 115 questions, the witness would select facial features from among seven preset masks and then explain how the suspect's face, hair, and complexion differed from the resulting mask.[207] Although this system led to the capture of a suspect in a high-profile Canadian case, it quickly fell into disuse because it was too messy and difficult to administer, particularly by comparison to the Identi-Kit.[208]

After American gun manufacturer Smith & Wesson acquired the rights market to distribute the Identi-Kit, it quickly spread to other departments around the world.[209] However, UK officials were dissatisfied with how long it took to generate a satisfactory composite ("half a day or longer") and the fact that the original kit did not include many of the hairstyles that had become popular among youth in the 1960s.[210] Another problem was that the original Identi-Kit's line drawings lacked the shading necessary to convey depth and dimensionality.[211] The resulting images could be considerably less recognizable than the work of a professional sketch artist.

In 1968, the U.K. government commissioned a photographer of "questionable credentials"—a man born Bill Ryan but who went by the name "Jacque Penry"—to develop a home-grown, photo-based alternative to the Identi-Kit.[212] After consulting the mugshot books maintained in a few police stations, Penry, an avowed physiognomist[213] and self-proclaimed "facial topographer," created a series of cutouts for each of five parts of the face (eyes, nose, mouth, chin, and hair) that could be assembled jigsaw-style to

---

205. Paul Lawrence, *Policing, 'Science,' and the Curious Case of Photo-Fit*, 63 HIST. J. 1007 (2020), https://doi.org/10.1017/S0018246X19000530; Tredoux et al., *supra* note 193, at 155.

206. TAYLOR, *supra* note 159, at 22.

207. *Id.*

208. *Id.*

209. Hopper, *supra* note 204.

210. Lawrence, *supra* note 205.

211. Davies & Valentine, *supra* note 167.

212. Tredoux et al., *supra* note 193, at 155–56.

213. In the late 1930s, Penry published a book called *Character from the Face*, in which he purported to be able to determine personality from a person's facial features. In the 1950s, he published another book in the same vein called *The Face of Man*. For a detailed description of Penry's beliefs on physiognomy see Lawrence, *supra* note 205.

create a composite image.[214] Penry's system, which resembled a children's boardgame he developed in 1939 ("Physogs"), was called Photo-FIT.[215]

Although the Identi-Kit and Photo-FIT were celebrated by the police departments that embraced them, both suffered from significant limitations from the moment they were introduced. To begin with, the range of features available in each kit was limited and not fully representative of the wide range of faces that exist in society.[216] Because both kits were assembled based on a single person's review of available mugshots, both were at great risk of being influenced by the biases of their creators. Notably, a common complaint about the original Photo-FIT, which Penry compiled in his mid-to-late 60s,[217] was that it did not include enough features from young people, giving most of the composites it produced a distinctly middle-aged look.[218] As Bertillon grasped in the late 1800s, what is needed to avoid such biases is (1) the ability to gauge where the average person stands in terms of each trait that determines their appearance, and (2) a sense of how much variation exists on either side of that average. It is not clear how much this insight guided the development of the Identi-Kit and Photo-FIT.

Moreover, neither kit was designed to allow operators to vary global characteristics like the age, shape, or size of a face, or the distance between features on a face, all of which can significantly impact the representativeness and recognizability of the composite.[219] Although operators developed workarounds to vary the size of the face relative to the features on it, none of these was easy to accomplish.[220] Further, as already noted, the original Identi-Kit lacked shading necessary to convey depth. In attempting to address this problem by using cut-outs from real photographs of people's faces, the Photo-FIT created a separate problem: distracting boundary-lines between the cut-outs that made up the composite.[221] Both systems were limited by the need for a separate operator to make selections on behalf of the eyewitness.[222] Finally, both systems required the eyewitness to begin the

214. Lawrence, *supra* note 205; Tredoux, et al. *supra* note 193, at 155–56.

215. Lawrence, *supra* note 205.

216. Graham Davies et al., *Facial Composite Production*, 85 J. Applied Psychol. 119, 119 (2000); Davies & Valentine, *supra* note 167.

217. Lawrence, *supra* note 205.

218. Davies & Valentine, *supra* note 167.

219. *Id.*

220. *Id.*

221. Davies et al., *supra* note 216, at 119.

222. Charlie D. Frowd et al., *EvoFIT: A Holistic, Evolutionary Facial Imaging Technique for Creating Composites*, 1 ACM Transactions Applied Perception 19, 22 (2004).

process of reconstructing a face by recalling and describing its individual features.[223] As discussed more in Chapter 3 on ***perception*** and ***memory***, people tend to process each other's faces more holistically.

c. Early Computer Technology

In the 1980s, computer technology emerged to address many of these problems at least to some degree. Early software packages like "Mac-a-Mug Pro" gave operators greater flexibility to manipulate the age, size, and shape of faces, as well as the distance between features on the face, and conveyed depth through shading without creating borderlines between different areas of the face, like the original Photo-FIT.[224] Because programmers had access to more robust databases, the programs they created were also more representative, at least as to white male faces.[225] Even so, these programs, like the manual kits that came before them, required eyewitnesses to recall and select facial features one at a time using a human operator as an intermediary.[226] The developers of the competing "E-FIT" software sought to address this issue by having the software make certain default feature choices based on the eyewitness's responses to certain multiple-choice questions.[227] Once the program had made its selections, they would appear on a model, and the witness could fine-tune each one by selecting from a range of algorithmically generated alternatives.[228] This system went a long way toward eliminating the "middle-man" problem of previous systems insofar as it replaced the human operator used in previous technologies with an algorithmic selection process. Even so, the program remained at odds with the holistic way humans see and remember faces because it required users to answer questions about facial features before refining the program's selections one feature at a time.[229]

---

223. *Id.*; Davies & Valentine, *supra* note 167.
224. Davies & Valentine, *supra* note 167.
225. *Id.*
226. *Id.*
227. *Id.*
228. *Id.*
229. Graham E. Pike et al., *Advances in Facial Composite Technology, Utilizing Holistic Construction, Do Not Lead to an Increase in Eyewitness Misidentifications Compared to Older Feature-Based Systems*, 10 Frontiers Psychol., Aug. 28, 2019, http://dx.doi.org/doi:10.3389/fpsyg.2019.01962.

d. Principal Components Analysis–Based Composite Software

A truly holistic alternative to feature-based composite construction did not emerge until the early 2000s, when software capable of using principal components analysis (PCA) to generate composite images was developed. PCA-driven composite software functions by means of an algorithm that allows it to distill a voluminous database of faces into a few representative "eigenfaces" by isolating principal components from the original set of faces.[230] These eigenfaces can then be combined in various ways to generate an array of composites. Specifically, by varying the "weight" that each eigenface receives in a given composite in a manner reminiscent of the technique Galton used to create "transformers" in the 1870s, *see supra*, the software can generate any face in the original database, as well as any one that occurs within the theoretical "space" defined by the variation between and among those faces. If the underlying database is sufficiently broad and representative, then the program theoretically could generate the face of any person in the population.

To generate a composite with PCA-based software, the eyewitness begins by selecting the face that looks most like the target's face from a grid of randomly selected options.[231] The precise number of options in the grid depends on the software. Once a face has been selected, the program uses an algorithm to generate a series of small variations on that face, and the witness again selects the face that looks the most like the target. As this process repeats, the faces in the grid begin to look more and more alike. When the witness can no longer say whether any one face looks more like the target than the others, the process is complete. One variation on this system involves having the eyewitness rank the faces they see in terms of how similar they are to the target face, rather than simply indicating which one they think looks most like the target face. Although PCA-based software is ubiquitous in the United Kingdom, it has never caught on among police departments in the United States, which continue to rely on computerized, feature-based composite technology.[232]

230. *Id.*
231. *Id.*
232. Tredoux et al., *supra* note 193.

3. *(How Long) Will Composites Endure?*

As noted in subsequent chapters of this book, sketches and composite images are riddled with the potential for case-altering bias. Any system that relies on a witness remembering and describing a person's facial features to someone else who is responsible for rendering them visually will be prone to inaccuracies, many of which are influenced by the expectations and stereotypes of both the witness and the artist/renderer. A sketch also may prejudice the accused by depicting him or her in an angry or menacing light. Thus, even assuming the sketch accurately reflects the dimensions and proportions of the perpetrator's face, something we can never really know, it still can have a lasting negative impact on how people perceive the perpetrator's state of mind at the time of the offense.

With all the drawbacks of police sketches and composite images, and the increasing availability of surveillance footage, one might guess that sketches and images are a dying art, like the live lineup. After all, surveillance cameras are pervasive and the images they generate have the distinct advantage of being totally unaffected by the vagaries of perception and memory.[233] However, for all their ubiquity, there are limits to what surveillance can capture. For the most part, they are mounted at a great distance from the people they monitor, so as to allow them to capture the widest area possible. As such, they may not be well positioned to capture facial features with the clarity needed to facilitate an identification.

It is perhaps for this reason that the composites and sketches still maintain modest relevance in American policing. At last check, just over a third of departments (35.5 percent) listed composite sketch preparation among their identification procedures.[234] Moreover, among those 112 agencies that reported using a composite sketch in 2010, the average number of composites prepared was three and the modal number was one.[235] The factors most

---

233. Todd Feathers, Ubiquitous Surveillance Cameras Are Changing Our Behavior, VICE, Jan. 17, 2020, https://www.vice.com/en/article/qjdbxm/ubiquitous-surveillance-cameras-are-changing-our-understanding-of-human-behavior. They were instrumental in allowing authorities to swiftly identify the Tsarnaev brothers in the wake of the Boston marathon bombing, leading many to advocate expanding surveillance capacity. *See, e.g.*, Stuart Caplan, *Is Ubiquitous Video Surveillance of Public Spaces Good Public Policy?*, ACLU OREGON https://www.aclu-or.org/en/ubiquitous-video-surveillance-public-spaces-good-public-policy (last visited March 16, 2024).

234. PERF SURVEY, *supra* note 8, at 66; *see also* IDENTI-KIT, https://identikit.net/ (last visited March 16, 2024) (noting that Identi-Kit software is used by 600 law enforcement departments).

235. PERF SURVEY, *supra* note 8, at 48.

likely to influence whether a sketch or composite was sought in a given case were "whether the witness [purports to have gotten] a particularly good view (66.1%), whether it is a high-profile case (53.8%), and whether there are few or no leads in the case (52.2%)."[236] Thus, the use of composite images and sketches appears to be a last-resort tactic that police use when they are under outside pressure to solve a case.

C. Field Views

Where police have not developed a suspect, an officer may accompany a witness to wherever that person might be located to see if the witness recognizes anyone.[237] For example, if the police suspect that a purse-snatcher is targeting a particular commercial space during the lunch hour, an officer "might take the eyewitness to the site and walk around with him or her during the lunch hour without [consciously] direct[] his or her attention to any specific individual."[238] As of 2010, this procedure was used by roughly one quarter of U.S. law enforcement agencies.[239]

Like other identification procedures, a field view's integrity can be compromised by an administrator's suspicions and suggestions. If the administrator sees someone during the field view who they think might be responsible for the crime under investigation—for instance, because that person has been arrested for a similar crime in the past—the administrator may give nonverbal cues that the witness picks up on subconsciously. Such cues can irrevocably taint the identification process. Although blind administration might solve this problem, there is no indication that any department has instituted such safeguards.

James McKenzie's Case

Field views seemingly used to be a lot more common. A field view figured prominently in the 1940s prosecution of James McKenzie for the rape and robbery of Vada Abarca in Washington, D.C. Mrs. Abarca had been working in a laundry service in

(continued)

236. *Id.* at 66.
237. *Id.* at 50.
238. Nat'l Rsch. Council, *supra* note 10, at 28.
239. PERF Survey, *supra* note 8, at 50.

James McKenzie's Case *(continued)*

Northwest D.C., when a man walked in and robbed her at gunpoint, before forcing her into a back room, where he raped her.[240] After a similar crime was reported several blocks away, the two complainants helped detectives search for the perpetrator by accompanying detectives on a ride through the neighborhood in the back of an unmarked police car.[241] When complainants saw Mr. McKenzie standing in front of another laundry service, they identified him immediately.[242] Thereafter, the police took him into custody and interrogated him.[243] Both complainants picked Mr. McKenzie out of a lineup the following day.[244] Mr. McKenzie was initially convicted and condemned to die, before the D.C. Circuit Court of Appeals reversed his conviction based on the trial judge's failure to alert his jury in plain English to the need to find the identification convincing beyond a reasonable doubt.[245] This holding will be discussed further in Chapter 3.

III. Surveillance-Based Identifications

As noted in the introduction to this chapter, the increased availability of surveillance is rapidly changing when, whether, and how police use eyewitness identification procedures in their cases. Even so, it is far too early to declare eyewitness identification obsolete. Although it is tempting to think that new technology will invariably decrease reliance on human powers of recognition, new technologies are not without their own drawbacks. Video surveillance rarely captures people's faces in fine enough detail to enable the factfinder in a criminal trial to make a confident identification. Since surveillance cameras tend to be positioned far away from the spaces they surveil, to maximize the size of the area under surveillance, they tend to capture fleeting glimpses of far-away faces under lighting conditions that may be less than ideal or less than conducive to comparison based on a known exemplar.

240. *McKenzie*, 126 F.2d at 534.

241. The 30-year-old manager of a different laundry service was similarly forced into a back room after being robbed at gunpoint. *Id.*

242. *2 Victims Help Trap D.C. Rape Suspect*, Wash. Post, 1, 13, June 27, 1941.

243. *Rape Suspect Identified in Police Line*, Wash. Post, 1, 5, June 28, 1941.

244. *Id.*

245. *McKenzie*, 126 F.2d at 534.

To ascertain the identity of the surveilled and/or compensate for the poor quality of images derived from surveillance, police may turn to some combination of facial recognition software, lay witnesses who purport to know a specific person's likeness well enough to recognize it in poor quality images, and/or experts who have been trained to compare faces across photos. Each of these techniques has its own drawbacks which in turn invite corroboration through more conventional eyewitness identification.

A. Facial Recognition Software

Without going into detail about how facial recognition software works, it suffices to say that at least some of it utilizes the same "principal components analysis" that was used to develop modern computerized facial composite software.[246] Precisely how many police departments use facial recognition software to generate identifications is unknown and unknowable, as some departments and officers who make use of facial recognition software either choose not to disclose that fact in their warrant applications or are forbidden to disclose their use of it by their contracts with the software companies.[247]

The use of artificial intelligence in this manner raises obvious questions about the reliability of the systems and algorithms used to enhance images and generate matches.[248] At least as of 2023, facial recognition was "far less accurate at identifying people of color and women than white men."[249] "[A] 2019 study by the National Institute of Science and Technology . . . found that many commercial face recognition algorithms were 10 to 100 times more inaccurate in identifying Asian and Black faces than white ones."[250] Already, it has led to a handful of confirmed wrongful arrests—each one of a different Black person—since it began spreading to police departments

246. *See, e.g.*, Kerri A. Thompson, *Countenancing Employment Discrimination: Facial Recognition in Background Checks*, 8 Tex. A&M L. Rev. 63, 71–73 (2020).

247. Kashmir Hill & Ryan Mac, *"Thousands of Dollars for Something I Didn't Do,"* N.Y. Times, March 31, 2023, https://www.nytimes.com/2023/03/31/technology/facial-recognition-false-arrests.html?action=click&module=RelatedLinks&pgtype=Article/.

248. *State v. Arteaga*, 476 N.J. Super. 36, 296 A.3d 542 (App. Div. 2023).

249. Tate Ryan-Mosely, *The Movement to Limit Face Recognition Tech Might Finally Get a Win,* MIT Technology Review, July 20, 2023, https://www.technologyreview.com/2023/07/20/1076539/face-recognition-massachusetts-test-police/.

250. *Id.*; Clare Garvie, *Garbage In, Garbage Out: Face Recognition on Flawed Data*, Geo. L. Ctr. on Priv. & Tech. (May 16, 2019), https://www.flawedfacedata.com.

across the country.[251] Eyewitness identification remains one way that police seek to corroborate the results of facial recognition software.

B. Image Comparison by Lay Witnesses

Another method used by police to overcome the flaws inherent in surveillance imagery involves asking someone familiar with the suspect's appearance whether they recognize the suspect in a piece of surveillance. To pursue this method, police must first develop a suspect. The opinions yielded by such inquiries are not "eyewitness identifications" because the identifying witnesses are not eyewitnesses to the crime. Rather, such witnesses are only competent to make identifications, insofar as they know enough about a suspect's appearance to be able to make an identification on the basis of such flawed and limited images.

Although identifications generated in this manner are not eyewitness identifications, they raise some of the same concerns about suggestion and reliability. When the police ask a citizen if they recognize someone from a set of images derived from surveillance, they necessarily suggest to the citizen their belief that the surveilled person is someone whom the citizen knows, who may have been involved in a crime. Often, even if the police do not come right out and say who they are investigating, the witness will be able to guess, based on the context of the inquiry and the person's general appearance in the surveillance. Combined with whatever pressure the citizen may feel to help the police advance their investigation, this ability to guess may lead some witnesses, consciously or subconsciously, to minimize any doubts they have about making an identification.

Those who make identifications based on surveillance from a crime scene may further be biased by their past experiences with those whom they identify. For instance, when attempting to determine the identity of someone in a piece of surveillance, police often turn to other members of law enforcement, who know the accused from their experience investigating, arresting, or supervising that person in a different case.[252] Given these drawbacks,

---

251. Kashmir Hill, *Eight Months Pregnant and Arrested After False Facial Recognition Match*, N.Y. Times (Aug. 6, 2023), https://www.nytimes.com/2023/08/06/business/facial-recognition-false-arrest.html/.

252. *See, e.g.*, *United States v. Fulton*, 837 F.3d 281 (3rd Cir. 2016); *United States. v. Jadlowe*, 628 F.3d 1 (1st Cir. 2010); *United States v. Henderson*, 68 F.3d 323 (9th Cir. 1995); *United States v. Stormer*, 938 F.2d 759 (7th Cir. 1991); *United States v. Barber*, 887 F.2d 266 (6th Cir. 1989); *United States v. Farnsworth*, 729 F.2d 1158 (8th Cir. 1984); *United States v.*

police likely will opt to corroborate any identification rendered under these circumstances with an eyewitness identification if possible.

C. Image Comparison by Analysts

To resolve the identity of a suspect in a piece of surveillance, police may also turn to forensic analysts who are trained to compare faces as they may appear in different kinds of photographs. "The FBI has been comparing facial images since at least the 1950s."[253] In 2000, the FBI merged its various photo- and video-analysis units to form a single Forensic, Audio, Video and Image Analysis Unit in Quantico, Virginia. Examiners in this unit compare samples submitted by other law enforcement agencies. As of 2012, the unit had around five employees specializing in facial comparison, all of whom had undergone a two-year training program. However, according to a 2019 article in the *Intercept*, the unit has since expanded.

Over the years, forensic facial-comparison analysts have relied on various techniques to enhance their facial-comparison ability, including (1) "feature classification," assigning facial features to descriptive categories; (2) "photographic anthropometry," comparing the angles and proportions of the spaces between specific facial landmarks (the corners of the eyes, nostrils, mouth, cheekbones, and jaw lines); (3) "morphology," analyzing the size, shape, and symmetry of various facial features and smaller parts thereof; and (4) "superimposition," merging two samples in an effort to better capture the similarities and differences between them.[254] In addition, like other forms of comparison analysis (fingerprints, firearms, etc.), facial comparison relies on the "ACE-V" principle, according to which examiners must:

- "Analyze" the unknown sample by blindly determining which aspects warrant comparison to the known sample;[255]

Allen, 787 F.2d 933 (4th Cir. 1986); *United States v. Butcher*, 557 F.2d 666 (9th Cir. 1977); *United States v. Calhoun*, 544 F.2d 291 (6th Cir. 1976).

253. Ava Kofman, *Losing Face: How Facial Recognition Mismatch Can Ruin Your Life*, INTERCEPT (Oct. 13, 2016), https://theintercept.com/2016/10/13/how-a-facial-recognition-mismatch-can-ruin-your-life/.

254. *Id.*

255. To minimize confirmation bias—the tendency to give greater weight to information that tends to confirm the existence of a "match"—there is widespread agreement that examiners should remain "blind" to known reference samples until they have determined which aspects of the questioned sample warrant comparison. PRESIDENT'S COMM. OF ADVISORS ON SCI. & TECH., FORENSIC SCIENCE IN CRIMINAL COURTS: ENSURING SCIENTIFIC VALIDITY OF FEATURE-COMPARISON METHODS 49 (2016) [hereinafter PCAST REPORT], https://obamawhitehouse.archives.gov/sites/default/files/microsites/ostp/PCAST/pcast_forensic_science_report_final.pdf.

- "Compare" the known and unknown samples to each other by examining the relevant points of comparison;[256]
- "Evaluate" the degree of similarity between the two samples according to a standard scale;[257] and
- "Verify" the analysis by transferring it to another examiner who repeats it to determine if the results can be replicated.[258]

Throughout this process, examiners must document each choice and observation they make.

Although courts have been permitting FBI analysts to opine regarding the identity of those captured on surveillance since the 1970s,[259] there is ample reason for skepticism regarding the scientific rigor of these methodologies. To begin with, although facial comparison techniques date back to Bertillon and Galton in the late 1800s, until very recently, there had never been any standards governing when or how to apply them. Nor had any scientific research been conducted to show whether any of these techniques actually improved an analyst's ability to compare faces. Although the purpose of "ACE-V" was to prevent examiner bias from affecting the outcome of forensic comparison analysis, it did not have the strongest track record in that regard.[260] A big problem with ACE-V was that although it requires verification of results, until recently, there were no standards requiring that verification be "blind." In other words, it was perfectly common and acceptable for the verifying examiner to know exactly what the original examiner concluded.

These problems came to a head in 2009, when the operating arm of the National Academy of Sciences, the National Research Council, published a report calling for more rigorous standards across all forensic disciplines. In addition to concluding that ACE-V is insufficient to ensure the scientific rigor needed for admissibility under *Daubert*,[261] the report specifically noted that a great deal of forensic evidence had been "introduced in criminal trials

---

256. Rueben Moreton, *Forensic Face Matching: Procedures and Applications*, *in* FORENSIC FACE MATCHING: RESEARCH AND PRACTICE (2021), https://doi.org/10.1093/oso/9780198837749.003.0007.

257. *Id.*

258. *Id.*

259. *United States v. Cairns*, 434 F.2d 644 (9th Cir. 1970); *see also United States v. Brown*, 501 F.2d 146 (9th Cir. 1974); *United States v. Brown*, 511 F.2d 920 (2d Cir. 1975).

260. NAT'L RSCH. COUNCIL, STRENGTHENING FORENSIC SCIENCE IN THE UNITED STATES: A PATH FORWARD 137–45 (2009), http://www.nap.edu/catalog/12589.html (outlining problems with ACE-V in the context of latent fingerprint examination).

261. *Id.* at 142.

without any meaningful scientific validation, determination of error rates, or reliability testing to explain the limits of the discipline."[262] The absence of an error rate was particularly problematic because it allowed unwarranted and unsupportable claims about the reliability of forensic methods to go unimpeached.[263] As such, the report called for research into whether such disciplines were actually founded on "reliable scientific principles," as well as the promulgation of "procedures and performance standards to guard against [the] bias and error" that are inherent in any discipline that relies on human observation.[264]

In response, the FBI formed the "Facial Identification Scientific Working Group" (FISWG) to recommend uniform standards and best practices.[265] The FISWG, in turn, helped to develop a "standard list of facial components and component characteristics to be assessed and evaluated during a morphological analysis"—the E3149 "Standard Guide for Facial Image Comparison List for Morphological Analysis"—while discouraging reliance on other methods such as feature classification, photographic-anthropometry, and superimposition, which have been proven either unreliable or fatally prone to inconsistent application.[266] However, FISWG's efforts to standardize human facial recognition have run into the same problem that brought down *Bertillonage* more than a century ago (and which continues to plague every pattern-matching disciplines to some degree): nobody knows just how common or distinctive a particular set of facial features really is.[267] The FBI and FISWG have been working to address this issue in a variety of ways, but it is unclear whether they will succeed in this endeavor.[268] Unless and until

262. *Id.* at 108.

263. *Id.* at 103.

264. *Id.* at 111.

265. Kofman, *supra* note 253.

266. *See* Facial Identification Scientific Working Group, Facial Comparison Overview and Methodology Guidelines, Version 2.0 (2022), https://fiswg.org/fiswg_facial_comparison_overview_and_methodology_guidelines_V2.0_2022.11.04.pdf.

267. *See* Kofman, *supra* note 253.

268. To address this problem, the FBI called for the creation of a database of faces, akin to others maintained by federal law enforcement (e.g., Automated Fingerprint Index System ("AFIS"), the Combined DNA Index System ("CODIS"), and National Integrated Ballistic Information Network ("NIBIN")), on the theory that it would allow the FBI to estimate how often certain features and feature combinations occur in the population. *See* Martin Paul Evison & Richard W. Vorder Bruegge, *The Magna Database: A Database of Three-Dimensional Facial Images for Research in Human Identification and Recognition*, 10:2 Forensic Science Communications (2008), https://archives.fbi.gov/archives/about-us/lab/forensic-science-communications/fsc/april2008/research/2008_04_research01.htm. The status of this proposal is unknown.

these reliability questions are resolved, there is no reason to think this technology will pose a threat to the role of traditional eyewitness identification in criminal investigation.

IV. Conclusion

As noted in the introduction to this chapter, more up-to-date information about how the police administer identification procedures to draw firm conclusions would greatly illuminate the question of how well or poorly police adhere to best practices related to eyewitness identification. However, what we do know leaves plenty of room for concern, especially for people in small jurisdictions serviced by smaller police departments. As of 2010, such departments were less likely to have incorporated best practices such as blind administration, preprocedure instructions, and documentation of confidence in the identification procedures they administered.[269] This disparity has devastating implications for those accused of crimes in small jurisdictions that lack the capacity for routine DNA testing and thus are more reliant on eyewitness identifications.

Moreover, what we know about police identification procedures, their history, and their outsized role in contributing to wrongful convictions suggests a strong need for oversight to ensure that, to the greatest degree possible, they serve as a genuine test of memory, rather than a hollow formality. As the foregoing discussion demonstrates, the identification procedures that police rely on to generate statements of identification were not decreed by prophets. Nor were they created by psychologists in laboratories in search of the least error-prone method for discerning genuine recognition.[270] With

---

In 2016, the President's Committee of Advisors on Science and Technology (PCAST) separately called for error rate calculations to inform determinations regarding the admissibility of forensic testimony and to prevent unwarranted claims regarding the value of comparison analysis and the likelihood of a "match," given certain similarities. PCAST Report, *supra* note 255. To establish such error rates, PCAST recommended "black-box studies," where "examiners are presented with many independent comparison problems—typically, involving 'questioned' samples and one or more 'known' samples—and asked to declare whether the questioned samples came from the same source as one of the known samples." *Id.* As yet, no forensic facial comparison "black box" study has been released.

269. Rachel L. Greenspan & Elizabeth F. Loftus, *Patterns in the Use of Best Practices for Eyewitness Identifications in the Field*, 29 Psychol. Crime & L. 161 (2023) https://doi.org/10.1080/1068316X.2021.2018436.

270. However, psychologists have suggested that the probative value of lineups would improve if police behaved more like scientists in administering them. Gary L. Wells & C.A. Elizabeth Luus, *Police Lineups as Experiments: Social Methodology as a Framework for Properly-Conducted Lineups*, 16 Person. & Soc. Psychol. Bull. 106 (1990), https://doi:10.1177/0146167290161008.

the notable exception of the lineup, which was adopted to address "judicial criticisms of the cruder methods of identification,"[271] police devised these methods to generate the evidence they need to close cases, and they have persisted, lo these many years, because they tend to do so more efficiently than the alternatives.

To break the cycle of the "[i]nnocent people" being unnecessarily deprived of their liberty, while "perpetrator[s] go[] free, and public confidence in the judicial system erodes,"[272] police need oversight and accountability: from experts who can identify best practices and suggestive practices and ascertain the degree to which specific procedures ascertain genuine recognition or induce mere willingness to identify; from commanders who can implement best practices and discourage suggestive ones through internal regulations and training; from supervisors who can promote adherence to best practices in individual cases; from advocates and attorneys who can expose when police practice falls short of best practice and tends toward the suggestive; from prosecutors who can encourage best practices and discourage suggestive ones through their decision not to prosecute certain cases; and from judges and juries who can do the same by suppressing evidence of suggestively generated identifications or by returning a verdict of acquittal.

271. Devlin Report, *supra* note 16, ¶ 5.29, at 112.
272. *2019 Third Circuit Task Force Report*, *supra* note 65, at 11 (citation omitted).

2
Admissibility of Eyewitness Identification

When may the government coerce someone's participation in a pretrial identification procedure? What rules govern such procedures? When may the government elicit the identification from a witness who has taken part in such a procedure? These questions have the potential to implicate many different areas of the law—from the United States Constitution and state constitutions, to the rules of evidence and holdings made pursuant to the supervisory jurisdiction of various appellate courts, to the internal regulations that govern how police investigate crime and interact with the public, more generally. Nevertheless, as a practical matter, U.S. Supreme Court jurisprudence predominates in this area,[1] in part because so many state courts have interpreted their state due process guarantees to provide no more protection against the risk of wrongful conviction due to misidentification than the federal Constitution.[2]

1. Nat'l Rsch. Council of the Nat'l Acads., Identifying the Culprit: Assessing Eyewitness Identification 32 (2014) [hereinafter Nat'l Rsch. Council].

2. *Proctor v. State*, 424 So.2d 705, 708–09 (Ala. Crim. App. 1982); *State v. Bracy*, 703 P.2d 464, 474–75 (Ariz. 1985); *Chism v. State*, 853 S.W.2d 255 (Ark. 1993); *People v. Clark*, 833 P.2d 561 (Cal. 1992); *People v. Weller*, 679 P.2d 1077, 1083 (Colo. 1984); *Younger v. State*, 496 A.2d 546, 550 (Del. 1985); *Turner v. United States*, 622 A.2d 667, 672 (D.C.1993);

In 1977, the Supreme Court established a two-part test for determining whether the Due Process Clause requires the exclusion of an eyewitness identification in a case called *Manson v. Brathwaite*. Under *Manson*, an identification must be excluded if a judge finds that the police used "impermissibly suggestive" conduct to obtain it, resulting in a "very substantial likelihood of irreparable misidentification" based on (1) the witness's opportunity to observe and (2) degree of attention, (3) the accuracy of the witness's prior description, (4) the level of certainty demonstrated at the confrontation, and (5) the time between the crime and the confrontation. This chapter considers the development of this test, before chronicling recent departures from it.

The *Manson* test derives from three cases decided on the same day in 1967—*United States v. Wade*, 388 U.S. 218 (1967), *Gilbert v. California*, 388 U.S. 263 (1967), and *Stovall v. Denno*, 388 U.S. 293 (1967). In *Wade* and *Gilbert*, the Court recognized the right to counsel during live pretrial confrontations between the accused and an eyewitness, and established a multifactor test for determining whether an eyewitness's ability to identify the defendant from the witness stand was attributable to the fact that

---

Collins v. State, 626 So.2d 991, 992 (Fla. Dist. Ct. App. 1993); *State v. Masaniai*, 628 P.2d 1018 (Haw. 1981); *State v. Hoisington*, 657 P.2d 17 (Idaho 1989); *People v. Miller*, 626 N.E.2d 1350 (Ill. 1993); *Hamlet v. State*, 490 N.E.2d 715, 720 (Ind. 1986); *State v. Thornton*, 506 N.W.2d 777, 779–80 (Iowa 1993); *State v. Holloman*, 837 P.2d 826 (Kan. Ct. App. 1992); *Wilson v. Commonwealth*, 695 S.W.2d 854, 857 (Ky. 1985); *State v. Robinson*, 386 So.2d 1374, 1377 (La. 1980); *State v. Rolls*, 599 A.2d 421, 423 (Me. 1991); *Small v. State*, 211 A.3d 236 (Md. 2019); *State v. Lambert*, 278 N.W.2d 57, 57 (Minn. 1979) (per curiam); *McNeal v. State*, 405 So.2d 90, 92–93 (Miss. 1981); *State v. Carter*, 572 S.W.2d 430, 435 (Mo. 1978); *State v. Johnson*, 674 P.2d 1077 (Mont. 1983); *State v. Richard*, 424 N.W.2d 859 (Neb. 1988); *Gehrke v. State*, 613 P.2d 1028 (Nev. 1980); *State v. Whittey*, 591 A.2d 1326 (N.H. 1991); *State v. Maes*, 665 P.2d 1169 (N.M. 1983); *State v. Richardson*, 402 S.E.2d 401 (N.C. 1991); *State v. Packineau*, 423 N.W.2d 148, 149–50 (N.D. 1988); *State v. Parker*, 558 N.E.2d 1164 (Ohio 1990); *Sherman v. State*, 675 P.2d 458, 459 (Okla. Crim. App. 1984); *Commonwealth v. Baker*, 614 A.2d 663 (Pa. 1992); *State v. Gomes*, 604 A.2d 1249, 1253 (R.I. 1992); *State v. Stewart*, 272 S.E.2d 628 (S.C. 1980); *State v. Phinney*, 348 N.W.2d 466, 468–69 (S.D.1984); *State v. Short*, 698 S.W.2d 81, 83 (Tenn. Crim. App. 1985); *Jackson v. State*, 657 S.W.2d 123, 130 (Tex. Crim. App. 1983); *Satcher v. Commonwealth*, 421 S.E.2d 821 (Va. 1992); *State v. Maupin*, 822 P.2d 355 (Wash. Ct. App. 1992); *State v. Woodall*, 385 S.E.2d 253 (W. Va. 1989); *State v. Roberson*, 935 N.W.2d 813 (Wis. 2019); *Alberts v. State*, 642 P.2d 447, 450 (Wyo. 1982). *But see State v. Harris*, 191 A.3d 119, 142 (Conn. 2018) (departing from the Supreme Court's test; noting that "courts in Alaska, Kansas, Massachusetts, New Jersey, New York, Utah and Wisconsin have held as a matter of state constitutional law that the *Biggers* framework insufficiently protects against the risk of misidentification, and the courts of Georgia and Oregon have reached the same conclusion as a matter of state evidentiary law."); *State v. Discola*, 184 A.3d 1177 (Vt. 2018) (same); *State v. Martinez*, 478 P.3d 880 (N.M. 2021) (same).

the police had arranged a pretrial identification procedure without counsel's presence or permission. In *Stovall*, the Court established the threshold principle that Due Process prohibits the admission of an eyewitness identification obtained by suggestive police practices. However, before considering these cases and how they led to *Manson*, it is worthwhile to consider the circumstances that led the Court to determine (or at the very least, coincided with its apparent determination) that a constitutional rule was needed.

*I. Pre-*Wade *Admissibility*

By the time the Court got around to imposing constitutional limits on eyewitness identification evidence in the late 1960s, jurists, scholars, and practitioners were keenly aware of the fallibility of such evidence, even if they were comparatively ignorant as to the root causes and full scope of the problem. Such fallibility had been documented in infamous cases throughout history. As Justice Brennan wrote in *Wade*, "the annals of criminal law [were] rife with instances of mistaken identification" by the early twentieth century.[3] Indeed, so "many" were these "cases of mistaken identity" by 1874, that one judge charged his jury to exercise "scrupulous care and caution" with respect to identifications, at least insofar as they appeared to conflict with other evidence.[4] A relatively short time later, the Pennsylvania Supreme Court observed that due to the myriad vagaries of perception, "identification [was] one of the least reliable facts testified to by actual witnesses who have seen the parties in question"[5] and that "[n]o class of testimony [was] more uncertain and less to be relied upon."[6]

By the turn of the twentieth century, scholars in the emerging field of psychology had begun to expose and document the limits of our ability to identify strangers after brief and stressful encounters. In a 1905 experiment, a Swiss professor named Rene-Édouard Claparède arranged for a masked

3. *United States v. Wade*, 388 U.S. 218, 228 (1967).

4. *Tisdale v. Mut. Ben. Life Ins. Co.*, 23 F. Cas. 1302, 1303 (C.C.D. Iowa 1874), *rev'd on other grounds*, 91 U.S. 238, 23 L. Ed. 314 (1875); *see also* 2 Charles C. Moore, Treatise on Facts § 1292, at 1366 (1908) (citing *Palmer v. Baird*, 29 N.B. Rep. 42, 55 (1888)) (noting Canadian judge's observation that "a person may be mistaken, and sometimes is, as to the identity of his best known friend," even "under circumstances when one would think a mistake could not very well occur"); 14 Law Notes: April, 1910 to March, 1911, at 125 (Thompson rev. 1911) (same).

5. *Estate of Bryant*, 176 Pa. 309 (1896).

6. *Commonwealth v. House*, 223 Pa. 487, 493 (1909).

man to break into his classroom and accost him during a lesson, thereafter asking his students to both describe the assailant and to pick his mask out of a lineup.[7] Claparéde expected his students to falter in their verbal descriptions, as he believed "it [would be] far easier to recognise something you have before seen than to describe it from memory."[8] Much to his surprise, however, they also struggled to identify the assailant's mask when it was presented in a lineup—of the twenty-three participants, only five positively identified the assailant's mask to the exclusion of all the others and only eight included it among a list of possible suspects; ten incorrectly excluded it altogether.[9] Consistent with these findings, Professor Frederick Welton Colegrove wrote in 1900 that "[m]ost people cannot easily remember faces."[10] Hugo Münsterberg, the German-born head of Harvard's psychology laboratory, had likewise called into question the relationship between eyewitness certainty and accuracy.[11] With the notable exception of Münsterberg's work, which drew sharp criticism from legal scholars and professionals, these works were fairly influential among legal scholars in the early twentieth century, garnering mention in prominent treatises.[12]

In 1904, an Englishman named Adolf Beck was pardoned following fifteen separate wrongful convictions over the course of two different criminal trials for defrauding women of their jewels.[13] In both trials, Beck was confidently identified by multiple eyewitnesses. After the first conviction, Beck served five years in prison. Days after the second conviction, police arrested the real culprit as he was attempting to pawn the spoils of his latest caper. Beck's ordeal led to public outcry and myriad reforms, including the creation of a Court of Criminal Appeal with the power to overturn criminal convictions infected by tainted identifications.[14] By contrast, the predecessor to this court was more limited in its ability to alter criminal judgments. Moreover, the Crown

---

7. Professor Ed. Claparede, "*What Is the Value of Evidence?*", 34 Strand 143, 147 (1907).

8. *Id.* at 148.

9. *Id.*

10. F.W. Colegrove, Memory: An Inductive Study 346 (1900).

11. Hugo Münsterberg, On the Witness Stand 55–56 (1908).

12. 2 Moore, Treatise on Facts § 1292, at 1366, *cited with approval in* 3 Wigmore, Evidence § 786a, at 205 (Chadbourn rev. 1970); 14 Law Notes, *supra* note 4, at 125; John H. Wigmore, *Professor Munsterberg and the Psychology of Testimony*, 3 Ill. L. Rev. 399, 433 (1909).

13. Regarding the facts of the Beck case, *see generally* Brian Cathcart, *The Strange Case of Adolf Beck*, Independent, Oct. 17, 2004, https://independent.co.uk/news/uk/crime/the-strange-case-of-adolf-beck-535209.html.

14. Felix Frankfurter, The Case of Sacco and Vanzetti 30 (1927).

commissioned an inquiry into the case, which led to the official pronouncement that "[e]vidence as to identity based on personal impressions, however *bona fide*, is perhaps of all classes of evidence the least to be relied upon, and therefore, unless supported by other facts, an unsafe basis for verdict of a jury."[15]

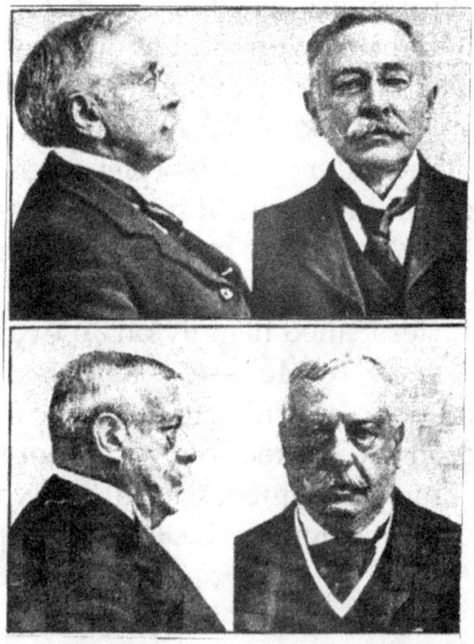

Adolf Beck (Top) and the Man Who Confessed to His Charges (Bottom). Scan from *Crimes and Punishment* magazine.

In 1927, civil libertarian and future Supreme Court Justice Felix Frankfurter released a book in his capacity as a Harvard law professor, chronicling the role of faulty identifications in the convictions of Nicola Sacco and Bartolomeo Vanzetti—Italian anarchists infamously executed for murdering the guard and paymaster at a shoe factory in Braintree, Massachusetts. In his book, Frankfurter wrote that "the identification of strangers is proverbially untrustworthy" and "runs all the grave hazards . . . due to the frailties and fallibilities of human observation and memory."[16] In 1932, another "well known" book by Edwin Borchard analyzed sixty-five wrongful convictions and concluded that twenty-nine of them had come about as a result of faulty eyewitness identification.[17]

15. *Id.*
16. *Id.* at 24, 30.
17. *Lawyers and Lineups*, 77 Yale L.J. 390, 391 (1967) (citing Edwin Borchard, Convicting the Innocent 1–6 (1932)); *see also id.* at 392 (citing *The Case Against Personal Identification*, 13 Fortnightly L.J. 87 (1943)).

Frankfurter's Musing on the Cross-Race Effect

One of Justice Frankfurter's more forward-thinking insights about Sacco and Vanzetti's case involved the fact that they belonged to a different ethnicity than the people who had identified them. Frankfurter argued that this factor undermined the reliability of each identification, noting one witness in particular who initially had mistaken one of the suspects for "a Portuguese fellow named Tony that he knew."[18] As noted in the ensuing chapters of this book, the tendency to experience greater difficulty or inaccuracy when making identifications across a racial or ethnic divide is called "own-race bias" or the "cross-race effect," and numerous empirical studies have documented its existence. Although Frankfurter leaned heavily on an overtly racist song—"All Coons Look Alike To Me"—to make his case for the prevalence of the cross-race effect,[19] modern research shows that it does not depend on the degree to which people harbor overtly racist attitudes. This phenomenon will be explored in greater detail in Chapter 6 on **system** and **estimator variables**.

Nevertheless, before *Wade*, American courts historically imposed few restrictions on the use of eyewitness identification in criminal cases. Rather, the American legal system's relationship to eyewitness identification was characterized by its blind faith in the jury's innate ability to determine the latter's reliability with assistance of duly probing cross-examination and appropriate instruction regarding the government's burden of proof beyond a reasonable doubt—in the words of Chief Judge David Bazelon of the D.C. Circuit, a willingness to "bravely assume[]" (to the detriment of the accused)

18. Frankfurter, *supra* note 14, at 31.

19. Frankfurter likened the struggle to differentiate between "men of foreign races" like Sacco and Vanzetti to the struggle of a woman to differentiate between her Black paramours in the racist minstrel song, "All Coons Look Alike to Me." Frankfurter, *supra* note 14, at 31. In the song, the narrator complains that his lover has left him for another "Nig" because "all coons look alike" to her. *Voices Across Time: United/Divided*, U. Pitt. Libr. Sys., https://voices.pitt.edu/TeachersGuide/Unit%206/Song%20Page%20AllCoonsLookAlike.htm. While Frankfurter argued that these lyrics "represent[ed] a deep experience of human fallibility," Frankfurter, *supra* note 14, at 31, the song's popularity was perhaps an even stronger bellwether regarding racial attitudes and the risk of cross-racial misidentification at the turn of the century.

"that the jury is capable of evaluating [the] reliability" of almost every identification, despite much evidence to the contrary.[20]

Bazelon wrote that this "brave[] assum[ption]" was, "no doubt, attributable at least in part to the perce[ption]," among judges and policymakers, that "the [criminal] process could [not] operate without identifications."[21] To drive this point home, he pointed to "the difference between [the legal system's] approach to polygraph tests and to identifications"—although identifications are "perhaps consistently less reliable than [the results of] lie detector tests, which [many courts] exclude[] for unreliability," authorities have never given serious consideration to barring identifications from criminal trials.[22] In Bazelon's view, the most likely explanation for this disparity was "the perceived differences in [the legal system's] need for the information"—while judges "have no difficulty conceiving of a criminal process that operates without the aid of lie detectors, even if [they] assume that lie detectors might in some instances enhance the process[,] . . . it is hard to see how the process could operate without identifications[.]"[23]

Bazelon's polygraph analogy is arguably flawed insofar as the problem with polygraphs is not just their unreliability, but also their potential to lull jurors into abandoning their duty to serve as lie detectors.[24] But even setting this example aside, there are many examples of the American willingness to "bravely assume" the jury's ability to weigh identification evidence, owing to the perception that the legal system could not function without it. For instance, American courts generally have adhered to the common law "one witness rule" whereby the uncorroborated testimony of one witness may be sufficient to sustain a conviction, thus "declining to follow the rule of the canon and civil law requiring a greater number of witnesses or corroboration."[25] This rule is expressly rooted in the "recogni[tion] that certain crimes are solitary," but no less deserving of punishment on that basis, and the further assumption that procedural "safeguards," like the right to

20. *United States v. Brown*, 461 F.2d 134, 145 n.1 (D.C. Cir. 1972) (en banc) (Bazelon, C.J., dissenting).

21. *Id.*

22. *Id.*

23. *Id.*

24. *See United States v. Scheffer*, 523 U.S. 303, 314 (1998) (Thomas, J.) (plurality opinion). *But see id.* at 318 (Kennedy J., concurring in part and concurring in judgment) (arguing to the contrary).

25. *Telfaire v. United States*, 469 F.2d 552, 554 (D.C. Cir. 1972) (per curiam); *United States v. Levi*, 405 F.2d 380, 383 (4th Cir. 1965).

trial by jury, will suffice to "dilute the danger of conviction of the innocent, a problem that concerns every civilized system of justice."[26]

The same "brave[] assum[ption]" lay at the heart of countless cases holding that all circumstances tending to affect the reliability of an identification are "customary grist for the jury mill,"[27] no matter how seriously they might undermine the integrity of the identification. Although, in the wake of the Beck incident, the newly established Court of Criminal Appeal showed some willingness to vacate convictions based on identifications shown to have been suggestively obtained,[28] the consensus among American courts was that such suggestiveness went to the weight of the resulting identification, not its admissibility.[29] Likewise, judges were (and are) hostile to the idea that the prosecution should be prevented from presenting evidence of an identification based on practical limitations on the eyewitness's ability to perceive a suspect.[30] Although, like all evidence, identifications are subject to the requirement that they have some probative value that is not substantially outweighed by the unfair prejudice that would result from admitting them, as a practical matter this principle was seldom used to exclude an

---

26. *Telfaire*, 469 F.2d at 554.

27. *Manson v. Brathwaite*, 432 U.S. 98, 116 (1977).

28. *See* Dickman's Case, 5 Cr. App. Rep. 135, 142-45 (1910) ("If we thought in any case that justice depended upon the independent identification of the person charged, and that the identification appeared to have been induced by some suggestion or other means, we should not hesitate to quash any conviction which followed."); FRANKFURTER, *supra* note 14, at 31 & n.1 (collecting cases). Given Frankfurter's professed admiration for the criminal system in England and his ascension to the U.S. Supreme Court, it is a wonder that the British example did not have more influence on the law in this area. *See, e.g., Malinski v. New York*, 324 U.S. 401, 419 (1945) (Frankfurter, J., concurring) ("Despite the fact that English criminal justice has serious inadequacies and lags behind some of our penological advances, it is undeniable that on the whole it is much more effective than ours.").

29. *See, e.g., Redmon v. Commonwealth*, 321 S.W.2d 397 (Ky. 1959); *see also* Daniel E. Murray, *The Criminal Lineup at Home and Abroad*, 1966 UTAH L. REV. 610, 616 (1966) (describing the weight/admissibility distinction as a "cliché").

30. *See, e.g., State v. Woodruff*, 67 N.C. 89, 92 (1872) ("The law allows persons to testify to such identity or to such resemblance who have had an opportunity of seeing such persons, if but for an instant."); *see also* 2 WIGMORE, EVIDENCE § 660(c), at 898–99 & n.1 (Chadbourn rev. 1979) (collecting cases; noting: "It has been properly held, for example, that a witness may testify to a person's identity from his voice alone, or from observing his stature, complexion, clothing, or other marks, or from the sight of a person's photograph[.]"); *Reid*, 187 A. at 266 ("[E]vidence of identification, . . . need not be positive and certain. A witness may testify that it is his belief, opinion, or judgment that the accused is the person who committed the crime. The indefiniteness and uncertainty in the testimony, of course, affects its weight." (quoting 2 WHARTON'S CRIMINAL EVIDENCE § 932, at 1626).

identification, except, perhaps, where it would be cumulative of other evidence presented.[31]

Similarly, although the rules of evidence have long required lay witnesses to refrain from offering opinions about the relevant facts at trial,[32] and although every identification is "a matter of opinion or belief concerning a fact,"[33] there has never been any doubt that the common law restrictions on lay opinion testimony did not in any way constrain testimony regarding the identity of a person or thing.[34] Jurists and scholars have long agreed that, although it is generally desirable to confine lay witness testimony to the facts underlying their opinions, it would be impractical to confine eyewitnesses to such a restriction because an identification may be reliable notwithstanding the eyewitness's inability to explain it; thus, imposing such a limitation would inevitably deprive the jury of some evidence that could genuinely be probative of identity.[35]

The most significant judicial restriction on identification evidence before *Wade* involved "the intricacies of the hearsay rule."[36] Notably, after a few influential turn-of-the-century cases suggested that evidence of extrajudicial identification might be inadmissible to the same degree as any other prior consistent statement offered by a witness—that is, inadmissible unless it had some tendency to rebut a claim that the in-court identification was recently fabricated[37] —consensus quickly emerged around the idea that pretrial identification procedures were far too probative and/or persuasive to keep from the jury on hearsay grounds, at least insofar as the identifying witness was available for cross-examination.[38]

31. STEVEN I. FRIEDLAND ET AL., EVIDENCE LAW AND PRACTICE 478 (2d ed. 2004).

32. Wigmore estimated that the general prohibition on such testimony emerged somewhere in the late 1700s or early 1800s. *See* 7 WIGMORE, EVIDENCE § 1917 at 1 (Chadbourn rev. 1978).

33. *Medsker v. State*, 152 N.E.2d 182, 183 (Ind. 1946).

34. 7 WIGMORE, *supra* note 32, § 1977 at 1; *accord Com. v. Reid*, 187 A. 263, 266 (Pa. Super. 1936) ("The opinion, belief, judgment, or impression of an ordinary witness as to the identity of a person or an object is admissible in evidence, provided such testimony is based upon his own knowledge and not upon information furnished by another. Identification may be made through the perception of any of the senses, and it is not essential that the witness should himself be free from doubt as to the correctness of his opinion.") (quoting 2 WHARTON'S CRIMINAL EVIDENCE § 1015, at 1776).

35. *See generally* 7 WIGMORE, EVIDENCE § 1977, at 190–200 (Chadbourn rev. 1978).

36. *Lawyers and Lineups*, 77 YALE L.J. 390, 391 (1967).

37. *Warren v. State*, 146 S.W. 477, 479 (Ark. 1915); *People v. Jung Hing*, 106 N. E. 105, 107, (N.Y. 1914). *But see Com. v. Connors*, 27 A. 366 (Pa. 1893) (charging the jury to consider evidence of the pretrial photographic lineup that took place).

38. *See, e.g.*, *State v. Buschman*, 29 S.W.2d 688, 691 (Mo. 1930); *People v. Savage*, 152 P.2d 240, 244 (Cal. App. 1944) (collecting cases).

Why did the American legal system have a mid-century change of heart on the admissibility of extrajudicial identification? To be sure, part of the explanation involves skepticism regarding the probative value of in-court identification. Extrajudicial identifications have always had the advantage of happening much closer in time to the offense under investigation, "affording less opportunity for deterioration or fading of the identifier's impressions or recollection and for changes in the appearance of the accused or guilty party, and thus enabling the identifier to be more certain or positive as to the identification."[39] More to the point, in-court identification has never been much of a test of the witness's ability to recall a particular suspect. Unless the defense makes a successful request for an alternate seating arrangement, the defendant reliably can be expected to occupy a chair next to the attorney with whom the witness is less or least familiar. This dynamic was further exacerbated by the prevalence of shackling and prison garb in early-twentieth-century courtrooms. As the Second Circuit remarked in a 1951 case, which held prior statements of identification admissible, "[i]dentification of the accused is frequently dubious and when made in open court sometimes has little testimonial value so that corroboration would seem to be properly allowed."[40]

Part of the explanation for this shift may also involve the increased perception of police officers as "professionals" capable of guaranteeing the kind of reliability that a modern criminal legal system demands.[41] By the mid-twentieth century, police lineups had been normalized through police dramas on radio and television and in film.[42] At the same time, law enforcement agencies were advocating that their officers could collect eyewitness identifications in the same "systematized or scientific" way that they collected "fingerprints, blood sample[s], clothing, and hair."[43] Whatever happened to

39. C.R. McCorkle, *Admissibility of Evidence as to Extrajudicial or Pretrial Identification of the Accused*, 71 A.L.R.2d 449 § 4[a] & n.17 (2023) (collecting cases).

40. *United States v. Forzano*, 190 F.2d 687, 689 (2d Cir. 1951).

41. *See, e.g.*, David Alan Sklansky, *The Persistent Pull of Police Professionalism*, NEW PERSPS. POLICING (2011), https://www.ojp.gov/pdffiles1/nij/232676.pdf.

42. *See, e.g.*, *The Lineup: Cop Killer* (CBS television broadcast, Nov. 12, 1954), https://www.youtube.com/watch?v=NFvCHedA7KQ (accessed Aug. 12, 2022); THE LINEUP (Columbia Pictures 1958), https://youtu.be/y776sAcJds4?t=962 (accessed Aug. 14, 2022); DESTINATION MURDER (RKO Radio Pictures 1950).

43. *United States v. Wade*, 388 U.S. 218, 227 (1967); *see also* David R. Papke, *A History of the Mugshot*, MARQUETTE U.L. SCH. FACULTY BLOG, https://law.marquette.edu/facultyblog/2013/10/a-history-of-the-mug-shot/ (noting that in the mid-1800s "some thought of the mug shot as a useful component in 'scientific law enforcement.'").

change the judicial perception of police identification procedures, by the mid-twentieth century, the mainstream view was that they were "ordinarily more reliable than an identification at the trial."[44] It was against this backdrop of renewed enthusiasm for extrajudicial identifications that Supreme Court regulation of eyewitness identification emerged.[45]

II. The Road to Manson

A. *Wade, Gilbert,* and the Right to Counsel

In *United States v. Wade*, 388 U.S. 218 (1967), and *Gilbert v. California*, 388 U.S. 263 (1967), the Supreme Court extended the Sixth Amendment right to counsel to postindictment, pretrial confrontations involving the accused. The Court had recently extended the right to counsel to those facing felony prosecution in state court in *Gideon v. Wainwright*, 372 U.S. 335 (1963), a burglary case that involved an eyewitness of questionable veracity.[46] In *Wade*, the Court confronted a conviction arising out of the robbery of a federally insured bank in Texas.[47] The robber had entered the bank wearing a disguise made of tape and forced the employees to fill a pillowcase with money at gunpoint.[48] Wade was subsequently arrested, indicted, and appointed counsel for his defense. While he was awaiting trial at the courthouse jail, an FBI agent arranged for him to appear in a lineup where two of the bank's employees identified him as the robber.[49] At the agent's direction, those in the lineup wore tape on their faces and spoke the words allegedly uttered by the perpetrator during the robbery.[50] The agent provided no notice to Wade's attorney before compelling Wade's participation in the lineup.[51] After the employees identified Wade at trial, he unsuccessfully moved

---

44. McCorkle, *supra* note 39, § 4[a]; *United States v. Denno*, 355 F.2d 731, 738 (2d Cir. 1966) ("Since courtroom identification, which usually takes place many months after the occurrence of the crime, is permissible, interests of the accused and society alike demand that the opportunity to identify be afforded at the earliest possible moment when the likelihood of an accurate identification is greatest.").

45. *Gilbert v. California*, 388 U.S. 263, 272 n.3 (1967).

46. Notably, at Gideon's retrial for burglarizing a pool hall, after the Supreme Court reversed his first conviction based on the failure to appoint counsel for his defense, his new lawyer successfully argued to the jury that the key government eyewitness had falsely accused Gideon to cover up his own involvement in the break-in. *See, e.g.*, Anthony Lewis, *The Silencing of Gideon's Trumpet*, N.Y. Times Mag., April 20, 2003, https://www.nytimes.com/2003/04/20/magazine/the-silencing-of-gideon-s-trumpet.html.

47. *United States v. Wade*, 388 U.S. 218 (1967).

48. *Id.* at 220.

49. *Id.*

50. *Id.*

51. *Id.* at 220, 223.

to strike their identifications under the Sixth Amendment and was thereafter convicted.[52]

Gilbert involved another bank robbery, this one in California.[53] As in *Wade*, police compelled Gilbert's participation in a postindictment lineup without notifying his court-appointed lawyer.[54] During the lineup, which took place in a large auditorium, "upwards of 100" witnesses were present, including some from other robberies where Gilbert had been a suspect,[55] and each was permitted to observe as the others narrowed down their selections.[56] As in *Wade*, Gilbert's mid-trial motion to strike any in-court identification was denied.[57] The jury found Gilbert guilty and condemned him to die, based on his involvement in other robberies.[58]

The Supreme Court granted certiorari in *Wade* and *Gilbert* to decide whether the Sixth Amendment guaranteed the right to counsel when, as in both cases, the government arranges a pretrial confrontation for purposes of allowing an eyewitness to identify the accused. In holding that it does, the Court reasoned that counsel's presence was required to afford a meaningful opportunity to expose any defects in an identification to a jury.[59] Counsel's presence during such confrontations was especially crucial, given the "proverbially untrustworthy" nature of eyewitness identification evidence as a whole.[60] In this regard, the *Wade* Court acknowledged that identifications are "peculiarly riddled with innumerable dangers and variable factors," such as the suggestive influence of overzealous investigators, which "might seriously, even crucially, derogate from a fair trial."[61] Such suggestion could "be created intentionally or unintentionally in many subtle ways" and "account[ed] for more miscarriages of justices than any other single factor" and "perhaps . . . more . . . than all such errors combined."[62]

---

52. *Id.* at 220.
53. *Gilbert v. California*, 388 U.S. 263 (1967).
54. *Id.* at 269.
55. *Id.* at 269–70.
56. *Id.* at 270 n.2 (quoting *Gilbert v. United States*, 366 F.2d 923 (1966)).
57. *Id.* at 271.
58. *Id.* at 265.
59. *Wade*, 388 U.S. at 223–24, 227.
60. *Id.* at 228 (quoting Felix Frankfurter, The Case of Sacco and Vanzetti 30 (1927)).
61. *Id.* at 228–29.
62. *Id.* (quoting Wall, Eye-Witness Identification in Criminal Cases).

Wade and *Gilbert* further held, contrary to the trial court's opinion in *Gilbert*,[63] that the remedy for violating the right to counsel during a pretrial confrontation would be the exclusion of any subsequent in-court identification by that eyewitness, unless the government could show that it had not been tainted by the pretrial procedure.[64] Accordingly, the *Wade* Court instructed lower courts to consider "various factors" that might bear on a witness's ability to make an identification independent of the pretrial confrontation: "for example, [1] the prior opportunity to observe the alleged criminal act, [2] any discrepancy between any pre-lineup description and the defendant's actual description, [3] any identification prior to lineup of another person, [4] the identification by picture of the defendant prior to the lineup, [5] failure to identify the defendant on a prior occasion, and [6] the lapse of time between the alleged act and the lineup identification."[65] The Court's decision to remand this case for consideration of these factors drew sharp criticism from Justice Black, who wrote that it would be "practically impossible" for anyone to determine whether an in-court identification was, or would probably be, tainted by exposure to the defendant during a pretrial line-up.[66] Justice Black was particularly hostile to this framework because it allocated the burden of proof to the government.[67] The Court would address this concern in subsequent cases.

Although *Wade* and *Gilbert* were rooted in the belief that defense lawyers had an important role to play in reining in the "innumerable dangers" associated with eyewitness identifications,[68] any hope that access to counsel would serve as a comprehensive solution to these problems evaporated a few years later, when the Supreme Court clarified that the right to counsel did not extend to any preindictment lineup[69] or any photo-array, regardless

63. "[T]he trial judge denied [Gilbert's] motion [to strike] on the ground that, assuming a violation [of the right to counsel], it would not in any event entitle Gilbert to suppression of the in-court identification." *Gilbert*, 388 U.S. at 271.

64. *Wade*, 388 U.S. at 240–41; *see also Gilbert*, 388 U.S. at 272 ("The admission of the in-court identifications without first determining that they were not tainted by the illegal lineup but were of independent origin was constitutional error.").

65. *Id.* at 241. By contrast, in *Gilbert*, the Court held that the government lost the right to avail itself of this independent source analysis, because they affirmatively relied on the out-of-court procedure to corroborate the in-court identification in their case-in-chief.

66. *Id.* at 248 (Black, J.) (concurring in part, dissenting in part).

67. *Id.* ("What kind of 'clear and convincing evidence' can the prosecution offer to prove upon what particular events memories resulting in an in-court identification rest?").

68. *Wade*, 388 U.S. at 228.

69. *Kirby v. Illinois*, 406 U.S. 682 (1972).

of when it occurred in relation to an indictment.[70] Given these parameters, any comprehensive solution to the problems outlined in *Wade* would need to rest on different authority. Although judges and commentators had done their best to encourage legislative solutions, none were forthcoming by the late 1960s when these issues were coming to a head.[71] The only other tool that the Supreme Court could bring to bear on this issue was the Due Process Clause, which up to then had been deployed to bar evidence obtained by means of outright brutality, as well as other subtler forms of coercion.[72]

B. *Stovall*, *Manson*, and the Right to Due Process

1. Stovall v. Denno, *388 U.S. 293 (1967)*

In *Stovall v. Denno*, 388 U.S. 293 (1967), the companion case to *Wade* and *Gilbert*, the Supreme Court recognized the due process right to a conviction free from the influence of "unnecessarily suggestive" police identification procedures.[73] Such a claim had succeeded in *Palmer v. Peyton*, 359 F.2d 199 (4th Cir. 1966), a federal habeas case decided one year earlier. Palmer, a Black man, had been convicted and sentenced to life imprisonment for raping a white woman in her home.[74] By the complainant's own admission, she did not get a good look at her attacker, who had been wearing a "purina chow bag" made of "heavy paper" "snugly" over his head, and had identified Palmer based solely on his "childlike voice," after listening to him repeat the words of her attacker from a separate room inside the police station.[75]

---

70. *United States v. Ash*, 413 U.S. 300 (1973). In hindsight, these holdings should come as no surprise. Appointment of counsel for the purpose of any pretrial identification procedure had been laughed off as a "'Disneyland' contention" as little as two years before *Wade* was decided. *Williams v. United States*, 345 F.2d 735, 736 (D.C. Cir. 1965).

71. *Wade*, 388 U.S. at 236 n.26.

72. *Leyra v. Denno*, 347 U.S. 556 (1954) (suppressing confession obtained by means of involuntary hypnosis); *Rochin v. California*, 342 U.S. 165 (1952) (suppressing evidence obtained by forcibly extracting the contents of the stomach); *Malinski v. New York*, 324 U.S. 401 (1945) (suppressing confession obtained by means of prolonged isolation, undressing, and implied threat of "shellacking); *Brown v. Mississippi*, 297 U.S. 278 (1936) (suppressing confession obtained by means of whipping and hanging from a tree).

73. *Stovall v. Denno*, 388 U.S. 293, 302 (1967).

74. *Palmer*, 359 F.2d at 200. Prior to these allegations, Palmer led a "peaceful married life" and "provided for his family reasonably well," *Man Convicted of Rape Escapes Death Penalty*, VIRGINIAN-PILOT, 17, Mar. 11, 1958, in a house that sat a few hundred yards from the victim's. *2nd Trial Begins for Man Accused of Woman Assault*, NORFOLK LEDGER-DISPATCH, 12, Jan. 10, 1958.

75. *Palmer*, 359 F.2d at 200 & n.2. The other evidence against Palmer was equally unimpressive. Although Palmer had been wearing an orange shirt consistent with the complainant's description of the attacker the day after the alleged attack, when he was arrested, multiple witnesses testified that he had been wearing something else the day before. *Id.* The Commonwealth

The Commonwealth of Virginia brought Palmer to trial for this rape on three separate occasions before obtaining a conviction.[76] At no point during this process was the complainant ever asked whether any of Palmer's other features or qualities conformed to her memory of the suspect.[77]

In holding that these circumstances required reversal of Palmer's convictions, the Fourth Circuit interpreted the Due Process Clause to bar state reliance on "identification[s] secured by a process in which the search for truth is made secondary to a quest for a conviction," to the same degree as evidence obtained by means of coercion or brutality.[78] Complainant's identification of Palmer fell into the former category because, before she made it, the police had told her that Palmer was a suspect; because "Palmer's was the only voice [she] was permitted to hear repeating the [perpetrator's] damning words"; and because her identification had been based on "voice alone," making it even more vulnerable to suggestion.[79]

A majority of the Supreme Court endorsed this interpretation of the Due Process Clause in *Stovall*.[80] That case involved a home invasion in Garden City, Long Island.[81] The assailant had stabbed a pair of married physicians, killing the husband and critically wounding the wife. Evidence at the scene

---

also proffered the testimony of a neighbor named Flythe who claimed, after being brought in for questioning by the police, that he saw Palmer leaving the victim's house and that Palmer had confessed the crime to him. *Id.* However, Flythe was never subjected to any form of identification procedure, despite his apparent status as a suspect. *Id.* It was only after being brought in that Flythe claimed to have heard Palmer's confession. *Id.*

76. After Mr. Palmer's first jury returned a guilty verdict and condemned him to die, the judge granted a new trial, which ended in a hung jury. *Id.* at 199. Perhaps to minimize his chances of receiving another death sentence, Palmer waived the jury for his third trial and was convicted and sentenced to life imprisonment. *Id.*

77. *Id.* at 201.

78. *Id.* at 202; *see also United States v. Stovall*, 355 F.2d 731, 738 (2d Cir. 1966) ("Although federal courts should be loath to interfere with state court evidentiary matters which go primarily to the weight of evidence admitted, it may be that an identification procedure could be so unfair as to amount to a violation of the Fourteenth Amendment's due process guarantee.").

79. *Palmer*, 359 F.2d at 202. In addition, the Fourth Circuit pointed to the discrediting fact that the "assailant [had been] of a different race [than the victim], and [had] spoke[n] through a heavy paper clothespin bag which doubtless muffled his voice; yet this same paper bag, in the possession of the police, was not worn by Palmer on the night of the identification." *Id.*

80. *Stovall*, 388 U.S. at 299 (citing *Palmer*, 359 F.2d 199) ("It remains open to all persons to allege and prove, as Stovall attempts to do in this case, that the confrontation resulted in such unfairness that it infringed his right to due process of the law."); *contra id.* at 305–06 (Black, J.) ("I dissent from [the] holding that a general claim of 'unfairness' at the lineup is 'open to all persons to allege and prove'" because "[s]uch a constitutional formula substitutes this Court's judgment of what is right for what the Constitution declares shall be the supreme law of the land.").

81. *Id.* at 295.

led the police to Stovall, who was quickly arrested and brought to an arraignment. However, when the arraignment was postponed so that Stovall could retain counsel, police brought him in handcuffs to the wife's hospital room, where she lay recovering from emergency surgery. With some prompting from law enforcement, she identified Stovall—the only Black man in a room filled with uniformed police officers—as the attacker, and later confirmed this identification for the jury at Stovall's trial.

On collateral review of Stovall's convictions and death sentence, the Supreme Court invoked *Palmer* to hold that although an identification may be "so unnecessarily suggestive and conducive to irreparable mistaken identification [as to] den[y] due process of law," Stovall's rights had not been violated, given the need to present him to the surviving victim quickly, while she could tell the police whether or not he was the perpetrator.[82] In reaching this conclusion, the Court acknowledged that single-suspect presentations had been "widely condemned" as suggestive for good reason, and that a traditional lineup would have been preferable insofar as it would have been less suggestive.[83] However, in the Court's view, the wife's inability to travel from the hospital to the jail foreclosed any possibility of presenting Stovall to her in such a lineup.[84] Hence, the Court affirmed Stovall's convictions and sentences.[85]

2. Simmons v. United States, *390 U.S. 377 (1968)*

After *Stovall*, the due process inquiry was arguably twofold, taking into account (1) whether the pretrial identification procedure was "suggestive" and/or "conducive to irreparable misidentification"—for instance, whether the witness received suggestive information about the suspect from the police before the procedure, or, as in the case of a single-suspect presentation, the procedure was inherently suggestive—and (2) whether use of such a suggestive procedure was "unnecessar[y]," based on the "totality of circumstances." Over the course of the next decade, however, the Court would refocus the inquiry on a third factor: (3) what the Court ultimately described as the "reliability" of the testimony offered to support the

82. *Id.* at 302. The Court also held that the right to counsel during a pretrial identification procedure announced in *Wade* and *Gilbert* was not so fundamental to the fair administration of justice; thus, it would not apply "retroactively" to convictions like Stovall's, which became "final" before *Wade* and *Gilbert* were decided. *Id.* at 298–301.

83. *Id.* at 302.

84. *Id.*

85. *Id.*

defendant's conviction—whether any unduly suggestive procedure was not only "conducive to irreparable misidentification" but had in fact produced "a very substantial likelihood of irreparable misidentification," based on a post hoc, judicial assessment of the strength of the witness's memory, ability to observe, and powers of observation.[86]

The Court took its first step toward this modification in *Simmons v. United States*, 390 U.S. 377 (1968), by holding that proof of "a very substantial likelihood of irreparable misidentification" would be required, whenever the defendant alleged that an in-court identification was tainted by an "impermissibly suggestive" pretrial photo-display.[87] *Simmons* involved another bank robbery.[88] After linking Simmons and a man named Andrews to the getaway car, FBI agents showed the bank's employees a series of group photos containing the two suspects, in an effort to see whether the witnesses recognized them.[89] In holding that use of the identifications obtained by virtue of this procedure did not violate due process, the Court acknowledged the danger inherent in showing eyewitnesses a series of group photos that have only one or two people in common: specifically, that the eyewitnesses will quickly deduce the suspect's identity.[90] Nevertheless, the Court declined to find this procedure unconstitutional because it was "essential" to helping the FBI determine whether its investigation into a serious felony was "on the right track,"[91] and because the "likelihood" that the eyewitnesses had identified Simmons by mistake was not "very substantial."[92] Rather, the "totality of circumstances"—including the witnesses' viewing opportunity, the well-lit conditions, the lack of any disguises, the fact that the identifications happened only a day after the robbery, and the witnesses' professed confidence in their identifications—"le[ft] little room for doubt that the identification of Simmons was correct."[93]

---

86. In making this transition, the Court contended that this factor was always present, even in *Stovall*, given its reference to the "totality of circumstances." *Manson v. Brathwaite*, 432 U.S. 98, 113 (1977). However, by the time the Court made this suggestion in *Manson*, it had already acknowledged in *Biggers* that it was "less clear from the Court's cases . . . whether . . . unnecessary suggestiveness alone requires the exclusion of evidence." *Neil v. Biggers*, 409 U.S. 188, 198–99 (1972).

87. *Simmons*, 390 U.S. at 380.

88. *Id.*

89. *Id.*

90. *Id.* at 384.

91. *Id.* at 384–85.

92. *Id.* at 384.

93. *Id.* at 385–86.

To this day, the Court's rationale for requiring a "very substantial likelihood of irreparable misidentification" in *Simmons* is somewhat murky. The opinion itself points to the "decisions of other courts on the question of identification by photograph,"[94] suggesting that the use of photographs might have carried some weight. *Stovall*, by contrast, involved an in-person confrontation, which the Court later held carries much greater risk of hidden and inarticulable prejudice than mere photographic display.[95] Because this distinction would ultimately carry an analytical difference under the Sixth Amendment, it seems plausible that the *Simmons* Court relied on it in opting to limit its holding to cases involving photographic display. On the other hand, later jurisprudence suggests that the real reason for the "very substantial likelihood" requirement in *Simmons* was that Simmons had been attempting to suppress in-court identifications, and thus, had no choice but to prove that they were tainted by the out-of-court procedures that preceded them.[96] By contrast, it was possible to read *Stovall* as having forgone the need to prove a specific "likelihood of . . . misidentification" because the government relied on the suggestive out-of-court identification directly by introducing it at trial.[97]

Whatever the rationale, the Court made no mention of this "very substantial likelihood" requirement in the two eyewitness identification cases that it decided in 1969 and 1970.[98] Even so, some lower courts began to take the position that a "very substantial likelihood of irreparable misidentification" based on the specific factors set forth in *Simmons* was a precondition to relief for any suggestively obtained identification under the Due Process Clause.[99] The "very substantial likelihood" requirement did not

94. *Id.* at 384 & n.5 (citing *People v. Evans*, 246 P.2d 636 (Cal. 1952)).

95. *Ash*, 413 U.S. at 317 (holding that photographic displays are less risky for the accused because they need not be present and thus cannot be tricked, misled, or overpowered into inculpatory behavior).

96. *Neil v. Biggers*, 409 U.S. 188, 198 (1972) (noting that the "very substantial likelihood" language "was coined as a standard for determining whether an in-court identification would be admissible in the wake of a suggestive out-of-court identification"); *accord Manson v. Brathwaite*, 432 U.S. 98, 122 (1977) (Marshall, J., dissenting) (same). There is good reason to take these statements with a grain of salt because neither of the authors (Justices Powell and Marshall) were a part of the majority that decided *Simmons*.

97. *Manson*, 432 U.S. at 122–23.

98. *Coleman v. Alabama*, 399 U. S. 1 (1970); *Foster v. California*, 394 U. S. 440, 442 (1969). Both involved pretrial, in-person confrontations, but only one of which involved an in-court identification.

99. *See, e.g., United States v. Telfaire*, 469 F.2d 552, 555 n.5 (D.C. Cir. 1972) (per curiam); *United States v. Levi*, 405 F.2d 380, 383 (4th Cir. 1968).

resurface again in the Supreme Court's case law until *Neil v. Biggers*, 409 U.S. 188 (1972), a case that did little to resolve the emerging circuit split on this question.

3. Neil v. Biggers, *409 U.S. 188 (1972)*

In *Biggers*, Nixon's newly minted conservative majority[100] held that the "very substantial likelihood" requirement would apply at least to those due process challenges to show-ups that took place *before* the Court's condemnation of the procedure in *Stovall*.[101] *Biggers* involved a cross-racial show-up identification that took place seven months after the complainant's initial report of rape but well before *Stovall*'s condemnation of the practice. The complainant, a white woman, had described her attacker as "fat and flabby, with smooth skin, bushy hair and a youthful voice."[102] In the seven months that followed her report, she viewed multiple lineups, show-ups, and photo-arrays without making an identification, before identifying sixteen-year-old Biggers, whom police had brought in on another rape charge.[103] The police decided to present Biggers in a show-up because they were having trouble finding suitable fillers.[104] Thereafter, the complainant identified Biggers based on his appearance or the "youth[ful]" sound of his voice or both.[105] She would later testify that she recognized him immediately and had no doubt that he was the perpetrator.[106]

On collateral review of Biggers's conviction,[107] the Supreme Court held that this show-up did not violate his right to due process because, much

100. *See, e.g.*, Kevin J. McMahon, Nixon's Court: His Challenge to Judicial Liberalism and Its Political Consequences (2011).

101. By this time, multiple circuit courts had already embraced this showing as a precondition of relief under the Due Process Clause.

102. *Biggers*, 409 U.S. at 193–94. There was some dispute as to whether her initial description also included other information that she had relayed during the habeas corpus proceedings, after Mr. Bigger's conviction. The Supreme Court resolved this dispute in favor of the complainant and the state of Tennessee. *Id.* at 194.

103. *Id.* at 194–95.

104. *Id.* at 195.

105. *Id.* at 194–95. There was some inconsistency on this point. There was no question that the complainant had asked the police to have Biggers speak her rapist's words, and she testified at trial that Biggers's voice "was the first thing that made her think" he was the culprit. *Id.* at 195 & n.4. However, a police officer remembered the identification coming before the complainant's request to hear Biggers speak the rapist's words. *Id.* Of course, even assuming this is true, and the complainant identified Biggers in some way before he spoke, it begs the question why she asked Biggers to speak if she was certain about her identification.

106. *Id.* at 195–96.

107. An equally divided Court had previously affirmed Biggers's conviction. *Biggers v. Tennessee*, 390 U.S. 404 (1968).

like the photographic displays at issue in *Simmons*, it did not give rise to a "substantial likelihood of misidentification."[108] Proof of this "substantial likelihood" was necessary, the Court reasoned, to avoid needlessly punishing the state's reliance on a show-up procedure that was not condemned until *after* Biggers's identification, when *Stovall* was decided.[109] In reaching this conclusion, the Court specifically rejected the notion that proof of unnecessary suggestiveness would suffice, absent a substantial likelihood of misidentification, to establish a due process violation or warrant evidentiary exclusion.[110] Rather, the only "purpose in imposing a strict rule barring evidence of unnecessarily suggestive confrontations would be to deter the police" from using it *in the future*.[111] In the Court's view, Biggers's case was ill-suited to advancing that policy interest because his identification had been obtained and introduced *before* the Court's condemnation of show-ups in *Stovall*.[112]

Harkening back to *Wade*'s test for whether an in-court identification had been tainted by denial of the right to counsel during a postindictment, pretrial lineup,[113] the Court further held that whether a "very substantial likelihood of misidentification" exists would depend on factors such as (1) the witness's opportunity to observe and (2) degree of attention, (3) the accuracy of her prior description, (4) the level of certainty demonstrated at the confrontation, and (5) the time between the crime and the confrontation.[114] As in *Wade*, these factors were in no way exhaustive or exclusive; rather, they were merely "include[d]" among those "to be considered in evaluating the likelihood of misidentification."[115] Applying these factors, a majority of justices found no such likelihood of misidentification, given the complainant's professed opportunity to observe, degree of attention, descriptive accuracy, and level of certainty.[116]

---

108. *Biggers*, 409 U.S. at 201. The only difference between this test and the one outlined in *Simmons* was that, whereas *Simmons* required proof of "a very substantial likelihood of *irreparable* misidentification," irreparability was irrelevant, whereas in *Biggers*, the government relied directly on the out-of-court identification. *Id.* at 198.

109. *Id.* at 199.

110. *Id.* at 198–99.

111. *Id.* at 199.

112. *Id.*

113. *See Wade*, 388 U.S. at 241. Interestingly, the Court did not cite *Wade* by name in this regard. Rather, it noted that the factors to be considered previously had been "indicated by [the Court's] cases." *Biggers*, 409 U.S. at 199–200.

114. *Id.*

115. *Id.* at 199–200.

116. *Id.* at 200–201.

4. Manson v. Brathwaite, *432 U.S. 98 (1977)*

The *Biggers* Court's analysis left lingering uncertainty about whether those bringing due process challenges to identification procedures that took place after *Stovall* would be required to show a "very substantial likelihood of misidentification." In *Manson v. Brathwaite*, 432 U.S. 98 (1977), the Court answered this question in the affirmative, clarifying that, with one important modification, the *Biggers* test would govern *all* cases where an unduly suggestive procedure was alleged, regardless of when the identification procedure took place and how the government intended to use it at trial.[117] In so doing, the Supreme Court doubled down on the willingness to "bravely assume[] that the jury is capable of evaluating [eyewitness] reliability" that has defined the American legal system's relationship to eyewitness identification from the beginning.[118]

Brathwaite had been convicted of selling heroin to an undercover officer through the partially open door of an apartment.[119] After the transaction, the undercover relayed a description of the seller ("colored man, approximately five feet eleven inches tall, dark complexion, black hair, short Afro style, . . . high cheekbones and a heavy build") to his colleague who, in turn, suggested Brathwaite as a suspect.[120] Two days later, the undercover officer consulted a picture of Brathwaite that the colleague had provided and determined him to be the seller.[121] On collateral review of Brathwaite's conviction,[122] the Second Circuit held that this single picture show-up should have been excluded from trial given its suggestive nature, reasoning that there was no need to consider the specific likelihood of misidentification because unlike the *Biggers* show-up, the procedure here had been conducted after *Stovall* was decided.[123]

The Supreme Court reversed, holding that "reliability is the linchpin in determining the admissibility of identification testimony for both pre- and post-*Stovall* confrontations."[124] In so holding, the court considered and

117. *Manson*, 432 U.S. at 114, 117.

118. *United States v. Brown*, 461 F.2d 134, 145 n.1 (D.C. Cir. 1972) (en banc) (Bazelon, C.J., dissenting in part and concurring in part).

119. *Manson*, 432 U.S. at 101–102.

120. *Id.* at 101.

121. *Id.*

122. In finding Brathwaite guilty, the jury rejected his alibi, complete with the testimony of his treating physician, that he had been physically incapacitated at the time of his alleged heroin sale. *Id.* at 102.

123. *See Brathwaite v. Manson*, 527 F.2d 363, 367–71 (2d Cir. 1975).

124. *Manson*, 432 U.S. at 114.

rejected the merits of adopting a "*per se* rule of exclusion" for cases involving identifications obtained by unnecessarily subjective means, akin to the "strict rule" discussed in *Biggers*.[125] Such *per se* rules had been adopted by a number of courts in the wake of *Biggers* and required exclusion of any identification obtained by unnecessarily suggestive means, regardless of any assessment of reliability.[126] Although such a rule was arguably needed to maintain a certain level of deterrence and reliability, the Court believed that it would "go[] too far" in that regard, insofar as it would also deprive juries of some evidence that a judge could consider sufficiently "reliable and relevant" for a jury's consumption.[127] Critically, although rejecting the *per se* rule would allow the government to benefit from "element[s] of untrustworthiness" that its own agents had injected into the identification process, the majority was "content to rely upon the good sense and judgment of American juries" to separate the good from the bad because, in its view, jurors were "not so susceptible that they [could not] measure intelligently the weight of identification testimony that has some questionable feature."[128]

Thus, the test for determining the admissibility of eyewitness identification evidence under the Due Process Clause was twofold. Under the first prong, the accused would have to show that police came about an identification by "unnecessary and suggestive" means.[129] Under the second, the accused would have to show that this conduct gave rise to a "very substantial likelihood of irreparable misidentification" based on the factors set forth in *Biggers*—(1) opportunity to observe and (2) degree of attention, (3) the accuracy of the prior description, (4) the level of certainty demonstrated at the confrontation, and (5) the time between the crime and the confrontation.[130] However, whereas in *Biggers* these factors were merely illustrative,[131] under *Manson* they became exclusive and exhaustive.[132] Moreover, this test would apply regardless of whether the evidence sought to be excluded was

125. *Id.* at 109.

126. *Id.* at 109110. Nevertheless, these courts tended to consider reliability in deciding whether to strike or suppress an in-court identification because it was tainted by a suggestive pretrial procedure. *Id.*

127. *Id.* at 112–13.

128. *Id.* at 116 ("[E]vidence with some element of untrustworthiness is customary grist for the jury mill.").

129. *See id.* at 99; *accord Perry v. New Hampshire*, 565 U.S. 228 (2012)

130. *Manson*, 432 U.S. at 114.

131. *Biggers*, 409 U.S. at 199 (noting that the relevant factors "include" those listed).

132. *Manson*, 432 U.S. at 114. More on this later.

a pretrial identification or an in-court identification following an allegedly suggestive procedure.[133] It would further apply regardless of whether the impermissibly suggestive procedure happened before or after the Court decided *Stovall.*

Echoing the majority's analysis in *Biggers*, a majority of the justices concluded that Brathwaite had failed to establish "a substantial likelihood of irreparable misidentification," given the undercover officer's trial testimony that he was able to get a good look at the seller (through the door of the apartment building where the transaction occurred) and that he was confident in his identification, combined with the fact that he had provided a verbal description of the seller and made an identification only two days later.[134] The dissent countered that these circumstances deserved no weight, given the cursory nature of the officer's initial description,[135] and the fact that his identification had been based on a single, potentially unrepresentative photograph, coupled with the suggestion of another officer (an experienced narcotics detective, who arguably projected a certain air of expertise about the local drug trade) that Brathwaite had in fact been the seller.[136] In the dissent's view, these circumstances were more than adequate to imply "a substantial likelihood of irreparable misidentification," and mandate suppression.[137]

5. Perry v. New Hampshire, *565 U.S. 228 (2012)*

The Court reaffirmed its commitment to the *Manson* framework in *Perry v. New Hampshire*, 565 U.S. 228 (2012), where it held that due process does

133. By contrast, courts have consistently declined to apply *Manson* to "first-time in-court" identifications, which are not preceded by any government-initiated identification procedure. *United States v. Gentile*, 530 F.2d 461, 467–69 (2d Cir.), *cert. denied*, 426 U.S. 936 (1976); *United States v. Davis*, 487 F.2d 112, 122 (5th Cir. 1973), *cert. denied*, 415 U.S. 981 (1974); *United States v. Hamilton*, 469 F.2d 880, 883 (9th Cir. 1972); *Middleton v. United States*, 401 A.2d 109 (D.C. 1979).

134. *Manson*, 432 U.S. at 114–16. In so doing, the majority placed great weight on the fact that the undercover officer who identified Brathwaite was no mere "casual or passing observer," but rather "a trained police officer on . . . specialized and dangerous duty," who was better equipped to perceive and remember the specific details of the perpetrator's face because he "himself was [also] a Negro." *Id.* at 115.

135. In the dissent's view, Brathwaite's West Indian heritage should have featured prominently in the officer's description, given the profound impact it would have had on Brathwaite's "appearance and accent." *Id.* at 132 (Marshall, J., dissenting). The dissent believed that it was especially unlikely that a Black person, like the identifying police officer, would neglect to mention Brathwaite's West Indian heritage. *Id.*

136. *Id.* at 132–36.

137. *Id.* at 130.

not require preliminary judicial inquiry into the reliability of an eyewitness identification that was not procured under unnecessarily suggestive circumstances arranged by law enforcement. *Perry* involved a report of someone trying to break into cars in the parking lot of an apartment building.[138] The first officer to arrive on the scene found Perry in the parking lot carrying multiple pieces of car stereo equipment.[139] When a second officer arrived, the first left to find the witness who had made the initial report, leaving Perry in the parking lot with the second officer.[140] Upon locating the witness in an apartment, the officer asked her to describe who she saw breaking into cars; the witness, in turn, identified Perry in the parking lot below.[141] The trial court found that these circumstances could not give rise to a due process violation because Perry's identification had not been orchestrated by police, but rather, was "spontaneous."[142]

The Supreme Court affirmed, reasoning that (more) purposeful "state action" or involvement in arranging the suggestive circumstances surrounding an identification had always been an implied prerequisite to relief under *Stovall* and its progeny. Harkening back to *Manson*,[143] the Court further reasoned that there was no need to extend due process protection to cases where police have come about an unreliable identification inadvertently because the jury can separate wheat from chaff using the procedural safeguards that are applicable at trial, like cross-examination and instructions on the reasonable doubt standard, as well as, in some cases and some jurisdictions, specialized jury instructions and expert testimony regarding the reliability of eyewitness identification testimony.[144] Justice Sotomayor disagreed with this analysis, further arguing that the majority's proposed distinction between accidental and purposeful state action was murky and apt to invite arbitrary results.[145]

138. *Perry*, 565 U.S. at 233.
139. *Id.*
140. *Id.* at 233–34.
141. *Id.* at 234.
142. *Id.* at 235 (internal quotation marks and citation omitted).
143. *Manson*, 432 U.S. at 116.
144. *Perry*, 565 U.S. at 245–46.
145. For his part, Justice Thomas maintained his long-held view that *Stovall* and its progeny were wrongly decided because the Due Process Clause is not "a secret repository of substantive guarantees against unfairness." *Id.* at 249 (Thomas, J., dissenting).

III. *What's Wrong with the* Manson *Test?*

From the moment *Manson* was decided, the test it announced has been the subject of intense criticism from scholars and advocates alike.[146] Indeed, given the backlash to *Neil v. Biggers*, 409 U.S. 188 (1972), it is fair to say that *Manson* has been under attack since before it was decided.[147] Time has only intensified these criticisms. In the last decade and a half, the test has begun to engender criticism from the high courts of several states, which have elected to interpret their state constitutions to provide more robust protections against the risk of wrongful conviction.[148] Judicial and scholarly criticisms of the *Manson* test have come to focus on three overlapping issues: (1) its reliance on outdated and unscientific assumptions about perception and memory, (2) its failure to deter suggestive law enforcement practices, and (3) its failure to stem the tide of wrongful convictions due to mistaken identifications.

A. Unscientific, Outdated, and Under-Inclusive

A persistent criticism of *Manson's* five-factor reliability test is that it is "untethered to any sound scientific knowledge."[149] That *Manson* is unmoored from the scientific perspective should come as no surprise as, "[a]t the time

146. *See, e.g.*, Note, *Manson v. Brathwaite: Looking for the Silver Lining in the Area of Eyewitness Identifications*, 35 Wash. & Lee L. Rev. 1079 (1978); Steven P. Grossman, *Suggestive Identifications: The Supreme Court s Due Process Test Fails to Meet Its Own Criteria*, 11 U. Balt. L. Rev. 53, 59–60 (1981); Wallace W. Sherwood, *The Erosion of Constitutional Safeguards in the Area of Eyewitness Identification*, 30 How. L.J. 439, 457 (1987); David E. Paseltiner, Note, *Twenty-Years of Diminishing Protection: A Proposal to Return to the Wade Trilogy's Standards*, 15 Hofstra L. Rev. 583, 589–90 (1987); Benjamin E. Rosenberg, *Rethinking the Right to Due Process in Connection with Pretrial Identification Procedures: An Analysis and a Proposal to Return to the Wade Trilogy's Standard*, 79 Ky. L.J. 259, 275–97 (1991); Dori Lynn Yob, Comment, *Mistaken Identifications Cause Wrongful Convictions: New Jersey's Lineup Guidelines Restore Hope, but Are They Enough?*, 43 Santa Clara L. Rev. 213, 229–31 (2002); Timothy P. O'Toole & Giovanna Shay, *Manson v. Brathwaite Revisited: Towards a New Rule of Decision for Due Process Challenges to Eyewitness Identification Procedures*, 41 Val. U.L. Rev. 109, 122–26 (2006); Richard A. Wise, et al., *A Tripartite Solution to Eyewitness Error*, 97 J. Crim. L. & Criminology 807, 870 (2007); Gary L. Wells & Deah S. Quinlivan, *Suggestive Eyewitness Identification Procedures and the Supreme Court's Reliability Test in Light of Eyewitness Science: 30 Years Later*, 33 L. & Hum. Behav. 1 (2009).

147. Harry M. Caldwell & Douglas S. Smith, *The Pre-Arraignment Lineup: Necessity of a Magistrate*, 3 Pepp. L. Rev. 82 (1976); Charles A. Pulaski, *Neil v. Biggers: The Supreme Court Dismantles the Wade Trilogy's Due Process Protection*, 26 Stan. L. Rev. 1097, 1104–10 (1974).

148. *State v. Martinez*, 478 P.3d 880, 897 (N.M. 2021); *Young v. State*, 374 P.3d 395, 421 (Alaska 2016); *State v. Lawson*, 291 P.3d 673, 685 (Or. 2012); *State v. Henderson*, 27 A.3d 872, 918 (N.J. 2011).

149. *Martinez*, 478 P.3d at 897.

of *Manson*, eyewitness science was still in its incipient stages."[150] Specifically, "[a]lthough scientists had documented problems with eyewitness memory since the early twentieth century, they had not yet developed research to reveal the range of variables that can reduce reliability in individual cases."[151] Moreover, "despite early legal work recognizing misidentification by eyewitnesses as a primary cause of wrongful conviction, the science of eyewitness identification remained largely stagnant until the late 1970s, just around the time the Supreme Court was articulating the current due process standard admission of eyewitness evidence in *Manson*."[152]

Indeed, as discussed at length in Chapter 4, this stagnation was the direct result of the backlash that one early pioneer of applied forensic psychology, Prof. Hugo Münsterberg, faced for suggesting that judges, lawyers, and juries had been operating under pervasive misconceptions about eyewitness reliability. The overwhelming response to this suggestion from the legal community was to insist that judicial precedents were a better source of insight into the vagaries of perception and memory than any experiment arranged by a psychologist because precedent reflected the time-tested wisdom of preeminent legal scholars and practitioners. Against this backdrop, it is unsurprising that "[t]he five [*Manson*] factors were drawn from earlier judicial rulings," like *Wade*, "and not from scientific research."[153]

Although it is unclear how the *Wade* Court derived its five-factor "independent source" test (because the Court did not include any citations to relevant authority in this part of its opinion),[154] it bears a striking resemblance to nineteenth-century scholarship on mistaken identifications, which tended to focus on the factors that influence perception, while relegating the impact of time on memory and the potential for postevent suggestion to an afterthought.[155] This kind of thinking was consistent with the widespread

150. Nicholas A. Kahn-Fogel, *The Promises and Pitfalls of State Eyewitness Identification Reforms*, 104 Ky. L.J. 99, 109 (2016).

151. *Id.* (citing James M. Doyle, True Witness: Cops, Courts, Science, and the Battle Against Misidentification 49–63, 83–99 (2005); citations omitted)).

152. Nicholas A. Kahn-Fogel, Manson *and Its Progeny: An Empirical Analysis of American Eyewitness Law*, 3 Ala. C.R. & C.L.L. Rev. 175, 184 (2012) (footnote and citation omitted).

153. Nat'l Rsch. Council, *supra* note 1, at 32.

154. *Wade*, 388 U.S. at 241.

155. James Ram, Treatise on Facts as Subjects of Inquiry 72 (3d ed. 1873) ("It may happen that a person has not taken a correct impression of another's countenance. If it was seen for an instant only, although by day, or was seen at night, or in twilight, or afar off, or was seen as one in a mass or throng, or by a person of short or otherwise defective sight, or by one intoxicated or affrighted; either of these circumstances—the instant of time, the darkness, the distance, the crowd, the defective sight, the intoxication, the terror—may cause the

misconception that mistaken identifications were almost always the result of "poor seeing, not poor memory,"[156] which, in turn, was a byproduct of the widespread misconception that shocking, stressful events produce vivid, "flashbulb" memories that not only contain more details than other kinds of memory but also are more accurate with respect to the details they contain.[157] Research tending to dispel this myth did not gain traction among psychologists until the late 1970s, around the time that *Manson* was decided.[158]

In the decades since *Manson*, researchers have conducted "over 2000 scientific studies . . . on the reliability of eyewitness identifications," leading to a better understanding of the factors that affect the reliability of eyewitness identification evidence.[159] "Research of this category identifie[d] principled and insurmountable limits of vision and memory that inevitably affect eyewitness accounts[] [and] bear on conclusions regarding accuracy,"[160] and "provided new insights into the fallibility of eyewitness identifications."[161] Significantly, this research has led to an overwhelming consensus among psychologists that "the *Manson* factors are woefully incomplete."[162] Decades of experimentation have "conclusively demonstrated" that the trustworthiness of an identification is influenced by many variables that escaped the Supreme Court's notice in 1979—including at least eight "system" variables within law enforcement control and seven "estimator" variables related to the observer and their opportunity to observe.[163] These variables are addressed at length in Chapter 6.

B. Fails to Deter and May Incentivize Suggestive Procedures

A related critique of *Manson* is that it "is so flexible as to be toothless, and . . . includes some factors that" not only fail to "give judges good information

impression to be defective, and consequently disable the person, . . . from identifying . . . the true countenance").

156. F.W. Colegrove, Memory: An Inductive Study 347 (1900).

157. *See, e.g.*, Fergus Craik & Larry Jacoby, *What Are Flashbulb Memories?*, MIT Press Reader, June 26, 2023, https://thereader.mitpress.mit.edu/what-are-flashbulb-memories/.

158. *Id.*

159. *Dennis v. Sec'y, Pa. Dep't of Corr.*, 834 F.3d 263, 335 (3d Cir. 2016) (McKee, C.J., concurring); *see also, e.g.*, *State v. Lawson*, 291 P.3d 673, 685 (Or. 2012) ("Since 1979 . . . there have been more than 2,000 scientific studies conducted on the reliability of eyewitness identification.").

160. Nat'l Rsch. Council, *supra* note 1, at xiii.

161. *State v. Mahmoud*, 147 A.3d 833, 837–38 (Me. 2016).

162. Kahn-Fogel, *The Promises and Pitfalls of State Eyewitness Identification Reforms*, *supra* note 150, at 109.

163. *Id.*

about the reliability of eyewitness identifications,"[164] but actively work to undermine the test's integrity. "[T]here appears to be broad consensus among commentators that three of the five *Manson* factors—view, attention, and certainty—are insufficiently independent from each other and from the suggestiveness of a given identification procedure to be accurate predictors of reliability and accuracy."[165] Simply put, "the more suggestive the procedure, the greater the chance eyewitnesses will seem confident and report better viewing conditions."[166]

The Case of Ronald Cotton

To appreciate just how badly reports of eyewitness confidence can be tainted by suggestive procedures, consider the case of Ronald Cotton. Mr. Cotton was arrested in connection with two rapes that followed a similar pattern: the assailant had broken into an apartment and cut the phone lines before raping his victims and taking their belongings.[167] One of the victims, a college student named Jennifer Thompson, created a composite sketch. After arresting Mr. Cotton based on his purported resemblance to the sketch, the police presented Mr. Cotton to Ms. Thompson in a photo-array. After examining it, Ms. Thompson reluctantly identified Mr. Cotton by stating, "I think this is the guy." When the lead detective said, "You're sure," Ms. Thompson responded, "Positive." Then, Ms. Thompson asked, "Did I do OK?" to which the detective responded, "You did great."

Thereafter, the police presented Mr. Cotton to Ms. Thompson in a live lineup, where she again hesitated to identify him, despite the fact that he was the only person in the lineup whose face had been presented in the prior photo array. After several minutes of examining the lineup, Ms. Thompson told the lead detective that Mr. Cotton "looks the most like him." When the lead detective again asked if Ms. Thompson was "certain," she said "Yes." The detective then added that Mr. Cotton was "the same person [she] picked from the photos," eliminating any residual doubt Ms. Thompson may have had about whether she chose the

164. Brandon L. Garrett, Convicting the Innocent 63 (2011).
165. *Martinez*, 478 P.3d at 897–98 (citations omitted).
166. *State v. Henderson*, 27 A.3d 872, 918 (N.J. 2011).
167. Regarding the facts of Mr. Cotton's case, *see generally, e.g.*, Nat'l Rsch. Council, *supra* note 1, at 10; and *Cotton's Wrongful Conviction: What Jennifer Saw*, Frontline, https://www.pbs.org/wgbh/pages/frontline/shows/dna/cotton/summary.html.

The Case of Ronald Cotton *(continued)*

right person. At Mr. Cotton's subsequent trial, Ms. Thompson expressed "absolute" certainty that he was her rapist. Thereafter, Mr. Cotton was convicted and sentenced to 54 years of imprisonment, despite the fact that the second victim had identified someone else. Mr. Cotton was exonerated more than a decade into his sentence, when DNA testing excluded him as a possible suspect and implicated another man. His case remains an enduring testament to the ways that suggestive identification procedures engender false confidence in the eyewitnesses who take part in them.

Insofar as judges could overcome the biasing potential of suggestive procedures by focusing on those factors in the analysis that are immune to suggestion—time between initial observation and identification and quality and consistency of preidentification description—the Supreme Court has arguably discouraged this kind of rigorous application of its test by making clear that such factors can always be disregarded or explained away when they contradict an eyewitness's self-report of certainty. Indeed, that is arguably what the Supreme Court did in both *Biggers* and *Manson*, when it cast aside concerns about how much time had passed before an identification occurred and/or how little information had been included in the eyewitness's initial description of the suspect, in order to focus on the confidence the eyewitnesses expressed in their identification and/or viewing opportunity.[168] Many jurists have latched onto these examples to conclude that "there can be no due process problem," as long as certain reliability factors can be "gleaned from the record," and thus refuse to treat the reliability inquiry as anything other than a rote exercise in cataloging evidence that tends to support the existence of reliability factors before summarily concluding that the identification is reliable.[169] Against this backdrop, there is widespread consensus that *Manson* does not deter and "may unintentionally reward suggestive police practices" by "encourag[ing] [courts] to admit identifications

168. *Manson*, 432 U.S. at 114–16; *Biggers*, 409 U.S. at 200–201.

169. O'Toole & Shay, *supra* note 146, at 113, 132; Garrett, Convicting the Innocent, *supra* note 164, at 68–70, 72.

based on criteria that have been tainted by the very suggestive practices the test aims to deter."[170]

C. Failure to Promote Reliability

No indictment of the *Manson* test would be complete without an examination of the considerable role that eyewitness identifications have played in wrongful convictions since *Manson* was decided. Indeed, the purpose of the *Manson* test was to provide for a baseline level of reliability in cases, while also preserving the government's ability to prosecute based on suggestively obtained identifications.[171] However, despite the opinion's Solomonic conceit, there is sound reason to believe that the test has failed to fulfill the first part of its mandate.

Arguably, the *Manson* test was doomed to fail in this regard, as it depends on proof that a suggestive practice resulted in a substantial likelihood of irreparable misidentification. As Justice Black admitted in his dissent to *Wade*, it is "practically impossible" for anyone to prove that an in-court identification was tainted by exposure to the defendant during a pretrial line-up.[172] As another jurist wrote, "[c]onsidering the complexity of the human mind and the subtle effects of suggestive procedures upon it, a determination that an identification was unaffected by such procedures must itself be open to serious question."[173] Thus, the natural consequence of the *Manson* Court's decision to allocate to the defense a burden to prove "a substantial likelihood of irreparable misidentification" was that a substantial percentage of mistaken identifications would fall through the cracks, leading to wrongful conviction.

Decades later, this prediction has been confirmed. Mistaken identifications have maintained a consistently significant role in DNA exonerations since 1989, when people began keeping track of such information.[174] As the

170. *Henderson*, 27 A.3d at 918.

171. *See Manson*, 432 U.S. at 112 (noting the "concern that the jury not hear eyewitness testimony unless that testimony has aspects of reliability"; arguing that the *Manson* test is "responsive to this concern").

172. *Wade*, 388 U.S. at 248 (Black, J.) (concurring in part, dissenting in part) ("How is a witness capable of probing the recesses of his mind to draw a sharp line between a courtroom identification due exclusively to an earlier lineup and a courtroom identification due to memory not based on the lineup?").

173. *Com. v. Johnson*, 650 N.E.2d 1257, 1263 (Mass. 1995)

174. *State v. Martinez*, 478 P.3d 880, 893 (N.M. 2021) (citing Jules Epstein, *The Great Engine That Couldn't: Science, Mistaken Identifications, & the Limits of Cross-Examination*, 36 STETSON L. REV. 727, 729–30 (2007); Sandra G. Thompson, *Judicial Blindness to*

recent Third Circuit Task Force on Eyewitness Identifications wrote in its 2019 report:

> Eyewitness misidentifications have been a factor in well over half of the cases that resulted in wrongful conviction later overturned by DNA evidence. Nearly seventy percent of the DNA driven exonerations in the United States involved eyewitness identifications. In fact, mistaken identifications "are responsible for more wrongful convictions than all other causes combined." Innocent people are convicted, the perpetrator goes free, and public confidence in the judicial system erodes.[175]

Recent data from the National Registry of Exonerations may complicate this narrative somewhat, insofar as they suggest that many DNA exonerations now happen before people go to trial or plead guilty.[176] Likewise, a shocking number of exonerations seem to involve knowingly fabricated identifications, where eyewitnesses contrive to falsely accuse someone in a way that the *Manson* test is powerless to correct.[177] Even so, there is little to suggest that *Manson* has done anything to enhance the reliability of the eyewitness identification evidence that juries receive. In light of the police's perverse incentive under *Manson* to maximize eyewitness confidence by amplifying suggestion,[178] it seems quite plausible that the *Manson* test has exacerbated the exact reliability concerns that the Court sought to address in the opinion.

* * *

Eyewitness Misidentification, 93 Marq. L. Rev. 639, 639 (2009); and Gary L. Wells & Eric P. Seelau, *Eyewitness Identification: Psychological Research & Legal Policy on Lineups*, 1 Psychol., Pub. Pol'y, & L. 765, 787 (1995), for the proposition that "As the [DNA] exonerations grew in number, the role of mistaken-identification testimony retained its prominence.").

175. *2019 Report of the United States Court of Appeals for the Third Circuit Task Force on Eyewitness Identifications*, 92 Temp. L. Rev. 1, 10–11 (2019); Wells & Quinlivan, *supra* note 146, at 1–2 ("All the DNA exoneration cases had the benefit of *Manson* when they were tried, which is at least some indication *Manson* did not work to prevent their wrongful convictions.").

176. *See* Kaitlin Jackson & Samuel Gross, *Tainted Identifications*, Nat'l Registry Exonerations (Sept. 22, 2016), https://www.law.umich.edu/special/exoneration/Pages/taintedids.aspx.

177. *Id.* On the other hand, where a witness knowingly succumbs to external pressure to identify a suspect, the *Manson* test is implicated.

178. *See supra* Section III.B.

To the aforementioned grievances, one might add *Manson's* overestimation of the jury's capacity to intelligently weigh eyewitness identification evidence. In rejecting a *per se* rule, the Court proclaimed that "[j]uries are not so susceptible that they cannot measure intelligently the weight of identification testimony that has some questionable feature."[179] As discussed further in the next chapter, decades of research have confirmed the suspicions of practitioners everywhere that juries struggle mightily to separate those situations where an eyewitness's confidence in an identification is a byproduct of suggestive police practices and those where it genuinely reflects the strength of an eyewitness's memory, even with the help of vigorous cross-examination, expert witnesses, and cautionary jury instructions.

In the end, *Manson* cannot be viewed as a comprehensive solution to the problem of misidentification because it only addresses one very small part of the problem: the use of identifications that lack the specific indicia of reliability enumerated in *Biggers* and *Manson.*[180] As the vast majority of eyewitness identifications fall outside of this category, and into the category that the Supreme Court designated "customary grist for the jury mill,"[181] the likelihood of wrongful conviction due to mistaken identification necessarily depends heavily on whether, in any given case, the jury is willing and able to "measure intelligently the weight of identification testimony that has some questionable feature."[182] The next two chapters examine two of the safeguards designed to promote such intelligent measurement: cautionary jury instructions and expert testimony.

179. *Manson*, 432 U.S. at 116.

180. *Id.* at 112; *see Henderson*, 27 A.3d at 919 (noting that *Manson's* "all-or-nothing approach does not account for the complexities of eyewitness identification evidence").

181. *Manson*, 432 U.S. at 116.

182. *Id.*

3
Jury Instructions

In any system of adjudication that relies primarily on lay juries to decide whether an eyewitness identification is trustworthy, the rate of wrongful conviction due to mistaken identification will depend on how well the judge instructs the jury on its task to determine whether the prosecution has proven "identity" beyond a reasonable doubt. All the more so in a system like ours, which presupposes that "the vast majority" of identifications will be received by a jury, warts and all, because the bar for establishing inadmissibility is so "high."[1] This is so because, as study after study has demonstrated, and court after court has recognized, jurors tend to report for jury duty harboring any number of misconceptions about what makes an identification more or less trustworthy.[2] Perhaps the most stubborn of these

1. *Perry v. New Hampshire*, 565 U.S. 228, 237 (2012) (Sotomayor, J., dissenting).

2. *See, e.g.*, *United States v. Brownlee*, 454 F.3d 131, 142 (3d Cir. 2006) ("[W]hile science has firmly established the inherent unreliability of human perception and memory . . . this reality is outside the jury's common knowledge, and often contradicts jurors' commonsense understandings.") (internal quotation marks and citations omitted); *United States v. Moore*, 786 F.2d 1308, 1312 (5th Cir. 1986) ("[T]he conclusions of the psychological studies are largely counter-intuitive, and serve to explode common myths about an individual's capacity for perception.") (internal quotations omitted)); *United States v. Smithers*, 212 F.3d 306, 312 n.1 (6th Cir. 2000) ("[B]ecause many of the factors affecting eyewitness impressions are counter-intuitive, many jurors' assumptions about how memories are created are actively wrong.") (internal quotations omitted); *Phillips v. Allen*, 668 F.3d 912, 916 (7th Cir. 2012) ("[O]ne point well established in the psychology literature is that most people's intuitions on the subject of identification are wrong."); *Jones v. United States*, 262 A.3d 1114, 1127–28 (D.C. 2021) ("[U]ltimately, scientific findings show that judicial

misconceptions involves the relationship between eyewitness confidence and accuracy. In evaluating the trustworthiness of an identification, jurors tend to rely heavily on an eyewitness's confidence on the witness stand, despite longstanding scientific consensus that such confidence can be easily manipulated and does not reliably indicate accuracy.[3] In addition, jurors tend "to believe that witnesses remember the details of violent events better than those of nonviolent ones," when, as further discussed in Chapters 5 and 6, "the opposite is true."[4] Likewise, jurors tend to be unaware of the well-documented human tendency toward diminished accuracy in identifying members of another race and to overestimate the duration of violent encounters.[5] These misconceptions have persisted despite increased public awareness regarding the fallibility of eyewitness identifications in general.[6]

---

intuition concerning jurors' knowledge of eyewitness testimony is flawed."); *Benn v. United States*, 978 A.2d 1257, 1268 (D.C. 2009) ("[J]urors, as a matter of common sense, are not fully aware of the factors that influence eyewitness testimony." (internal quotation marks and citation omitted)); *State v. Guilbert*, 49 A.3d 705, 720 (Conn. 2012) (noting "widespread judicial recognition that eyewitness identifications are potentially unreliable in a variety of ways unknown to the average juror."); Brandon L. Garrett et al., *Factoring the Role of Eyewitness Evidence in the Courtroom*, 17 J. Empirical L. Stud. 556, 557 (2020), https://doi.org/10.1111/jels.12259 ("Many studies have shown that jurors are not aware of the limitations of eyewitness testimony that memory researchers have studied.") (citing, e.g., Sarah L. Desmarais & J. Don Read, *After 30 Years, What Do We Know about What Jurors Know? A Meta-Analytic Review of Lay Knowledge Regarding Eyewitness Factors*, 35 L. & Hum. Behav. 200 (2011), https://doi.org/10.1007/s10979-010-9232-6; Daniel J. Simmons & Christopher F. Chabris, *What People Believe about How Memory Works: A Representative Survey of the U.S. Population*, PLoS One (Aug. 3, 2011), https://doi.org/10.1371/journal.pone.0022757; Tanja Rapus Benton et al., *Eyewitness Memory Is Still Not Common Sense: Comparing Jurors, Judges and Law Enforcement to Eyewitness Experts*, 20 Appl. Cog. Psychol. 115 (2006), https://doi.org/10.1002/acp.1171; Brian L. Cutler & Steven D. Penrod, Mistaken Identification: The Eyewitness, Psychology, and the Law (1995)); Richard S. Schmechel et al., *Beyond the Ken? Testing Jurors' Understanding of Eyewitness Reliability Evidence*, 46 Jurimetrics 177 (2006); Patrick M. Wall, Eye-Witness Identification in Criminal Cases 19 (1965) ("[I]n general, juries are unduly receptive to identification evidence and are insufficiently aware of its dangers."); Glanville Williams, Proof of Guilt 95 (1955) ("It would be pleasant, but unduly optimistic, to think that the danger inherent in identification evidence by comparative strangers to the accused is now generally recognised. The fact is that juries do not recognise its unreliable nature, and there is still no practice of cautioning juries upon it. Nor are juries given any adequate instruction on the limitations of the identity parade."); Hugo Münsterberg, On the Witness Stand 44 (1908) ("The public in the main suspects that the witness lies [and] may forget a thing, but it would not believe that he could remember the wrong thing. The confidence in the reliability of memory is so general that the suspicion of memory illusions evidently plays a small role in the mind of the jury man[.]"); *id.* at 63 ("[I]ndividual differences" in perception and memory "can be tested today by the methods of experimental psychology far beyond anything which common sense and social experience suggest[.]").

3. Garrett et al., *supra* note 2, at 557.
4. *Benn*, 978 A.2d at 1268.
5. *Id.*; *see, e.g.*, Jordan Abshire & Brian H. Bornstein, *Juror Sensitivity to the Cross-Race Effect*, 27 L. & Hum. Behav. 471 (2003); Schmechel et al., *supra* note 2, at 195–204.
6. *See Benn*, 978 A.2d at 1268.

(How) Do Jurors Scrutinize Identifications?

Moreover, it is not just that jurors do not always know what makes an identification reliable; they also struggle to integrate and apply their knowledge when faced with a confident eyewitness. The psychologist Hans Gross once summed up this difficulty with an anecdote about "a man who claimed in spite of absolute darkness to have recognized an opponent who punched him in the eye."[7] Gross claimed that the man "was altogether believed" (presumably, by a factfinder in a trial) "simply because it was assumed that the punch was so vigorous that the wounded man saw sparks by the light of which he could recognize the other."[8] Gross went on to stress the absurdity of believing that a punch might cause actual "sparks," noting that even "Aristotle knew that such sparks are only subjective."[9] Even so, he argued that this incident should be "a notable warning" about the human capacity to scrutinize eyewitness identifications.[10]

Since the time of Gross's anecdote over a century ago, psychologists' understanding of how juries process identifications has grown more sophisticated and less dependent on anecdotes. However, the picture of the jury that emerges from more recent research is only slightly rosier than the one painted by Gross's anecdote.

In a 1974 study, Loftus presented three groups of mock jurors with evidence from "a grocery store robbery in which the owner and his granddaughter were killed."[11] The first group heard that there were no eyewitnesses; the second heard that the defendant had been identified by a single eyewitness who defense counsel argued was mistaken; and the third group heard about the same identification but was told it had been "discredited" by a defense impeachment suggesting that the eyewitness had not been wearing his glasses during the robbery and that his uncorrected vision was so poor (worse than 20/400) that he could not possibly have seen the robber's face.[12] Perhaps unsurprisingly, those jurors who heard about the identification were much more inclined to

(continued)

7. Hans Gross, Criminal Psychology § 98, at 426–27 (1918).
8. *Id.* § 98, at 427.
9. *Id.*
10. *Id.*
11. Elizabeth F. Loftus, 15 Jurimetrics J. 188, 189 (1975).
12. *Id.*

(How) Do Jurors Scrutinize Identifications? *(continued)*

convict, even in the third group who seemingly had very strong reasons to doubt the accuracy of the identification.[13] However, because those reasons came from a defense lawyer, it is hard to know just how much the results of this study reflect the jury's helplessness vis-à-vis the identification or its unwillingness to trust defense counsel.

Subsequent research circumvented this methodological issue by studying what happens when eyewitnesses expressly concede the factors that undermine their identifications. Consistent with Loftus's findings, this body of research suggests that jurors tend to be most influenced by eyewitness confidence on the witness stand, even when they are told by a judge and/or an expert that such confidence can be very misleading.[14] Jurors are inclined to give lesser but still significant weight to eyewitness confidence at the time of an initial identification.[15] However, where confidence at the time of trial and confidence at the time of identification are in conflict, jurors seem to prioritize confidence at the time of trial.[16] Moreover, no other factor tends to have a significant impact on juror inclination to accept an identification, even when juries are expressly told by a judge and/or an expert that these factors warrant serious consideration.[17] Although, for reasons discussed in Chapter 7, it would be premature to conclude on this basis that jurors cannot rigorously scrutinize in-court identifications even with the help of good jury instructions and expert testimony, this research lends credence to Gross's century-old observation that people are strongly predisposed toward believing identifications, even in the face of circumstances that tend to strongly undermine their reliability.

Although jury instructions are but one tool that can be brought to bear on juror misconceptions about eyewitness identifications, there is reason to believe that they have a special role to play in this regard. As Supreme Court precedent in this area reflects, the assistance of counsel to expose an

13. *Id.* at 189–90 (noting that while only 18 percent of the first group voted to convict, 72 percent voted to convict in the second and 68 percent voted to convict in the third).
14. Garrett et al., supra note 2, at 570–71.
15. *Id.*
16. *Id.*
17. *Id.* at 571.

identification's hidden elements of untrustworthiness is a necessary but insufficient condition to reducing the likelihood of wrongful conviction, as juries may "not trust representations or arguments by counsel"—least of all where, as here, they contradict the juror's common sense and lived experiences.[18] Likewise, although expert witnesses "can help jurors evaluate whether their beliefs about the reliability of eyewitness testimony are correct,"[19] "jurors tend to assume that experts are biased in favor of the side that called them" and may be distracted from considering the merit of an expert's opinion by unrelated "peripheral cues," like the expert's credentials or any other factor that triggers bias (for instance, the expert's race or gender).[20]

Jury instructions, by contrast, are not "opinions" that a jury will feel free to disregard based on what law school the judge attended, their style of dress, or whether they tripped over certain words in addressing the jury. Likewise, instructions do not suffer from the appearance of partisanship. Although there is ample reason to be circumspect about the jury's ability to set aside the preconceptions about eyewitness identification even with the help of expert opinion testimony and carefully crafted jury instructions,[21] the opportunity to disabuse even a single juror of even a single misconception that may prevent such rational parsing is too valuable to forgo on the grounds that it will not solve the problem entirely. Thus, as the Supreme Court acknowledged in *Perry*, the jury system's fairness and integrity depends on the availability of "jury instructions on . . . the fallibility of eyewitness identifications," which specifically "warn the jury to take care in appraising identification evidence."[22] But under what circumstances should these cautionary instructions be administered and what warnings should they include?

---

18. *Jones*, 262 A.3d at 1122.

19. *United States v. Bartlett*, 567 F.3d 901, 906 (7th Cir. 2009).

20. Edie Greene & Natalie Gordon, *Can the "Hot Tub" Enhance Jurors' Understanding and Use of Expert Testimony?*, 16 Wyo. L. Rev. 359, 368 (2016), https://scholarship.law.uwyo.edu/wlr/vol16/iss2/6. Indeed, most juries are instructed to weigh an expert's opinion just like that of any other witness and to give it whatever weight they deem appropriate. *See, e.g.*, Kevin F. O'Malley et al., 1A Federal Jury Practices and Instructions § 14:01 (6th ed.).

21. Garrett et al., *supra* note 2, at 558; *see also, e.g.*, Fiona Leverick, *Jury Instructions on Eyewitness Identification Evidence: A Re-Evaluation*, 49 Creighton L. Rev. 555 (2016).

22. *Perry*, 565 U.S. at 233, 246; *see also, e.g.*, P. Devlin, Report to the Secretary of State for the Home Department of the Departmental Committee on Evidence of Identification in Criminal Cases ¶ 8.4, at 150 (recommending that "the trial judge should be required . . . to direct the jury that it is not safe to convict upon eye-witness evidence unless the circumstances of the identification are exceptional or the eye-witness evidence is supported by substantial evidence of another sort; and . . . to indicate to the jury the circumstances, if any, which they might regard as exceptional and the evidence, if any, which they might regard as supporting the identification.").

In practice, although many jurisdictions encourage judges to caution jurors regarding the perils of eyewitness identification as a matter of course, the failure to do so will not result in the reversal of a conviction unless the identification in question was both contested and uncorroborated.[23] Several courts have held that specialized identification instructions are unnecessary given adequate instruction on the prosecution's burden of proof beyond a reasonable doubt, and the need to determine eyewitness credibility.[24] In most of the country, those jurors who receive a cautionary instruction tend to hear that, in evaluating the reliability of an eyewitness identification, they should consider the same five factors that govern a trial judge's determination of reliability of an identification under *Manson*: namely, (1) opportunity to observe; (2) "strength" of the identification, based in part on how much time passed before it occurred; (3) whether there were any prior inconsistent identifications; (4) the identifying witness's general credibility; and (5) whether there was any defect in the identification procedure itself. This approach was innovated by the United States Circuit Court of Appeals for the District of Columbia in *United States v. Telfaire*, 469 F.2d 552 (D.C. Cir. 1972) (per curiam).[25] Before considering the merits of this regime, it is worthwhile to consider just how it came about.

I. How Did We Get Here?

The notion that a jury might need special guidance from a judge to assess the reliability of an eyewitness identification predates Supreme Court case law in this area by a considerable margin. As noted in the previous chapter, in 1874, Judge James Love of the U.S. District Court for the District of Iowa charged a civil jury to exercise "scrupulous care and caution" with respect to identification evidence they received, insofar as it contradicted other evidence, given how "many cases of mistaken identity occur."[26] In that case, the plaintiff, Hattie B. Tisdale, sought to collect on her husband's life insurance policy, after he failed to return from a trip to Chicago. However, the ink had barely dried on the policy when he went missing, and the insurance company sought to defeat

23. Vitauts M. Gulbis, J.D., *Necessity of, and Prejudicial Effect of Omitting, Cautionary Instruction to Jury as to Reliability of, or Factors to Be Considered in Evaluating, Eyewitness Identification Testimony—State Cases*, 23 A.L.R.4th 1089, § 2[a] (2024).

24. *Id.*

25. Thomas D. Albright & Brandon L. Garrett, *The Law and Science of Eyewitness Evidence*, 102 B.U. L. Rev. 511, 552–58, 606–27 (2022).

26. *Tisdale v. Mut. Ben. Life Ins. Co.*, 23 F. Cas. 1302, 1303 (C.C.D. Iowa 1874), *rev'd on other grounds*, 91 U.S. 238 (1875).

Mrs. Tisdale's claim by showing that her husband had been spotted in Baxter Springs, Kansas, several months after his supposed death. At the request of at least one party (Mrs. Tisdale, presumably), Judge Love provided the following instruction "as to the question of identification" and "whether the jury [could] rely upon the identification" offered by the defense:

> This matter scarcely admits of legal definition. The truth is that we do ordinarily rely upon our recollection of other men. . . . Nevertheless, experience shows that we often make mistakes in this way, and so many cases of mistaken identity occur that it is our duty to receive such evidence to show error. Then the jury must receive and consider evidence of personal identity which is inconsistent with other evidence in the case with scrupulous care and caution. This is all, gentlemen, that the court can say upon this question of identity. It does not admit of anything like a precise legal definition, in my opinion.[27]

By the 1920s and 1930s, some authorities in the British Commonwealth came to consider specialized cautionary instructions like this one a necessary means of addressing suggestive law enforcement practices in cases where they believed that evidentiary exclusion was unwarranted. Such instructions were consistent with the longstanding common law tradition allowing judicial commentary on the weight of the evidence and the credibility of witnesses.[28] Pursuant to this tradition, judges routinely exercised their discretion to warn juries regarding any "defects which may have been present in the identification procedure" (for instance, the use of too few photos to obtain a photographic identification), as well as any other "warning signs" regarding the likelihood of mistaken identification.[29] As Lord Chief Justice of England, the Right Honourable Gordon Hewart extended this tradition even further by suggesting, in the 1924 case of Thomas Dwyer and Allen Ferguson, that the administration of such warnings was a formal

27. *Id.* at 1303–04.

28. *See, e.g.*, *Quercia v. United States*, 289 U.S. 466, 469 (1933) (noting the trial judge's prerogative at common law "to direct" the jury "in matters of law emerging upon the evidence . . . and also, in matters of fact to give them a great light and assistance by his weighing the evidence before them, and observing where the question and knot of the business lies, and by showing them his opinion even in matters of fact; which is a great advantage and light to laymen.'" (quoting HALE, HISTORY OF THE COMMON LAW, 291, 292 (internal quotation marks omitted))).

29. WALL, *supra* note 2, at 193.

requirement under law, rather than a matter confided to the judge's discretion. There, after reversing Dwyer and Ferguson's convictions based on the use of single-suspect photographic displays, Lord Hewart opined that the identifying witnesses' testimony would have been suspect, even had a proper lineup or array been administered.[30] He went on to state that where such witnesses testify at trial, their in-court identifications should "at any rate . . . be taken subject to" the discrediting fact "that [they have] previously seen the [suspect's] photograph."[31] Many prominent authorities took these words to suggest that the trial court had a duty to "at least caution the jury" about the perils of eyewitness identifications made under such circumstances.[32]

Lord Hewart's colleagues would later retreat from this interpretation.[33] However, in 1937, the high court of Australia held that it was reversible error to fail to "clearly warn[]" the jury about the "dangers" of a single-suspect photographic display because it created a "possibility of error . . . SO substantial as to make the conviction unsafe . . . according to the accepted view" of both jurists and scientists.[34] For these purposes, it would not suffice for a judge to "treat the matter as one depending upon a choice between rival systems [or] different 'schools of thought.'"[35] Rather the court's duty was to "give the weight of [its] judicial authority to a statement of the dangers."[36] By the 1940s, Canadian judges had followed suit.[37]

30. R. v. Dwyer & Ferguson [1925], 2 K.B. 799, 803 ("[W]here [such] a process has been gone through, no matter with what care, it is quite evident that afterwards the witness who has so acted in relation to a photograph is not a useful witness for the process of identification.").

31. *Id.*; *see also* R. v. Phillips (1924), 18 Cr. App. R. 151 (C.C.A.) ("The evidence of identification in this case was weak. It is not, of course, to be said that a person is not to be convicted on the testimony of one witness identifying him, but where the circumstances are those of the present case—where the identifying witness is a stranger to the defendant and the physical circumstances are those to which reference has been made—it is right that the attention of the jury should be directed to the weakness of the evidence.").

32. Williams, *supra* note 2, at 97; *see also* 7 Wigmore, Evidence § 786, at 203 & n.7 (Chadbourne rev. 1978).

33. Williams, *supra* note 2, at 97 (citing R. v. Hinds, [1932] 2 K.B. 664).

34. Davies & Cody v. R., 57 Commw. L.R. 170, 182 (Austl. 1937).

35. *Id.*

36. *Id.*

37. R. v. Baldwin (1944), 82 C.C.C. 15 (Ont. C.A.) (holding that although "[e]vidence as to identity, given by witnesses who have seen photographs of an accused after his arrest, . . . is not, by reason of such fact, rendered inadmissible, . . . it is the duty of the trial judge under such circumstances to call the attention of the jury to what has happened, and properly to caution the jury."); R. v. Bagley (1926), 2 W.W.R. 513, 515 (B.C.C.A.) (MacDonald, C.J., dissenting) (arguing that the verdict was unsustainable because, while the trial judge "referred several times to the fact that photos were shown to the several witnesses . . . he made no comment upon the effect of that on the weight of the witnesses' testimony.").

Lord Chief Justice Hewart.

A. The Pre-*Telfaire* Era

And yet, for all of this authority, and the widespread impression that eyewitness identifications were "proverbially untrustworthy,"[38] American judges remained largely resistant to cautioning criminal juries about the perils of eyewitness identifications until the *Wade* trilogy was decided.[39] Although in the states, this resistance was part of a larger movement to depart from the common law by amending state constitutions to expressly ban "inappropriate judicial comment on the evidence,"[40] cautionary

38. *United States v. Wade*, 388 U.S. 218, 228 (1967) (quoting FELIX FRANKFURTER, THE CASE OF SACCO AND VANZETTI 30 (1927) (internal quotation marks omitted)).

39. WALL, *supra* note 2, at 198–99 ("[I]t is surely not a general practice of American criminal trial courts to warn juries of the dangers of identification evidence in general, and the defects present in the identification evidence offered in the particular case then on trial."); *id.* at 196 (noting that it was "not common for [an American] trial judge to . . . point out whatever dangers may exist with respect to the identification testimony"). Even so, there were some jurisdictions where the failure to instruct "the dangers that may exist with respect to [eyewitness] identification testimony" was "occasionally criticized by an appellate court, and . . . sometimes even cited as ground for reversal." *id.* at 196. As discussed further below, the Pennsylvania Supreme Court was especially "strict" on this issue, but was assuredly an outlier. *Id.* 196–98 & nn. 59–64 (collecting cases). Likewise, the high courts of New York and Illinois had indicated that such cautionary instructions were advisable. *Id.* at 198–99 nn.65–67 (collecting cases).

40. NAT'L RSCH. COUNCIL OF THE NAT'L ACADS., IDENTIFYING THE CULPRIT: ASSESSING EYEWITNESS IDENTIFICATION 41 & n. 52 (2014) [hereinafter NAT'L RSCH. COUNCIL] (citing *Brodes v. State*, 614 S.E.2d 766, 769 & n.6 (Ga. 2005) (surveying state case law)); Myron Atkinson, Jr. & LaVern C. Neff, *Evidence-Jury Trials-Weight of Evidence-Credibiity of Witnesses-Judicial Comment Thereon*, 27 N.D. L. REV. 199, 200–201 (1951).

instructions about eyewitness identification were just as rare in federal court, perhaps owing to a general judicial reluctance to draw attention to weaknesses in the prosecution's case.[41]

Hence, early litigation in this area focused less on the right to an instruction of the kind that the (alleged) widow Tisdale had received and more on the right to an instruction calling attention to the government's burden to prove the specific issue of "identity" beyond a reasonable doubt. Such were the facts in *McKenzie v. United States*, 126 F.2d 533 (D.C. Cir. 1942) (per curiam), where the D.C. Circuit reversed James McKenzie's conviction and death sentence in a racially charged, headline-grabbing rape case, based on the trial judge's "failure [or refusal] to say in plain words that if the circumstances of the identification were not convincing, [the jury] should acquit."[42] Despite this outcome, courts quickly dismissed the case as an outlier because of the uniquely compelling circumstances involved: Mr. McKenzie's conviction had come in a capital case, had "rested largely on the testimony of the complaining witness," and had been undermined by "a strong case for the defense" (see the text box that follows).[43] Moreover, the judge's error in omitting the identification instruction had been exacerbated by the remainder of the instructions, which suggested to the jury that the decision to acquit or convict rested on its willingness to believe Mr. McKenzie's relatively weak alibi.[44] By contrast, in noncapital cases that did not present the same extenuating circumstances, it sufficed to charge the jury that they alone were the arbiters of witness credibility and that the government bore the burden of proof beyond a reasonable doubt as to every element of the offense.[45]

41. *Ballard v. United States*, 237 F.2d 582, 583 (D.C. Cir. 1956) (no abuse of discretion where the trial court refused to admonish the jury regarding the risks of accomplice testimony); *Shettel v. United States*, 113 F.2d 34, 36 (D.C. Cir. 1940) (same, where the judge refused to admonish the jury regarding the unreliability of "professional detectives"); *see also United States v. Moss*, 410 F.2d 386, 387 (3d Cir. 1969) (collecting cases; finding no reversible error from the failure to administer a specialized cautionary instruction on eyewitness identification).

42. *McKenzie*, 126 F.2d at 536.

43. *Obery v. United States*, 126 F.2d 533, 536 & n.3 (D.C. Cir. 1956).

44. *McKenzie*, 126 F.2d at 536.

45. *Obery*, 126 F.2d at 536 & n.3; *accord Jones v. United States*, 307 F.2d 190, 192 & n.2 (D.C. Cir. 1962).

The Trial of James McKenzie

The prosecution of James McKenzie, a 21-year-old Black man, for the rape and robbery of Vada Abarca, a white woman, ranks among the most sensational and racially charged episodes in D.C. history.[46] Mrs. Abarca had been working in a laundry service, when a man walked in, robbed her at gunpoint, and then forced her into a back room, where he raped her.[47] The next day, Katherine Harper, the manager of a different laundry service, was similarly forced into a back room after being robbed at gunpoint.[48] Unlike Mrs. Abarca, however, Ms. Harper's ordeal had ended when her assailant accidentally shattered the plate glass in the front door.[49]

Facing an unprecedented "wave of unsolved sex crimes" (including the suspected rape and murder of a 23-year-old War Department stenographer),[50] the Captain of the Metropolitan Police Department led a task force of dozens in the "most intensive [manhunt] in the annals of the Washington police department," "raid[ing] . . . juke joints, pool rooms, and beer parlors" and subjecting "scores" of young black men to arrest and interrogation, before the complainants happened to see Mr. McKenzie during a ride-along.[51] They had been riding in a car with two detectives when they saw him in front of another laundry service. Upon seeing him, Mrs. Abarca reportedly screamed "My God! That's the man" and collapsed in "hysterics."[52] After Ms. Harper seconded the identification, the police took him into custody, interrogated him, and placed him in a lineup, where the complainants identified him again.[53]

(continued)

46. *But see, e.g., Fisher v. United States*, 328 U.S. 463 (1946) (holding that the defendant was not entitled to an instruction on diminished capacity in his trial for murdering a librarian at the National Cathedral where he worked as a janitor, after she berated him and called him a "black nigger"); *Laney v. United States*, 294 F. 412 (D.C. Cir. 1923) (holding that the defendant was not entitled to claim self-defense for opening fire on an angry "mob" that chased him through the streets, throwing sticks and stones, and yelling "catch the nigger" and "kill the nigger").

47. *McKenzie*, 126 F.2d at 534.

48. *Id.*

49. *See, e.g., Fiend Strikes Again*, WASH. POST, 1, June 26, 1941.

50. *Sex Crimes in Overcrowded Washington Continue Unsolved*, AUSTIN AMERICAN, 8, June 26, 1941.

51. *2 Victims Help Trap D.C. Rape Suspect*, WASH. POST, 1, 13, June 27, 1941.

52. *Jury Confined by Judge in Assault Case*, WASH. POST, 14, July 29, 1941.

53. *Rape Suspect Identified in Police Line*, WASH. POST, 1, 5, June 28, 1941.

The Trial of James McKenzie *(continued)*

In "one of [D.C.'s] most rapid prosecutions on record," Mr. McKenzie was brought to trial thirty-five days after Mrs. Abarca reported the incident to police.[54] The U.S. Attorney for the District of Columbia elected to prosecute Mr. McKenzie personally, announcing the decision to seek the death penalty immediately after the case was indicted.[55] T. Whitfield Davidson, who would later decry the "amalgamation of the races" in rejecting Dallas Public Schools integration plan, presided over the trial.[56]

Mrs. Abarca's identification was undermined by several circumstances related to her initial description of the attacker: while she said he was between thirty and thirty-five, Mr. McKenzie looked younger, and insofar as her description had included any distinctive characteristics, she had based her identification on generic ones: Mr. McKenzie's dark glasses and long arms.[57] Apart from her identification, the only evidence tying Mr. McKenzie to the offense was dubious hair and blood analysis performed by D.C.'s inexperienced, volunteer coroner.[58] Police never recovered any proceeds or instrumentalities of the crime from Mr. McKenzie or any place he was known to frequent.[59] Meanwhile, laundry service workers continued to report suspicious behavior by someone who fit the perpetrator's description well after Mr. McKenzie's arrest.[60]

With all of this working in Mr. McKenzie's favor, his attorney staked the defense on a shaky alibi and a risky attempt to discredit Mrs. Abarca's identification by showing that another eyewitness had contradicted Ms. Harper's identification of Mr. McKenzie.[61] This gambit required the defense to reveal that Ms. Harper also had been attacked and had identified Mr. McKenzie as her attacker, two facts which the prosecution had omitted from its case in chief. The plan backfired when Judge Davidson

54. *Two Facing Chair After Speedy Trials*, AFRO-AMERICAN (BALTIMORE), 12, Aug. 9, 1941.

55. *Death Penalty Will Be Asked for Assault on Laundry Clerk*, WASH. POST, 9, July 9, 1941.

56. *Borders v. Rippey*, 184 F. Supp. 402 (N.D. Tex. 1960).

57. *McKenzie*, 126 F.2d at 535–36.

58. *Dr. Rosenberg's Laboratory Provides Clews in Assault*, WASH. POST, 5, June 28, 1941.

59. *McKenzie*, 126 F.2d at 536.

60. *See, e.g.*, *1 Policeman Shot, 2 Bitten as Prisoner Grabs Another's Gun*, WASH. POST, 1, June 29, 1941.

61. *McKenzie*, 126 F.2d at 535.

The Trial of James McKenzie *(continued)*

ruled that defense counsel would not be allowed to elicit the contradictory identification.[62]

In his closing argument, the U.S. Attorney told the jury: "These crimes have got to be stopped, . . . and you are the ones that can stop them. I ask for you for a verdict that will make the streets of Washington safe for women."[63] A jury comprised entirely of white men voted to convict Mr. McKenzie and condemn him to die after only an hour and forty-eight minutes of deliberations.[64] There is some indication that Judge Davidson stymied the appeal by failing to include his instructions to the jury in the record on appeal.[65] Against this backdrop, and no doubt mindful of the hostile atmosphere in which Mr. McKenzie's trial occurred, the D.C. Circuit held that Judge Davidson reversibly erred by failing to say "plainly" to the jury that it "*should* acquit" "if the circumstances of the identification were not convincing."[66]

Over the next two decades, *Telfaire's* development was aided by two eventualities. The first was doctrinal: in *Levine v. United States*, 261 F.2d 747 (1958), the D.C. Circuit joined the Fifth and Sixth Circuits in recognizing, as a general proposition, that judges are required to instruct the jury on any theory of the defense that would support acquittal as long as it is supported by the evidence.[67] Before *Levine*, the court had only applied this rule in the self-defense context.[68] *Levine* clarified that "it applies as well to situations," like the case of a purportedly unreliable identification, "where

62. In holding that Judge Davidson had not committed reversible error in failing to admit this evidence, the D.C. Circuit panel wrote that counsel's "zeal outran his discretion." *Id.* However, the exoneree Ronald Cotton would prevail on a similar claim of error decades later. *State v. Cotton*, 351 S.E.2d 277, 280 (N.C. 1987) (granting a new trial where the judge excluded evidence that someone else raped in a similar attack on the same night had identified another person).

63. *D.C. Woman's Attacker Is Condemned to Death*, WASH. POST, 1, July 30, 1941.

64. *Two Facing Chair After Speedy Trials*, *supra* at 54; *Neighbors Say Bashful Bubbles McKenzie May Die for Crime He Didn't Commit*, AFRO-AMERICAN (BALTIMORE), 10, Aug. 16, 1941.

65. *Lawyers Believe Client Mistaken for Another Man*, PITTSBURGH COURIER, Oct. 4, 1941.

66. *McKenzie*, 126 F.2d at 536 (emphasis added).

67. *Levine*, 261 F.2d at 748–49 (quoting *Calderon v. United States*, 279 F. 556, 558 (5th Cir. 1922); *Marson v. United States*, 203 F.2d 904, 912 (6th Cir. 1953)).

68. *See Meadows v. United States*, 82 F.2d 881 (D.C. Cir. 1936).

special facts present an evidentiary theory which if believed defeats the factual theory of the prosecution."[69]

The second concerned the composition of the court. In 1962, a liberal shift in the composition of the D.C. Circuit paved the way for progressive reform in a number of areas related to the criminal legal system, including eyewitness identification. That year, David Bazelon, "a consistent advocate of safeguarding the rights of persons accused of crimes,"[70] succeeded the "conservative" Wilbur Kingsbury Miller to become the Circuit's Chief Judge.[71] At the same time, the Senate confirmed J. Skelly Wright to serve alongside Bazelon. A reform-minded liberal from Louisiana, Judge Wright once joked that he was "probably the only judge on any federal court of appeals who [could] call Judge David L. Bazelon conservative."[72] No doubt emboldened by a simultaneous progressive shift in the composition of the U.S. Supreme Court,[73] the left-leaning judges of Bazelon's D.C. Circuit targeted a number of issues affecting those who had been historically underserved by the legal system, including those facing criminal prosecution. In the wake of this realignment, eyewitness identification reform came swiftly.

Notably, in *Salley v. United States*, 353 F.2d 897 (D.C. Cir. 1965), the D.C. Circuit reemphasized the need for juries to be instructed on the burden to prove the specific issue of identity, in certain cases where it was at issue. Salley had been charged with selling drugs to an undercover police officer and requested an instruction to the effect that identity "is an element of every crime," which the government must "prove beyond a reasonable doubt," and that the jury had an obligation to acquit if it was not "satisfied beyond a reasonable doubt of the accuracy of the witness' identification of the defendant."[74] The trial court rejected this proposal, instead giving a "boiler plate" instruction regarding the government's burden of proof as to "every element of the offense."[75] The D.C. Circuit reversed Salley's conviction, holding that the trial court had an obligation to instruct

69. *Id.* at 748.

70. Lawrence Meyer, *Judge Bazelon*, WASH. POST, May 15, 1979, https://www.washingtonpost.com/archive/politics/1979/05/15/judge-bazelon/f7fa5790-2178-4498-bdef-cfdf953302bf/.

71. Inez Smith Reid, *Historical Links: The Remarkable Legacy and Legal Journey of the Honorable Julia Cooper Mack*, 8 U.D.C. L. REV. 303, 325 (2004), https://digitalcommons.law.udc.edu/cgi/viewcontent.cgi?article=1165&context=udclr.

72. J. Skelly Wright, *A Colleague's Tribute to Judge David L. Bazelon on the Twenty-fifth Anniversary of His Appointment*, 123 U. PA. L. REV. 250, 250 (1974).

73. *See* Al Kamen, *U.S. Court's Liberal Era Ending*, WASH. POST, Jan. 27, 1985.

74. *Salley*, 353 F.2d at 898–99 & n.2.

75. *Id.* at 898 & n.1.

the jury that they "should acquit" "if there was reasonable doubt as to the identification of the defendant as the person who made the sale."[76] The court reasoned that such an instruction was required given the involvement of an undercover agent who "file[d] for as many as 100 warrants after his tours of duty, which generally last for a number of months."[77] Against this backdrop, "the possibility of error due to mistake and the fallibility of human memory [was] obvious."[78]

As with *McKenzie*, the D.C. Circuit quickly limited *Salley's* holding to the uniquely compelling circumstances of an undercover agent trying to remember one person out of hundreds who participated in "unrelated narcotics purchases."[79] By contrast, robbery victims who professed to have gotten good looks at those who robbed them did not raise the same degree of concern for the judges.[80] Nevertheless, by 1966, "claims . . . that the issue of identification was inadequately treated in the instruction to the jury" had become so numerous that the D.C. Circuit considered them a "recurring problem."[81] Likewise, scholarly consensus had begun to develop around the need for a cautionary instruction "in every case where identification is an important issue."[82] Thus, in *Jones v. United States*, 361 F.2d 537 (D.C. Cir. 1966), the court held that "special instruction on identification . . . adapted to the evidence in [a] particular case" should be given whenever "the defendant has placed [identity] in issue" in one of several ways,[83] and further

76. at 899 (emphasis added).

77. *Id.* at 898.

78. *Id.* at 898–99.

79. *Jones v. United States*, 361 F.2d 537, 542 (D.C. Cir. 1966).

80. *Id.*; *see also Macklin v. United States*, 409 F.2d 174 (D.C. Cir. 1969). *But see Gregory v. United States*, 369 F.2d 185, 190 (D.C. Cir. 1966) (holding that the instructions to the jury were "deficient" because "no charge on identification was given" despite the fact that identification was "the only real issue" and "there was a division among the eyewitnesses as to whether or not the defendant on trial was the bandit").

81. *Jones*, 361 F.2d at 542.

82. Wall, *supra* note 2, 199–200 ("[T]he trial judge should be required to warn the jury of the dangers of identification in general and to instruct them to receive it with caution. Where the original identification is obtained in a suggestive manner, he should call this fact to the jury's attention explaining its significance. If any danger signals are present in the case, such as an identifying witness's previous failure to identify the defendant he should give appropriate instructions on that point as well. His failure to follow this rule in cases where it applies should result in the reversal of the conviction, unless the appellate court finds that the proof of guilt was so strong that the jury would have convicted the defendant even if the proper warning had been given."); *see also* 7 Wigmore, Evidence § 2033, at 259 (3d ed. 1940) (arguing that "the true way" to "protect litigants from the unrestrained and inexperienced mental processes of the jury" is to allow judicial commentary on the evidence).

83. The defendant could place identity in issue "either by his own direct denial, by the production of alibi witnesses, or by impeachment of opposing witnesses." *Jones*, 361 F.2d at 542.

"asks for a special instruction on identification."[84] "The instruction should point out":

1. "[T]hat the evidence raises the question of whether the defendant was in fact the criminal actor and necessitates the juror's resolving any conflict in testimony upon this issue"; and
2. "[T]hat the burden of proof is upon the prosecution with reference to every element of the crime charged, . . . includ[ing] . . . the identity of the defendant as the perpetrator of the crime."[85]

This approach was endorsed by multiple federal circuit courts of appeal, including the Fourth Circuit, which adopted this language verbatim in articulating a model identification instruction.[86] Judges Edward Devitt and Charles Blackmar similarly included a charge based on this language in their second edition of the *Federal Jury Practice and Instruction* series.[87] Meanwhile, the D.C. Bar Association's Junior Bar Section introduced its own collection of pattern jury instructions—the *Criminal Jury Instructions for the District of Columbia*—containing its own "Mistaken Identity" charge with slightly different language:

> The burden is on the Government to prove beyond a reasonable doubt, not only that the offense was committed as alleged in the indictment, but also that the defendant is the person who committed it. You must be satisfied beyond a reasonable doubt of the accuracy of the identification of the defendant before you may convict him. If the circumstances of the identification are not convincing beyond a reasonable doubt, you must find the defendant not guilty.[88]

These instructions were a far cry from the days when judges refused to call attention to the government's burden to prove "identity" in plain English. Still, it did not take long for judges to conclude they did not go far enough.

84. *Id.*
85. *Id.*
86. *See United States v. Levi*, 405 F.2d 380 (4th Cir. 1968); *see also Pallotta v. United States*, 404 F.2d 1035, 1039 (1st Cir. 1968); *Cullen v. United States*, 408 F.2d 1178, 1181 (8th Cir. 1969); *McGee v. United States*, 402 F.2d 434, 436 (10th Cir. 1968).
87. *United States v. Barber*, 442 F.2d 517, 526 n.10 (3d Cir. 1971) (quoting E. DEVITT & C. BLACKMAR, FEDERAL JURY PRACTICE AND INSTRUCTION (2d ed. 1970)); *Macklin v. United States*, 409 F.2d 174, 178 (1969); *accord* NAT'L RSCH. COUNCIL, *supra* note 40, at 41.
88. *United States v. King*, 461 F.2d 152, 158 n.1 (D.C. Cir. 1972) (Bazelon, C.J., concurring) (quoting JUNIOR BAR SECTION OF THE BAR ASSOC. OF THE DISTRICT OF COLUMBIA, CRIMINAL JURY INSTRUCTIONS FOR THE DISTRICT OF COLUMBIA No. 126 (1966) ("Mistaken Identity").

In the wake of *Wade*, *Gilbert*, and *Stovall*, many federal judges (especially those in the D.C. Circuit, who presided over more street-crime cases involving eyewitness identifications than their counterparts elsewhere) criticized these pattern instructions for their failure to offer the jury any guidance on how to resolve the myriad questions of reliability that the 1967 *Wade* trilogy had identified, but left unresolved.[89] Thus, in *Macklin v. United States*, 409 F.2d 174 (1969), the D.C. Circuit (Wright, J.) observed that the Bar Association's "mistaken identity" charge should be "supplemented by observations on identification evidence as discussed in *Wade*, *Gilbert*, and *Stovall*," and administered to juries "as a matter of routine," regardless of whether it was requested by the defense.[90] Three years later, however, when no such modifications were forthcoming, the D.C. Circuit took matters into its own hands. The result was the model instruction appended in *United States v. Telfaire*, 469 F.2d 552 (D.C. Cir. 1972) (per curiam).

The Emergence of Pattern Jury Instructions

The development of specialized cautionary jury instructions on eyewitness identification coincides with a period of "increasing [judicial] reliance on form language for jury instructions."[91] The earliest American judges tended to devise their own jury instructions, with party input and an eye toward precedent. By the mid-twentieth

(continued)

89. *Barber*, 442 F.2d at 518 (describing Devitt & Blackmar's instruction as "skeletal"); *United States v. Telfaire*, 469 F.2d 552, 557 (D.C. Cir. 1972) (per curiam) (noting that the D.C. Bar Association's "mistaken identity" instruction did "little more than incorporate one sentence modeled on [the court's] 1942 opinion in *McKenzie*"); *King*, 461 F.2d at 156–57 (Bazelon, C.J., concurring) (noting "I do not see how we can turn over to the jury this critical question without even trying to acquaint it with the risks involved or the information now available that could illuminate its inquiry"; describing the D.C. Bar Association's "mistaken identity" instruction as "vacuous and unhelpful"; chastising the court for failing to "even take the trouble to provide the jury with meaningful information about the pitfalls of the identification process"); *United States v. Brown*, 461 F.2d 134, 145 n.1 (D.C. Cir. 1972) (Bazelon, C.J., dissenting) ("More information is needed to assist the jury's resolution of identification issues . . . ."); *United States v. Washington*, 413 F.2d 409, 411 (D.C. Cir. 1969) (Fahy, J., dissenting) (arguing that the failure to give an appropriate instruction on eyewitness identification pursuant to *Macklin* constitutes reversible error).

90. *Macklin*, 409 F.2d at 178.

91. *Barber*, 442 F.2d at 527.

The Emergence of Pattern Jury Instructions *(continued)*

century, however, members of the bench and bar were clamoring for compilations that were "trial-tested and appellate-approved."[92]

In the federal system, these prayers were answered with the release of *Federal Jury Practice and Instructions* by West Publications. This treatise began as "a sort of hobby" for Judge William C. Mathes of the Southern District of California, who started collecting jury instructions in order to "facilitate oft-repeated acts in [his] day-to-day work."[93] In 1957, after about a decade of compiling, he published the fruits of his "hobby" in the Federal Rules Decisions.[94] A few years and one revision later,[95] it was incorporated into the first edition of *Federal Jury Practice and Instructions*, which Judge Mathes coauthored with Judge Edward Devitt.[96] In 1970, Judge Devitt coauthored a new edition of the treatise containing the *Jones* instruction with Charles Blackmar.[97] "The treatise, now written by a new generation of authors, has grown to nine volumes, is in its [sixth] edition, and is widely cited."[98] Its success speaks to just how thoroughly dependent on pattern jury instructions the judicial system has become, for both good and ill.

As Judge Aldisert wrote, "increas[ed] reliance on form language for jury instructions" was a double-edged sword that had the potential to impact the judicial system both positively and negatively.[99] On the one hand, the act of creating a model instruction "serves a useful function of survey and synthesis, to distill outstanding judgments on matters that have been pondered by this and other courts."[100] Likewise, reliance on such instructions helps to promote judicial efficiency (by reducing the amount of time that judges have to spend crafting jury instructions), as

92. *Id. at* 527–28.

93. Hon. William C. Mathes, *Some Suggested Forms for Use in Criminal Cases*, 20 F.R.D. 231 (1958).

94. *Id.*

95. Hon. William C. Mathes, *Jury Instructions and Forms for Federal Criminal Cases*, 27 F.R.D. 39 (1961).

96. William Mathes & Edward Devitt, Federal Jury Practice and Instructions (1965 & Supp. 1968).

97. *See Barber*, 442 F.2d at 526 n.10 (quoting E. Devitt & C. Blackmar, Federal Jury Practice and Instruction (2d ed. 1970)).

98. Tom Singer, *To Tell the Truth, Memory Isn't That Good*, 63 Mont. L. Rev. 337, 350 (2002).

99. *Barber*, 442 F.2d at 527.

100. *United States v. Telfaire*, 469 F.2d 552, 561 (D.C. Cir. 1972) (per curiam) (Leventhal, J., concurring).

The Emergence of Pattern Jury Instructions *(continued)*

well as greater stability and reliability in the administration of justice.[101]On the other hand, if judges are not careful, they may become unduly inflexible and overly dependent on "skeletal, pattern instructions" that fail to "assure the essential particularity demanded by the facts" of each case.[102] "Jury instructions should be drawn with reference to the particular facts of the case on trial, and ought not be conveyed merely in boilerplate abstractions."[103]

This double-edged sword dynamic has influenced the development of eyewitness identification instructions in multiple ways. The deficiency of early pattern identification instructions helped to inspire the creation of the *Telfaire* instruction, and pattern jury instruction compilations have eventually helped it to spread to additional jurisdictions. At the same time, it could be argued that the *Telfaire* instruction's ready availability in printed volumes helped to discourage judges from attempting any changes that might have improved it.

B. The *Telfaire* Era

Compared to *McKenzie* and *Salley*, the two cases that inspired previous developments in this area, the facts of *Telfaire* are quite unremarkable. Melvin Telfaire was convicted of robbing a man whom others had lured onto the dimly lit, third-floor landing of a hotel under false pretenses.[104] The complainant had identified Mr. Telfaire in the hotel lobby immediately after reporting the incident to police, a process that took roughly thirty minutes.[105] Confronting these facts on appeal, a three-judge panel of the D.C. Circuit held that Mr. Telfaire's right to have the jury instructed on his defense of mistaken identity had been satisfied by the trial court's instructions on the government's twofold burden: (1) to prove every element of the offense, including identity, beyond a reasonable doubt; and (2) to rebut Mr. Telfaire's defense of alibi, also beyond a reasonable doubt.[106] In the court's view, Mr. Telfaire's case presented "none of the special difficulties

101. *Barber*, 442 F.2d at 527–28.
102. *Id.* at 528.
103. *United States v. Holley*, 502 F.2d 273, 276 (4th Cir. 1974) (internal quotation marks and citations omitted).
104. *Telfaire*, 469 F.2d at 555 n.4.
105. *Id.*
106. *Id.* at 556.

often presented by identification testimony that would require additional information be given to the jury" because the complainant had "adequate opportunity to observe" and had made a "spontaneous identification" soon thereafter.[107]

Despite the ease with which it dispatched Mr. Telfaire's claim of instructional error, the panel (Chief Judge Bazelon, Judge Harold Leventhal, and Judge Arlin Adams of the Third Circuit, by designation) nevertheless used the case to promulgate a new eyewitness identification instruction for prospective use, holding that such a "supplement to [its] prior rulings" was "require[d]," given the failure of the current instruction to "take note of the discussion in *Wade* and subsequent cases."[108] Building on an approach innovated by the Pennsylvania Commonwealth and later adopted by the Third Circuit Court of Appeals,[109] the *Telfaire* panel proffered an instruction that "emphasiz[ed]" the government's burden to prove "identity," while encouraging (but not requiring) the jury to "consider" those factors the Supreme Court deemed relevant to determining whether an eyewitness's recollection was tainted by exposure to the defendant during an illicit identification procedure, specifically: (1) whether "the witness had the capacity and an adequate opportunity to observe the offender"; (2) whether, given the "strength" and circumstances of the identification, it was "the product of [the eyewitness's] own recollection" or a suggestive procedure that preceded it; and (3) whether the eyewitness had failed to identify the defendant at any time in the past.[110] In addition, the instruction told the jury that it

107. *Id.*

108. *See id.* at 557 (citing *Macklin*, 409 F.2d 174).

109. Under the Pennsylvania approach, whenever the eyewitness was "not in a position to clearly observe the assailant, or [was] not positive as to identity," or the identification was "weakened by qualification or by failure to identify defendant on one or more prior occasions," judges were bound to both "warn the jury that the testimony as to identity must be received with caution," *Com. v. Kloiber*, 106 A.2d 820, 827 (Pa. 1954), and "specially direct the attention of the jury" to whatever evidence was relevant in this regard. *Com. v. Ronello*, 89 A. 553, 555 (Pa. 1913); *accord Com. v. Wilkerson*, 203 A.2d 235, 237 (Pa. Super. 1964). The Third Circuit's decision to adopt this approach in an effort to transcend "skeletal pattern instructions and assure the essential particularity demanded by the facts surrounding each identification" helped inspire the *Telfaire* court's instruction. *Telfaire*, 469 F.2d at 557 (quoting *Barber*, 442 F.2d at 528). However, whereas the Pennsylvania approach counseled "caution" with respect to any identification that was uncertain or undermined by poor viewing conditions or a past failure to make an identification, *Kloiber*, 106 A.2d at 827, the *Telfaire* instruction only advocated "great care" regarding those that "may have been influenced" by a prior suggestive procedure. *Telfaire*, 469 F.2d at 558.

110. *Telfaire*, 469 F.2d at 558–59; *see also id.* at 559 n.3 (Bazelon, C.J., concurring) (noting that "the question of independent source" is "essentially an issue of reliability"). In so doing, the court also held that the same factors would determine whether a single eyewitness's uncorroborated identification was sufficient to sustain the government's burden of proof as to identity. *See id.* at 555 n.5 (quoting *United States v. Levi*, 405 F.2d 380, 383 (4th Cir. 1968)).

"should consider" a fourth factor: (4) the requirement to "consider the credibility of each identification witness in the same way as any other witness, consider whether he is truthful, and consider whether he had the capacity and opportunity to make a reliable observation on the matter covered in his testimony."[111] Consistent with the *Macklin* court's view that such an instruction should be "routine[ly]" given,[112] the *Telfaire* panel advised that the failure to administer its instruction "would constitute a risk in future cases that should not be ignored unless there [was] strong reason in the particular case."[113]

The *Telfaire* Instruction

One of the most important issues in this case is the identification of the defendant as the perpetrator of the crime. The Government has the burden of [proving] identity, beyond a reasonable doubt. It is not essential that the witness himself be free from doubt as to the correctness of his statement. However, you, the jury, must be satisfied beyond a reasonable doubt of the accuracy of the identification of the defendant before you may convict him. If you are not convinced beyond a reasonable doubt that the defendant was the person who committed the crime, you must find the defendant not guilty.

Identification testimony is an expression of belief or impression by the witness. Its value depends on the opportunity the witness had to observe the offender at the time of the offense and to make a reliable identification later. In appraising the identification testimony of a witness, you should consider the following:

1. Are you convinced that the witness had the capacity and an adequate opportunity to observe the offender?

   Whether the witness had an adequate opportunity to observe the offender at the time of the offense will be affected by such matters as how long or short a time was available, how far or close the witness was, how good were lighting conditions, whether the witness had had occasion to see or know the person in the past.

(continued)

111. *Id.* at 559.
112. *Macklin*, 409 F.2d at 178.
113. *Telfaire*, 469 F.2d at 557; *see also id.* at 561 & n.1 (Leventhal, J., concurring).

The *Telfaire* Instruction *(continued)*

[In general, a witness bases any identification he makes on his perception through the use of his senses. Usually[,] the witness identifies an offender by the sense of sight—but this is not necessarily so, and he may use other senses.]

2. Are you satisfied that the identification made by the witness subsequent to the offense was the product of his own recollection? You may take into account both the strength of the identification, and the circumstances under which the identification was made.

   If the identification by the witness may have been influenced by the circumstances under which the defendant was presented to him for identification, you should scrutinize the identification with great care. You may also consider the length of time that lapsed between the occurrence of the crime and the next opportunity of the witness to see [the] defendant, as a factor bearing on the reliability of the identification.

   [You may also take into account that an identification made by picking the defendant out of a group of similar individuals is generally more reliable than one which results from the presentation of the defendant alone to the witness.]

3. [You [may] take into account any occasions in which the witness failed to make an identification of the defendant, or made an identification that was inconsistent with his identification at trial.]

4. Finally, you must consider the credibility of each identification witness in the same way as any other witness, consider whether he is truthful, and consider whether he had the capacity and opportunity to make a reliable observation on the matter covered in his testimony.

   I again emphasize that the burden of proof on the prosecutor extends to every element of the crime charged, and this specifically includes the burden of proving beyond a reasonable doubt the identity of the defendant as the perpetrator of the crime with which he stands charged. If after examining the testimony, you have a reasonable doubt as to the accuracy of the identification, you must find the defendant not guilty.[114]

---

114. *Telfaire*, 469 F.2d at 558-59.

II. *What's Wrong with the* Telfaire *Instruction?*

Upon its release in 1972, the *Telfaire* instruction was embraced by many as a template for modern cautionary instructions on eyewitness identification both within and without the federal system.[115] The *Telfaire* panel's decision to focus the jury on those factors that the *Wade* Court identified as relevant to whether an eyewitness's recollection of a perpetrator was forever tainted by a prior identification procedure likewise received a measure of validation from the Court's holding in *Manson v. Brathwaite*, 432 U.S. 98 (1977), that these factors alone would determine whether an identification was sufficiently reliable to warrant admissibility.

Even so, the *Telfaire* instruction has aged poorly in light of the past fifty years (and counting) of scientific research on eyewitness identifications, much like the Supreme Court case law that underlies it. As already noted, over the past several decades, certain system and estimator variables have become widely known to affect the reliability of eyewitness identification. The *Telfaire* instruction, in turn, has drawn sharp criticism for "omit[ting] some of the[se] system and estimator variables," including "stress, the perpetrator's use of a weapon, and the racial or ethnic difference between the perpetrator and the witness."[116] Moreover, the instruction "is vague as to the . . . relevance" of those factors that it does mention, and does not explain the myriad ways that they can impact perception and memory.[117] Finally, the *Telfaire* instruction "appears (erroneously) to associate confidence with identification accuracy."[118]

---

115. *See, e.g.*, Thomas D. Albright & Brandon L. Garrett, *The Law and Science of Eyewitness Evidence*, 102 B.U. L. Rev. 511, 552–58, 606–27 (2022); *People v. Wright*, 45 Cal. 3d 1126, 1139 & n.10, 755 P.2d 1049 (1988) (noting that the *Telfaire* instruction was "well[] known" and "ha[d] been approved in most federal circuits" and several states); *State v. Clopten*, 223 P.3d 1103, 1110 (Utah 2009) (describing the *Telfaire* instruction as a "pioneer[ing]" effort); *State v. Malmrose*, 649 P.2d 56, 64 (Utah 1982) (Stewart, J. dissenting) (noting the state and federal courts that adopted the *Telfaire* instruction or its equivalent). *But see, e.g.*, *State v Edwards*, 600 P.2d 566 (Wash. App. 1979) (describing the *Telfaire* instruction as "impermissibly slanted"); *State v. Classen*, 571 P.2d 527, 533 (Or. App. 1977), *rev'd*, 590 P.2d 1198 (Or. 1979) (stating that the instruction is "prolix, . . . tends to overemphasize the issue, and . . . contains elements that amount to comments on the evidence").

116. Supreme Judicial Court Study Group on Eyewitness Evidence, Report and Recommendation to Justices 54 (2013) [hereinafter Study Group Report], https://www.mass.gov/doc/supreme-judicial-court-study-group-on-eyewitness-evidence-report-and-recommendations-to-the/download.

117. Leverick, *supra* note 21, at 564; *accord, e.g.*, Study Group Report, *supra* note 116, at 54.

118. Leverick, *supra* note 21, at 564; *accord, e.g.*, Study Group Report, *supra* note 116, at 54.

Among those jurisdictions still clinging to *Telfaire's* basic architecture, these criticisms are matters of urgent concern that carry additional weight given the *Telfaire* panel's implicit acknowledgment that their proffered instruction *should* evolve in light of future developments in the understanding of eyewitness identification. Specifically, in their respective concurrences, Chief Judge Bazelon and Judge Leventhal debated the merits of including a cautionary instruction for cases where the eyewitness and suspect were not members of the same race. Bazelon wrote that such a model instruction was needed urgently because "the available data, while not exhaustive, unanimously support[ed] the widely held common sense view that members of one race have greater difficulty in accurately identifying members of a different race."[119] Although Leventhal believed that this topic was not yet "ripe" for "distillation" in a model instruction given the state of the existing science, he conceded that further research and "consideration" might ultimately vindicate Bazelon's proposal.[120] Thus, even among the judges who wrote the *Telfaire* instruction, there was some basic agreement that it might be incomplete. Against this backdrop, and in light of the scientific developments discussed in subsequent chapters of this book, it could not be clearer that the basic *Telfaire* framework is in desperate need of reevaluation.

---

119. *Telfaire*, 469 F.2d at 559 (Bazelon, C.J., concurring). Chief Judge Bazelon believed that including an instruction on the cross-race effect was especially important because "a significant percentage of the identifications in this jurisdiction are inter-racial." *Id.* To this end, he proposed the following instruction:

In this case the identifying witness is of a different race than the defendant. In the experience of many it is more difficult to identify members of a different race than members of one's own. If this is also your own experience, you may consider it in evaluating the witness's testimony. You must also consider, of course, whether there are other factors present in this case which overcome any such difficulty of identification. For example, you may conclude that the witness has had sufficient contacts with members of the defendant's race that he would not have greater difficulty in making a reliable identification.

Id. at 561.

120. *Id.* ("The issue of inter-racial identifications is not ripe for this kind of distillation of wisdom" because it involves "a matter on which there [was] only 'meager data' and assertion of 'common sense' views that merit further consideration.") (citations omitted). Judge Leventhal also believed that given the "divisive" nature of the issue, the court should wait to resolve it until it was squarely presented on the facts of a case, and/or a committee comprised of trial judges, lawyers, and social scientists had weighed in on the question. *Id.* at 562–63. Five years later, when the Supreme Court decided *Manson*, the majority did not share any of Judge Leventhal's reservations about the cross-race effect, emphasizing the same-race nature of the identification in finding that it was sufficiently reliable. *Manson*, 432 U.S. at 115.

4
EXPERTS

Alongside evidentiary exclusion (Chapter 2) and cautionary jury instructions (Chapter 3), expert testimony is vital to preventing wrongful conviction due to mistaken identification.[1] This is so because, as discussed in the preceding chapter, jurors may harbor any number of misconceptions about what makes an identification reliable when they report for jury duty.[2] Moreover, although it is important not to underestimate the importance of jury instructions, it is at least equally important to be realistic about their limitations. Even assuming jury instructions are properly crafted, such that they do not merely draw attention to those factors that may affect the reliability of an identification but further explain their potential significance, instructions are at best an awkward means by which to convey all the "data and information" that a juror may need to apply this information to the facts of a case.[3] Even if a judge can be persuaded that such "data and information"

1. *Perry v. New Hampshire*, 565 U.S. 228, 247 (2012) ("In appropriate cases, some States also permit defendants to present expert testimony on the hazards of eyewitness identification evidence.") (citing *State v. Clopten*, 223 P.3d 1103, 1113 (Utah 2009) ("We expect . . . that in cases involving eyewitness identification of strangers or near-strangers, trial courts will routinely admit expert testimony [on the dangers of such evidence].")).

2. *See supra* Chapter 3, note 2.

3. Fredric D. Woocher, *Did Your Eyes Deceive You? Expert Psychological Testimony on the Unreliability of Eyewitness Identification*, 29 STANFORD L. REV. 969, 1004 (1977).

are appropriate fodder for a jury instruction, they may feel less than qualified to relay it to the jury.[4] The jury may not wait until the final deliberations to decide whether an identification is trustworthy.[5] Although this issue can be addressed by arranging for cautionary instruction on eyewitness identification to come either immediately before or after any proof of identification the jury receives, this will not solve the problem entirely, as jurors may need more context that only an expert can provide in order to give effect to the instruction. For all these reasons, expert testimony has an important role to play in preventing wrongful conviction due to mistaken identification.

So, when is the defense allowed or entitled to rely on expert testimony to rebut an eyewitness identification? To some degree, the answer to this question depends on the legal standard governing the admissibility of specialized opinion or expert testimony in the forum jurisdiction. If the jurisdiction is one of the shrinking number that "still follows the admissibility standard of general acceptance within the scientific community, as exemplified in *Frye v. United States* [293 F. 1013 (D.C. Cir. 1923)], the party advancing the expert proof will have to demonstrate that the opinions held are based upon research and principles which are generally accepted in the scientific community."[6] "If the forum jurisdiction applies a more relaxed standard" consistent with *Daubert v. Merrell Dow Pharmaceuticals, Inc.*, 509 U.S. 579 (1993), "counsel will still have to demonstrate that the testimony is based on scientific principles and research which have achieved some degree of scientific reliability."[7]

However, "[i]n general and in all jurisdictions, the issue of whether to allow expert testimony on the issue of eyewitness identification continues to be left to the sound discretion of . . . trial judge[s]," who, "[f]or a variety of reasons," tend to view such testimony "with distaste."[8] "Most trial judges are still reluctant to allow one witness to offer an opinion on the credibility of another."[9] Moreover, they "hesitate to allow an expert to invade what has long been considered an exclusive province of the jury, and abhor the notion of inviting a plethora of experts to do battle over whether the testimony of a given

4. *Id.* at 1004–05.
5. *Id.* at 1005.
6. Hon. D. Duff McKee, *Challenge to Eyewitness Identification Through Expert Testimony*, 35 Am. Jur. Proof of Facts 3rd 1, § 8 (Dec. 2023 update).
7. *Id.*
8. *Id.*
9. *Id.*

witness is truthful, reliable, and accurate."[10] "In practice, . . . courts continue to exclude more of this evidence than they allow, despite a battering from academic commentators."[11] The general justification for this hostility "continue[s] to be that the weaknesses of eyewitness identification can be ferreted out through cross examination, and that evaluations of credibility and reliability are for the jury to determine, without the help of a so-called expert."[12]

I. How Did We Get Here?

Much like cautionary jury instructions, the idea for using expert testimony to combat misconceptions about eyewitness testimony dates back to the late nineteenth century. At that time, courts across Europe and the United States were accustomed to relying on forensic psychiatrists called "alienists" to inform their decisions regarding matters of insanity and mental competency.[13] These alienists were clinicians, whose opinions were rooted in their observations of the patients in their care. The concept of applied psychologists who could formulate opinions based on experiments conducted in a controlled environment was essentially foreign. When these experts began to offer their opinions regarding the reliability of ordinary eyewitnesses, who did not suffer from any apparent psychological abnormalities, the legal system reacted with predictable skepticism.

The first of these experts was a German psychologist named Albert von Schrenck-Notzing, who raised concerns about the eyewitness accounts offered during an extremely high profile triple-homicide case in 1896.[14] Schrenck-Notzing had trained under Wilhelm Wundt, the "Father of Experimental Psychology," with a specialization in suggestion.[15] At trial, he urged that even "normal men" may be susceptible to "very particular forms of error and deception" caused by their environment,[16] and that the prose-

10. *Id.*

11. *Id.*

12. *Id.*; *see also* Note, *The Province of the Jurist: Judicial Resistance to Expert Testimony on Eyewitnesses as Institutional Rivalry*, 126 HARV. L. REV. 2381, 2383–84 (2013).

13. *See, e.g.*, Kenneth J. Weiss & Yan Xuan, *You Can't Do That! Hugo Münsterberg and Misapplied Psychology*, 42–43 INT'L J. L. & PSYCHIATRY 1, 1 (2015), https://doi.org/10.1016/j.ijlp.2015.08.001.

14. Graham Davies & Gisli H. Gudjonsson, *Looking Back: Psychologists in the Witness Box*, PSYCHOLOGIST (July 5, 2013), https://www.bps.org.uk/psychologist/looking-back-psychologists-witness-box.

15. *Wilhelm Maximilian Wundt*, STANFORD ENCYCLOPEDIA PHIL. (June 16, 2006), https://plato.stanford.edu/entries/wilhelm-wundt/.

16. MATTHEW HALE, JR., HUMAN SCIENCE AND SOCIAL ORDER: HUGO MÜNSTERBERG AND THE ORIGINS OF APPLIED PSYCHOLOGY 113 (1980).

cution's eyewitnesses had been influenced by the sensational coverage of the case in the newspapers—a phenomenon he called "retroactive memory falsification."[17] Although the biasing potential of such postevent information is by now well established,[18] Schrenck-Notzing's testimony was not well received by the trial judge, who found the defendant guilty without hesitation.[19] Thereafter, Schrenck-Notzing abandoned expert testimony altogether to pursue research.[20]

Yet another of Wundt's students inspired the famed French psychologist Alfred Binet to research the suggestibility of child witnesses.[21] Binet's work in this area, made popular by his 1900 monograph *La Suggestibilité*, broke new ground by demonstrating the impact of leading questions on child memory.[22] Binet would later become famous as the "father of the IQ test."[23] Nevertheless, and although Binet was "qualified as a lawyer, [he] was never permitted to testify in the French courts."[24]

A. Münsterberg Throws Down His Gauntlet

It was against this backdrop that another Wundt protégé named Hugo Münsterberg released his book *On the Witness Stand* in 1908, advocating broader judicial acceptance of applied psychology in a number of areas, including as it related to eyewitness identification. Prior to the book's publication, Münsterberg made two ill-fated attempts to involve himself in high-profile cases as the head of Harvard's Psychology laboratory. The first involved an intellectually disabled man named Richard Ivens, who was charged with raping and murdering the wife of a prominent Chicago businessman.[25] Ivens had discovered the woman's body near the barn where he

---

17. Davies & Gudjonsson, *supra* note 14.
18. *Id.*
19. *Id.*
20. *Id.*
21. *Id.*
22. *Id.*
23. *See, e.g.*, Robert S. Siegler, *The Other Alfred Binet*, 28 Dev. Psychol. 179, 179 (1992), https://doi.org/10.1037/0012-1649.28.2.179.
24. Davies & Gudjonsson, *supra* note 14. Binet's failure as a testifying expert is less surprising when one considers his lack of formal training in psychology or university affiliation. Siegler, *supra* note 23, at 186. Even so, this did not seem to hold him back in other aspects of his career. *Id.*
25. *See, e.g.*, Romeo Vitelli, *The Problem with Richard Ivens (Part One of Two)*, Providentia (June 26, 2016), https://drvitelli.typepad.com/providentia/2016/06/the-case-of-richard-ivens.html; *see also* Harry Olson, *Crime and Heredity*, 7 J. Am. Judicature Soc. 37, 44, 54 (1923) (admitting the prosecution's awareness of Ivens's intellectual disabilities).

Professor Hugo Münsterberg.

tended his father's horses, and had been arrested and subjected to hours of interrogation after reporting the discovery to the police. Upon his confession, Ivens was convicted and condemned to die. Thereafter, a local psychologist weighed in on his behalf and recruited Münsterberg to do the same.[26] However, the Illinois Supreme Court and Board of Pardons upheld Ivens' conviction and sentence, even after Münsterberg opined that his confession was certainly false.[27] After Ivens's execution, Münsterberg criticized the authorities' collective failure to heed the assessments of applied psychologists like himself, while taking the word of state psychiatrists that Ivens could distinguish right from wrong and was prone to violence due to his "feeble-minded[ness]."[28] After these statements were made public, defenders of the verdict accused Münsterberg of practicing armchair psychology without having examined Ivens directly.[29]

These criticisms only made Münsterberg more eager to prove his methods on a grand stage. It was perhaps for this reason that, in 1907, he accepted an invitation from *McClure's* magazine to examine a professional hitman named Harry Orchard, who had implicated the powerful union leader "Big

---

26. Weiss & Xuan, *supra* note 13, at 3; Eilis S. Magner, *Wigmore Confronts Munsterberg: Present Relevance of a Classic Debate*, 13 Sydney L. Rev. 121, 123 (1991).

27. Weiss & Xuan, *supra* note 13, at 3–4.

28. *See, e.g.*, Raymond T. Bye, Capital Punishment in the United States 90–91 (1919).

29. Ludy T. Benjamin Jr., A History of Psychology in Letters 100 (2006).

Bill" Haygood in a plot to murder the former governor of Idaho.[30] With the sitting governor's blessing, Münsterberg administered a word association test to Orchard from the secure facility where he was being held during Haygood's trial, and based on how long Orchard took to respond to certain trigger words associated with his testimony, Münsterberg concluded that he was telling the truth.[31] Although his agreement with *McClure's* stipulated that these results would not be published until after the trial, Münsterberg leaked them to a reporter on his way back to Harvard, sparking headlines across the country.[32] Around the same time, the *New York Times* associated him with plans to develop a precursor to the polygraph, using some of the same principles he applied to Orchard.[33] Despite all this, the jury, which had been sequestered during its deliberations, voted to acquit Haygood, further spoiling the publicity that Münsterberg hoped to gain by involving himself in the case.[34] Although he abandoned the plan to publish an article about the case, Münsterberg nevertheless received criticism—from the mainstream media, the criminal defense bar, and those friendly to the cause of organized labor—for the leak and the apparent interest he took in his assessment of Orchard's credibility.[35]

Having twice failed to improve perceptions of applied psychology through his work in high-profile cases, Münsterberg attempted to do so through his writing. In *On the Witness Stand*, a collection of essays published in 1908, he argued that judicial skepticism toward experimental psychology was indefensible because it had progressed so far toward understanding the factors that dictate the witness reliability and because judges had proven themselves so receptive to so many dubious kinds of "scientific" testimony. He noted that "while the alienist [was] always a welcome guest in the court room, the psychologist is still a stranger there" and that judges "would rather listen for whole days to the 'science' of the handwriting experts than allow a witness to be examined [by a psychologist] with regard to his memory and his power of perception, his attention and his associations, his volition and his suggestibility, with methods which are in accord with the exact work

30. Weiss & Xuan, *supra* note 13, at 4.

31. *See, e.g.*, Margaret Münsterberg, Hugo Münsterberg, His Life and Work 145 (1922).

32. Weiss & Xuan, *supra* note 13, at 4; Magner, *supra* note 26, at 124.

33. Magner, *supra* note 26, at 124; *Invents Machines for 'Cure of Liars': Prof. Munsterberg Experiments to Reduce Knowledge of Truth to a Science*, N.Y. Times, Sept. 11, 1907.

34. Weiss & Xuan, *supra* note 13, at 4.

35. *Id.*

of experimental psychology."[36] With respect to eyewitness identification, he continued:

> Modern law welcomes, for instance, for identification of criminals all the discoveries of anatomists and physiologists as to the individual differences; even the different play of lines in the thumb is carefully registered in wax. But no one asks for the striking differences as to those mental details which the psychological experiments on memory and attention, on feeling and imagination, on perception and discrimination, on judgment and suggestion, on emotion and volition, have brought out in the last decade.[37]

One of the book's most important and inflammatory insights concerned the relationship between eyewitness accuracy and the "subjective feeling of certainty."[38] In this regard, Münsterberg noted a recent experiment by a "well-known psychologist" (later revealed to be Louis William Stern), where children were asked to describe a picture they had seen for 15 seconds, and then to underline those parts of the description they felt capable of attesting to under oath; in the end, the underlined portions were no more accurate than the rest.[39] Münsterberg noted that his own experiments similarly had shown that eyewitness certainty depends "largely" on "the vividness of the image" or its level of "congruity" with the witness's "past experiences."[40] However, "[t]he most surprising result," in his view, had been "that the feeling of certainty [stood] in no definite relation to the attention with which the objects [were] observed."[41] It seemed that by focusing on certain aspects of a memory, eyewitnesses could trick themselves into believing that they had paid close attention to something, even when they had not.[42] Against this backdrop, Münsterberg concluded that "correlations between attention, recollection, and feeling of certainty" were "complex" in ways that defied the "self-made psychology of the

36. Hugo Münsterberg, On the Witness Stand 46 (1908).
37. *Id.* at 63.
38. *Id.* at 55.
39. *Id.* at 54–55.
40. *Id.* at 55–56.
41. *Id.* at 56.
42. *Id.* ("If we turn our attention with strongest effort to certain parts of a complex impression, we may yet feel in our recollection more certain about those parts of which we hardly took notice than about those to which we devoted our attention.").

average juryman" and the "scanty psychological statements which judge and attorney find in the large compendiums on Evidence."[43]

Given his professed affinity for experimentation, one might expect Münsterberg to shy away from diagnosis in his writing. Even so, he seemed to relish the opportunity to pathologize the legal system's aversion to psychological expertise. In attempting to explain how such aversion could persist, despite the progress psychologists had made toward understanding eyewitness reliability, Münsterberg pointed to the legal system's need for a kind of diagnostic certainty that psychology was ill-equipped to provide: the ability (or willingness) to say that a specific piece of testimony was definitely true or false. In Münsterberg's view, psychology's incompatibility with this kind of certainty did not undermine its scientific validity or potential as a forensic discipline. Rather, to Münsterberg, it was the law that needed to change, by evolving beyond its dependence on a veneer of certainty that did not comport with human behavior. Thus, he wrote: "It is so much easier everywhere to be satisfied with sharp demarcation lines and to listen only to a yes or no; the man is sane or insane, and if he is sane, he speaks the truth or he lies. The psychologist would upset this satisfaction completely."[44]

There is no question that many of Münsterberg's ideas were ahead of their time, particularly those related to the counterintuitive relationship between eyewitness certainty and accuracy. As detailed more thoroughly in Chapter 5, the notion that "the feeling of certainty" may depend less on how well an event is perceived and more on some combination of how vividly it is remembered and how well the memory conforms to the rememberer's expectations regarding what happened has been confirmed by countless experiments over the last century. Even so, there is critical consensus that his condemnation of the legal profession for failing to adopt what John Henry Wigmore called "expert tests of testimonial certitude" was premature.[45] As Wigmore—Münsterberg's harshest and most influential legal critic—would write, the prevailing view among Münsterberg's contemporaries was that these methods, while promising, had yet to be proven viable in the forensic context.[46] Some, like the word association test Münsterberg used on Harry Orchard, never would prove viable, in part because the Fifth Amendment

43. *Id.*

44. *Id.* at 46.

45. John H. Wigmore, *Professor Muensterberg and the Psychology of Testimony: Being a Report of the Case of* Cokestone v. Muensterberg, 3 ILL. L. REV. 399, 410 (1909).

46. *Id.* at 414–15.

right against self-incrimination limits a judge's ability to compel someone to undergo psychological examination.[47] The word association method further would age poorly in light of its connections to the polygraph, which has yet to prove itself sufficiently reliable to warrant admissibility in most courts.[48] Combined with his apparent disregard for the Constitution and basic rules of evidence, Münsterberg's enthusiasm for this kind of automated lie detection arguably undermined his credibility as an ambassador for common sense reform in other areas, prompting nicknames like "Professor Monsterwork."[49]

However, Münsterberg's most costly blunder as the de facto spokesperson for the emerging field of forensic psychology was his failure to anticipate how the legal profession would respond to his overenthusiastic criticism. This backlash was foreseeable, as Münsterberg leveled his criticisms of common-law truth seeking at a time of peak legal formalism—a school of thought that conceived of law as an "exact science" akin to physics, and called for dogmatic adherence to logic and precedent, above any other complexity that the "human element" might introduce.[50] We are still living in an era of jurisprudence defined by the schism between law and psychology that coincides with the publication of *On the Witness Stand* in 1908. The Supreme Court's implicit hostility to the psychological perspective on eyewitness reliability in *Manson v. Brathwaite*, 432 U.S. 98 (1977), and its progeny is almost certainly a byproduct of the schism.

B. The Legal System Responds

Owing to the public's growing fascination with all disciplines that promised insight into the confounding aspects of human behavior, *On the Witness Stand* was (and remains) a considerable commercial success.[51] However, to say that it failed to persuade skeptics in the legal profession to put more faith in applied psychology would be an understatement. Indeed, insofar as

---

47. *Id.* at 431.

48. Kenneth J. Weiss et al., *Frye's Backstory: A Tale of Murder, a Retracted Confession, and Scientific Hubris*, 42 J. Am. Acad. Psychiatry. L. 226 (2014).

49. Matthew Hale, Jr., Human Science and Social Order: Hugo Münsterberg and the Origins of Applied Psychology at 117 & n.33 (1980).

50. Dragan Milovanovic, A Primer in the Sociology of Law 89, 92 (1988).

51. Such fields of study included psychology, as well spiritualism, faith healing, hypnotism, astrology, and telepathy. Hale, *supra* note 49, at ix–x. Regarding the commercial success of On the Witness Stand, *see* Hale, *supra* note 49, at 115; Weiss & Xuan, *supra* note 13, at 9; Davies & Gudjonsson, *supra* note 14.

Münsterberg sought to win over lawyers and judges,[52] his efforts backfired spectacularly, as the book was panned—widely, though perhaps not uniformly—by prominent members of the legal profession. One of the tamest responses came from Yale law professor and future Connecticut governor Simeon E. Baldwin, who wrote in his review for the journal *Science* that Münsterberg had given judges, lawyers, and juries too little credit for knowing what makes testimony more or less reliable.[53]

Charles C. Moore, whose *Treatise on Facts* went to print the same year as *On the Witness Stand*, took his criticism a step further. In his article *Yellow Psychology* (a reference to the style of journalism that emphasized sensationalism over accuracy), Moore likened Münsterberg to "[a]n old Thibetan magician" offering "a formula which would enable [someone] to perform miracles" and accused him of peddling a "Northwest Passage to the truth," referring to the hypothetical trans-Arctic waterway, the pursuit of which had killed many European explorers.[54] Moore went on to state that, when it came to understanding what makes testimony more or less reliable, "the judges have the psychologists 'beaten by a mile'" because unlike psychologists who rely on classroom experiments (Münsterberg), "[the] judge's class room is the court room," where "year after year, he conducts or presides over experiments of living and momentous consequence."[55] Judges further benefit from access to countless judicial "opinions discussing the fidelity of human observation and memory, some of them written by men whose names will perish only with the civilization of the world," which, in Moore's view, trumped anything a psychologist could offer.[56] Thus, he argued that

52. One could argue that in describing lawyers as uniquely "obdurate" among professionals who stood to benefit from recent advances in psychology, he went out of his way to alienate and condescend to members of the legal profession. MÜNSTERBERG, *supra* note 36, at 10.

53. Simeon E. Baldwin, *On the Witness Stand: Essays on Psychology and Crime. By Hugo Münsterberg, Professor of Psychology, Harvard University. Pp. 269. New York, the McClure Co. 1908*, 29 Sci. 301 (1909), https://www.science.org/doi/10.1126/science.29.738.301.

54. Charles C. Moore, *Yellow Psychology*, 11 LAW NOTES 125, 125 (1907). Although this article was published before *On the Witness Stand*, it addressed an essay published in *McClure's* magazine that Münsterberg incorporated into the book.

55. *Id.*

56. *Id.* After all, what psychologist could claim a better understanding of witness reliability than Chief Justice John Marshall or Lord Stowell? *Id.* But, as Moore was quick to point out, such expertise was not limited to the likes of those esteemed judges. Even the average "native Southern Judge" knew more about the "memories and mental characteristics of the negro race" than a psychologist could possibly tell him. *Id.* ("A psychologist will tell you, peradventure, that 4.1144 per cent of eleven negro women, whom he catechised, recollected such and such a class of incidents in their childhood. But a native Southern judge knows a thing or two about the memories and mental characteristics of the negro race, and says so when occasion arises.").

expert testimony regarding whether "a witness is or is not a trustworthy observer," should be no more welcome in a courtroom than the opinion of Sir Arthur Conan Doyle (author of Sherlock Holmes) regarding a person's guilt or innocence.[57]

Moore's flare for rhetoric notwithstanding, the most significant critique of Münsterberg's work came from John Henry Wigmore, dean of Northwestern University Law School. By the time of his response to Münsterberg, Wigmore already had published an influential treatise on evidence and was well on his way to becoming the foremost authority on that subject in the country.[58] Rather than responding to Münsterberg in the traditional essay format, Wigmore elected to present his criticisms as the report of a fictious libel case: "*Cokestone v. Muensterberg*."

From its opening paragraph, the article cast Münsterberg as a foreign-born interloper in the American legal system, casting stones at treasured Anglo-American legal traditions from the comfort of his ivory-tower laboratory. The name "Cokestone" was a reference to Lord Coke and William Blackstone, two of the most highly venerated figures in the history of the common law.[59] The article described "Muensterberg" as "a professor of psychology in the faculty of arts and sciences of the Ancient and Honorable University of Cambridge, Bay State," referring to Harvard, and noted that the trial had taken place in the "Wundt County" Court in "Windyville, Illiana," references to Münsterberg's mentor, Wilhelm Wundt, and the City of Chicago, where Wigmore taught, and where Münsterberg made his first unsuccessful foray into forensic psychology in the *Ivens* case.[60] The trial took place on April Fool's Day, 1909. Whereas "Muensterberg's" defense team consisted of "Mr. R. E. Search," "Mr. Si Kist," and "Mr. X. Perry Ment," the venerable "Cokestone" was represented by "Simplicissimus Tyro"—Latin terminology that translates to "the simplest beginner."[61] Thus, Wigmore used "cloddish professorial attempts at humor" to draw attention to those aspects of Münsterberg's biography that made him seem most out of touch.[62]

57. Charles C. Moore, *Psychology in the Courts*, 11 Law Notes 185, 186 (1908). On the other hand, Moore embraced the work of other psychologists like Rene-Édouard Claparéde and F.W. Colegrove, whose work better aligned with the way that judges and lawyers conceived of memory and perception. *See* 2 Charles C. Moore, Treatise on Facts § 1292, at 1366 (1908).

58. Weiss & Xuan, *supra* note 13, at 5; Magner, *supra* note 26, at 127.

59. *See, e.g.*, Magner, *supra*, at 127.

60. Weiss & Xuan, *supra* note 13, at 5 (internal quotation marks and citations omitted).

61. Magner, *supra* note 26, at 127; Wigmore, *supra* note 45, at 400–01.

62. James M. Doyle, *Ready for Psychologists: Learning from Eyewitness Errors*, 48 Court Rev. 4, 4 (2012), https://digitalcommons.unl.edu/ajacourtreview/379.

John Henry Wigmore.

The article imagined how "Muensterberg" would respond to being confronted—on the witness stand—regarding the allegedly libelous claims of his book: that is, that there were "precise experimental and psychological methods for ascertaining and measuring testimonial certitude" which were "fully accepted and indorsed by psychologists" but which had been unreasonably ignored or rejected by the legal profession writ large.[63] In this vein, Wigmore targeted both the word association test that Münsterberg had used on Orchard, and certain "expert tests of testimonial certitude" pioneered by Louis William Stern—the same Stern whose research on eyewitness certainty

63. Wigmore, *supra* note 45, at 401.

Münsterberg had included in *On the Witness Stand*.[64] In addition to noting the surprising disconnect between certainty and accuracy, Stern hypothesized that certain observer characteristics, such as age, sex, intelligence, and education might be more probative of reliability than subjective certainty.[65] In this way, Stern's work anticipated some of the estimator variables that are discussed in Chapter 6 of this book. However, while Stern believed that psychologists would eventually "be able to construct a scale on which to rank individuals according to their reliability" that would be of "inestimable value" to the legal profession,[66] he had been very careful to note that this work was still in its early stages.[67] Seizing upon these statements, Wigmore argued rather convincingly that Münsterberg had jumped the gun and it was still too early to trust Stern's observer characteristics in a forensic context.[68]

Wigmore concluded his critique by proffering and applying a six-part test to determine whether any of the techniques referred to in *On the Witness Stand* should be admitted in a court of law: "(1) Does it offer something new? (2) Are its rules exact? (3) Are its tests concrete, not merely abstract? (4) Are the conditions of its use practical? (5) Are its results yet even agreed upon? (6) Has it yet taken all available means of verifying its relative efficiency?"[69] Turning to the first prong, Wigmore argued that Münsterberg had given the legal scholars far too little credit for knowing what makes witness statements more or less reliable, citing numerous examples from law and literature where those who lacked Münsterberg's specialized training in psychology had intuited some of the observations that Münsterberg had touted as ground breaking.[70]

However, for Wigmore, the problem with Stern's "expert tests of testimonial certitude," was not just that they offered factfinders no insight beyond what good, common sense might suggest or that they had been insufficiently

---

64. *Id.* at 410. Wigmore further attacked Münsterberg's penchant for publishing in "popular magazines," which were conducive to elevating his own status as a public intellectual, rather than in scientific journals where he might encounter serious scholarly criticism, *See id.* at 411–12.

65. Hale, *supra* note 49, at 113.

66. *Id.*

67. Wigmore, *supra* note 45, at 414–15.

68. *Id.*

69. Weiss & Xuan, *supra* note 13, at 6 (quoting Wigmore, *supra* note 45, at 417). In this way, Wigmore's critique marked an important milestone in evidence law, anticipating contemporary standards for expert admissibility—"general acceptance" under *Frye v. United*, 293 F. 1013 (D.C. Cir. 1923) and the more flexible, testability-focused inquiry of *Daubert v. Merrell Dow Pharmaceuticals, Inc.*, 509 U.S. 579 (1993). *Id.*

70. Wigmore, *supra* note 45, at 418–20.

vetted, insofar as they did offer something new. The problem was also, as Münsterberg predicted,[71] that these methods promised no definitive answer to the question whether specific testimony was accurate, only lab-tested information about its likelihood of being accurate.[72] In other words, while "[p]sychological experiments . . . yield statistical, probabilistic results" and "can tell you what happens eight times in ten," "[t]he question for the courts is never 'Will [someone in the eyewitness's] position be right 80 percent of the time?' but rather [']is *this* witness right, *this* time?'"[73] Psychiatrists, by contrast, offered definitive diagnoses.

To his credit, Münsterberg not only anticipated this criticism but also included a response to it in *On the Witness Stand*, by advocating a system whereby psychologists could evaluate an eyewitness's truth-telling capacities by subjecting that person to a series of pretrial tests.[74] Arguably, such an individualized evaluation could lay better claim to being "definitive" in ways that might appease skeptics like Wigmore. However, this proposal failed to account for practical limitations on judicial ability to compel psychological examination.[75] Moreover, to Wigmore, psychology's indefiniteness was not something that could be solved by individualized testing. Simply put, although "Stern [could] conduct tests to measure [a witness's] capacities for perception, memory, and recall[,] . . . his experiments [would still] only tell us (at best) that [the] witness . . . is *relatively* likely to be accurate a certain percentage of times." "No examination [could] say that [the witness] is *always* wrong or always right, or *definitely* right this time," which was the only question Wigmore deemed relevant.[76]

C. Psychology Retreats and Regroups

For several decades after Wigmore's article, research into forensic psychology "stalled," both in general and as related to the specific issue of eyewitness identification.[77] Although, to be sure, there are multiple explanations for this

71. MÜNSTERBERG, *supra* note 36, at 46.

72. Wigmore, *supra* note 45, at 420–25.

73. JAMES M. DOYLE, TRUE WITNESS: COPS, COURTS, SCIENCE, AND THE BATTLE AGAINST MISIDENTIFICATION 29 (2005).

74. MÜNSTERBERG, *supra* note 36, at 46.

75. Even setting aside any limits the Constitution might impose, imagine how strenuously the prosecution would object to the victim of a violent crime being compelled to undergo psychological examination.

76. DOYLE, *supra* note 73, at 29. The merits of this argument are addressed in Chapter 6.

77. Weiss & Xuan, *supra* note 13, at 1; *see also* Davies & Gudjonsson, *supra* note 14 (noting that "with [Münsterberg's] death [in 1916] much of the research interest in psychology and the law in the USA died with him.").

gap (including the emergence of behaviorism as the predominant school of thought in psychology),[78] conventional wisdom holds that Wigmore's article was at least partly responsible.[79] As one scholar put it, Wigmore's "satirical response is still remembered by psychologists as the blood-thirsty slaughter of psychology as a discipline by the greatest evidence scholar that Anglo-American tradition ever produced: a grisly paradigm of the kind of welcome social scientists should expect from the legal system and its practitioners."[80] "If this is what you get from the great Wigmore, researchers reasoned, just imagine the treatment you will receive from an ordinary legal tribesman."[81]

Researchers did not return to the specific questions of eyewitness reliability that inspired *On the Witness Stand* until the early 1970s, when psychologists such as Robert Buckhout and Elizabeth Loftus "picked up Munsterberg's fallen banner."[82] Both had much greater success as expert witnesses than Münsterberg, who died suddenly in 1916, having never testified in a trial.[83] In 1972, Dr. Buckhout's testimony played an important role

78. Magner, *supra* note 26, at 130–31.

79. Weiss & Xuan, *supra* note 13, at 1 ("Forensic psychology's development was stalled by resistance from within legal authorities, including John Henry Wigmore, the leading expert on evidence."); *id.* at 8 ("The question of expert witness input on assessing eyewitness testimony remained dormant, due partly to Wigmore, until the 1960s." (citation omitted)).

80. Doyle, *supra* note 62, at 4. The sad irony is that Wigmore ultimately did believe that the law could better reflect the lessons of applied psychology, just not in the ways that Münsterberg advocated. He concluded his response to Münsterberg by chastising the legal profession for failing to take any interest in what psychology had to teach about "crime prevention." Wigmore, *supra* note 45, at 433 ("No country in the civilized world was probably so far behind in the scientific study of criminal law as affected by the contributory sciences of sociology, anthropology, psychology, and medicine."). Likewise, Wigmore hoped that applied psychology would progress in other areas that would allow it to inform the law, and spent much of his career working toward that goal. Doyle, *supra* note 62, at 4.

81. Doyle, *supra* note 62, at 4.

82. *Id.* at 5; *accord* Davies & Gudjonsson, *supra* note 14 ("Interest only revived when cognitive psychology became the dominant paradigm in the 1970s, with its emphasis upon a greater engagement with 'real world' issues. Research such as that conducted by Elizabeth Loftus and Robert Buckhout (1935–1990) highlighted again the vulnerability of witness testimony[.]"). *But see* James Marshall, Law and Psychology in Conflict (1969).

83. Despite Wigmore's scathing review, Münsterberg retained his interest in forensic psychology, and the defense bar maintained its interest in his work. Weiss & Xuan, *supra* note 13, at 6; Lionel R.C. Haward, *The Psychologist as Expert Witness* 44, *in* Psychology, Law and Legal Processes (1979). In 1916, he consulted on the case of a young man accused of robbing and murdering his father in Cambridge, Massachusetts, where the prosecution's case depended on the identification of a streetcar driver who did not know the defendant. Weiss & Xuan, *supra* note 13, at 6–7. Münsterberg watched the streetcar driver's testimony and may have offered opinions about how to cross-examine him. *Id.* at 7. Still, he was not called to testify. *Id.* The jury voted to acquit, and a few months later, Münsterberg died in the middle of a lecture. *Id.* By all accounts, Münsterberg died a lonely man, having alienated his colleagues with his (pro-German) views in the lead-up to World War I, and his opposition to women serving on jury. *See* Siegreid L. Sporer, *Lessons from the Origins of Eyewitness Testimony Research in Europe*, 22 App. Cog. Psych. 737 (2008), https://doi.org/10.001/acp.1479.

in bringing about the acquittal of civil rights activist Angela Davis on capital felony charges of murder, kidnapping, and conspiracy.[84] Davis had been charged with executing an armed assault on a Marin County courthouse, which had left four dead.[85] Although Davis had circumstantial ties to the attack and its perpetrators,[86] the only evidence suggesting her direct involvement was an eyewitness who claimed to have seen her driving the van that the attackers used to make their escape.[87] Dr. Buckhout testified that the identification had been procured by a suggestive photo-array, consisting of "three pictures of [Angela Davis] from an outdoor rally, two police 'mug shots' of other women with their names displayed, a picture of a 55-year old woman," and two more pictures that were easy to distinguish from Ms. Davis's.[88] Seemingly as a direct result, a jury composed entirely of white men voted to acquit Davis after thirteen hours of deliberation.[89]

Due to the extremely high-profile nature of Davis's trial,[90] and Dr. Buckhout's role in it,[91] the case did much to rekindle the public's interest in eyewitness identification research.[92] Dr. Buckhout followed up this public relations triumph with an article in *Scientific American*, bringing even more attention to the problem of unreliable identifications in American courtrooms.[93] Meanwhile, Dr. Loftus offered her services to a young Seattle woman accused of killing her abusive boyfriend and published an article recounting the case and her research shortly after the jury voted to acquit.[94]

---

84. McKee, *supra* note 6, § 4; Doyle, *supra* note 62, at 5; Elizabeth F. Loftus, *Eyewitness Science and the Legal System*, 14 Ann. Rev. L. Soc. Sci. 1, 3 (2018), https://doi.org/10.1146/annurev-lawsocsci101317-030850.

85. *See, e.g.*, Antonio Mejía-Rentas, *How Angela Davis Ended Up on the FBI Most Wanted List*, History.com (Jan. 25, 2023), https://www.history.com/news/angela-davis-fbi-most-wanted-list.

86. *Id.*

87. *Id.*

88. Robert Buckhout, *Eyewitness Testimony*, 15 Jurimetrics J. 171, 179 (1974).

89. Mejía-Rentas, *supra* note 85.

90. *See, e.g.*, *id.*

91. *See, e.g.*, Earl Caldwell, *Trial Hears News Upset Miss Davis*, N.Y. Times 13, May 24, 1972, https://www.nytimes.com/1972/05/24/archives/trial-hears-news-upset-miss-davis-witness-says-first-word-of.html.

92. Loftus, *supra* note 84, at 3; Doyle, *supra* note 62, at 5.

93. Robert Buckhout, *Eyewitness Testimony*, Sci. Am., 23, Dec. 1974.

94. *See* Elizabeth F. Loftus, *Reconstructing Memory: The Incredible Eyewitness*, 15 Jurimetrics J. 188, 193 (1975), http://www.jstor.org/stable/29761487. The woman had claimed self-defense, and a key question for the jury was whether she had shot her boyfriend immediately after retrieving a gun from their bedroom, as she claimed, or, alternatively, she had waited as long as five minutes to shoot, as the government's witness contended. *Id.*; Ann Marsh & Greta Lorge, *How the Truth Gets Twisted*, Stanford Mag., Nov./Dec. 2012, https://stanfordmag.org/contents/how-the-truth-gets-twisted.

D. The "Beyond the Ken" Era Begins

Although these cases helped win support for the second wave of eyewitness research among members of the criminal defense bar, they did little to win over skeptical judges. In 1973, shortly after Angela Davis's acquittal, the Ninth Circuit Court of Appeals held that the trial court had not abused its discretion in excluding the defense's proposed eyewitness expert testimony in *United States v. Amaral*, 448 F.2d 1148 (9th Cir. 1973). Amaral had been charged with bank robbery and sought to present the testimony of a psychologist regarding the effect of stress on perception and more generally the unreliability of eyewitness identification.[95] The Ninth Circuit held that such testimony would be inadmissible unless the defense (1) offered a "qualified witness" (2) to testify on a "proper subject" that lay outside of the jury's common sense understanding, (3) by means of "generally accepted" scientific principles, and further showed (4) that the testimony's probative value would outweigh any unfair prejudice that would come from admitting it.[96] In the court's view, Amaral's proffer failed to clear the second of these hurdles because the jury was "superbly equipped" to evaluate the impact of stress on the witnesses during the robberies and because the "legal system places primary reliance for the ascertainment of truth on the 'test of cross-examination.'"[97]

Amaral drew criticism for its failure to give trial judges meaningful guidance on how to apply and interpret the four criteria it set forth.[98] Even so, it became an influential template for deciding eyewitness expert admissibility,[99] in those jurisdictions that did not preemptively bar such testimony altogether, based on the purported need to protect the jury's prerogative to determine witness credibility.[100]

For the next decade, preclusion of eyewitness expert testimony was routinely upheld by appellate courts across the country, on the grounds

95. *Amaral*, 488 F.2d at 1150, 1152.

96. *Id.* at 1152.

97. *Id.* at 1153 (quoting *United States v. De Sisto*, 329 F.2d 929 (2d Cir. 1964)).

98. Elizabeth F. Loftus, Eyewitness Testimony 195 (1996); Fredric D. Woocher, *Did Your Eyes Deceive You? Expert Psychological Testimony on Eyewitness Identification*, 29 Stanford L. Rev. 969 (1977), https://www.jstor.org/stable/1228141.

99. *United States v. Brown*, 540 F.2d 1048, 1053–54 (10th Cir. 1976); *United States v. Watson* 587 F.2d 365 (7th Cir. 1978); *United States v. Fosher*, 590 F.2d 381 (1st Cir. 1979); *United States v. Thevis*, 665 F.2d 616 (5th Cir. Unit B 1982); *United States v. Purham*, 725 F.2d 450 (8th Cir. 1984).

100. *See, e.g.*, *People v. Johnson*, 38 Cal. App. 3d 1, 112 Cal. Rptr. 834 (1974); *United States v. Benitez*, 741 F.2d 1312, 1315 (11th Cir. 1984).

that, as a general matter, eyewitness reliability is not beyond the "ken" or comprehension of the average laymen.[101] During this time, Dr. Buckhout's own testimony came to be viewed with great skepticism and disfavor in the federal court system.[102] Then, in *State v. Chapple*, 600 P.2d 1208 (Ariz. 1983), the Arizona Supreme Court made history by finding an abuse of discretion based on the erroneous preclusion of eyewitness expert testimony. Chapple had been convicted of killing three people in connection with a drug deal gone wrong.[103] The only evidence connecting him to the murders had been the identifications of two sibling eyewitnesses who had never seen him before or after the incident, except for when they picked his photo out of an array more than a year later.[104] Both witnesses had failed to identify Chapple in previous photo-arrays conducted closer in time to the incident.[105] Both had received immunity for their roles in the underlying drug transaction in exchange for testifying against Chapple.[106] To support his defense of mistaken identification, Chapple offered the testimony of Dr. Loftus on a number of issues, including the "forgetting curve" (the fact that forgetting happens more quickly right after a witnessed event), the effect of stress on perception, unconscious transference, the tendency to assimilate postevent information, and the complex relationship between eyewitness accuracy and confidence.[107] After the trial court excluded this testimony on the government's motion, the Arizona Supreme Court reversed, adopting the *Amaral* test, but determining that Dr. Loftus's testimony *did* concern a "proper subject" beyond the average laymen's comprehension, contrary to every other appellate court that had considered a similar question previously.[108] Even so, the opinion emphasized that its holding was limited to the

---

101. *Fosher*, 590 F.2d at 384; *State v. Valencia*, 575 P.2d 335, 337 (Ariz. App. Ct. 1977); *People v. Guzman*, 121 Cal. Rptr. 69, 71–72, 47 Cal. App. 3d 380, 385–86 (1975); *Dyas v. United States*, 376 A.2d 827, 831–32 (D.C. 1977); *Nelson v. State*, 362 So. 2d 1017, 1021 (Fla. App. Ct. 1978); *State v. Porraro*, 404 A.2d 465, 471 (R.I. 1979); *People v. Dixon*, 410 N.E.2d 252, 256 (Ill. App. 1980); *Caldwell v. State*, 594 S.W.2d 24, 28 (Ark. App. Ct. 1980).

102. *Thevis*, 665 F.2d at 641–42 (upholding the exclusion of Buckhout's testimony excluded); *Fosher*, 590 F.2d at 382–84 (same); *United States v. Brown*, 501 F.2d 146 (9th Cir. 1974), *rev'd on other grounds sub nom. United States v. Nobles*, 422 U.S. 225 (1975) (same); *United States v. Collins*, 395 F. Supp. 629 (M.D. Pa.), *aff'd*, 523 F.2d 1051 (3rd Cir. 1975) (same).

103. *Chapple*, 600 P.2d at 1210–12.

104. *Id.* at 1212.

105. *See id.* at 1217.

106. *Id.* at 1212.

107. *Id.* at 1220–21.

108. *Id.*; *see id.* at 1222–24 (finding that the trial court had abused its discretion in determining otherwise).

"peculiar facts" of the case presented, which had turned entirely on the identifications at issue; that it did not "intend to 'open the gates' to a flood of expert evidence" on eyewitness reliability; and that it had "no quarrel" with the exclusion of such testimony in "the vast majority of cases."[109] Thereafter, courts began to rule similarly.[110]

E. Enter *Daubert v. Merrell Dow Pharmaceuticals, Inc.*, 509 U.S. 579 (1993)

In 1993, the Supreme Court issued a landmark decision in *Daubert v. Merrell Dow Pharmaceuticals, Inc.*, 509 U.S. 579 (1993), clarifying that the standard for expert admissibility under the Federal Rules of Evidence was intended to be more "liberal," "permissive," and "flexible" than it had been under the common law.[111] Although this opinion raised hopes that eyewitness expert testimony might find greater purchase in federal court than it had previously, *Daubert* has yet to "liberal"-ize any aspect of the gatekeeping that judges perform with respect to eyewitness identification experts, least of all their determinations of whether such expertise lies beyond the ken of the average lay juror.

In *Daubert*, the Court held that pursuant to Rule 702, judges could no longer exclude expert testimony based solely on its lack of "general acceptance" in the relevant scientific community, as they had been able to under *Frye v. United*, 293 F. 1013 (D.C. Cir. 1923). Coincidentally, *Frye's* strict "general acceptance" standard arose out of a murder case where the defendant sought to introduce evidence of systolic blood pressure analysis, "a crude precursor to the polygraph machine,"[112] which had been developed by one of Münsterberg's students, William Marston.[113] Without citing Wigmore's rebuke of Münsterberg directly,[114] the D.C. Circuit affirmed the

---

109. *Id.* at 1224.

110. *See, e.g.*, *United States v. Downing*, 753 F.2d 1224 (3d Cir. 1984); *United States v. Smith*, 736 F.2d 1103, 1105 (6th Cir. 1984); *United States v. Moore*, 786 F.2d 1308, 1312 (5th Cir. 1986).

111. *Daubert*, 509 U.S. at 588–89.

112. *Id.* at 585.

113. For a more thorough accounting of Marston's involvement in Frye's case, see, e.g., Jill Lepore, *On Evidence: Proving* Frye *as a Matter of Law, Science, and History*, 124 Yale L.J. 1092 (2015), https://www.yalelawjournal.org/article/on-evidence-proving-frye-as-a-matter-of-law-science-and-history; Kenneth J. Weiss et al., *Frye's Backstory: A Tale of Murder, a Retracted Confession, and Scientific Hubris*, 22 J. Am. Acad. Psychiatry & L. 226 (2014), https://jaapl.org/content/42/2/226.

114. Wigmore's article seemed to figure prominently in the government's attempt to discredit Marston at the trial level. *See* Lepore, *supra* note 113. In an interesting turn, it was Dr. Marston and Mr. Frye's defense team that sought Wigmore's advice to shape their proffer of evidence. *Id.*

decision to bar this evidence because it had "not yet gained such standing and scientific recognition among physiological and psychological authorities as would justify the courts in admitting expert testimony deduced from the discovery, development, and experiments thus far made."[115]

For the next seventy years, "'general acceptance' . . . [was] the dominant standard" in courtrooms across the country "for determining the admissibility of novel scientific evidence at trial."[116] Nevertheless, it was heavily criticized for excluding reliable and probative analyses that had been developed for the litigation context, and thus had not been submitted for publication in a peer-reviewed journal.[117] At the same time, because rigorous scientific testing was not necessarily a prerequisite to "general acceptance," the test allowed some junk science, like the paraffin gunshot residue analysis, to escape meaningful scrutiny.[118] Moreover, the lack of a uniform definition for "general acceptance" gave rise to inconsistent outcomes, allowing judges to use the test to further "their own views about the reliability of particular forensic techniques."[119] Finally, because "general acceptance" depends on publication in peer-reviewed journals, the test could be manipulated by deep-pocketed interest groups (like big corporations and the Law Enforcement Assistance Administration) who had the money to finance their own research and publications.[120]

These problems came to a head when the parents of Jason Daubert and Eric Schuller sued Merrell Dow Pharmaceutical, Inc., alleging that the company's prenatal, antinausea medication, Bendectin, had caused their children to suffer from birth defects.[121] Dow, in turn, moved for summary judgment, arguing that the plaintiffs could not prove causation, given that peer-reviewed research had uniformly ruled out any causal link between Bendectin and the kinds of birth defects that the plaintiffs suffered.[122] In response, the plaintiffs proffered the testimony of experts who had identified a causal connection by reinterpreting the data underlying the studies

115. *Daubert*, 509 U.S. at 586.

116. *Id.* at 585.

117. *See, e.g.*, Paul C. Gianelli, *The Admissibility of Novel Scientific Evidence:* Frye v. United States, *a Half-Century Later*, 80 Colum. L. Rev. 1197, 1223–25 (1980).

118. *Id.*

119. *Id.* at 1221.

120. *Id.* at 1232.

121. *Daubert*, 509 U.S. at 582.

122. *Id.*

referred to in Dow's motion.[123] The district court and Ninth Circuit found that this "reanalysis" could not satisfy *Frye's* "general acceptance" standard because it had never been published in a peer-reviewed journal.[124] The Supreme Court reversed, holding that "general acceptance" was not the *sine qua non* of expert admissibility under Rule 702, which required courts to consider other factors, such as testability, peer-reviewed publication, and the existence of a known error rate in determining scientific validity.[125]

In reaching these conclusions, the *Daubert* Court made several observations about the admissibility standard under Rule 702, which suggested that it might look more favorably upon eyewitness expert testimony than the common law had up to that point. Specifically, the Court emphasized that one of Rule 702's key purposes had been "relaxing the traditional barriers to 'opinion' testimony" under the common law.[126] Thus, its standards for relevance and admissibility were more "liberal," "flexible," and "permissive" than they had been under the common law.[127] Further, in explaining Rule 702's "flexible" approach to admissibility, the Court cited with approval the Third Circuit's analysis in *United States v. Downing*, 753 F.2d 1224 (3d Cir. 1984), a case that interpreted Rule 702 to "*require*[] . . . that expert testimony on eyewitness perception and memory be admitted at least in some circumstances."[128] In this regard, the Third Circuit specifically noted that although many courts ruled eyewitness expert testimony inadmissible because it involved questions that a jury could evaluate on its own, there were "serious doubts" about whether this logic was consistent with "the liberal standard of admissibility mandated by Rule 702."[129]

Despite these calls for flexible, permissive, and liberal administration, *Daubert* has done little to change how federal judges evaluate eyewitness expert admissibility. Some have been inclined to construe *Daubert's* holding narrowly, noting that while it mandates a "flexible" determination of whether the science underlying an opinion is valid, it does not necessarily call for the same flexibility with respect to the separate "beyond the ken"

123. *Id.* at 583.
124. *Id.*
125. *Id.* at 592–95.
126. *Id.* at 588–89 (internal quotation marks and citations omitted).
127. *Id.*
128. *Downing*, 735 F.2d at 1232; *see Daubert*, 509 U.S. at 594 n.12 (citing *Downing*, 735 F.2d at 1238–39 to explain the "flexible" nature of the underlying inquiry).
129. *Downing*, 735 F.2d at 1230; *see also id.* at 1226 ("Fed. R. Evid. 702 . . . contemplates a liberal view toward the admissibility of expert testimony generally.").

determination that so frequently torpedoes proffers of eyewitness expert testimony.[130] Thus, *Daubert's* impact in this arena has been limited at best.[131]

II. What's Wrong with the Status Quo?

In courtrooms across the United States, attempts to marshal eyewitness expert testimony to support a defense of mistaken identification are routinely beset by a number of obstacles. Chief among them is the general impression among judges that expert testimony is not needed to help a jury parse the reliability of an identification, even where the identification raises questions that are likely beyond the average juror's comprehension based on available research. True, in the decades since *Chapple*, many courts have joined the Arizona Supreme Court in recognizing that questions of eyewitness reliability may exceed the average lay person's comprehension to at least some degree.[132] Still, some have not. Notably, the Eleventh Circuit has effectively declined to reconsider the "per se rule of inadmissibility" it adopted in 1984, based on its finding that "the jury can adequately weigh the[] problems [of perception and memory] through common-sense evaluation."[133] While

130. *See generally United States v. (Fred) Smith*, 122 F.3d 1355, 1358–59 (11th Cir. 1997); *see also Parker v. United States*, 249 A.3d 388, 403 (D.C. 2021) (noting that D.C.'s shift to a *Daubert*-like standard did not "change the fact that the trial court [retained] discretion" to determine whether particular eyewitness expert testimony "would ultimately be unhelpful to the jury" because it did not "fit" the evidence presented).

131. *But see United States v. (Andreas) Smith*, 621 F. Supp. 2d 1207, 1211 (M.D. Ala. 2009) ("A per se proscription against all eyewitness-identification expert testimony is irreconcilable with the United States Supreme Court's decision in *Daubert*[.]").

132. *See, e.g., Downing*, 753 F.2d 1224; *United States v. (James) Smith*, 736 F.2d 1103, 1105 (6th Cir. 1984); *United States v. Moore*, 786 F.2d 1308, 1312 (5th Cir. 1986); *United States v. Smithers*, 212 F.3d 306, 312 (6th Cir. 2000); *United States v. Mathis*, 264 F.3d 321 (3rd Cir. 2001); *United States v. Brownlee*, 454 F.3d 131, 142 (3d Cir. 2006); *People v. McDonald*, 690 P.2d 709 (Cal. 1984); *State v Bell*, 788 P.2d 1109 (Wash. App. 1990); *State v. Copeland*, 226 S.W.3d 287, 290, 299–300 (Tenn. 2007); *People v. Abney*, 13 N.Y.3d 251, 266, 918 N.E.2d 486, 494 (2009); *State v. Clopten*, 223 P.3d 1103 (Utah 2009); *Benn v. United States*, 978 A.2d 1257, 1268 (D.C. 2009); *Minor v. United States*, 57 A.3d 406 (D.C. 2012); *In re L.C.*, 92 A.3d 290 (D.C. 2014); *see also Jones v. United States*, 262 A.3d 1114 (D.C. 2021) (holding counsel ineffective for failing to hire an eyewitness identification expert).

133. *United States v. (Fred) Smith*, 122 F.3d 1355, 1358 (11th Cir. 1997) (quoting *Thevis*, 665 F.2d at 641); *see also United States v. Holloway*, 971 F.2d 675, 679 (11th Cir. 1992) ("The established rule of this circuit is that such testimony is not admissible."); *United States v. Benitez*, 741 F.2d 1312, 1315 (11th Cir.1984) ("[Defendant's] contention that the district court incorrectly excluded expert testimony concerning identification also lacks merit because such testimony is not admissible in this circuit."). It is arguable that the Eleventh Circuit case law misinterprets *Thevis*, insofar as it extracts a categorical bar from fact-bound analysis. The *Thevis* court's observation that "the jury can adequately weigh these problems [of perception and memory] through common-sense evaluation," *Thevis*, 665 F.2d at 641, must be viewed in light of the facts there presented. *See, e.g., Armour & Co. v. Wantock*, 323 U.S. 126, 132–33 (1944)

acknowledging that this logic is less than sound as applied to topics that lie "demonstra[bly]" beyond the jury's "common sense" comprehension, such as "the lack of correlation between a witness's level of certainty [at trial] and the accuracy of their identification,"[134] the Eleventh Circuit nevertheless has adhered, on stare decisis grounds, to a rule whereby eyewitness expert testimony is either categorically inadmissible or perpetually subject to discretionary exclusion, such that it cannot be the basis for a finding of reversible error.[135]

Although this rule is an extreme example, the notion that jurors need no help from an expert to scrutinize most identifications is all too pervasive in this area of jurisprudence.[136] The prevailing view in the federal system is that because of this innate proficiency, eyewitness expert testimony need only be admitted to address a "narrow" category of exceptional issues that may arise with respect to the reliability of an identification.[137] "Despite a general trend toward admitting expert evidence on factual matters and mounting scientific research challenging jurors' ability to assess eyewitness evidence reliably, courts continue to affirm the sufficiency of the jury's lay knowledge in order to deny the utility of more rarefied knowledge on eyewitness identifications."[138]

Moreover, many appellate courts remain resistant to the notion that expert testimony may assist the trier of fact in determining eyewitness reliability because they are concerned that full-throated endorsement of this principle will open the floodgates to expensive, time-consuming expert battles. Because of this concern, some courts have expressly limited eyewitness

---

(admonishing that "words of [judicial] opinions are to be read in the light of the facts of the case under discussion"). *Thevis* dealt with a proffer of "general[ized] testimony "as to problems with eyewitness identification," as well as testimony regarding the fact "that pilots *as a group* were not better equipped than ordinary witnesses to make identifications." *Thevis*, 665 F.2d at 641. Confined to its facts, *Thevis* does not support a *per se* bar on all conceivable eyewitness identification expert testimony. Rather, it merely implies that similar testimony should not be admitted.

134. *United States v. (Charles) Smith*, 148 F. App'x 867, 872 n.8 (11th Cir. 2005).

135. *Id.*; *see United States v. (Andreas) Smith*, 621 F. Supp. 2d 1207, 1214 (M.D. Ala. 2009) (noting that *Thevis* does not necessarily bar the admission of eyewitness expert testimony).

136. *See United States v. Rodriguez-Felix*, 450 F.3d 1117, 1125 (10th Cir. 2006) ("Jurors, assisted by skillful cross-examination, are quite capable of using their common-sense and faculties of observation to make this reliability determination."); *United States v. Labansat*, 94 F.3d 527, 530 (9th Cir. 1996) ("Any weaknesses in eyewitness identification testimony can ordinarily be revealed by counsel's careful cross-examination of the eyewitnesses.").

137. *United States v. Harris*, 995 F.2d 532, 535 (4th Cir.1993); *United States v. Stevens*, 935 F.2d 1380, 1400 (3d Cir. 1991); *(Fred) Smith*, 122 F.3d at 1359.

138. Note, *The Province of the Jurist*, *supra* note 12, at 2383.

expert admissibility to cases where the government's case depends solely on an eyewitness identification, separate and apart from whether the expert testimony concerns an issue with great potential to confound the average juror. Indeed, two years after it decided *Chapple*, the Arizona Supreme Court clarified that its holding was limited to the "peculiar facts of that case" where "the question of guilt . . . hinge[d] solely on the testimony of eyewitnesses."[139] Many courts have held similarly.[140] To this day, only the Utah Supreme Court has expressed an "expect[ation] . . . that in cases involving eyewitness identification of strangers or near-strangers, trial courts will routinely admit expert testimony."[141]

In excluding, or affirming the exclusion of, eyewitness expert testimony, some courts have also cited concerns that attend almost all other kinds of expert testimony, including that the jury will be unduly impressed by an expert's credentials or confused by their testimony.[142] However, it is difficult to imagine that these concerns would carry the same weight if judges

139. *State v. Poland*, 698 P.2d 183, 194 (Ariz. 1985).

140. *United States v. Watkins*, 66 F.4th 1179, 1185 (8th Cir. 2023) (finding no abuse of discretion where "the government presented significant evidence, in addition to the eyewitness testimony, that Watkins possessed the firearms"; noting, with approval, the district court's similar reasoning); *United States v. Nickelous*, 916 F.3d 721, 724–25 (8th Cir. 2019) (finding no abuse of discretion in part "because the conviction did not rest solely" on the eyewitness testimony); *People v. Young*, 7 N.Y.3d 40, 45, 850 N.E.2d 623, 626–27 (2006) ("[I]f this case turned entirely on an uncorroborated eyewitness identification, it might well have been an abuse of discretion to deny the jury the benefit of Brigham's opinions."); *McDonald*, 690 P.2d at 727 ("[L]ike the court in *Chapple*, 'we do not intend to 'open the gates' to a flood of expert evidence on the subject.' We expect that such evidence will not often be needed, and in the usual case the appellate court will continue to defer to the trial court's discretion in this matter.").

141. *Clopten*, 223 P.3d at 1113; *see also id.* 1112 ("We expect this application of rule 702 will result in the liberal and routine admission of eyewitness expert testimony, particularly in cases where, as here, eyewitnesses are identifying a defendant not well known to them."); *id.* at 1118 ("We therefore hold that, in cases where eyewitnesses are identifying a stranger and one or more established factors affecting accuracy are present, the testimony of a qualified expert is both reliable and helpful, as required by rule 702. Such eyewitness expert testimony should therefore be routinely admitted, regardless of whether the trial judge decides to issue a cautionary instruction.").

142. *See* Note, *The Province of the Jurist*, *supra* note 12, at 2384 & nn.23–24 (citing *United States v. Jones*, 689 F.3d 12, 19 (1st Cir. 2012); *United States v. Langan*, 263 F.3d 613, 621 (6th Cir. 2001); *United States v. Brien*, 59 F.3d 274, 277 (1st Cir. 1995)); *see also, e.g.*, *Commonwealth v. Simmons*, 662 A.2d 621, 631 (Pa. 1995) (affirming exclusion of expert testimony because it "would have given an unwarranted appearance of authority as to the subject of credibility"); McKee, *supra* note 6, § 13 ("Some courts have expressed a fear that presenting expert evaluation of eyewitness testimony will improperly influence juries against such testimony," insofar as "the jury may be unduly impressed by the credentials and presence of the expert witnesses, or may become confused or misled by the technical testimony, and will unfairly discount or disregard perfectly good testimony from the actual witnesses.").

could be persuaded that expert testimony was needed to assist the jury in the first place.

This "beyond the ken" problem has only been exacerbated by the fact that expert admissibility determinations remain entirely within the trial court's discretion. As the First Circuit cautioned in an influential 1979 case, "a trial court can, in its discretion, conclude that scientific evaluation either has not reached, or perhaps cannot reach a level of reliability such that scientific analysis of a question of fact surpasses the quality of common-sense evaluation inherent in jury deliberations."[143] Because of this extremely deferential standard of appellate review that would apply to such a determination, the defendant would have no recourse for such a determination on appeal. Thus, "trial judges have little to fear from appellate courts if they decide to block the subject of such expert testimony at the gate."[144]

Preclusion of Expert Testimony in *Flowers v. State*, 240 So. 3d 1082 (Miss. 2017)

Contemporary hostility toward eyewitness expert testimony is demonstrated by the Mississippi Supreme Court's opinion in *Flowers v. State*.[145] Curtis Flowers was tried on six separate occasions in connection with the 1996 murder of four furniture store employees in Winona, Mississippi.[146] The first three trials ended in death sentences that were overturned by the Mississippi Supreme Court.[147] The next two ended in mistrial after the jury was unable to reach a verdict.[148] The sixth and final trial resulted in a death sentence that the United States Supreme Court vacated based on the prosecution's unlawful pattern of excluding African Americans from the jury.[149] Thereafter, the charges against Mr. Flowers were dismissed.

Mr. Flowers' convictions had rested largely on circumstantial evidence and the identification of a white man named Porky

(continued)

143. *Fosher*, 590 F.2d at 383.
144. McKee, *supra* note 6, § 8.
145. 240 So. 3d 1082 (Miss. 2017)
146. *Id.* at 1091.
147. *Id.* at 1093.
148. *Id.*
149. *Flowers v. Mississippi*, 588 U.S. 284 (2019).

Preclusion of Expert Testimony in *Flowers v. State*, 240 So. 3d 1082 (Miss. 2017) *(continued)*

Collins, who reported having seen two Black men arguing outside of the furniture store shortly before the murders.[150] Collins told police that after he "circled the block and returned to where he saw the men arguing . . ., the men were headed toward [the furniture store]."[151] Collins eventually identified Flowers as one of the men he saw after reviewing a photo array that the police had prepared.[152] However, Collins's identification was undermined by a number of factors, including the fact that he had no reason to have been paying close attention to those he saw outside of the furniture store.[153] The photo array containing Mr. Flowers was further suggestive insofar as his photo made him look bigger and darker skinned than the fillers.[154]

Mr. Flowers sought the help of an expert in psychology–Dr. Jeffrey Neuschatz—to opine on the significance of these factors.[155] The defense proffered Dr. Neuschatz's expertise on a variety of topics related to Mr. Collins's identification, including (1) how memory works; (2) [the] effect of exposure time on reliability of memory; (3) effect of appearance changes and disguises on identification; (4) the phenomenon of unconscious transference where one situation is confused with another; (5) problems with cross-racial identifications; (6) problems with post identification feedback; and (7) problems with suggestive line-up procedures.[156]

The defense further proffered (via Dr. Neuschatz's affidavit) "thirty-three studies," each of which tended to show that his methods had attained "general acceptance in the field of psychology."[157] The state, for its part, made no attempt to rebut this showing.[158]

---

150. *Flowers*, 240 So. 3d at 1094.

151. *Id.*

152. *Id.* at 1097.

153. Parker Yesko, *Why the Eyewitness IDs of Curtis Flowers May Not Be Reliable*, In the Dark, June 19, 2018, https://www.apmreports.org/story/2018/06/19/why-eyewitness-id-of-curtis-flowers-may-not-be-reliable.

154. *Id.*; *see also Flowers*, 240 So. 3d at 1098.

155. *Flowers*, 240 So. 3d at 1103-04.

156. *Id.* at 1174 (King, J., dissenting).

157. *Id.*

158. *Id.* at 1174-75.

Preclusion of Expert Testimony in *Flowers v. State*, 240 So. 3d 1082 (Miss. 2017) *(continued)*

Nevertheless, the trial court ruled Dr. Neuschatz's testimony inadmissible, reasoning that it would not "assist the jury in the least bit" because Mr. Flowers had been granted "extensive cross-examination of Mr. Collins" and because other witnesses more familiar with Mr. Flowers than Mr. Collins had placed him near the scene.[159] The trial court further reasoned that Dr. Neuschatz's testimony was inadmissible under *Daubert* because, notwithstanding his affidavit and the studies cited therein, the defense had proffered insufficient information to establish general acceptance of his methods.[160]

A majority of the Mississippi Supreme Court, in turn, affirmed this ruling under the highly deferential "abuse of discretion" standard because, although Dr. Neuschatz's affidavit had cited numerous studies, he had not *attached* those studies to his affidavit for the trial judge to review.[161] The court further found that his opinions might have confused the jury, insofar as they ran counter to the judge's pretrial ruling that the photo-array viewed by Collins was not unconstitutionally suggestive.[162] Finally, the appellate court endorsed the trial court's reasoning that cross-examination had been sufficient to expose what was wrong with Collins's identification and because Collins's identification was not sufficiently "critical" to the prosecution's case.[163] Although the dissenting justices did their best to expose the gaps in the majority's reasoning on this issue,[164] and although Mr. Flowers later won his freedom at the U.S. Supreme Court in light of his meritorious *Batson* objection, the Mississippi Supreme Court's application of *Daubert* to Dr. Neuschatz's testimony appears to remain good law in the State of Mississippi.

159. *Id.* at 1104.
160. *Id.* at 1105.
161. *Id.*
162. *Id.* at 1105-06 & n.4
163. *Id.* at 1106-07.
164. *Id.* at 1174-76 (King, J., dissenting).

5

Vagaries of Perception and Memory

In the half-century since the Supreme Court decided its seminal eyewitness identification cases, certain factors have become widely known to affect the reliability of this kind of evidence. Before launching into an in-depth discussion of these reliability factors and considering how the legal system might better address them, it is worth pulling back to consider how we form, store, and access memories, and what happens in the mind of an eyewitness when that person purports to identify someone else as the perpetrator of a crime. Establishing these core principles should help illuminate further discussion of the factors that impact eyewitness reliability, which can exert their influence at different stages of perception and memory.

A recurring theme in this discussion will be that the eye is not a camera, and memory is not a stable archive of our past experiences because our eyes and brain do not mechanically reproduce the light in our field of vision and store it in a durable format for later use. Rather, they render a three-dimensional environment from the "tiny distorted upside-down image" that is projected onto the back of the retinas when light shines through them.[1]

---

1. V.S. Ramchandran, A Brief Tour of Human Consciousness: From Imposter Poodles to Purple Numbers 8 (2004).

Our brains then selectively incorporate information about these renderings into a set of malleable, dynamic, long-term memories that are subject to change in unpredictable ways every time we access them. Although no ink has been spared in explaining the ways that human perception and memory deviate from their mechanical counterparts,[2] it is nevertheless a crucial point of departure for any conversation about eyewitness reliability.

I. Visual Perception

Scientists divide the process by which we acquire visual information from our environment into three stages: sensation, attention, and perception. Sensation refers to the process by which we detect light and extract raw image data from it.[3] Attention refers to the process by which we focus consciously and subconsciously on what is relevant to our current cognitive and behavioral demands.[4] Perception is what happens when our conscious mind renders raw image data into recognizable objects with semantic meaning and emotional valence. Visual information can be lost or distorted at each of these stages.

A. Sensation

Sensation begins when light enters the eye through the lens. The lens, in turn, focuses and projects light onto the retina at the back of the eye, creating a "retinal image."[5] The retinal image then "activat[es]" neurons in the optic nerve (photoreceptors),[6] prompting them to send electrochemical signals about the image to the primary visual cortex in the brain.[7] These signals contain data about the contrasting orientation, movement, brightness, and color of the different kinds of light that the image contains.[8] The brain

---

2. *2019 Report of the United States Court of Appeals for the Third Circuit Task Force on Eyewitness Identifications*, 92 TEMP. L. REV. 1, 24 (2019) [hereinafter *2019 Third Circuit Task Force Report*].

3. NAT'L RSCH. COUNCIL OF THE NAT'L ACADS., IDENTIFYING THE CULPRIT: ASSESSING EYEWITNESS IDENTIFICATION 46 (2014) [hereinafter NAT'L RSCH. COUNCIL].

4. *See, e.g.*, Gillian Murphy & Ciara M. Greene, *Perceptual Load Affects Eyewitness Accuracy and Susceptibility to Leading Questions*, FRONTIERS PSYCHOL. 1, Aug. 30, 2016, https://doi.org/10.3389/fpsyg.2016.01322; Gillian Murphy et al., *Twenty Years of Load Theory: Where Are We Now, And Where Should We Go Next?*, 23 PSYCHONOMIC BULL. REV. 1316 (2016), https://doi.org/10.3758/s13423-015-0982-5; NAT'L RSCH. COUNCIL, *supra* note 3, at 53.

5. NAT'L RSCH. COUNCIL, *supra* note 3, at 50.

6. *Id.*

7. *see, e.g.*, Mohit Gupta et al., *Neuroanatomy*, Visual Pathway, https://www.ncbi.nlm.nih.gov/books/NBK553189/.

8. NAT'L RSCH. COUNCIL, *supra* note 3, at 50; Charles D. Gilbert, *Intermediate-Level Visual Processing and Visual Primitives*, in PRINCIPLES OF NEUROSCIENCE 602 (5th ed. 2012).

combines these data to construct "basic image features"—that is, line segments that we integrate into objects in three-dimensional space through the magic of our uniquely human powers of perception.[9] Light thus rendered has been "sensed."

As our sight depends on contrasts between and among different kinds of light in our field of vision, it is limited by factors that impede our ability to detect such contrast. They include visual impairments such as color blindness, myopia, and poor contrast sensitivity, as well as environmental factors such as how much time we spend looking at an object (**exposure duration**), how close to it we are when we see it (**distance**), and how well it is illuminated (**lighting conditions**).[10] These factors are discussed in greater detail in Chapter 6 on **estimator variables.**

In addition, the anatomy of the human eye places certain limitations on our ability to glean visual information from the environment:

- Notably, vision is sharpest at the center of our gaze,[11] which corresponds to a part of the retina called the "fovea" that is densely packed with photoreceptors.[12] This heightened foveal clarity explains why we tend to move our eyes along with the words of a sentence as we read it, as you, reader, are probably doing right now.[13] At the same time, our ability to resolve contrast suffers dramatically as little as ten degrees from the center of our gaze.[14] The resulting difference does not just make peripheral vision blurrier. It alters our perception of basic features such as size, shape, and, in the realm of human faces, sex and gender.[15]
- Further, although vision tends to rely on two types of photoreceptors—cones that enable us to see color and rods that enable us to see everything else (light/dark contrast, shape, movement, etc.)—the fovea has

---

9. NAT'L RSCH. COUNCIL, *supra* note 3, at 50.

10. *Id.*

11. *Id.* at 51.

12. Emma E.M. Stewart et al., *A Review of Interactions Between Peripheral and Foveal Vision*, 20 J. VISION 1 (2020), https://doi.org/10.1167/jov.20.12.2; *see also* Eric H. Chudler, *The Retina*, NEUROSCIENCE FOR KIDS, https://faculty.washington.edu/chudler/retina.html (last visited Jan. 2, 2023).

13. NAT'L RSCH. COUNCIL, *supra* note 3, at 51.

14. *Id.*

15. Nonie J. Finlayson et al., *Spatial Heterogeneity in Bistable* Figure-*Ground Perception*, 11 I-PERCEPTION 1, 2 (2020), https://doi.org/10.1177/2041669520961120; Arash Afraz et al., *Spatial Heterogeneity in the Perception of Face and Form Attributes*, 20 CURRENT BIOLOGY 2112 (2010), https://doi.org/10.1016/j.cub.2010.11.017.

only cones.[16] Cones require more light than rods to activate; thus, "[i]n light that is too dim to activate cones," we experience "a blind spot at the cent[er] of our visual field," corresponding to where the fovea is.[17]

- Moreover, "[b]ecause photoreceptors are located on the back side of the retina, away from the light," some are obstructed by ocular blood vessels.[18] The shadows that these blood vessels cast on the photoreceptors behind them "create a pattern of blindness in the field of vision," corresponding to where the blood vessel is located.[19]
- Finally, every eyeball has a blind spot where the optic nerve exits the retina to connect to the brain.[20] At this part of the retina, there are no photoreceptors, and thus, there is no ability to see.[21]

So how does our vision work so seamlessly, when our eyes have so many "seams?" That we generally do not notice the anatomical imperfections is a testament to how well our brains have adapted to compensate for them. Even so, the manner by which we compensate has important implications for the reliability of eyewitness identification. We compensate for the unevenness and incompleteness of the visual information we receive by reorienting our gaze and attention to take in more of the environment, by taking "averages" of the visual information we receive, and by drawing inferences about what we cannot see based on our experiences and expectations.[22] As moving around our eyes and attention is key to our ability to see well, it is important to scrutinize an eyewitness's **viewing opportunity** to ensure it allowed for such thorough appraisal.[23] Moreover, as discussed later, although visual inferencing is key to our ability to process the visual world smoothly, it can lead our perceptions astray.

B. Attention

Because our environments contain an overwhelming amount of visual information—and because we are better equipped to survive when we can respond to it quickly—humans and other visually dominant primates process

---

16. Stewart et al., *supra* note 12; Chudler, *supra* note 12; David H. Hubel, *Vision in Dim Light*, NATURE at 32, July 3, 1997, https://www.nature.com/articles/40308.
17. Hubel, *supra* note 16, at 32.
18. Stewart et al., *supra* note 12.
19. Daniel L. Adams & Jonathan C. Horton, *Shadows Cast by Retinal Blood Vessels Mapped in Primary Visual Cortex*, 298 SCIENCE 572 (2002), https://doi.org/10.1126/science.1074887.
20. Stewart et al., *supra* note 12.
21. Adams & Horton, *supra* note 19.
22. Stewart et al., *supra* note 12.
23. *See* NAT'L RSCH. COUNCIL, *supra* note 3, at 51.

visual stimuli selectively and prioritize what is relevant to their current behavioral needs.[24] Our capacity to focus more on what seems more relevant, while ignoring what seems less relevant is called "selective attention."[25] It is a finite cognitive resource that objects in our field of vision compete to occupy.[26]

1. *Selective Enhancement*

Selective attention has "top-down," observer-driven components, as well as "bottom-up," stimulus-driven components.[27] The top-down components include our ability to shift our focus to a particular space in our field of vision, even without shifting our gaze—for instance, shifting our focus to a person's nametag in the middle of a conversation, while maintaining eye contact so as not to reveal that we forgot the person's name in the first place.[28] Bottom-up attention refers to any number of intrinsic qualities, such as color contrast and novelty, that make an object stand out from its surroundings—for instance, the way a red apple might stand out in a sea of green leaves, especially to someone who is hungry.[29]

However an object garners attention, the result is the same: we see it more clearly and in richer detail. Visual attention allows the brain to selectively enhance the contrast of attended stimuli, making them stand out more from their surroundings.[30] The brain accomplishes this feat by boosting sensitivity to signals sent from the parts of the retina corresponding to the attended visual information.[31] Thus, we can selectively enhance what we see without shifting our gaze, even when lighting is poor.[32] At the same time, this kind of artificial enhancement can distort our perception.[33]

---

24. *Id.* at 53 ("[T]he informational content of [our field of vision] vastly exceeds what can be attended at any point in time[.]").

25. *See, e.g.*, Murphy & Greene, *supra* note 4; Murphy et al., *supra* note 4; NAT'L RSCH. COUNCIL, *supra* note 3, at 53.

26. NAT'L RSCH. COUNCIL, *supra* note 3, at 53.

27. Charles E. Connor et al., *Visual Attention: Bottom-Up Versus Top-Down*, 14 CURRENT BIOLOGY, R850 (2004), https://doi.org/10.1016/j.cub.2004.09.041; NAT'L RSCH. COUNCIL, *supra* note 3, at 52.

28. Marisa Carrasco, *How Visual Spatial Attention Alters Perception*, 19 COGNITIVE PROCESSING 77 (2018), https://link.springer.com/article/10.1007/s10339-018-0883-4.

29. Connor et al., *supra* note 27.

30. NAT'L RSCH. COUNCIL, *supra* note 3, at 52.

31. Vahid Mehrpour et al., *Attention Amplifies Neural Representations of Changes in Sensory Input at the Expense of Perceptual Accuracy*, NATURE COMM., May 1, 2020, https://www.nature.com/articles/s41467-020-15989-0; John H.R. Maunsell, *Neuronal Mechanisms of Visual Attention*, 1 ANNU. REV. VISION SCI. 373 (2015) https://doi.org/10.1146/annurev-vision-082114-035431.

32. NAT'L RSCH. COUNCIL, *supra* note 3, at 52.

33. Mehrpour et al., *supra* note 31.

2. *Inattentional Blindness*

On the other hand, when objects in our field of vision struggle to command attention, we are more likely to overlook them altogether. Such unattended content is effectively invisible to us because it does not penetrate our consciousness and will not be stored in long-term memory.[34] This phenomenon, whereby people miss objects in their field of vision, even those that are obvious, unusual, or unexpected, is called "inattentional blindness."[35] It can be triggered by any number of engrossing tasks, as documented by YouTube magicians and psychology professors alike.[36] It is an important phenomenon in the context of eyewitness identification because it can also be induced by the kind of visual complexity that may attend a crime scene and by highly stressful, fear- or anxiety-inducing stimuli, such as weapons.

a. Visual Complexity and Perceptual Load

Selective attention helps us navigate complex environments by allowing us to parse them one object at a time in order of apparent relevance.[37] But there are limits to our capacity to grapple with visual complexity. Selective attention can be compromised by environments that impose a "high perceptual load" on us because they contain large amounts of visually complex stimuli in close proximity to one another.[38] When confronted with such environments, we tend to zero in on what most effectively draws our attention, while overlooking what does not.[39] Under these circumstances, inattentional blindness is more likely.[40]

For this reason, high perceptual load may reduce an eyewitness's ability "to accurately perceive the facial features of a perpetrator" in a "visually complex scene, such as a sporting event."[41] Recent research shows that

---

34. Nat'l Rsch. Council, *supra* note 3, at 53.
35. Alia N. Wulff & Ayanna K. Thomas, *The Dynamic and Fragile Nature of Eyewitness Memory Formation: Considering Stress and Attention*, Frontiers Psychol., April 13, 2021, https://doi.org/10.3389/fpsyg.2021.666724.
36. Daniel J. Simons, The Monkey Business Illusion, https://www.youtube.com/watch?v=IGQmdoK_ZfY; Professor Ross, Brain Games – Inattentional Blindness (Double Dutch), https://www.youtube.com/watch?v=TSsuwZvom3g.
37. Murphy & Greene, *supra* note 4, at 1.
38. Nat'l Rsch. Council, *supra* note 3, at 53–54; Murphy & Greene, *supra* note 4, at 1.
39. Murphy & Greene, *supra* note 4, at 1.
40. Nat'l Rsch. Council, *supra* note 3, at 54; Murphy & Greene, *supra* note 4, at 1.
41. Nat'l Rsch. Council, *supra* note 3, at 54.

high perceptual load can impair an observer's ability to identify peripheral characters from the scene of a crime, even when the observer is expressly instructed to "pay close attention" to the scene before witnessing the crime, which seldom happens during a real world criminal encounter.[42] In any case, perceptual load has important implications for how we define what it means to get a "good look" at someone in the course of a highly stressful, fast-moving criminal encounter.

b. Stressful/Emotional Content

Finally, stimuli that elicit strong emotional, fight-or-flight responses, such as weapons, have a great potential to "hijack" our attention.[43] This explains, at least in part, why the presence of such provocative stimuli may prevent us from "acquiring greater visual information about the face of the perpetrator."[44] As applied to the specific example of weapons, this phenomenon is called "**weapon focus**" and will be discussed further in the chapter on **estimator variables.**

C. Perception

Once we have sensed and attended a pattern of light, our conscious mind can perceive it. "Perception" is what happens when we convert basic image features into coherent objects in a three-dimensional space, with emotional and behavioral significance that our conscious minds can comprehend and remember, such as a human face.[45] Perception involves multiple structures of the brain.[46] Like the processes underlying sensation and attention, the processes underlying perception are imperfect. They give rise to bias and distortion because they are constructive and categorical in nature.

1. Perception Is Constructive

Scientists describe perception as the outcome of a "constructive" process because they believe that our brains literally piece the perceived object together from photoreceptor data, using expectations and experience as a

---

42. Murphy & Greene, *supra* note 4, at 1.
43. Nat'l Rsch. Council, *supra* note 3, at 55.
44. *Id.*
45. *See, e.g., id.*
46. *Id.* at 55–56.

guide.[47] Our brains do this to compensate for the natural limits that biology places on our ability to acquire visual information from the environment. As discussed in Section I.A, the human eye is a structurally flawed mechanism for conveying data about the light in our field of vision. Because so much visual information is lost by the time our brains begin visual processing, and because what remains "is often noisy . . . and ambiguous," we use experience and expectation to "fill in the blanks, reconcile ambiguities, and leave clear and coherent percepts."[48] This process allows us to navigate the world with "certainty of perception in the face of noise and ambiguity," but exposes us to a certain risk of perceptual error.[49]

a. Expectation-Related Bias

The constructive nature of perception has troubling implications for eyewitness identifications because it suggests a natural tendency to resist visual information that defies expectation. The power of expectation to override perception was demonstrated in a couple of classic experiments involving playing cards. In the first, subjects were briefly shown a set of twelve aces of all four suits and asked to report the number of spades.[50] Most subjects reported three, but there were five: three that were black and two "trick" cards that were the same color red as the hearts and diamonds in the display.[51]

In the second experiment, subjects were asked to describe a series of playing cards, which included some color-swapped trick cards (e.g., black ace of diamonds and red six of clubs).[52] The cards were shown one at a time, at progressively longer intervals, until participants successfully identified

---

47. Dr. Saul McLeod, *Visual Perception Theory,* SIMPLY PSYCHOLOGY (2018), https://www.simplypsychology.org/perception-theories.html.

48. NAT'L RSCH. COUNCIL, *supra* note 3, at 57; *accord* Dr. Saul McLeod, *supra* note 47; Peggy Seriès & Aaron R. Seitz, *Learning What to Expect (in Visual Perception)*, 7 FRONTIERS HUM. NEUROSCI. 1, Oct. 24, 2013, https://www.frontiersin.org/articles/10.3389/fnhum.2013.00668/full.

49. NAT'L RSCH. COUNCIL, *supra* note 3, at 57; *accord* Dr. Saul McLeod, *supra* note 47; Seriès & Seitz, supra note 48 at 1.

50. Robert Buckhout, *Eyewitness Testimony*, 15 JURIMETRICS J. 171, 176 (1975), https://www.jstor.org/stable/29761486.

51. *Id.*

52. Jerome S. Bruner & Leo Postman, *On the Perception of Incongruity: A Paradigm*, 18 J. PERSONALITY 206, 209 (1949), https://onlinelibrary.wiley.com/doi/abs/10.1111/j.1467-6494.1949.tb01241.x.

each card twice. As in the "twelve aces" version of the experiment, subjects experienced considerable difficulty identifying the trick cards.[53] When confronted with an incongruous color/suit combination, even one they had seen multiple times, subjects tended to misjudge the suit (e.g., calling a heart for a spade or vice versa), misjudge the color (e.g., describing red as purple, rusty black, or grayish), or insist that the card did not belong to any familiar suit.[54] These results led Bruner and Postman to conclude that "perceptual organization is powerfully determined by expectations built upon past commerce with the environment" and that "[w]hen such expectations are violated by the environment, the perceiver's behavior can be described as resistance to the recognition of the unexpected or incongruous."[55]

Since Bruner and Postman's playing cards, scientists have learned a great deal about when and how expectations influence perception. Our brains "continuously extract[] and learn[] the statistical regularities of the environment," to form expectations that affect us at various levels of sensory processing and consciousness.[56] These processes happen "automatically and without awareness."[57] These expectations, in turn, color our perceptions, exerting their strongest influence when viewing opportunities are limited and "available sensory inputs are ambiguous" and subject to "multiple competing interpretations."[58]

i. ***Structural and Contextual Expectations*** Some expectations are structural, impacting our perception in the same way in all situations.[59] For example, because we spend our whole lives under the sun and other overhead light sources, we have a well-documented tendency to expect our environments to be lit from above.[60] This assumption allows us to instantaneously detect shadow, resolve object contours, and perceive depth.[61]

53. *Id.* at 210.
54. *Id.* at 214–20.
55. *Id.* at 222.
56. Seriès & Seitz, *supra* note 48, at 1.
57. *Id.*
58. *Id.* at 1, 3.
59. *Id.* at 2.
60. *Id.*
61. *See, e.g.*, Abigail Croydon et al., *The Light-From-Above Prior Is Intact in Autistic Children*, 161 J. Experimental Child Psychol. 113, 116 (2017), https://www.sciencedirect.com/science/article/pii/S0022096516302351.

However, like any assumption, it can lead us astray.[62] For instance, the "light-from-above" prior can distort our perception of human faces when the light and shadow do not behave as we initially expect or make it harder to recognize a face that was illuminated differently the first time we saw it. "[F]ace recognition processes are sensitive to either the direction of lighting or the resultant pattern of shading," and can be easily disrupted by shadows.[63] This has obvious bearing on how we evaluate the quality of the **lighting conditions**, as noted in Chapter 6 on **estimator variables.**

Other expectations are contextual, reflecting our tendency to use environmental cues to resolve perceptual ambiguity.[64] One part of the environment that we frequently leverage in this regard is ourselves. A recent study shows that whether a person first sees the "old" or "young" woman in the famous (and unfortunately named) "My Wife and My Mother-In-Law" picture depends on the viewer's age; younger viewers tend to register the younger woman first, and older viewers tend to register the older woman first.[65] Although this tendency could be attributable to our disproportionate exposure to people our own age, that explanation would not account for the fact that our perception of the emotion conveyed by a person's facial expression tends to be equally self-referential.[66] It is not hard to see how our self-referential tendencies might impact our perception of a perpetrator during a brief encounter. For this reason, the characteristics of a witness and the perpetrator, including **age** and **race**, warrant special attention in attempting to evaluate the reliability of an identification.

---

62. Seriès & Seitz, *supra* note 48, at 2.

63. Wendy L. Braje et al., *Illumination Effects in Face Recognition*, 26 Psychobiology 371 (1998), https://link.springer.com/content/pdf/10.3758/BF03330623.pdf; *accord* Simone Favelle et al., *About Face: Matching Unfamiliar Faces Across Rotations of View and Lighting*, i-Perception 1, Nov. 29, 2017, https://journals.sagepub.com/doi/full/10.1177/2041669517744221.

64. Seriès & Seitz, *supra* note 48, at 2.

65. Michael E.R. Nicholls et al., *Perception of an Ambiguous Figure Is Affected by Own-Age Social Biases*, Sci. Reports, Aug. 23, 2018, https://doi.org/10.1038/s41598-018-31129-7.

66. Katharina A. Schwarz et al., *Why Are You Looking Like That? How the Context Influences Evaluation and Processing of Human Faces*, 8 Soc. Cognitive & Affective Neurosci. 438 (2013), https://doi.org/10.1093/scan/nss013.

"My Wife and My Mother-In-Law" by William Ely Hill (1915), a famous optical illusion, appeared in *Puck*, 78, no. 2018 (1915 Nov. 6), p. 11.

Another important contextual expectation involves our expectation of continuity and/or repetition from the environment. This expectation is manifest in our tendency to resolve perceptual ambiguity by reference to apparent patterns.[67] However, and especially when combined with distracting stimuli (like weapons), these expectations can dull our ability to detect important changes in the environment, for instance, where someone else has taken the perpetrator's place at the scene of a crime. This phenomenon is called "change blindness" and it has been demonstrated in a variety of experiments.[68] In one study, participants who watched video of a theft that

67. Elizabeth F. Loftus, Eyewitness Testimony 43–45 (2d. ed. 1996) (when viewing an ambiguous drawing that could be interpreted either as a rat or a human face, people are more likely to see the rat if they have just seen drawings of other animals, and the human face, if they have just seen drawings of other faces).

68. Kally J. Nelson et al., *Change Blindness Can Cause Mistaken Eyewitness Identification*, 16 Legal & Criminological Psychol. 62 (2011), https://doi.org/10.1348/135532509X482625; Deborah Davis et al., *"Unconscious Transference" Can Be an Instance of "Change Blindness,"* 22 Applied Cognitive Psychol. 605 (2008), https://doi.org/10.1002/acp.1395; Graham Davies & Sarah Hines, Change Blindness and Eyewitness Testimony, 14 J. Psychol.: Interdisciplinary & Applied, 423 (2007), https://doi.org/10.3200/JRLP.141.4.423-434.

was immediately followed by footage of a lookalike exiting the building were overwhelmingly unable to detect the change between individuals and were thus far more likely to identify the lookalike in a lineup than those who had seen the same person commit the theft and leave the building.[69]

*ii. **The Influence of Stereotype*** The biasing power of expectation warrants serious concern in the eyewitness identification context, not just because we may misperceive briefly encountered, strangely lit faces, but also because the expectations that inform our perceptions may be informed by negative stereotypes about specific races and genders.[70] As discussed throughout this chapter, our perception is sensitive to categorization by race and gender, and when we encounter ambiguous visual information about someone we perceive to be involved in a crime, we may be inclined to resolve it in favor of a preconceived notion about what the perpetrator looks like.

Allport and Postman demonstrated the biasing power of racial stereotypes by having subjects describe a photo that showed a confrontation between a white man armed with a razor blade and an unarmed Black man.[71] After viewing the photo, one subject described it to another, who passed it along to another, and so on.[72] By the sixth or seventh retelling, the razor blade tended to migrate into the hands of the unarmed Black man.[73] An updated version of the study in the 1980s found a similar effect.[74] Among other things, these studies underscore the need for police to separate witnesses when they arrive at the scene of a reported crime. This topic is discussed in the next chapter.

That people tend to hold certain stereotypes about the appearance of those who commit certain crimes has been suggested most recently by a series of experiments showing a tendency among people of all races to misattribute stereotypically pan-African features—darker skin tones, broader noses, and fuller lips—to those suspected of crimes that evoke negative stereotypes about Black people.[75] In one study, before watching a short video of a Black

---

69. Nelson et al., *supra* note 68.
70. Buckhout, *supra* note 50, at 176; *see also* LOFTUS, *supra* note 67, at 37–39.
71. *See* LOFTUS, *supra* note 67, at 37–39.
72. *Id.*
73. *Id.*
74. ELIZABETH F. LOFTUS ET AL., EYEWITNESS TESTIMONY: CIVIL AND CRIMINAL § 2.11, at 36–37 (4th ed. 2007).
75. Paul G. Davies et al., *Victims' Race and Sex Leads to Eyewitness Misidentification of Perpetrator's Phenotypic Stereotypicality*, 7 SOC. PSYCHOL. & PERSONALITY SCI. 491 (2016) https://www.sciencedaily.com/releases/2016/05/160512212415.htm; Danny Osborne & Paul G. Davies, *Crime Type, Perceived Stereotypicality, and Memory Biases: A Contextual Model of Eyewitness Identification*, 28 APPLIED COGNITIVE PSYCHOL. 392 (2014), https://doi.org/10.1002/acp.3009;

man walking out of a building, a subset of the participants was advised that he was suspected of committing a certain crime.[76] For half of this subset, the crime (pimping) was one proven to evoke negative stereotypes about Black people, according to a recent survey.[77] For the other half, the crime (computer hacking) was more often linked to white perpetrators in the same survey.[78] After a distraction task, participants viewed a range of mugshots generated by manipulating the suspect's photograph to make his features more or less consistent with stereotypes about Black people.[79] From this array of altered mugshots, participants were asked to select the one that most resembled the person they saw in the video.[80] While the control group (who had not been told about any crime) and those who believed they were identifying a computer hacker were generally accurate in their identifications, those primed with the pimping accusation tended to choose stereotype-consistent mugshots.[81] When this experiment was repeated with different Black and white exemplars (drive-by-shooting and serial murder, respectively), results were comparable.[82] Another follow-up study showed that these effects could be exacerbated or negated by information about the race and sex of the victim.[83]

These findings suggest that exposure to a certain kind of crime or involvement in certain kinds of criminal investigation may prime negative racial stereotypes in a way that could compromise the accuracy of an eyewitness's memory and/or descriptions of a perpetrator to police, composite sketch artists, or a jury. All of this increases the likelihood of misidentification and wrongful conviction in ways that will be explored later. For now, it suffices to state that we, as humans, may harbor negative stereotypes about the appearance of those who end up involved in certain types of crimes, and that, based on what we know about the constructive nature of perception, these stereotypes may affect how we perceive a perpetrator as well as how we remember him.

Danny Osborne & Paul G. Davies, *Eyewitness Identifications Are Affected by Stereotypes About a Suspect's Level of Perceived Stereotypicality*, 16 Group Processes & Intergroup Rel. 488 (2013), https://doi.org/10.1177/1368430212454927.

76. Osborne & Davies, *Eyewitness Identifications Are Affected by Stereotypes About a Suspect's Level of Perceived Stereotypicality*, *supra* note 75, at 494.

77. *Id.* at 494; *see id.* at 491 (describing the pretesting procedure to determine the crimes that evoked black and white stereotypes).

78. *Id.* at 494.

79. *Id.* at 494–95.

80. *Id.* at 495–96.

81. *Id.* at 496.

82. *Id.* at 497.

83. Davies et al., *supra* note 68.

b. Viewpoint Specificity

Although perception and memory are constructive, inference-laden processes, there may be certain limits on what we can construct and infer. For this reason, our ability to recognize unfamiliar faces is profoundly sensitive to lighting and perspective and can be thrown off by visual information that is "unique to a specific angle of view."[84] This makes sense, as "[t]he retinal pattern generated by a face viewed directly from the front differs considerably—with changes in aspect ratio and relative placement of facial features—from that generated by a face viewed from an oblique side angle."[85] "A profile view, for example, has one less eye, eyebrow and cheek" than a front view, but "provides information regarding the protuberance of the nose not directly available from a front view."[86] "Viewing a face from . . . above or below . . . (as might be the case if the criminal were standing over you, or below you on the stairs) also yields retinal distortions of facial features."[87] "The appearance of a face can change at least as dramatically with changes in lighting direction."[88] Researchers have shown that changes in lighting and viewpoint can result in more objective "image variance" than changes to the identity of the person in a picture.[89]

Viewpoint dependency has obvious implications for how we evaluate the quality of an eyewitness's opportunity to observe a perpetrator. Although a certain logic would suggest that looking at someone head-on is enough to ensure reliable future identifications—after all, this is how we prefer to carry on conversations—recent research suggests that we derive more useful information about faces from seeing them at a forty-five-degree angle.[90]

Moreover, changing the angle from which we perceive an unfamiliar face can profoundly undermine our ability to recognize it again: rotations about the vertical/Y axis (which happen when you nod your head up and down) exerting greater negative impact than rotations about the horizontal/X axis (which occur when you shake your head back and forth).[91] Rotations about

84. Nat'l Rsch. Council, *supra* note 3, at 56.
85. *Id.*
86. Favelle et al., *supra* note 63, at 2.
87. Nat'l Rsch. Council, *supra* note 3, at 56.
88. Favelle et al., *supra* note 63, at 2.
89. *Id.*
90. Simone Favelle & Steven Palmisano, *View Specific Generalisation Effects in Face Recognition: Front and Yaw Comparison Views Are Better Than Pitch*, PLOS ONE, Dec. 18, 2018, https://doi.org/10.1371/journal.pone.0209927.
91. *Id.* at 2.

the Z axis (the most extreme version of which is total inversion of the face so that it is upside down) tend to affect familiar face recognition more than unfamiliar face recognition, suggesting that we rely on different biological mechanisms to process familiar and unfamiliar faces.[92]

2. *Perception Is Categorical*

Perceptual distortions also arise from our natural tendency to categorize what we perceive. To help us navigate the complexity of the world around us, our brains lump objects into categories based on prior associations, taking into account factors such as the object's purpose, properties, meanings, or emotional significance.[93] Our natural tendency to categorize means it is easier for us to discriminate between objects in different categories.[94] A paradigmatic example of this effect involves the colors of the rainbow.[95] Because color categorization is such a dominant feature of our perception, we tend to perceive naturally occurring rainbows as discrete bands of color rather than a gradual continuum, even though as an objective matter, the light frequency in a rainbow changes smoothly.[96] The rainbow appears as a set of discrete bands in part because it is easier for us to tell two shades apart when they cross a color boundary than when they do not.[97] Thus, a shade of green and a shade of yellow may seem to contrast more than two different shades of green or two different shades of yellow, even when the difference in wavelength for both pairs is identical.[98]

By the same token, we are less attuned to differences between objects that fall into the same category.[99] This effect is compounded in memory where objects are often "encoded . . . as a category type, . . . without specific detail."[100] Thus, our memory of an object tends to be heavily influenced by how we classify it in the first place.

---

92. *Id.*

93. NAT'L RSCH. COUNCIL, *supra* note 3, at 58.

94. *Id.*

95. James M. Beale & Frank C. Keil, *Categorical Effects in the Perception of Faces*, 57 COGNITION 217, 218 (1995), https://doi.org/10.1016/0010-0277(95)00669-x; Daniel T. Levin & Bonnie L. Angelone, *Categorical Perception of Race*, 31 PERCEPTION 567, 567 (2002), https://doi.org/10.1068/p3315.

96. Beale & Keil, *supra* note 95, at 218.

97. *Id.*

98. *Id.*

99. NAT'L RSCH. COUNCIL, *supra* note 3, at 59.

100. *Id.* at 58.

For all these reasons we may have trouble differentiating between faces and facial features that we group into the same perceptual categories.[101] We categorize faces based on a variety of criteria—some as narrow as facial hair and bone structure; others as broad as gender and race.[102] Because these categories fail to capture the full complexity and variety of human appearance, certain details can be lost when we view a face during the short time it may take that person to commit a crime.[103] Our ensuing memory of the face will be less precise, and when we go to retrieve it, we may unknowingly resort to categorical "exemplars" or "gists" from memory that check the same boxes.[104] Our difficulty drawing subtle distinctions between objects in the same "category" ultimately helps to account for the **cross-race effect**, whereby identifications tend to be more accurate when they involve members of the witness's own race than when they involve members of a different race.[105] This phenomenon is discussed further in the next chapter.

II. Memory

Once an event (e.g., a crime) or an object (e.g. the perpetrator's face) has been perceived, aspects of the resulting perception may filter into long-term memory and become available for use during future cognitive tasks (e.g., to identify or exclude a suspect during an identification procedure). We store information about our sensory experiences separately from the motor skills that enable us to walk, run, talk, play an instrument, tie our shoes, or ride a bicycle. The latter kind of memory is "procedural" because we do not need our conscious minds to access it—once you learn how to tie your shoes, you can do it without thinking about the individual steps.[106] By contrast, perceptual memory is "declarative" insofar as we need our conscious minds to access them.[107] Long-term declarative memory is a network of interconnected "semantic," fact-based content and "episodic," event-based content.[108] New perceptual experiences create memory by generating "new content" and "new associations between existing content" in long-term memory.[109]

---

101. *Id.*
102. *Id.* at 58–59.
103. *Id.* at 59.
104. *Id.*
105. *Id.* at 59, 96–97; Levin & Angelone, *supra* note 95, at 567.
106. Nat'l Rsch. Council, *supra* note 3, at 59.
107. *Id.* at 59.
108. *Id.* at 61.
109. *Id.*

Scientists tend to describe the process of forming and recalling declarative memories in terms of three processes: encoding, storage, and retrieval.[110] As with the phases of perception, information can be lost or distorted during each of these processes. "The basic teaching of [contemporary] research [on memory] is that" the contents of these memories and the associations between them are not anywhere near as durable as once believed.[111] "[C]ontrary to popular belief, the brain does not work like a video camera, or create 'flashbulb' memories impervious to change."[112] Rather, "the fidelity of our memories for real events may be compromised by many factors at all stages of processing, from encoding through storage, to the final stages of retrievals."[113] Perceptual information can be lost and permanently forgotten during encoding. New knowledge and experience prompt our brains to start forgetting old. The act of retrieval itself can distort or compromise the contents of memory.

A. Encoding (and Consolidation)

Encoding refers to the process by which our perceptual experiences filter into long-term memory.[114] Scientists believe, and research tends to support, that encoding is carried out largely by the hippocampus.[115] During encoding, perceptual information is initially stored in short-term memory, which has a limited capacity, decays quickly, and is highly susceptible to interference from subsequent thoughts, emotions, and perceptions.[116] Short-term memory enables us to take action and make decisions based on recent perceptions; it also serves as the repository for long-term memories when we draw on them to complete a task—for instance, deciding whether we recognize a particular person as the perpetrator of a crime we witnessed.[117]

Once perceptual information has filtered into short-term memory, some version of it may become part of long-term memory, which is larger and

---

110. *Id.* at 60; *2019 Third Circuit Task Force Report*, *supra* note 1, at 25. *But see* Elizabeth F. Loftus et al., *supra* note 74, § 2.2, at 12–13 (referring to acquisition, retention, and retrieval); Loftus, *supra* note 67, at 21 (same).

111. *2019 Third Circuit Task Force Report*, *supra* note 1, at 24.

112. *Id.* at 24.

113. Nat'l Rsch. Council, *supra* note 3, at 60.

114. *Id.* at 60.

115. *See, e.g.*, John T. Wixted, *The Psychology and Neuroscience of Forgetting*, 55 Annu. Rev. Psychol. 235, 241–42 (2004).

116. Nat'l Rsch. Council, *supra* note 3, at 61; *2019 Third Circuit Task Force Report*, *supra* note 1, at 25.

117. Nat'l Rsch. Council, *supra* note 3, at 60.

more durable, though not without its limitations, as discussed further later in Section II.B. on storage. The process by which unstable short-term memory becomes (more) stable long-term memory is called "consolidation" because, through it, new memories are not merely stored alongside old ones; they are integrated into the existing network of associations that comprises our long-term memory.[118]

To achieve this integration, the brain undergoes two sets of changes.[119] The first set stabilizes new memory in, and between, the neurons of the hippocampus.[120] This process is called synaptic consolidation and happens in a matter of seconds, minutes, or hours, depending on the kind of memory involved.[121] While the process is ongoing, memories are unstable and susceptible to permanent loss or distortion.[122] In the second set of changes, the brain reallocates responsibility for storing and maintaining new memory to the neocortex.[123] This process is called system consolidation and plays a vital role in optimizing long-term memory storage and retrieval.[124] System consolidation happens while we sleep,[125] and can go on for days, months, or even years.[126]

Scientists believe that memories are especially vulnerable to bias and distortion during encoding and consolidation for a few reasons. As noted, short-term memory has a limited capacity and a rapid rate of decay, and new memories are highly unstable before synaptic consolidation is complete.[127] Because consolidation relies on the same finite resources in the hippocampus

---

118. *See, e.g.*, Yadin Dudai, *The Neurobiology of Consolidations, Or, How Stable Is the Engram?*, 55 Annu. Rev. Psychol. 51 (2004), https://doi.org/10.1146/annurev.psych.55.090902.142050.

119. Yadin Dudai et al., *The Consolidation and Transformation of Memory*, 88 Neuron 20, 20 (2015), http://dx.doi.org/10.1016/j.neuron.2015.09.004; Marcus Vinicius Costa Alves & Orlando Francisco Amodeo Bueno, *Retroactive Interference: Forgetting as an Interruption of Memory Consolidation*, 25 Trends Psychol. 1055, 1060 (2017), https://doi.org/10.9788%2FTP2017.3-07En.

120. *See, e.g.*, Alves & Bueno, *supra* note 119, at 1060.

121. *Id.*; Dudai, *supra* note 118, at 56; Zrinka Sosic-Vasic et al., *When Learning Disturbs Memory: Temporal Profile of Retroactive Interference of Learning on Memory Formation*, Frontiers Psychol., Feb. 16, 2018, https://doi.org/10.3389/fpsyg.2018.00082 ("first 12 min after learning are highly important for memory consolidation").

122. Alves & Bueno, *supra* note 119, at 1060; Dudai, *supra* note 118, at 51.

123. Bueno & Alves, *supra* note 119, at 1060; Dudai, *supra* note 118, at 51; Nat'l Rsch. Council, *supra* note 3, at 61.

124. Dudai et al., *supra* note 119, at 21; Dudai, *supra* note 118, at 55.

125. Björn Rasch & Jan Born, *About Sleep's Role in Memory*, 93 Phys. Rev. 681 (2013), https://doi.org/10.1152/physrev.00032.2012.

126. Bueno & Alves, *supra* note 119, at 1060.

127. Nat'l Rsch. Council, *supra* note 3, at 61.

as other "normal mental activity," what we think, feel, or experience before and after an event may interfere with our ability to form a stable memory of that event, resulting in irrevocable memory loss or distortion.[128] Finally, because consolidation is a selective process that prioritizes certain kinds of information over others, some information may be lost or distorted when the process has run its course. These issues are addressed in turn in the following.

1. *Proactive Interference*

Proactive interference occurs when existing memory interferes with the consolidation of new memory. The hallmark of this kind of encoding error is resistance to new information. It is most likely to occur when the new and existing memory traces concern the same subject.[129] Thus, we may quickly and easily forget a new password right after we reset it. In the laboratory, this phenomenon has been demonstrated in experiments that require subjects to memorize multiple sets of related word pairs. When participants are asked to memorize different pairs involving some of the same words (e.g., knee-bend and knee-bone), they will have more trouble memorizing the second pairing than those who did not have to memorize the initial pairing or whose initial pairing did not overlap with the second pairing.[130]

In extreme cases, proactive interference not only impedes consolidation of new information in working memory; it can also allow old(er) information to intrude on working memory during the encoding process. Scientists believe this sort of intrusion may help explain a specific kind of "unconscious transference" that occurs when an eyewitness misidentifies a bystander as the perpetrator of a crime during an identification procedure.

As discussed further later, "unconscious transference" refers to any situation where an eyewitness mistakenly identifies someone who is familiar but

---

128. Ronald L. Davis & Yi Zhong, *The Biology of Forgetting: A Perspective*, 95 Neuron 490, 492 (2017), https://doi.org/10.1016/j.neuron.2017.05.039.

129. *See, e.g.*, Oliver Kliegl & Karl-Heinz T. Bauml, *Buildup and Release from Proactive Interference: Cognitive and Neural Mechanisms*, 120 Neurosci. & Biobehavioral Rev. 264 (2021), https://doi.org/10.1016/j.neubiorev.2020.10.028.

130. *See, e.g.*, Larry L. Jacoby et al., *Learning to Diminish the Effects of Proactive Interference: Reducing False Memory for Young and Older Adults*, 38 Memory & Cognition 820 (2010), https://doi.org/10.3758/MC.38.6.820; Patricia L. Ebert & Nicole D. Anderson, *Proactive and Retroactive Interference in Young Adults, Healthy Older Adults, and Older Adults with Amnestic Mild Cognitive Impairment*, 15 J. Int'l Neuropsychol. Soc. 83 (2009), https://doi.org/10.1017/S1355617708090115.

innocent.[131] Anecdotal and experimental evidence suggests that the phenomenon is not limited to bystanders and people who are present at the time of encoding.[132] Nevertheless, there is widespread agreement that the presence of such individuals may increase the chances of transference because of how encoding works.[133]

One of the most high-profile examples of this phenomenon involved someone who was not a bystander in the traditional sense. In 1975, an Australian psychologist named Donald Thomson was accused of rape by someone who had seen him give a live address about eyewitness identification on national television.[134] The victim had been watching Thomson's address when she was attacked in her home.[135] During the address, Thomson "described his own face and height to illustrate a point about eyewitness identification, and the rape victim later provided that exact description to the police."[136] A few weeks later, Thomson was visited by the police, having been reported as a possible match.[137] Thomson was eventually cleared of wrongdoing upon confirmation of his alibi that he was giving a televised speech at the exact time of the rape.[138] However, when Thomson initially explained his alibi and insisted that the Deputy Commissioner of the Police and the President of Civil Liberties could confirm it, "the officers sneered 'And I suppose that Jesus Christ was there too!'"[139]

Experiments "strong[ly]" suggest that unconscious transference can occur when a bystander resembles a target more than other lineup choices.[140] In one study, subjects viewed one of two videos of a preschool class,

---

131. *See* Section II.C.2.a.ii; Loftus, *supra* note 67, at 142–43.

132. Loftus, *supra* note 67, at 142–43. *But see* David F. Ross et al., *Unconscious Transference and Mistaken Identity: When a Witness Misidentifies a Familiar but Innocent Person*, 79 J. Applied Psychol. 918 (1994), https://doi.org/10.1037/0021-9010.79.6.918/.

133. Francis A. Gilligan et al., *The Theory of "Unconscious Transference": The Latest Threat to the Shield Laws Protecting the Privacy of Victims of Sex Offenses*, 38 Bos. Coll. L. Rev. 107 (1996).

134. Annelies Vredeveldt & Colin Getty Tredoux, *Composite Communication: How Dissemination of Facial Composites in the Media Affects Police Investigations*, 1 Memory, Mind & Media 1, 8 (2022), https://doi.org/10.1017/mem.2022.4; "Don't Forget to Remember," Sci. Am., Dec. 22, 2003, https://www.scientificamerican.com/article/dont-forget-to-remember/#:~:text=In%20the%20book%20I%20tell,moment%20this%20woman%20was%20raped; Erika Hayaski, "The End of Eyewitness Testimonies," Newsweek.com, Nov. 19, 2014, https://www.newsweek.com/2014/11/28/end-eyewitness-testimonies-285414.html.

135. "Don't Forget to Remember," *supra* note 134.

136. Vredeveldt & Tredoux, *supra* note 134.

137. *Id.*

138. *Id.*

139. *Id.*

140. *Id.* at 923.

which culminated in a surreptitious theft from a teacher's purse.[141] Both videos began with a teacher reading to a group of students. However, to test for transference, the experiment varied this reading teacher's identity. In the control video, the person reading to the students was the female teacher whose belongings were taken. In the "transference" video, a male teacher who "moderately" resembled the eventual thief was reading to the students. After watching the video, subjects attempted to identify the thief in a lineup where either the thief was present (target-present), the male teacher was present (target-absent), or both were present (both present).

When viewing the target-absent lineup, those who saw the male teacher reading (the transference group) were almost three times more likely to misidentify the male teacher as those who did not (the control group).[142] Moreover, most of those who made this error had mistakenly assumed or inferred (despite visual evidence to the contrary), that the thief *was* the male teacher, as soon as they saw him walk into the cafeteria.[143] For this reason, researchers attributed the transference they observed in this experiment to the subjects' "conscious inference" regarding the thief's identity, which both blinded them to the distinguishing aspects of the thief, who had been on screen for the same amount of time as the teacher (thirty-four seconds), and allowed information about the teacher's appearance to be encoded in its place.[144]

Studies suggest that we are more prone to proactive interference as we get older; with each passing year, it gets harder to remember new passwords. This factor is significant insofar as it suggests that older eyewitnesses may be more prone to bystander transference. This topic will be addressed when **age** is discussed in the next chapter regarding **estimator variables.**

---

141. Ross et al., *supra* note 132, at 922.

142. *Id.* The transference group misidentified the male teacher 61 percent of the time. The control group did so only 22 percent of the time. The magnitude of this discrepancy suggests that the transference group was not just thrown off by the male teacher's "moderate" resemblance to the culprit, which would have affected the control group as much as the transference group; rather, the transference group was more inclined to misidentify the teacher because they had seen him earlier in the video.

143. *Id.*

144. *Id.* at 923–24; *see also id.* at 922 (noting the amount of time the perpetrator had been on screen). It is also possible and perhaps even probable that perception and attention were involved, as the expectation of repetition tends to dull one's appreciation for finer detail. *See id.* at 924. Again, this is not to say that transference cannot happen under other circumstances. Those circumstances are discussed further later in the chapter.

2. *Retroactive Interference*

Retroactive interference occurs when what we think, feel, or experience after a perceptual event prevents us from effectively consolidating and remembering the event. It is tied to the serial position effect, whereby we remember the last item in a series better than any other item. Memory is particularly susceptible to interference from shocking, attention-grabbing, stress-inducing stimuli, such as weapons, during encoding.[145] When such stimuli arise, our memories of what preceded them may never be fully consolidated into long-term memory or may contain distortions once consolidated.[146] This vulnerability helps explain how **weapon focus** can prevent us from acquiring visual information about the perpetrator's face in the midst of a stressful encounter, as noted earlier and discussed in more detail in the following chapter.[147]

3. *Selective Encoding and Consolidation*

Like the many cognitive processes underlying perception, memory consolidation is a selective process. "How the brain determines that some information is necessary and should be stored, while others can be discarded, is a fascinating enigma."[148] However, it appears that "[t]he sleeping brain often preferentially consolidates salient (e.g. emotional, novel, rewarding) memories."[149] Powerful emotions like fear and anxiety tend to enhance the encoding process, producing more vivid memories that we hold with greater confidence and a stronger subjective "sense of recollection."[150] Such memories are more strongly encoded because of "stress hormones (glucocorticoids)" that strengthen or "potentiat[e] . . . the neuronal processes underlying memory consolidation and storage."[151]

The notion that stressful, emotional memories tend to be etched more firmly into our brains may seem at odds with the idea that stress and weapon focus can deprive us of visual information about a crime and its perpetrator, but it is not. Although stress may make it easier for us to remember getting robbed at gunpoint, for instance, there is no evidence

145. Nat'l Rsch. Council, *supra* note 3, at 61.
146. *Id.* at 61.
147. *Id.* at 55.
148. Orly Lazarov & Carolyn Hollands, *Hippocampal Neurogenesis: Learning to Remember*, Progress Neurobiol., Feb. 6, 2016, https://doi.org/10.1016/j.pneurobio.2015.12.006.
149. *Id.*
150. Nat'l Rsch. Council, *supra* note 3, at 64–65.
151. *Id.* at 64.

to suggest that it makes us any better at dividing our attention between the gun and the person holding it or at retaining information about that person's appearance once they produce a gun.[152] The relationship between stress, encoding, and subjective confidence is explored further in the next chapter.

B. Storage, Decay, and Active Forgetting

Storage refers to the process by which our brains maintain information encoded in long-term memory.[153] Although long-term memory is larger and more durable than its short-term counterpart, it is nevertheless susceptible to decay and distortion over time.[154] To better understand why, consider the prevailing biological explanation for how and why we remember and forget: the synaptic model of memory.[155]

According to this model, memory operates by means of communication across billions of neurons in the brain.[156] These neurons communicate with each other across synapses, which number in the thousands on any given neuron.[157] Our brains consolidate new perceptual experiences into long-term memory by strengthening synaptic connections between specific neurons to create an interconnected array or circuit of neurons that scientists call a "cell assembly" or "memory engram."[158] In turn, the neurons that make up the engram undergo (sub-)molecular changes that make them more excitable

---

152. *Id.* at 55 ("[I]t is often the case that the attended emotional stimuli are not the ones with relevant informational content."); *id.* at 64 ("Despite the vividness and the sense of reliving that characterizes retrieval of emotional memories, there are many indications that such memories are just as prone to errors. . . . [E]motional memories are often inaccurate in detail."); *see also* Elizabeth A. Phelps & Tali Sharot, *How (and Why) Emotion Enhances the Subjective Sense of Recollection*, 17 Current Directions Psychol. Sci. 147 (2008), https://www.ncbi.nlm.nih.gov/pmc/articles/PMC3051358/ (author's manuscript) ("Emotion boosts memory accuracy to an extent but affects the subjective sense of recollection even more. The result is vivid memories for emotional events that are held with confidence but that may be surprisingly inaccurate in their details.").

153. Nat'l Rsch. Council, *supra* note 3, at 62; *2019 Third Circuit Task Force Report*, *supra* note 1, at 25.

154. Nat'l Rsch. Council, *supra* note 3, at 62.

155. Jesse J. Langille & Richard E. Brown, *The Synaptic Theory of Memory: A Historical Survey and Reconciliation of Recent Opposition*, Frontiers Sys. Neurosci., Oct. 26, 2018, https://www.frontiersin.org/articles/10.3389/fnsys.2018.00052/full.

156. *See, e.g.*, *id.*, at 1; Jeneen Interlandi, *New Estimate Boosts the Human Brain's Memory Capacity 10-Fold*, Sci. Am., Feb. 5, 2016, https://www.scientificamerican.com/article/new-estimate-boosts-the-human-brain-s-memory-capacity-10-fold/.

157. Langille & Brown, *supra* note 155, at 1; Interlandi, *supra* note 156.

158. Langille & Brown, *supra* note 155, at 1.

and easier to activate.[159] These processes, collectively known as long-term potentiation, happen largely while we sleep.[160]

Memory thus consolidated can be retrieved by firing synapses to activate the engram/assembly.[161] In this way, retrieval strengthens the relevant synaptic pathways between the neurons in the engram, thereby preserving and perpetuating access to the memory. However, when pathways go unused, they eventually weaken, causing the associated memories to fade.[162] This process of natural memory decay is one of a few that scientists refer to as "passive forgetting."[163] Moreover, recent research suggests that our brains engage in multiple kinds of "active forgetting" to facilitate future learning, memory acquisition, and emotional regulation.[164] Although scientists are still grappling with the underlying biological mechanisms, a growing body of research suggests that new information prompts us to both remember (by activating new engrams) and forget (by inhibiting old ones).[165]

The bottom line is that we can stave off forgetting by retrieving and rehearsing old memories, but each time we do, we expose them to the possibility of retrieval-related distortion and forgetting, as explained in more detail in the following section. All of this suggests that an eyewitness's "**retention interval**"—the time between the witnessed event and the identification procedure—may be an important indicator of whether or not that person's identification is trustworthy. This topic is explored in the next chapter.

C. Retrieval (and Reconsolidation)

Retrieval refers to the process by which we recall stored memories into consciousness, where they can guide action and decision making.[166] As noted

---

159. *Id.*

160. Jens G. Klinzing et al., *Mechanisms of Systems Memory Consolidation During Sleep*, 22 Nature Neurosci. 1598 (2019).

161. Langille & Brown, *supra* note 155, at 1.

162. Davis & Zhong, *supra* note 128.

163. *Id.* at 492 ("[T]he term passive forgetting has often been used to describe the biological decay of memory traces due to constitutive molecular turnover (natural decay)[.]"). In addition, the term "passive forgetting" has been used to describe certain retrieval errors discussed in the next section, that is, "the incidental accumulation across time of similar memory traces that impede proper retrieval of the wanted one; and changes in the memory's context between acquisition and retrieval that impairs efficient recall." *Id.*

164. *Id.*; Michael C. Anderson & Justin C. Hulbert, *Active Forgetting: Adaptation of Memory by Prefrontal Control*, 72 Annu. Rev. Psychol. 1 (2021), available at https://doi.org/10.1146/annurev-psych-072720-094140.

165. Davis & Zhong, *supra* note 162; Anderson & Hulbert, *supra* note 164.

166. Nat'l Rsch. Council, *supra* note 3, at 65.

earlier, scientists believe that retrieval requires activation of specific engrams or cell assemblies in the neocortex.[167] Retrieval can be triggered by a conscious effort to bring forth a memory that fits specific criteria, or a stream of consciousness that results in inadvertent retrieval, as when thinking about a crime inadvertently leads to remembering the perpetrator.[168]

1. *Eyewitness Identification as a Form of Object Recognition*

a. In General

Eyewitness identification belongs to a specific category of memory retrieval called object recognition, which requires us to compare the qualities of someone or something we see in front of us with the remembered qualities of someone or something we (believe that we) have encountered previously. Viewed in this way, it is easy to see why identifications are so persuasive. Compared to other forms of retrieval, such as trying to draw or describe someone from memory, recognition is very simple: one need only say whether someone is contextually familiar, a simple yes or no question. "Because we often identify familiar individuals with ease, we tend to think we are generally very good at face recognition."[169] And in a certain way we *are* very good at it. "We are better able to distinguish between the differences of faces and their components than between any other kind of objects."[170] We can remember a staggering number of human faces and a staggering amount of information about each face.[171] Indeed, our facial recognition expertise is so profound that an entire region of our brain (the right fusiform face area) has either adapted or evolved to specialize in this task.[172]

However, even setting aside the possibility of errors in perception and encoding, recognition is not nearly as foolproof as we tend to think. Depending on the circumstances, recognition testing (where a subject is asked whether a particular item was included in a list that they were previously asked to study or memorize) can produce more errors than free-response

167. Langille & Brown, *supra* note 155, at 1.

168. *See* Nat'l Rsch. Council, *supra* note 3, at 65.

169. *Id.* at 68–69.

170. Nicole-Simone Werner et al., *The Neuroscience of Face Processing and Identification in Eyewitnesses and Offenders*, Frontiers Behav. Neurosci., Dec. 6, 2013, https://doi.org/10.3389/fnbeh.2013.00189.

171. *Id.*

172. *Id.*; Edwin J. Burns et al., *P-Curving the Fusiform Face Area: Meta-Analyses Support the Expertise Hypothesis*, 104 Neurosci. & Biobehav. Rev. 209 (2019), https://doi.org/10.1016/j.neubiorev.2019.07.003.

testing (where the subject is asked to list items from memory).[173] The fact that a criminal investigation may require the eyewitness to engage in multiple forms of retrieval (e.g., verbal description or image composition) before attempting to recognize the perpetrator only complicates the matter. In addition, even assuming we are facial recognition "experts,"[174] decades of scientific research has shown that our expertise tends to falter when it comes to those with whom we are relatively unfamiliar.[175] Lack of familiarity decreases our ability to recognize a face under different circumstances and viewing conditions.[176] Neuroimaging likewise confirms that unfamiliar faces do not resonate as strongly with the part of our brain that we appear to rely on for facial recognition (the right fusiform face area) as familiar faces.[177] Whether it is because we have richer memories of familiar faces,[178] or because we can process them more holistically than unfamiliar faces,[179] we tend to recognize familiar faces with greater ease and accuracy than unfamiliar faces. Finally, individual recognition ability can vary widely from person to person.[180] All of this suggests that eyewitness identification warrants a great deal more skepticism than the other kinds of recognition we perform effortlessly on a daily basis.

b. Signal Detection Theory

Because eyewitness identification is a form of object recognition, signal detection theory (SDT), the leading theory on how people make diagnostic classification decisions, looms large. SDT supposes that, like any diagnostic classification, eyewitness identification is a kind of hypothesis test. An identification occurs whenever the information presented about someone is enough to convince us to accept the hypothesis that they are the same person

173. *See, e.g.*, Roy Lachman & William H. Field, *Recognition and Recall of Verbal Materials as a Function of Degree of Training*, 2 Psychonomic Sci. 225 (1965).

174. Werner et al., *supra* note 170.

175. Nat'l Rsch. Council, *supra* note 3, at 69.

176. Robert A. Johnston & Andrew J. Edmonds, *Familiar and Unfamiliar Face Recognition: A Review*, 17 Memory 577 (2009), https://doi.org/10.1080/09658210902976969.

177. Katja Weibert & Timothy J. Andrews, *Activity in the Right Fusiform Face Area Predicts the Behavioural Advantage for the Perception of Familiar Faces*, 75 Neuropsychologia 588 (2015), https://doi.org/10.1016/j.neuropsychologia.2015.07.015.

178. *Id.*

179. Sarah Mohr et al., *Early Identity Recognition of Familiar Faces Is Not Dependent on Holistic Processing*, 13 Soc. Cognitive & Affective Neurosci. 1019 (2018), https://doi.org/10.1093/scan/nsy079.

180. Nat'l Rsch. Council, *supra* note 3, at 69.

we saw commit a witnessed crime.[181] Depending on the circumstances, we might need to feel more or less convinced before accepting such a hypothesis—if we are more worried about the consequences of misidentification, we may need more convincing; if we are more worried about the consequences of freeing the guilty party, we may need less.[182] Thus, for any given eyewitness, the likelihood of both correct and mistaken identification depends on two receiver operating characteristics (ROCs): (1) sensitivity to the true perpetrator's defining characteristics, also known as "discriminability," "detectability," or "diagnostic accuracy," and (2) "response bias" or how certain the eyewitness needs to feel in order to make an identification.[183]

From all of this, it is clear that requiring greater certainty (adopting a more conservative response bias) will tend to make people less likely to identify in general, thereby reducing the chances of either correct or false identification.[184] What was less well appreciated until recently is that adopting stricter identification criteria will also increase the *ratio* of correct identifications to false identifications (the diagnosticity ratio).[185] Thus, given a close enough resemblance between the perpetrator and those presented during an identification procedure, being choosier necessarily promotes a kind of accuracy, in the sense that it increases the odds that anyone identified will be the actual perpetrator.[186]

Given this realization, some have suggested that, although conservative response criteria may be desirable given everything at stake in an eyewitness identification, they can be achieved through a variety of methods, including the instructions that precede an identification procedure.[187] Thus, there may be little reason to prefer an identification procedure that promotes accuracy by inducing caution. This topic is addressed in the next chapter, throughout the conversation on **system variables**.

More generally, researchers have pointed to the need for additional or alternative ways of measuring and thinking about eyewitness accuracy—ways that, unlike diagnosticity ratio, cannot be affected by response bias.[188] As an

---

181. *Id.* at 80; THOMAS D. WICKENS, ELEMENTARY SIGNAL DETECTION THEORY 4 (2001), https://doi.org/10.1093/acprof:oso/9780195092509.001.0001.

182. NAT'L RSCH. COUNCIL, *supra* note 3, at 80; *see also* WICKENS, *supra* note 181 at 6–8.

183. NAT'L RSCH. COUNCIL, *supra* note 3, at 80, 84; WICKENS, *supra* note 181 at 10; John T. Wixted & Laura Mickes, *A Signal-Detection-Based Diagnostic-Feature-Detection Model of Eyewitness Identification*, 121 PSYCHOL. REV. 262 (2014), https://doi.org/10.1037/a0035940.

184. NAT'L RSCH. COUNCIL, *supra* note 3, at 82.

185. *Id.*

186. *Id.*; *see also* Wixted & Mickes, *supra* note 183, at 264–65.

187. NAT'L RSCH. COUNCIL, *supra* note 3, at 86; Wixted & Mickes, *supra* note 183, at 266.

188. NAT'L RSCH. COUNCIL, *supra* note 3, at 86; Wixted & Mickes, *supra* note 183, at 266.

alternative, these researchers propose using ROC curves to measure whether different identification procedures actually affect diagnostic accuracy, while removing response bias from the equation.[189] Although such calculations are typically performed for individual test subjects and based on controlled response biases,[190] researchers theorize that it is possible to measure diagnostic accuracy for all of the participants in an experiment at the same time, provided they have given a statement regarding their confidence in any identification made during the experiment.[191] This methodology and its implications are discussed further in the discussion on **system variables** in the next chapter.

2. *Retrieval as a Source of False Memory*

Perhaps the most significant discovery about eyewitness reliability during the last century is that the contents of memory can be affected by the process of retrieving them. Retrieval can distort what we remember or, in extreme cases, give rise to false memories that are indistinguishable from real memories because reactivation may render memory unstable or "labile," as it was at the time of encoding.[192] Reactivated memories eventually restabilize during a reconsolidation process like the consolidation that occurs when a memory is first encoded.[193] However, before that process is complete, reactivated memories are susceptible to the biasing influence of what we think, feel, want, expect, or have learned from other sources, both before and after the events we want to remember.[194]

a. False Memory as a Source of Misidentification

"False memories are far more common than the law imagines, and they can be as vivid and realistic as true memories of actual events."[195] Indeed,

---

189. Nat'l Rsch. Council, *supra* note 3, at 86-87; Wixted & Mickes, *supra* note 171, at 266.

190. Wixted & Mickes, *supra* note 183, at 264, 266.

191. *Id.*; Nat'l Rsch. Council, *supra* note 3, at 86–87. A number of statistical and mathematical assumptions are implicit in this framework. Some of them are listed here. Wickens, *supra* note 181, at 10.

192. Nat'l Rsch. Council, *supra* note 3, at 62, 66; *see also, e.g.*, Maria Carmen Inda et al., *Memory Retrieval and the Passage of Time: From Reconsolidation and Strengthening to Extinction*, 31 J. Neurosci. 1635, 1635 (2011), https://doi.org/10.1523/JNEUROSCI.4736-10.2011.

193. Maria Carmen Inda et al., *supra* note 192.

194. *Id.* Although such plasticity may seem like the ultimate disadvantage where memory is concerned, scientists believe it has evolutionary advantages. *Id.*

195. C. J. Brainerd & Valerie F. Reyna, *Fuzzy-Trace Theory, False Memory, and the Law*, 6 Pol. Insights from Behav. & Brain Sci. 79, 81 (2018), https://doi.org/10.1177/2372732218797143.

as noted further in the accompanying figure, psychologists believe that widespread false memory is to blame for the "Mandela Effect," which happens when a large group of people remembers that something happened or looked a certain way that does not conform to the historical record of the remembered event or object.[196]

The Mandela Effect

The Mandela Effect was given its name by a woman named Fiona Broome, who had a vivid false memory of South African antiapartheid activist turned president Nelson Mandela dying as a political prisoner in the 1980s, despite the fact that he lived until 2013.[197] Ms. Broome coined the term after discovering that there were many others who shared her false belief. Psychologists now suspect that those, like Ms. Broome, who harbor strong false memories regarding Mr. Mandela's death have merely transposed information about the death of another antiapartheid activist named Steve Biko onto their memory of Mr. Mandela's life.[198] At first blush, this phenomenon may seem unrelated to the topic of eyewitness identification, insofar as our ability to recall when Nelson Mandela died (or, for that matter, the name of a popular children's book series . . . sorry to say, it's "Beren*stain* Bears," not "Beren*stein* Bears") depends on a "semantic" memory system that is seemingly distinct from the "episodic" memory system we rely on to remember what people look like.[199] Even so, research suggests that both kinds of memory are susceptible to contamination via the same processes. In this regard, consider that many examples of the Mandela Effect involve misremembered pop-culture iconography like the Fruit of the Loom logo.[200] Although the company does not feature a cornucopia in its logo, many insist that the picture is accurate.

---

196. *See* Rose Goodpasture, *The Mandela Effect: Why Do So Many People Have the Same False Memories?*, CogBlog, Apr. 28, 2022, https://web.colby.edu/cogblog/2022/04/28/the-mandela-effect-how-do-we-all-have-the-same-false-memories/; Deepasri Prasad & Wilma A. Bainbridge, *The Visual Mandela Effect: Evidence for Specific Shared False Memories in Popular Iconography*, 21 J. Vision 2121 (2021), https://doi.org/10.1167/jov.21.9.2121.

197. Goodpasture, *supra* note 196.

198. *Id.*

199. *But see* Daniel L. Greenberg & Mieke Verfaellie, *Interdependence of Episodic and Semantic Memory: Evidence from Neuropsychology*, 16 J. Int'l. Neuropsychol. Soc. 748 (2010), https://doi.org/10.1017/S1355617710000676.

200. Goodpasture, *supra* note 196.

False memory can lead to misidentification in a number of ways. Information gleaned from police, prosecutors, other witnesses, and the media may "intru[de]" on an eyewitness's recollection of a witnessed crime or its perpetrator.[201] "A memory that reflects witnessing person X at location Y on a particular evening might be readily and notably updated by subsequent learning that location Y is the home of a business associate of person X."[202] Likewise, eyewitnesses may "unconsciously smooth over perceptual inconsistencies" related to the perpetrator's appearance that have been created by factors such as lighting and viewing angle.[203]

*i. **Expectation-Related Bias*** Retrieval may further allow stereotype-driven expectations about a perpetrator's appearance to seep into memory. This is so because "people recall stereotype-consistent information better than stereotype-inconsistent information."[204] Recall the series of experiments discussed earlier, wherein, after watching a short video of someone walking out of a building, subjects tended to misattribute stereotypically Black features to him, but only when they had previously learned that he was suspected of a stereotypically Black crime.[205] Another follow-up study showed that these effects could be exacerbated or negated by information about the race and sex of the victim.[206] In this version of the experiment, identifications were most accurate when participants believed they were identifying the suspect of a non-Black crime (serial murder) and when they believed the victim of the Black crime (drive-by shooting) was a Black male.[207] On the other hand, participants tended to exaggerate the stereotypicality of the suspect's features when they believed the victim of the drive-by shooting was white and/or female.[208] Because subjects only received information about the victim after watching the video, they concluded that that "eyewitnesses . . . reconstruct[ed] their original memory of the suspect during the retrieval process to better exemplify their stereotypes about who commits what types of crimes."[209]

---

201. Nat'l Rsch. Council, *supra* note 3, at 66.
202. *Id.* at 62.
203. *Id.* Recall that these factors can cause significant variation in the appearance of a person's physical attributes, including, height, weight, and eye and hair color.
204. Davies et al., *supra* note 75.
205. *See supra* Section I.C.1.a. & nn.71–79.
206. Davies et al., *supra* note 75.
207. *Id.*
208. *Id.*
209. *Id.*

ii. Unconscious Transference Another phenomenon related to false memory that is particularly relevant to eyewitness identifications is unconscious transference. As noted briefly earlier, unconscious transference occurs when an eyewitness mistakenly identifies someone who is familiar but ultimately innocent.[210] The first publicized case involved the robbery of a ticket agent at a train station.[211] In the ensuing lineup, the agent identified a sailor, who was fortunate enough to have an ironclad alibi. When confronted about his apparent misidentification, the ticket agent maintained that he had seen the sailor before, and he had—the sailor was stationed near the railroad station and had bought tickets from the agent a few times before the robbery. Thus, the ticket agent apparently confounded his connection to the sailor when he saw him in the lineup.[212]

In the wake of these high-profile examples, scientists have demonstrated transference in a number of laboratory scenarios. A common thread through the high-profile examples noted above is that the transferred party was lucky enough to have an ironclad and unshakeable alibi. It stands to reason that not everyone has been so lucky and that some of those who have been sent to prison based on poorly corroborated eyewitness testimony in the past can attribute their misfortune to transference. Transference is an important concept—one that demands urgent policy consideration—not simply because it helps to explain how those who are simply familiar to an eyewitness might end up accused of a crime, but also because it helps to explain why police should not expose an eyewitness to the image of a suspect before an identification procedure, if that procedure is to be considered reliable or to retain any of its purported probative value. This issue will be taken up at length in the upcoming chapter.

b. Theories of False Memory

Of course, knowing that such distortions are possible only gets us so far. From a forensic or legal perspective, the real question is whether there are circumstances that make such distortions more or less likely to occur, as the existence or absence of these circumstances would have a natural tendency to bear on the reliability of specific identifications. To begin with, research suggests that "[r]econsolidation . . . is more likely to occur when"

210. Loftus, *supra* note 67, at 142.
211. *Id.*
212. *Id.*

we are confronted with new information about a remembered event that has strong behavioral implications.[213] New information about the perpetrator of a crime would seem to fit this criterion very well. To understand the other circumstances that influence the likelihood of retrieval-related distortion, consider two generally accepted scientific explanations for false memory, the source monitoring framework (SMF) and fuzzy-trace theory (FTT).[214]

*i. **Source Monitoring Framework*** The source monitoring framework (SMF) proceeds from the understanding that memory encoding and retrieval are both constructive processes where thoughts, expectations, and inferences about our observations can be brought to bear.[215] SMF proposes that, at least on some level, false memories begin with a breakdown in source monitoring: the process we use to attribute remembered information to a source.[216] Source monitoring is how we tell the difference between real and imagined events (whether you remembered to set an alarm or only thought about doing so) and also how we distinguish what we observed personally from what we only heard about after the fact.[217]

As it relates to false memory, the core insights of the SMF are twofold. The first is that source monitoring is inherently inferential. Unlike the files on a computer, the kernels of information that make up memory are not tagged with "metadata" at the time of encoding that would enable our brains to say where, when, and how they were encoded.[218] Thus, we must rely on our memory of context clues capable of shedding light on this question. Such circumstances naturally include sensory information from the encoding event—for example, the sound of someone's voice as they relayed the target information. However, such information is not always available, and where it is not, we cannot help but draw inferences from other, less reliable information.

---

213. Dudai et al., *supra* note 119, at 21.

214. *See* C.J. Brainerd & Valerie F. Reyna, *Fuzzy-Trace Theory, False Memory, and the Law*, 6 Pol'y. Insights from Behav. & Brain Sci. 79, 79 (2018), https://doi.org/10.1177/2372732218797143 (noting the general acceptance of fuzzy-trace theory).

215. Karen J. Mitchell & Marcia K. Johnson, *Source Monitoring 15 Years Later: What Have We Learned From FMRI About the Neural Mechanisms of Source Memory?*, 135 Psychol. Bull. 638 (2009), https://doi.org/10.1037/a0015849.

216. D. Steven Lindsay & Marcia K. Johnson, *False Memories and the Source Monitoring Framework: Reply to Reyna and Lloyd (1997)*, 12 Learning & Individual Differences 145, 146 (2000), https://doi.org/10.1016/S1041-6080(01)00035-8.

217. *Id.*

218. *Id.* at 146–47.

The second insight from the SMF is that most source monitoring happens unconsciously.[219] Just as we instantaneously attribute sensory information (like a voice) to a source (the speaker) when we perceive it in real time, so too might we make instantaneous hindsight judgments about the nature and origin of information stored in memory. Accordingly, false memory arises when we make one of these instantaneous judgments incorrectly. This is most likely to occur when the circumstances used to attribute the memory to a source are ambiguous (in that they suggest more than one possible source) or misleading (in that they suggest the wrong source), or when the circumstances of retrieval either "discourage[] careful source monitoring" or encourage reliance on circumstances that do not reliably shed light on the source.[220]

All of this suggests that police must use great caution in their attempts to elicit information from eyewitnesses, lest they suggest information or "discourage[] careful source monitoring."[221] It further supports that unstructured, private reflection and memory rehearsal can allow memory distortions and false memories to creep in. This topic is discussed further in the discussion of **leading questions** in the next chapter on **system variables.** In this regard, the **retention interval** (how long after the event an attempt at retrieval is made) is a matter of great concern. This topic is also discussed in the next chapter.

ii. Fuzzy-Trace Theory According to the fuzzy-trace theory (FTT), false memories are attributable, not simply to a breakdown in source monitoring, but rather (or also) to overreliance on a specific kind of memory that facilitates distortion. The FTT proceeds from the revelation that perceptions are simultaneously encoded at high and low levels of specificity, resulting in two separate memory "traces": a "verbatim trace" that captures "precise . . . representations" of what we perceive, and a "gist trace" that captures "vague,

219. *Id.* at 147.

220. *Id.* In this regard, consider just how often people misattribute jokes and anecdotes, when attempting to retell them in a social setting. Did you hear that story on a podcast or read it in a magazine? If directly called upon to name a source, you may realize you cannot, but less considered reflection may lead you through a series of subconscious inferences that results in false attribution to a plausible source—whoever was around or whatever was in front of you when you think you learned the joke or story. Perhaps, the best we can do is hope that we that we do not end up telling other people the stories and jokes they told us too often.

221. *Id.*

meaning-based . . . representations."[222] Thus, the person who sees a Coke bottle on the breakfast table, can immediately recall it as "a Coke bottle on the breakfast table" and "a soft drink in the kitchen."[223]

The retrieval process yields a mix of gist and verbatim information, with the precise ratio depending on how well each trace is remembered and recalled.[224] Importantly, while verbatim traces can help us reject suggestive postevent information, gist traces often do not. In the example, a person's memory of "a soft drink in the kitchen" could support both the accurate recollection that there was "a Coke bottle on the breakfast table" and the false memory that there was a "Pepsi can on the kitchen counter."[225] Thus, if "Pepsi can/kitchen counter" is suggested in some later encounter, the gist trace will not help the observer to rule it out. Likewise, when the gist is combined with the knowledge that the homeowner prefers Pepsi to Coke or cans to bottles, it could also lead to a false "Pepsi" or "can" memory. Hence, the observer's susceptibility to a false "Pepsi can/kitchen counter" memory depends on the degree to which retrieval yields the verbatim "Coke bottle/ breakfast table" trace.

The gist-dependent false memory process can undermine the reliability of an eyewitness identification because, as discussed in the section on categorical perception, *see supra* Section I.C.1., each person is simultaneously encoded into memory with precision and as a series of categorical judgments or "gists" about their appearance and defining traits.[226] To be sure, such judgments include categorizing people by race and sex.[227] In this way, the FTT helps explain the **cross-race effect**, whereby people are less accurate when it comes to recognizing members of a different race. However, such judgments go beyond race and sex, and apply to every quality or trait one might notice. A witness trying to identify a perpetrator based on the

---

222. Valerie F. Reyna et al., *How Fuzzy-Trace Theory Predicts True and False Memories for Words, Sentences, and Narratives*, 5 J. Appl. Res. Memory & Cognition 1 (2016), https://doi.org/10.1016/j.jarmac.2015.12.003. Scientists used to believe that gist memory was simply a byproduct of the cognitive processing that happens after perceptual information has been encoded—in other words, that we couldn't decide what something meant until after we perceived and encoded it. At least to some certain degree, gist and verbatim memory exist independently of one another. People can store the gist of the events after processing only a fraction of the details.

223. C.J. Brainerd & Valerie F. Reyna, *supra* note 214, at 79, 81.

224. *Id.*

225. *Id.*

226. *Id.* at 83.

227. *Id.*

perpetrator's "striking blue eyes" may need to contend with the fact that they remember the gist (that the eyes were "striking" and "blue") better than the eyes themselves.[228]

Moreover, the FTT has shed light on some of the circumstances that promote gist-dependent false memories. Studies suggest that one's ability to recall the verbatim trace may depend on how retrieval is initiated. Retrieval attempts that focus more on the meaning and feeling (like counseling sessions) are less conducive to verbatim trace retrieval. In addition, our susceptibility to gist-dependent false memory may also depend on the **retention interval.** "[V]erbatim memories fade more rapidly than gist."[229] Thus, we become more prone to false memory as time goes on. The FTT may further help explain **age**-related differences in memory, insofar as small children may be less adept at using verbatim traces to filter out misinformation and the elderly tend to rely on more heuristic-based retrieval processes that lend themselves to gist.[230] Both of these factors will be discussed in greater detail in the next chapter.

3. *Retrieval Cues, Retrieval Environment, and State-Dependent Memory*

The success or failure of retrieval—whether it brings the target memory into consciousness—may depend on the effectiveness of a retrieval cue.[231] Retrieval cues facilitate remembering by virtue of a link between the cue and the target memory that is established at the time of encoding.[232] In the context of eyewitness identification procedures, such cues include the aspects of the suspect's likeness and, perhaps, their voice and mannerisms, if the suspect is being presented as part of a live or videotaped lineup.

The environment itself may also serve as a cue to enhance retrieval.[233] Studies show that retrieval tends to work better when an observer's mood

228. *See id.*

229. *Id.* at 81.

230. *See id.*; Deborah Davis & Elizabeth F. Loftus, *Age and Functioning in the Legal System: Perception Memory and Judgment in Victims, Witnesses and Jurors*, *in* HANDBOOK OF HUMAN FACTORS IN LITIGATION 11–22 (Y. Ian Noy & Waldemar Karwowski eds. 2005).

231. *See, e.g.*, Rebecca L. Wheeler & Fiona Gabbert, *Using Self-Generated Cues to Facilitate Recall: A Narrative Review*, FRONTIERS PSYCHOL., Oct. 27, 2017, https://doi.org/10.3389/fpsyg.2017.01830.

232. *Id.*

233. *Id.*

or setting approximates that which existed at the time of encoding.[234] Moreover, studies have shown that the memory boost we get from reinstating the context of encoding can be achieved by having a witness imagine aspects of the encoding environment, like the "layout of the scene, the weather, the people and objects that were nearby," as well as the witness's "thoughts, feelings, and reactions."[235] This technique is called mental reinstatement, and it has shown some promise for improving performance on certain recognition tasks. For instance, in one experiment, a group of store clerks was better at picking past customers out of a lineup when they were directed to mentally "reconstruct [each] customer's face and . . . transaction," and given a physical cue, that is, "a piece of non-picture identification from the customer."[236] In another experiment, those who viewed a video of an armed robbery were better able to remember "what the robber looked like" if they "mentally reinstate[d] the encoding context . . . of [the] video," including "the surrounding environment and [their] thoughts/feelings at the time."[237] Participants in a third experiment "were more likely to correctly identify the culprit from a crime video when participants both encoded and retrieved in the same room."[238]

Such findings suggest that there may be some advantage to the fact that show-ups and field views occur at the scene of the crime and raise questions as to whether police should be pursuing reinstatement of context (mental or physical) to enhance eyewitness memory more often. These questions will be taken up at length in the upcoming chapter regarding system variables. However, a significant body of research suggests that the negative emotions that may accompany reinstatement of the eyewitness context are sufficient to neutralize any memory enhancement.[239] For example, in one experiment,

234. Nat'l Rsch. Council, *supra* note 3, at 65–66, 84. Similar relationships have been observed with respect to intoxication and other altered states of consciousness. *Id.* at 84.

235. Wheeler & Gabbert, *supra* note 231.

236. Ryan C. Yeung et al., *The Influence of Social Anxiety Provoking Contexts on Context Reinstatement Effects*, 74 Q. J. Experimental Psychol. 1170, 1170 (2021), https://doi.org/10.1177/1747021821998489 (citing Carol Krafka & Steven Penrod, *Reinstatement of Context in a Field Experiment on Eyewitness Identification*, 49 J. Personality & Soc. Psychol. 58 (1985), https://doi.org/10.1037/0022-3514.49.1.58).

237. *Id.* (citing Laura Hammond et al., *Facilitating Eyewitness Memory in Adults and Children with Context Reinstatement and Focused Meditation*, 3 J. Investigative Psychol. & Offender Profiling 117 (2006), https://doi.org/10.1002/jip.47).

238. *Id.* (citing Carol K. Wong & J. Don Read, *Positive and Negative Effects of Physical Context Reinstatement on Eyewitness Recall and Identification*, 25 Appl. Cognitive Psychol. 2 (2011), https://doi.org/10.1002/acp.1605).

239. *Id.* at 1171.

where subjects viewed a slideshow of a cyclist's encounter with a pick-up truck that ended either neutrally (with the cyclist passing unharmed) or gruesomely (with the cyclist bleeding on the ground in front of the truck), mental reinstatement only enhanced recall for those who saw the neutral ending.[240] Likewise, although context reinstatement seems to improve recognition of unfamiliar faces, this effect is cancelled out where the encoding context is one that produces stress, anxiety, or other negative emotions.[241] Such emotions tend to undermine retrieval, regardless of whether they accompany encoding or arise as a result of context reinstatement.

These findings have led scientists to theorize that, in addition to generally undermining retrieval, *see infra* Section II.C.4, negative emotions may also interfere with the brain's ability to bind target stimuli, such as faces, to a surrounding context during encoding.[242] Regardless of the explanation, there is little reason to believe that reinstatement would enhance recall for all or even most eyewitnesses. Rather, it seems more likely that a specific subset—perhaps, bystanders far removed from any danger—may benefit from targeted reinstatement of context—that is, evoking that which is unlikely to reignite any negative emotions that may have been experienced.

4. *Retrieval Interference*

Just as certain factors tend to enhance retrieval, others tend to hinder or interfere with it. In the realm of eyewitness identification, two sources of retrieval interference are particularly salient. The first involves "motivated forgetting," which occurs when "memories . . . threaten a positive self-image, run counter to strongly-held beliefs or attitudes, or evoke sadness, guilt, or embarrassment," as may happen when someone suddenly and unexpectedly becomes the victim of a crime.[243] Confronted by the specter of such memories and the emotions they could cause, we may try to suppress them, consciously or unconsciously.

A second kind of retrieval interference involves retrieval-induced forgetting, which occurs when partial retrieval of a memory leads us to forget

240. *Id.* (citing Jeffrey M. Brown, *Eyewitness Memory for Arousing Events: Putting Things into Context*, 17 APPL. COGNITIVE PSYCHOL. 93 (2003), https://doi.org/10.1002/acp.848).

241. *Id.* (citing Natascha Rainis, *Semantic Contexts and Face Recognition*, 15 APPL. COGNITIVE PSYCHOL. 173 (2001), https://doi.org/10.1002/1099-0720(200103/04)15:2<173::AID-ACP695>3.0.CO;2-Q); *id.* at 1181–83.

242. *Id.* at 1181.

243. Davis & Zhong, *supra* note 128.

the part that has not been retrieved.[244] This effect has been demonstrated in a variety of experiments. In one, subjects were presented with a slide show designed to simulate the search for a missing wallet through the bedroom where it was last seen.[245] The bedroom contained, among other items, eight different sweatshirts and eight different textbooks. After viewing the slide show, the experimental group answered a series of true/false questions about half of the sweatshirts or half of the textbooks, while the control group engaged in a series of distraction tasks. Finally, both groups were asked to name as many of the sweatshirts and textbooks as they could. In the end, postevent interrogation enhanced recall of items that were asked about but undermined recall of those that were not. Such experiments suggest that closed-ended questions regarding what a perpetrator looked like may hinder future recall of features about which there is no inquiry.

Unlike encoding interference, which is thought to promote permanent memory loss due to the instability of unconsolidated memory, retrieval interference need not be permanent and can be reversed by reactivating the blocked memory.[246] Nevertheless, retrieval interference warrants serious concern in the eyewitness identification context for two reasons. The first is that memories are more susceptible to long-term decay when we do not access them. Thus, retrieval interference may facilitate long-term, permanent forgetting, even if it need not result in short-term permanent forgetting in the same way, or to the same degree, as encoding interference.

The second cause for concern raised by retrieval interference is that we do not know precisely how long it takes for an eyewitness memory consolidate or the degree to which consolidation and retrieval can overlap for a given memory. Thus, scientists have suggested that retrieval interference in the immediate aftermath of an event could in fact be a source of disruption for memory encoding that leads to permanent memory loss. All of this underscores the need for police to use interview strategies that avoid closed-ended questions when attempting to elicit a suspect description. This topic will be taken up further in the next chapter.

---

244. John S. Shaw et al., *Retrieval-Induced Forgetting in an Eyewitness-Memory Paradigm*, 2 PSYCHONOMIC BULL. & REV. 249 (1995).

245. *Id.*

246. Davis & Zhong, *supra* note 128, at 492.

III. Conclusion

To sum up, perception and memory are not merely a lens and an archive. The human eye does not create a "point-by-point" record of the light that strikes it, like a camera.[247] Rather, it "contains sophisticated retinal circuitry that decomposes the retinal image into signals representing contrast and movement,"[248] resulting in visual information that is uneven, incomplete, and "noisy," and subject to the whim of our selective attention.[249] Our brains compensate for gaps in what we sense by making educated guesses about the characteristics of the objects in our field of vision. For this reason, our perception "is commonly influenced as much by expectations from prior experience with the world as it is by the precise patterns of light cast upon the retina."[250]

Likewise, human memory bears little resemblance to a brick-and-mortar library, with a selection of different media sitting on shelves waiting to be checked out, returned, or augmented by the addition of new titles. Nor can it be compared to a computer hard drive that is constantly being accessed, rewritten, and reorganized to make room for new information. Computer files are programmed to maintain their integrity until overwritten and have metadata to indicate where and when they originated. Neither of those things is true of our memories, which can seamlessly incorporate new information, each time they are retrieved. Our memory is a dynamic ecosystem of information, rather than an archive in the traditional sense.

247. Charles D. Gilbert, *The Constructive Nature of Visual Processing*, at 1, in PRINCIPLES OF NEURAL SCIENCE (5th ed. 2014), https://neurology.mhmedical.com/content.aspx?bookid=1049&sectionid=59138653.

248. Gilbert, *Intermediate-Level Visual Processing and Visual Primitives*, *supra* note 8.

249. Stewart et al., *supra* note 12.

250. NAT'L RSCH. COUNCIL, *supra* note 3, at 46.

6
On the Validity of System and Estimator Variables

In the decades since *Manson*, researchers have conducted "over 2000 scientific studies . . . on the reliability of eyewitness identifications."[1] This research, in turn, has "identifie[d] principled and insurmountable limits of vision and memory that inevitably affect eyewitness accounts[] [and] bear on conclusions regarding accuracy,"[2] while "provid[ing] new insights into the fallibility of eyewitness identifications."[3] As a result of this research, experts have identified certain system and estimator variables that are likely to impact the reliability of an eyewitness identification. The term "system variable" refers to those determinants of eyewitness reliability that lie within the control of law enforcement and include the use of various safeguards against the risk of undue suggestion in the administration of identification procedures. The term "estimator variable" refers to those determinants of

1. *Dennis v. Sec'y, Pa. Dep't of Corr.*, 834 F.3d 263, 335 (3d Cir. 2016) (McKee, C.J., concurring); *see also, e.g.*, *State v. Lawson*, 291 P.3d 673, 685 (Or. 2012) ("Since 1979 . . . there have been more than 2,000 scientific studies conducted on the reliability of eyewitness identification.").

2. Nat'l Rsch. Council of the Nat'l Acads., Identifying the Culprit: Assessing Eyewitness Identification xiii (2014) [hereinafter Nat'l Rsch. Council].

3. *State v. Mahmoud*, 147 A.3d 833, 837–38 (Me. 2016).

eyewitness reliability that are not entirely within law enforcement control, for example, how much time passed before the identification occurred, how long the eyewitness was able to see the perpetrator, and whether or not they belong to the same racial or ethnic group. What follows is a brief explanation of why these generally accepted system and estimator variables warrant the consideration of a judge or jury whenever the reliability of an eyewitness identification is in question.

I. Preliminary Objections

A. (Why) Should We Trust Mock-Witness Studies?

Before proceeding any further, it is worth addressing two preliminary objections to the use of system and estimator variables that have been recycled many times since they were uttered in response to Münsterberg at the turn of the twentieth century. The first of these criticisms, advanced by Charles C. Moore, among many others, concerns the use of "class room" experiments involving mock eyewitnesses to mock crimes to assess the reliability of an actual eyewitness to an actual crime.[4] Criticisms of experimental eyewitness identification research tends to focus on a few perceived shortcomings, including (1) the use of stimuli (such as video recordings of staged crimes) that do not replicate the stress of witnessing an actual crime, (2) the use of college-student eyewitnesses who do not reflect a fair cross-section of the population, and (3) the inability to replicate the effect of knowing that someone's liberty or life is at stake during an identification procedure.[5]

These criticisms raise questions of "ecological" and "external" validity—how closely a study mirrors real-world circumstances and how well its findings apply to the outside world—that have been capably addressed elsewhere by experts who are better qualified to do so.[6] This book will not

4. Charles C. Moore, *Yellow Psychology*, 11 LAW NOTES 125, 125 (1907).

5. *See* Gary L. Wells, *Applied Eyewitness-Testimony Research: System Variables and Estimator Variables*, 36 J. PERSONALITY & SOC. PYSCHOL. 1546, 1551 (1978); Gary L. Wells et al., *Eyewitness Evidence: Improving Its Probative Value*, 7 PSYCHOL. SCI. PUB. INT. 45, 50 (2006). Another issue raised by Wells involved the failure to replicate the "self-selection" that occurs when someone identifies themself to police as an eyewitness. Wells, *Applied Eyewitness-Testimony Research*, *supra*, at 1551. He worried that the absence of this "self-selection" in experimentation would make mock witnesses appear less accurate than actual eyewitnesses, insofar as actual eyewitnesses could be said to uniformly believe in their own ability to make an identification before attempting one. *Id.* Psychological experiments seem to have accounted for this difficulty by having mock eyewitnesses declare their level of confidence in the identifications they make and controlling for that confidence when they attempt to interpret their results.

6. *See, e.g.*, RESEARCH METHODS IN FORENSIC PSYCHOLOGY (Barry Rosenfeld & Steven D. Penrod eds., 2011); Roy S. Malpass & Patricia G. Devine, *Realism and Eyewitness Identification*, 4 L. & HUM. BEHAV. 347 (1981).

attempt to replicate that work. At the same time, two basic responses to this line of criticism are worth noting. The first is that not everything that serves to make a study less realistic also serves to undermine its applicability to the real world. Notably, there are good reasons to believe that the factors above need not substantially detract from the real-world applicability of system and estimator variable research. First, as discussed in the previous chapter and much more later in this chapter, there is little reason to believe that stress promotes more accurate identifications and much reason to believe that the opposite is true. And insofar as scientists need to induce stress for an experiment (for instance, to study the effect of stress on the accuracy of identifications), they have ways of doing so (staging a crime for participants to witness). Second, "college students [tend to be] less suggestible and more accurate . . . relative to the general population."[7] As such, eyewitness identification research might paint a rosier picture of eyewitness reliability than is warranted.[8] Third, although knowing that someone might lose liberty or life might lead to more careful identifications, archival data from real cases confirm that eyewitnesses make mistakes in the real world that can be explained at least in part by system and estimator variables.

The second response is that, in drawing conclusions about what tends to influence the reliability and accuracy of eyewitness identifications, psychologists are loathe to extrapolate from a single experiment and may not be satisfied with a meta-analysis of multiple studies. Rather, to verify the findings of the experiments they conduct, psychologists use multiple experimental designs, field research, and archival data from real cases.[9] It is "[o]nly when [psychologists] have converging results from . . . diverse methods of inquiry [that they] feel confident in generalizing to the forensic context, where any such assertions may have serious ramifications."[10]

B. (Why) Are System and Estimator Variables Sufficiently Precise to Warrant the Attention of Judges and Juries?

The second objection can be traced back to Wigmore, and relates to the utility of eyewitness research given its tendency to produce only general

7. Wells et al., *supra* note 5, at 50.

8. *Id.*

9. *See, e.g.*, Gary Wells & Steven D. Penrod, *Eyewitness Identification: Strengths and Weaknesses of Alternative Methods*, *in* Research Methods in Forensic Psychology (Barry Rosenfeld & Steven D. Penrod eds., 2011).

10. John C. Yuille et al., *Eyewitness Memory of Police Trainees for Realistic Role Plays*, 79 J. Appl. Psychol. 931, 945–46 (1994).

statements about the likelihood of accuracy. Recall that although Professor Gary Wells codified the system/estimator variable distinction in 1978,[11] the quest to identify those determinants of eyewitness reliability that are susceptible to independent observation and measurement began much earlier. As discussed in Chapter 4, at the turn of the twentieth century, the psychologist Louis William Stern hypothesized that characteristics such as age, sex, intelligence, and education might better predict eyewitness accuracy than an eyewitness's certainty about the memory in question.[12] Stern's attempt to use this information to "construct a scale on which to rank individuals according to their reliability"[13] drew strong criticism from the likes of Wigmore, who believed that such a scale could not be of any real use to a factfinder in court since it could not yield a *definitive* answer to the question whether a specific witness's testimony or identification was accurate.[14] Rather, because perception and memory are fairly unpredictable, it could at best enable general statements about the likelihood of accuracy.

So, was Wigmore right? Is psychology too imprecise to be useful in the context of an admissibility determination or a jury's deliberations? Is the value of injecting more of it into the various processes of criminal adjudication too marginal to justify the cost of prolonging those processes (by adding expert witness testimony and/or lengthening jury instructions) in order to do so? While some have argued "yes,"[15] the answer should be "no" for a couple of reasons.

---

11. *See* Wells, *Applied Eyewitness-Testimony Research*, *supra* note 5, at 1546, 1548.

12. Matthew Hale, Jr., Human Science and Social Order: Hugo Münsterberg and the Origins of Applied Psychology 113 (1980).

13. *Id.*

14. John H. Wigmore, *Professor Muensterberg and the Psychology of Testimony: Being a Report of the Case of Cokestone v. Muensterberg*, 3 Ill. L. Rev. 399, 421–23 (1909); *see also* James M. Doyle, True Witness: Cops Courts, Science, and the Battle Against Misidentification 29 (2005); *Young v. State*, 374 P.3d 395, 417 (Alaska 2016) ("[W]e recognize that the science of eyewitness identifications is 'probabilistic'; it cannot say for certain whether any particular identification is accurate but rather identifies the variables that are relevant to evaluating the risk of a misidentification."); *State v. Lawson*, 291 P.3d 673, 685 (Or. 2012) ("We recognize that the scientific research is 'probabilistic'—meaning that it cannot demonstrate that any specific witness is right or wrong, reliable or unreliable, in his or her identification."); *State v. Henderson*, 27 A.3d 872, 894 (2011) ("[E]yewitness identification research remains probabilistic, meaning that science cannot say whether an identification in an actual case is accurate or not. Instead, science has sought to answer, in the aggregate, which identification procedures and external variables are tied to an increased risk of misidentification.").

15. *See, e.g.*, Hon. D. Duff McKee, *Challenge to Eyewitness Identification Through Expert Testimony*, 35 Am. Jur. Proof of Facts 3rd § 13 (Dec. 2023 update) ("The difficulty is that there is no practical way for any expert to assess the accuracy or credibility of the eyewitness account of any specific witness, and no way to equate the specific eyewitness' specific recollections against the expert's general evaluation and the factors surrounding it.").

To begin with, Wigmorean skepticism about the utility of psychology, given humanity's inherent unpredictability, tends to fall away when the topic of inquiry shifts from the question whether eyewitness memory can be trusted to the question of which punishments and pretrial restraints will best promote public safety. We live in a society where judicial determinations regarding confinement routinely rely on probabilistic risk assessment, which Wigmore helped bring about. Indeed, he concluded his attack on Münsterberg by chastising the legal profession (via the aptly named "Judge Wiseman") for failing to take a more interdisciplinary approach to "the Prevention of Crime," when "sociology, anthropology, psychology," and "the modern science of Criminology" had so much to offer.[16] Although Wigmore took as a given that these disciplines had more to teach lawyers about crime prevention than it had to teach them about witness credibility, it is not clear why this should be true, given that most criminal judges spend as much time assessing incorrigibility as they spend determining eyewitness reliability. Ultimately, there is no reason to think that psychology will be any more helpful in determining whether someone is likely to reoffend or endanger society than it is in determining whether an eyewitness has told the truth. Both inquiries involve traits and behaviors that cannot be predicted with absolute certainty.

Moreover, Wigmore's critique sets the bar for "helpfulness" too high. In criminal trials, psychology's helpfulness to the factfinder does not depend on its ability to establish *definitively* that a specific identification is false. Rather, because the prosecution retains the burden to prove identity beyond a reasonable doubt throughout a trial, it suffices for psychology to supply the jury with (nonspeculative) reason(s) to doubt the accuracy of an identification.[17] Nor, for that matter, does any judicial determination of inadmissibility depend on *definitive* proof that an identification is mistaken. Rather, even under *Manson*, it suffices that the "likelihood of irreparable misidentification" is "very substantial."[18] Without question, psychology can illuminate such inquiries. As Wells keenly observed in 1978, general statements about the likelihood of eyewitness accuracy add value in a judicial system, insofar as we have reason to believe that judges and jurors are apt

16. Wigmore, *supra* note 14, 433.

17. *Victor v. Nebraska*, 511 US 1, 19–20 (1994); *In re Winship*, 397 U. S. 358, 364 (1970); *Jackson v. Virginia*, 443 U. S. 307, 315–316 (1979).

18. *Manson v. Brathwaite*, 432 U.S. 98, 135 (1977) (internal quotation marks omitted).

to trust eyewitness identifications too much or for the wrong reasons—we do, so it does.[19]

II. System Variables

System variables are circumstances within the control of law enforcement that have some impact on the accuracy of an identification and the reliability of the process used to obtain it.[20] "There is substantial agreement that a number of system variables can affect the reliability of identifications."[21] Recent research underscores the importance of system variables as a framework for understanding suggestive police practices. The "pristine conditions" hypothesis predicts that "high confidence suspect identifications will almost invariably be very accurate, even if viewing conditions (i.e., estimator variables) are poor," so long as the identification procedure itself is conducted under "pristine conditions." Pristine conditions include five of the system variables discussed in the following sections:

1. The use of a double-blind or blinded lineup
2. Appropriate pre-lineup instructions
3. No suggestion that the perpetrator is included, including only one suspect per procedure, ensuring the suspect does not "stand out"
4. Ensuring that fillers are not "duds" who look unlike the perpetrator
5. Using a blind administrator to obtain a witness's statement of confidence immediately after the identification decision prior to the witness receiving any verbal or nonverbal feedback about their identification[22]

As explained further below, there is scientific consensus that each of these factors bear heavily on the reliability of an identification.

---

19. *See* Gary L. Wells, *Applied Eyewitness-Testimony Research, supra* note 5, at 1551; *see also Lawson*, 291 P.3d at 685 ("[W]e believe that it is imperative that law enforcement, the bench, and the bar be informed of the existence of current scientific research and literature regarding the reliability of eyewitness identification because, as an evidentiary matter, the reliability of eyewitness identification is central to a criminal justice system dedicated to the dual principles of accountability and fairness."). This insight is consistent with widespread recognition that "scientific certainty" is not actually a helpful concept or a pre-requisite to admissibility in the context of expert opinion evidence. *See* Danielle Weiss Gerald LaPorte, *Uncertainty Ahead: A Shift in How Federal Scientific Experts Can Testify*, Nat'l Institute Just. J., Apr. 2018, https://www.ojp.gov/pdffiles1/nij/250699.pdf.

20. *2019 Report of the United States Court of Appeals for the Third Circuit Task Force on Eyewitness Identifications*, 92 Temp. L. Rev. 1, 54–55 & nn.278–80 (2019) [hereinafter *2019 Third Circuit Task Force Report*].

21. *Id.*

22. *Id.*

A. Blind Administration

To ascertain the reliability of an identification, judges and juries should first consider whether and to what degree administration of the underlying procedure was blind. There is widespread agreement that wherever feasible, lineups and photo-arrays should be presented in "double blind" fashion—by an administrator with no connection to the case and no knowledge of what the suspect looks like—to minimize the risk of administrator influence.[23] Where double-blind administration is not feasible (for instance, because a smaller department cannot spare the manpower), administrators should "blind" themselves to the suspect's location in the lineup.[24] For simultaneous lineups, this can be accomplished by using a computer to randomize the order of the lineup and a physical barrier, such as a wall or a screen, to block the administrator's view of the lineup.[25] Alternatively, administrators can utilize blinded sequential presentation, whereby photographs are placed into separate folders, shuffled, and handed to the witness one by one, so that the folder blocks the administrator's view.[26]

Such blind administration serves three equally important purposes. First, it prevents the administrator from communicating the location of the suspect in the lineup or array, which may happen verbally, nonverbally, consciously, and/or subconsciously if administration is not blind.[27] In past experiments, nonblind administrators have proven themselves "more likely to tell the witness to examine the lineup carefully, to take another look at the lineup after the witness failed to make an identification, and to remove a picture from consideration slowly if the witness rejected it as the suspect than were double-blind administrators."[28] Nonblind "administrators sometimes even told the witnesses that they knew

---

23. Memorandum from Sally Yates, Deputy Attorney General, to Heads of Department Law Enforcement Components, All Department Prosecutors 140, § 5.1 at 2 (Jan. 6, 2017), https://www.justice.gov/file/923201/download [hereinafter Yates Memo]; *2019 Third Circuit Task Force Report*, *supra* note 20, at 13, 22; Nat'l Rsch. Council, *supra* note 2, at 106.

24. Yates Memo, *supra* note 23, § 5.2 at 3.

25. *Id.*, § 5.3 at 3.

26. Police Exec. Rsch. F., A National Survey of Eyewitness Identification Procedures in Law Enforcement Agencies (2013), [hereinafter PERF Survey], https://www.policeforum.org/assets/docs/Free_Online_Documents/Eyewitness_Identification/a%20national%20survey%20of%20eyewitness%20identification%20procedures%20in%20law%20enforcement%20agencies%202013.pdf.; Yates Memo, *supra* note 23, § 5.3 at 3; Nat'l Rsch. Council, *supra* note 2, at 27.

27. Margaret Bull Kovera & Andrew J. Evelo, *Improving Eyewitness-Identification Evidence Through Double-Blind Lineup Administration*, 29 Curr. Dir. Psychol. Sci. 563 (2021), https://doi.org/10.1177/09637214209693.

28. Sarah M. Greathouse & Margaret B. Kovera, *Instruction Bias and Lineup Presentation Moderate the Effects of Administrator Knowledge on Eyewitness Identification*, 33 L. & Hum. Behav. 70, 81 (2009).

who the suspect was, giving a very overt cue to the witness that the administrator had knowledge that could help them choose the suspect."[29] "Even when lineup administrators scrupulously avoid comments that could identify which person is the suspect, unintended body gestures, facial expressions, or other nonverbal cues [can] inform the witness of his or her location in the lineup or photo array."[30]

Second, it prevents the administrator from giving the witness feedback following their selection, which, again, may happen verbally, nonverbally, consciously, and/or subconsciously, if administration is not blind.[31] When a witness receives positive feedback after selecting the suspect in a lineup or array, it serves to artificially boost their confidence in the selection in ways the accused cannot hope to refute at trial or in a suppression hearing. Available research indicates that nonblind administrators are more likely to engage in this kind of suggestion. For instance, in a 2001 study by Garrioch and Brimacombe, participants were asked to view a target absent lineup where the administrator was either misled to believe that the perpetrator had been placed in a specific position in the lineup, or alternatively was given no information about the perpetrator's position in the lineup.[32] By the end of the experiment it was clear that administrator beliefs regarding the perpetrator's location had influenced the participants' level of confidence in the identifications they made:

> [W]hen witnesses chose the lineup member who the lineup administrator had been led to believe was the perpetrator, the witnesses reported being much more confident than when the lineup administrator had no expectations about which person was the perpetrator. Videotapes of the lineup administrators' behaviors showed different patterns of post-identification nonverbal or paralinguistic behaviors as a function of lineup administrators' expectations about which lineup member was the perpetrator. These influences of the lineup administrators' expectations on the confidence of the witnesses occurred despite the fact that there were no incentives or other motivations on the part of the lineup administrators.[33]

29. *Id.*
30. NAT'L RSCH. COUNCIL, *supra* note 2, at 106.
31. *Id.*
32. John T. Wixted & Gary L. Wells, *The Relationship Between Eyewitness Confidence and Identification Accuracy: A New Synthesis*, 18 PSYCHOL. SCI. PUB. INT. 10 (2017), https://doi.org/10.1177/1529100616686966 (citing Lynn Garrioch & C.A. Elizabeth Brimacombe, *Lineup Administrators' Expectations: Their Impact on Eyewitness Confidence*, 25 L. & HUM. BEHAV. 299, 307–08 (2001)).
33. *Id.*

Finally, blind administration promotes unbiased reporting of the factors relevant to the reliability of the procedure, including the selection, any contemporaneous statements regarding confidence, the condition of the witness, and the conditions where the lineup or array was administered.[34] For all these reasons, blind administration is one of three agreed-upon "pristine conditions" that must be satisfied for an eyewitness's contemporaneous assessment of confidence regarding an identification to correlate with the accuracy of that identification.

In the past, attempts to elevate blind administration to the status of a system variable have been criticized as insufficiently grounded in scientific evidence that nonblind administration undermines eyewitness accuracy. Proponents of this view suggest that the widespread embrace of blind administration as a policy recommendation "has more to do with the historical importance of blind testing in other fields than the existence of a definitive empirical base involving lineup testing."[35] However, "[m]ore than 20 years since double-blind administration was first recommended, we now have direct evidence for the superiority of double-blind identification procedures for generating witness identifications" and "[t]here are now *substantial* data demonstrating that administrators' knowledge of which lineup member is the suspect causes them to emit behaviors that are directed toward the suspect and subsequently influence the choices that witnesses make from the lineups," and "positive feedback that . . . can increase [witness] confidence, attenuating the relationship between witness confidence and witness accuracy."[36] Thus, contrary to the minority view, the weight of scientific evidence supports that blind administration, *vel non*, is a circumstance relevant to assessing the reliability of an identification and that blind administration protocols are worth pursuing as a reform in those jurisdictions where they have not been implemented already.

B. Preprocedure Instructions

The reliability of an identification further depends on whether, before the procedure, the eyewitness harbored any false expectation that the perpetra-

---

34. *Id.*

35. *2019 Third Circuit Task Force Report*, *supra* note 20, at 34 (quoting Scott E. Gronlund et al., *Conducting an Eyewitness Lineup: How the Research Got It Wrong*, in 63 The Psychology of Learning and Motivation 1, 30 (Brian Ross ed. 2015) (internal quotation marks omitted)). *Id.* at 33 & n.50 (quoting Greathouse & Kovera, *supra* note 28, at 81 (internal quotation marks omitted).

36. Kovera & Evelo, *supra* note 27.

tor would necessarily be presented in the ensuing identification procedure. "Before a show-up, lineup, or photo array, there is substantial agreement that law enforcement should carefully instruct witnesses so as to minimize any impression that the perpetrator will necessarily be among the individuals displayed."[37] Allowing an eyewitness to believe that the police have "the guy" and "just need for [the eyewitness] to come [identify] him," creates an expectation of identification that has proven capacity to undermine the reliability of an identification procedure in ways that are difficult to ameliorate or expose later on in the case.[38] The negative impact of such a suggestion is threefold: "it increase[s] the risk of false identifications, it increase[s] eyewitness confidence in their incorrect identifications, and most importantly, it increase[s] witnesses' retrospective judgments on testimony-relevant variables," like how well they saw the perpetrator.[39]

To ward off eyewitness expectation of necessarily encountering the true perpetrator during the identification procedure, a clear majority of experts, judges, and practitioners, including the Department of Justice and the International Association of Police Chiefs, recommends advising eyewitnesses that the perpetrator may or may not be in the lineup, that the investigation will continue regardless of whether the witness makes an identification, and that it is just as important to free the innocent as it is to convict the guilty.[40] Researchers refer to preprocedure instructions that include these admonitions as "unbiased." In past studies, unbiased instructions have been shown to reduce the rate at which eyewitnesses mistakenly identify innocent suspects in target absent lineups.[41]

In the wake of the emerging consensus that unbiased instructions are needed to neutralize the expectation of identification that may attend an identification procedure, some have argued that unbiased instructions have not been proven sufficiently necessary to ensuring eyewitness accuracy and may end up discouraging eyewitnesses from making accurate identifications. Proponents of this view claim that unbiased instructions have never been shown to promote greater accuracy than so-called "neutral" instructions that are silent as to the matters addressed in the "unbiased" instructions,

---

37. *2019 Third Circuit Task Force Report*, *supra* note 20, at 14.

38. *Id.* at 48 & n.234 (quoting Wixted & Wells, *supra* note 32, at 17).

39. *Id.* at 48 n.235 (quoting Deah S. Quinlivan et al., *Do Pre-Admonition Suggestions Moderate the Effect of Unbiased Lineup Instructions*, 17 LEGAL & CRIMINOL. PSYCHOL. 165, 174 (2010)).

40. *Id.* at 48–49.

41. *Id.*

except for noting that the witness may indicate that the perpetrator is "not present."[42] The paradigmatic example of such an instruction would be telling a witness to make a selection, "if you see the [target] in the lineup" but otherwise, to indicate that the target is "not present." However, this claim is demonstrably false. Notably, in a 2006 study, Brewer and Wells compared "unbiased" instructions to a slightly "biased" alternative that was silent as to whether the perpetrator was in the lineup and did not mention the participant's ability to render a nonidentification response ("Now we would like you to try to identify the [target]. Please indicate your decision by clicking on a face.").[43] However, even in this experimental condition, participants had the option to indicate that the target was "Not Present" by clicking a button on the same screen as the computerized photo-array they were viewing. This button would seem to constitute an "acknowledg[ment] [of] the potential correctness of a no-identification response,"[44] comparable to that of the neutral instruction.[45] Indeed, having express "Not Present" options has been found to affect response bias in recognition tasks.[46] Thus, the results of this study, which found that those who received unbiased instructions were more accurate, cannot be dismissed as easily as the opposition contends.[47]

Opponents of unbiased instructions further contend that they are unnecessary because police have no duty "to correct [an eyewitness's] false assumption" about the perpetrator being present in a lineup, show-up, or photo-array.[48] This argument assumes that police bear no responsibility for the suggestiveness of an identification procedure, so long as they do not

---

42. *Id.*

43. Neil L. Brewer & Gary L. Wells, *The Confidence-Accuracy Relationship in Eyewitness Identification: Effects of Lineup Instructions, Foil Similarity and Target-Absent Base Rates*, 12 J. Experimental Psych. Applied 11-30 (2006), https://doi.org/10.1037/1076-898X.12.1.11.

44. *2019 Third Circuit Task Force Report*, *supra* note 20, at 51.

45. *Id.*

46. Joseph Clare & Stephan Lewandowsky, *Verbalizing Facial Memory: Criterion Effects in Verbal Overshadowing*, 30 J. Experimental Psych.: Learning, Memory, & Cognition 739 (2004) (finding that the effect of verbalization on eyewitness accuracy depended on whether an "not present" option was provided or withheld); Brian L. Cutler & Steven D. Penrod, Mistaken Identification: The Eyewitness, Psychology, and the Law 119 (1995), https://www.ojp.gov/pdffiles1/Digitization/159775NCJRS.pdf (noting that the effect of giving a more biased instruction in an experiment may have been canceled out by the fact that "all eyewitnesses are explicitly given the option of indicating that the thief is not in the lineup.").

47. Although it is true that earlier studies focused on more badly biased alternatives, that is because they were attempting to ascertain the impact of badly biased instructions used by police.

48. *2019 Third Circuit Task Force Report*, *supra* note 20, at 52.

actively encourage it. However, just as the police may not present a suspect in suggestive clothing, simply because they did not dress him in it, so too are they bound to mitigate the risk of suggestion that necessarily arises when they summon a witness to participate in an identification procedure, thereby implying that they have "the guy" and "just need for [the eyewitness] to come [identify] him." For all of these reasons, the use of unbiased instructions warrants consideration by judges and juries as a system variable.

C. Preprocedure Interviews

To maximize their chances of solving a reported crime, there is no question that police must attempt to interview an eyewitness as soon as possible after a crime has been reported to document the eyewitness's description of the perpetrator, as well as any other circumstances relevant to capacity to make an accurate identification, including the viewing conditions and how well the witness knows the perpetrator, if at all.[49] However, the manner in which police go about this task—whether and how they ask certain questions and perhaps even the order in which they ask them—can profoundly impact eyewitness memory, the likelihood of misidentification, and level of confidence.

1. Suggestive Questioning

It is widely agreed that in the process of obtaining information about a reported crime and its perpetrator(s), police should refrain from asking leading questions or suggesting information learned from other sources to a witness.[50] As noted in Chapter 3, details suggested by a police officer can become etched into memory as if personally observed by the witness through "source memory failure."[51]

That questions can distort memory has been documented with several experiments conducted over the span of three decades.[52] In this regard, the work of Elizabeth Loftus and her colleagues is particularly significant. In one study, they demonstrated the tendency of witnesses to report that the

49. *Id.* at 65.
50. *Id.*
51. *Id.*
52. Robert B. Michael & Maryanne Garry, *Ordered Questions Bias Eyewitnesses and Jurors*, 23 PSYCHONOMIC BULL. & REV. 601, 601 (2016), https://doi.org/10.3758/s13423-015-0933-1 (citing Elizabeth F. Loftus, *Planting Misinformation in the Human Mind: A 30-Year Investigation of the Malleability of Memory*, 12 LEARNING & MEMORY 361 (2005), https://doi.org/10.1101/lm.94705).

cars involved in an accident had been traveling at a faster rate of speed when a question suggested that the cars had *smashed* into each other, rather than *hit* each other.[53] In another, after watching a video of a traffic accident, witnesses were more likely to report seeing a broken headlight that had not been present during the video, when they were asked whether they had seen *the* broken headlight, instead of *a* broken headlight.[54] In a third, "participants who viewed a face and then heard a description of the face that was attributed to another witness later incorporated the verbal expressions of that witness into their description, even when the description was in error."[55]

In the context of ascertaining a perpetrator's description, suggestive questions include attempts to confirm information acquired from other sources (e.g., "Did the man have red hair with long sideburns?"), and questions that assume information that the witness has not mentioned ("This man with the red hair and long sideburns, did he have any facial hair?").[56] In the extreme, eyewitnesses may come to embrace false narratives about how they came about such suggested information, thus compromising their recollection of other relevant details.[57] Consider the eyewitness who, over time, becomes convinced that he got a good look at the perpetrator's face because he has incorporated elements of another person's description into his memory: "I must have gotten a good look because I distinctly remember that mole." Such false memories are particularly difficult to expose in the *Manson* framework because, even if suggestive questioning is revealed, the accused must show its impact on the witness. Moreover, the fact that the description was accurate in some respects may be used to suggest that the identification is nevertheless reliable because the eyewitness got a good look at the perpetrator.

---

53. *Id.* (citing Elizabeth F. Loftus & John C. Palmer, *Reconstruction of Automobile Destruction: An Example of the Interaction Between Language and Memory*, 13 J. VERBAL LEARNING & VERBAL BEHAV. 585 (1974), https://doi.org.10.1016/S0022-5371(74)80011-3).

54. *Id.* (citing Elizabeth F. Loftus & Guido Zanni, *Eyewitness Testimony: The Influence of the Wording of a Question*, 5 BULL. PSYCHONOMIC SOC'Y 86 (1975), https://doi.org/10.1016/0010-0285(75)90023-7).

55. Christian A. Meissner et al., *Person Descriptions as Eyewitness Evidence*, *in* 2 HANDBOOK OF EYEWITNESS PSYCHOLOGY: MEMORY FOR PEOPLE 16 (R.C.L. Lindsay et al., eds., 2007), https://labs.psych.ucsb.edu/schooler/jonathan/sites/labs.psych.ucsb.edu.schooler.jonathan/files/pubs/eyewitness_evidence.pdf (citing Elizabeth F. Loftus & Edith Greene, *Warning: Even Memory for Faces May Be Contagious*, 4 L. & HUM. BEHAV. 323 (1980), https://doi.org/10.1007/BF01040624).

56. *Id.*

57. *2019 Third Circuit Task Force Report*, supra note 20, at 65.

However, it is difficult to overstate the biasing potential of suggestive interview techniques because so much of the investigation depends on the description of the perpetrator that an eyewitness provides. Police use such descriptions to "locat[e] . . . suspect[s] in the immediate aftermath of an incident," "to identify potential suspects from mug books, to construct sketches or composites of a suspect, and as a basis for selecting fillers when . . . constructing a lineup identification parade."[58] Most importantly, the verbal description elicited by a police officer can become "'frozen' into [the] witness's recollection,"[59] through a process called "verbal overshadowing."[60] In this regard, it is both noteworthy and surprising that, in several recent experiments, the act of describing a face seemed to make people slightly more likely to misidentify it in a subsequent lineup.[61] Researchers hypothesize that this happens in part because "verbalization" causes people to produce "self-generated misinformation," which in turn impacts their memory of the face.[62] It is crucial that police not compound this problem by suggesting their own misinformation.

2. *Interview Structure and its Impact on the Accuracy and Completeness of a Description*

Although it is widely agreed that police should avoid leading questions, there is some diversity of opinion as to how best to achieve this goal and, more generally, how best to optimize the accuracy and completeness of the information obtained during an interview. It has long been agreed that while open-ended, free-response questions tend to produce more accurate responses, closed-ended questions tend to yield broader information.[63] By most accounts, police tend to use a combination of the two to elicit eyewitness descriptions, in a technique sometimes referred to as funneling.[64] The interview may begin with police asking the witness "what happened?" before proceeding to ask a few open-ended questions about what the perpetrator

58. Meissner et al., *supra* note 55, at 3–4.
59. Elizabeth F. Loftus, Eyewitness Testimony 97 (2d ed. 1996).
60. Meissner et al., *supra* note 55, at 22–26.
61. *Id.* at 22.
62. *Id.* at 23, 25.
63. Loftus, *supra* note 59, at 90–92.
64. *See* Ronald P. Fisher et al., *Interviewing Witnesses and Victims*, in Forensic Psychology in Context: Nordic and International Approaches 56–57 (Elizabeth F. Loftus & P.A. Granhag, eds., 2010), https://faculty.washington.edu/sjross2/documents/FisherRoss&10-interviewing%20witnesses%20and%20victims.pdf; Meissner et al., *supra* note 55, at 16.

and their features looked like.[65] However, at some point—either because of doubts about the level of detail that such questions are capable of eliciting or because of concern about the delay they could inject into an investigation—the format of the questions inevitably shifts to direct, short-answer questions about the topics of interest to the police (What color were his eyes? What color was his skin? How tall was he? How much did he weigh?).[66] It is here that the risk of suggestive questioning and inference-based responding peaks, as police may be tempted to test information acquired from other sources and round out what they think they need to know.

In the wake of the realization that this kind of interview structure may systematically promote suggestive questioning, two leading alternatives have emerged: the cognitive interview and the feature checklists.[67] The cognitive interview framework forbids the use of leading or suggestive questions or volunteering of information and seeks to reduce the likelihood of suggestion by forcing interviewers to approach the interview as a narrative-, rather than agenda-driven exercise.[68] In this regard, the cognitive interview methodology encourages police to (1) reinstate the context of the original event and (2) encourage comprehensive reporting, while asking the witness to (3) recount the event "in a variety of temporal orders" and (4) "from a variety of perspectives."[69] The success of this method in promoting more accurate and comprehensive memory retrieval has been documented in numerous studies.[70]

In addition, systematic "feature checklists" may help police elicit more complete descriptions while preventing the possibility of leading, suggestive questions.[71] Compared to cognitive interviewing, feature checklists present at least one advantage and at least one disadvantage vis-à-vis the suspect description. On the one hand, feature checklists are easier to administer and have already been implemented in a few departments in other countries,

65. Fisher et al., *supra* note 64, at 57.

66. *Id.*

67. *2019 Third Circuit Task Force Report*, *supra* note 20, at 65–66; Gary L. Wells et al., *Policy and Procedure Recommendations for the Collections and Preservation of Eyewitness Identification Evidence*, 44 L. & Hum. Behav. 1, 10–11 (2020).

68. *2019 Third Circuit Task Force Report*, *supra* note 20, at 65–66; Fisher et al., *supra* note 64, at 58.

69. Meissner et al., *supra* note 55, at 19; *accord 2019 Third Circuit Task Force Report*, *supra* note 20, at 65; Fisher et al., *supra* note 64, at 58.

70. Wells et al., *supra* note 67, at 10–11.

71. Meissner et al., *supra* note 55, at 16; *2019 Third Circuit Task Force Report*, *supra* note 20, at 66.

seemingly without causing any major disruption.[72] On the other hand, feature checklists have some potential to overwhelm witnesses, causing them to guess or offer uninformative, "neutral" responses in lieu of remembered information.[73] As a result, descriptions generated from feature checklists tend to contain "more incorrect features" than those generated from free recall.[74] Importantly, such inaccuracies may have some potential to "overshadow" memory, as discussed earlier. Thus, studies suggest that, compared to the free recall, feature checklists tend to undermine accuracy. At the same time, there do not appear to be studies comparing feature checklists to cognitive interviewing directly. Such research would help illuminate this issue greatly.

In any case, regardless of how police elicit an eyewitness's description of a perpetrator, the fact that their methods can have such a profound effect on the content and scope of the descriptions suggests that the nature of the description itself should carry less weight than it does under the *Manson* framework.[75]

Does the Order of Questions Induce False Confidence?

A recent study suggests that the order of questions in an interview can affect both an eyewitness's beliefs about the strength and accuracy of his or her own memory and an outside observer's assessment of the same. To test this hypothesis, researchers had subjects watch a video depicting a crime (an electrician stealing from the house where he had been working), and then answer a series of questions about it after completing a set of distraction tasks.[76] Subjects received the questions in either

(continued)

72. Meissner et al., *supra* note 55, at 16–17.
73. *Id.* at 17.
74. *Id.*
75. Fisher et al., *supra* note 64, at 57.
76. Michael & Garry, *supra* note 52.

Does the Order of Questions Induce False Confidence? *(continued)*

ascending or descending order of difficulty based on a predetermined ranking. During the test each subject rated their level of confidence in each response. Afterward, each subject rated the strength and accuracy of their recollection. Even controlling for variation in each person's objective accuracy, those who got the easy questions first were significantly more confident in their recall.[77] These results led researchers to conclude that we tend to decide how well we remember an event based the ease of the initial retrieval attempt and that we tend not to revise those assessments based on subsequent retrieval attempts.[78]

Question order similarly affected mock juror confidence in each witness's recollection. When asked to read a transcript of the first group's responses and rate the probable accuracy of those responses, mock jurors who reviewed more confident answers to easier questions first tended to believe that witnesses were more accurate on the whole.[79] The effect was similar in magnitude to what happens when a witness professes absolute certainty regarding their recollection or adds in additional details.[80]

As the authors of this study concluded, "[t]his collection of results paints a worrying picture of the malleability of beliefs about memory accuracy."[81] Notably, these findings suggest that the structure of on-scene interviews may systematically lead eyewitnesses to overrate their ability to recognize a perpetrator in a subsequent encounter.[82] As noted already, police officers tend to ascertain witness descriptions by "funneling"—asking open-ended, free response questions ("Can you tell me what he looked like?") before proceeding to closed-ended questions to which the witness may not know the answers ("Did he have any distinguishing marks or tattoos?").[83] At least in theory, these open-ended questions are easier to answer than those that

(continued)

77. *Id.* at 602–03.
78. *Id.* at 607.
79. *Id.* at 604, 606.
80. *Id.* at 607.
81. *Id.*
82. *Id.* at 608.
83. Fisher et al., *supra* note 64, at 56–57.

Does the Order of Questions Induce False Confidence? *(continued)*

call for specific information that the witness may be unable to recall. If our beliefs about how well we remember someone are tied to the ease of the first question we answer in that regard, then eliciting a description in this way could systematically bias witnesses toward the belief that they remember the perpetrator well—perhaps even well enough to recognize them again or reconstruct their face from memory, as required to create a composite sketch.

The study further suggests that police officers may react to the ease with which an eyewitness answers early questions by inferring that the witness remembers the perpetrator well. Thus, they may be prone to overestimating the witness's memory to the same degree as the witness themself. It is not clear if such overestimates have a lasting effect on confidence or if we simply come up with a new estimate of how well we retain each memory based on how well we have recalled it in the moment.[84] If the former is true, it suggests that a witness's confidence in the accuracy of an identification may depend, at least in part, on the order of questions in the initial interview. But, crucially, even if the former is not true, there are still profound implications for show-ups and composites, both of which tend to occur closer in time to when the police ascertain a description from the witness. According to a recent survey, the factor most likely to influence whether a sketch is prepared in a given case is an officer's impression of "whether the witness had a particularly good view."[85]

The results of this study require replication before they will warrant the same weight as the thoroughly vetted and overwhelmingly agreed-upon scientific principles that underly other system and estimator variables. However, assuming these results can be reproduced, they should give practitioners even further pause about the reliability of show-ups and composite sketches at bare minimum.

---

84. Michael & Garry, *supra* note 52, at 608.
85. PERF SURVEY, *supra* note 26, at 66.

D. Exposure to Other Eyewitnesses and Media

Just as police should refrain from suggesting information about the perpetrator or the witnessed event to an eyewitness and also refrain from suggesting that the perpetrator will necessarily be included in a to-be-administered identification procedure, so too should they take steps to prevent other eyewitnesses from doing the same. "Research demonstrates that an eyewitness may be influenced by being exposed to co-witness's description of a facial feature, learning that a co-witness made an identification, or learning that a co-witness made an identification confidently."[86]

For these reasons, judges, practitioners, and scholars recommend that upon arriving at the scene, police separate witnesses so that they do not contaminate each other's memories, and interview witnesses separately.[87] Moreover, police should refrain from transporting multiple witnesses to the location of the show-up at the same time, and refrain from additional show-up procedures once a suspect has been identified by one witness.[88] Police should arrange for witnesses to remain separate throughout any identification procedure that is administered in the case, including at the time that instructions are given.[89] Police should shuffle the order of any lineup or photo-array before it is presented to another witness and likewise, refrain from discussing any other identification procedure within the hearing of a witness.[90] Finally, upon termination of the procedure, police should caution witnesses to refrain from discussing the identification procedure with any other witness, and to avoid the news media, social media, and other sources of information about the case.[91]

Although, in the wake of *Perry v. New Hampshire*, 565 U.S. 228 (2012), it seems doubtful that the police's failure to abide by these recommendations would be enough to satisfy the "state-action/-arrangement" test under *Manson*,[92] they nevertheless remain highly relevant to the reliability of any identification under review.

---

86. *2019 Third Circuit Task Force Report*, *supra* note 20, at 62 (footnote omitted).
87. *Id.* at 63.
88. *Id.*
89. *Id.* at 63–64.
90. *Id.* at 64.
91. *Id.*
92. *See, e.g.*, *State v. Webster*, 104 A.3d 203 (N.H. 2014) (rejecting the claim that the requirement for "improper conduct" by law enforcement had been shown by the release of the defendant's photo to the media before interviewing the witnesses); *see also, generally*, 2 Wayne R. LaFave et al., Criminal Procedure § 7.4(d) (4th ed.) (collecting cases).

E. Construction of a Lineup or Photo-Array

1. Filler Selection and Formatting

Lineups and photo-arrays should be constructed and administered in such a way that does not allow the suspect to "stand out" from the fillers. In this regard, the formatting of the suspect's photograph in an array, including any obvious indication that a mugshot was used, may be just as important as the suspect's appearance, if not more important. "A lineup or photo array in which the suspect stands out from the . . . fillers may make it apparent to the witness which person is the suspect, thereby influencing the witness and possibly causing him or her to make an identification based upon the fact that one person stood out," rather than his or her memory of the perpetrator's appearance.[93] Moreover, where the suspect stands out, it may falsely elevate the eyewitness's confidence in an identification that would otherwise be more tentative.[94] Such falsely elevated confidence is all but irresistible to juries and can very easily lead to wrongful conviction, despite the best efforts of the accused to counter that false confidence with cross-examination and expert testimony.[95]

Nor, for similar reasons, should a filler be permitted to stand out from others in the lineup or array. Available research indicates that such distinctiveness tends to lull the observer into false confidence regarding the ease of the identification task, making them less cautious and more confident in their ultimate selection than the circumstances warrant and they might otherwise be.[96] Researchers refer to this phenomenon as the "dud effect."[97] Recent research by some particularly skeptical researchers has confirmed its existence.[98]

---

93. *2019 Third Circuit Task Force Report*, *supra* note 20, at 35–36.
94. *Id.* at 36.
95. *Id.*
96. *Id.*
97. *Id.*
98. Steve D. Charman et al., *The Dud Effect: Adding Highly Dissimilar Fillers Increases Confidence in Lineup Identifications*; 35 L. & Hum. Behav. 479 (2011), https://doi.org/10.1007/s10979-010-9261-1; Maciej Hanczakowski et al., *The Dud Alternative Effect in Memory*, 21 Psychonomic Bull. & Rev. 543 (2014), https://doi.org/10.3758/s13423-013-0497-x; *see also* Ryan J. Fitzgerald et al., *The Effect of Suspect-Filler Similarity on Eyewitness Identification Decisions: A Meta-Analysis*, 19 Psychol. Pub. Pol'y & L. 151 (2013), https://doi.org/10.1037/a0030618.

2. *Description Matching Versus Suspect Matching*

Beyond these two principles, there is some disagreement as to whether fillers should be selected based on how much they resemble the suspect or, alternatively, how well they fit the description of the perpetrator that the eyewitness provided.[99] Although suspect matching is more common, the majority view among experts holds that fillers should be selected based on the description provided but permitted to deviate in ways that do not concern the description, so that eyewitnesses can use subtle differences in the appearances of the target and fillers to guide their choice.[100] This view is based in part on a 1993 study, which found that, compared to suspect-matched filler selection, description-matched filler selection tended to maximize correct identification without increasing the risk of false identification.[101] The opposition view does not advocate for suspect matching *per se*. Rather, they argue that there is insufficient empirical support for recommending either approach, given that the results of the 1993 study have not been replicated.[102]

From a judicial perspective, this dispute may be largely academic because, for the purpose of determining whether a lineup is so unduly suggestive or unreliable as to warrant exclusion from trial or disregard by the factfinder, the question whether the suspect "stands out" as determined by relevant scientific measures (see following) is much more important than whether the police used description matching or suspect matching to construct the lineup in the first place.[103] In any case, notwithstanding the rigor of the minority argument, there is sound reason to prefer description matching, even assuming we lack an empirical basis to say it will yield more accuracy: namely, suspect matching confers a great deal of discretion on individual officers to determine a suspect's defining traits and to assess how well a filler approximates those traits. That discretion may be abused, consciously or

---

99. *2019 Third Circuit Task Force Report*, *supra* note 20, at 35, 41.

100. Fitzgerald et al., *supra* note 98, at 151. To paraphrase Gary Wells, eliminating every difference between the suspect and the fillers would result in a lineup full of clones, where everyone had an equal chance of being selected no matter how well the witness remembered the perpetrator. In such a lineup, even if that person was in the lineup and the eyewitness remembered them perfectly well, they would still be chosen only one sixth of the time, assuming there were five fillers. By contrast, the fillers would have a five in six chance of being mistakenly identified. Obviously, this is an extreme hypothetical that could not occur. Even so, it explains why scientists believe there is a tipping point past which suspect-filler similarity is actually detrimental to the process.

101. *Id.*

102. *Id.*; *2019 Third Circuit Task Force Report*, *supra* note 20, at 41.

103. At the same time, it would be interesting to know whether mock witnesses tend to rate description-based fillers as more suggestive than the suspect-based fillers.

subconsciously, by an officer who wants to make the strongest case possible. Likewise, the officer may simply have a poor eye for faces. In either case, the fairness and probative value of the lineup may suffer.

By contrast, requiring officers to adhere to whatever description the witness provides would relieve them of some of the discretion inherent in the suspect-matching paradigm. As noted in Chapter 1, the task of selecting fillers based on a suspect description has been simplified a great deal by the availability of computerized photo databases that allow police to filter out photographs based on certain features. From a due process and equal protection standpoint, this has value, even if it does not promote greater diagnostic accuracy. In other words, making the process less arbitrary and susceptible to the whims and abilities of a single decision-maker is a valid policy objective.[104] Thus, there is merit to the majority recommendation for description matching that is not undone by a lack of conclusive empirical support.

3. *Measuring and Expressing the Suggestiveness of a Lineup or Array*

Researchers have developed a few methods of measuring and expressing whether a lineup or array is suggestive, biased, or unfair, and if so, to what degree. These methods tend to involve having mock witnesses assess how much a suspect stands out from the fillers in the lineup or array, if at all.[105] "The mock-witness task generally involves presenting a lineup and a description of a perpetrator to [a group of randomly selected] people who have not seen the perpetrator and then asking these people to select the lineup member who best matches the description."[106] If the mock witnesses select the suspect significantly more often than they select the fillers, the lineup or array is biased. The logic behind this test is that, in a truly unbiased lineup or array where everyone fits the description provided equally

104. To be sure, the question whether suspect matching is too discretionary to be desirable is a hypothesis worth testing in an experimental setting. However, it seems difficult to test under the design parameters of previous experiments, where a single experimenter made all of the lineups. Indeed, this experimental design hurdle may explain why the studies conducted have yielded such varied outcomes: some experimenters might just have a better eye for faces when it comes to selecting suspect-matched fillers and leading to more accuracy from their suspect-matched lineups.

105. Jungwon Lee et al., *Validity of Mock-Witness Measures for Assessing Lineup Fairness*, 28 Psychol. Crime & L. 215 (2021), https://www.researchgate.net/publication/350459067_Validity_of_mock-witness_measures_for_assessing_lineup_fairness.

106. Jamal K. Mansour et al., *Evaluating Lineup Fairness: Variations Across Methods and Measures*, 41 L. & Hum. Behav. 103 (2017), https://doi.org/10.1037/lhb0000203.

well, every person should have an equal chance of being identified, based solely on that description.

The results of such a mock-witness assessment can be conveyed in a few ways. The simplest method involves dividing the total number of mock witnesses (n) by the number of mock witnesses who select the suspect (D).[107] The result of this calculation (n/D) is the "functional size" of the lineup, which reflects how many viable options there are in the lineup or array.[108] If, notwithstanding the fact that there are five fillers in a lineup, a suspect is chosen as the best match by half of the mock witnesses who have seen the description used to generate the lineup, then the functional size of the lineup is only two, meaning that for all intents and purposes, the suspect is one of only two viable choices.[109] Another way of evaluating the degree of bias inherent in a lineup is to take an average of how often each filler is overlooked compared to how often it would have been selected in an unbiased lineup, and subtract this number from the actual number of people in the lineup, minus any of the fillers who were not selected at all.[110] This calculation is called the effective size.[111] Another method involves having people rate the degree of similarity between the various faces that make up a lineup according to a standard scale.[112] More recently researchers have been adapting the computer technology that underlies facial recognition software to test and express the level of similarity between fillers and identification targets.[113]

Obviously, picking a suspect out of a lineup that amounts to a toss-up between two people is far less impressive than picking the suspect out of a lineup that contains five other viable options. A lineup with a functional size

107. *See, e.g.*, Roy S. Malpass & R.C.L. Lindsay, *Measuring Lineup Fairness*, 13 Appl. Cognitive Psychol. S1, S2 (1999), https://doi.org/10.1002/(SICI)1099-0720(199911)13:1+<S1::AID-ACP678>3.0.CO;2-9.

108. *Id.*

109. *Id.*

110. *Id.* at S3.

111. *Id.*

112. Lee et al., *supra* note 105 (citing Neil Brewer & Gary L. Wells, *The Confidence-Accuracy Relationship in Eyewitness Identification: Effects of Lineup Instructions, Foil Similarity, and Target-Absent Base Rates*, 12 J. Experimental Psychol.: Appl. 11 (2006), https://doi.org/10.1037/1076-898X.12.1.11).

113. *Id.* (citing Amanda N. Bergold & Paul Heaton, *Does Filler Database Size Influence Identification Accuracy?*, 42 L. & Hum. Behav. 227 (2018), https://doi.org/10.1037/lhb0000289; and Colin Tredoux, *A Direct Measure of Facial Similarity and Its Relation to Human Similarity Perceptions*, 8 J. Experimental Psychol. 180 (2002), https://doi.org/10.1037/1076-898X.8.3.180).

of one should be considered no more reliable than a show-up identification. Indeed, such a lineup should be considered even more offensive to due process than a show-up, because unlike the show-up, the lineup is not attended by any of the exigent circumstances that could justify using a suggestive procedure. Thus, this functional size calculation can add vital context to a judge's determination whether to admit an identification and a jury's determination as to how much weight it deserves.

The aforementioned metrics have been criticized for not taking into account how well an eyewitness may remember the perpetrator. Such criticisms point out that, unlike a mock witness (or a computer algorithm, for that matter), an actual eyewitness may be so familiar with a perpetrator that their choice cannot be influenced by the construction of the lineup. Under these circumstances, critics argue, it would be wrongheaded to prevent the jury from considering an identification or instructing them that it may be unreliable. However, research has shown that even moderately strong memories of a perpetrator are insufficient to neutralize the suggestiveness of a lineup.[114] Thus, mock witness evaluations are a valid indicator of eyewitness behavior and lineup fairness.

F. Sequential v. Simultaneous Presentation

As noted in Chapter 1, a photo-array or lineup may be viewed sequentially (one at a time) or simultaneously (all at once). As recounted in the most recent guidance from the Department of Justice on the use of photo-arrays, the simultaneous presentation of lineups and arrays was standard practice in American law enforcement agencies throughout most of the twentieth century.[115] However:

> In the late 1980s, psychological research began to suggest that sequential methods, in which witnesses are shown one photo at a time, would be better at preventing erroneous identifications without reducing the rate of correct identifications. As a result, several police agencies, . . . turned to the sequential method for photo arrays.[116]

---

114. *Id.*
115. Yates Memo, *supra* note 23, at 7.
116. *Id.* at 7.

More recent research has called the superiority of sequential presentation into question.[117] As a result, "there is no general [scientific] agreement as to whether showing an eyewitness a series of photos [or people] sequentially is preferable to showing [them] simultaneously."[118]

The current scientific debate regarding these two modes of lineup and photo-array presentation concerns whether sequential presentation has a benign or detrimental effect on eyewitness accuracy and response bias, that is, how certain an eyewitness needs to be before deciding they recognize the perpetrator. On the one hand, sequential presentation has been proven to yield a higher "diagnosticity ratio," meaning a higher ratio of correct to false identifications.[119] As discussed in Chapter 3, this means, necessarily, that the probative value of a sequential identification is higher than that of a simultaneous identification, as those identified through sequential presentation are more likely to be guilty than those identified through simultaneous presentation.[120] In this way, "the sequential method comes closer to satisfying the popular criterion that those identified as guilty are actually guilty."[121]

On the other hand, it is not clear that sequential presentation actually improves the ability to recognize someone from memory (diagnostic accuracy) and there is reason to believe that sequential presentation may actually impair this ability.[122] Some studies suggest that being able to see more than one face at a time helps eyewitnesses focus on the traits that have "diagnostic value"—that is, those that will actually help the eyewitness recognize the perpetrator or distinguish the innocent.[123] In light of this research, some have argued that sequential presentation does not make people more accurate, just more reluctant to choose, and that police would be better off inducing appropriate levels of caution by other means, for instance, by giving preliminary instructions to the effect of those already mentioned.[124] For

117. *Id.* at 7–8.

118. *2019 Third Circuit Task Force Report*, *supra* note 20, at 74 (citing Nat'l Rsch. Council, supra note 2, at 3, 24; Yates Memo, *supra* note 23, at 8).

119. *Id.*

120. John T. Wixted & Laura Mickes, *A Signal-Detection-Based Diagnostic-Feature Model of Eyewitness Identification*, 121 Psychol. Rev. 262, 264, 266 (2014), https://doi.org/10.1037/a0035940; Nat'l Rsch. Council, *supra* note 2, at 86–87.

121. *2019 Third Circuit Task Force Report*, *supra* note 20, at 74–75.

122. Wixted & Mickes, *supra* note 120, at 271.

123. *Id.*

124. *Id.*

its part, the American Psychology-Law Society has not weighed in on this controversy.[125]

This book does not attempt to resolve the ongoing scientific debate regarding simultaneous and sequential presentation. Nor could it. However, as scientists conduct different experiments to test their competing hypotheses, and policymakers grapple with the results, two points seem important to keep in mind.

First, insofar as sequential presentations make people more reluctant to choose, that is not necessarily a bad thing. There is no dispute that identifications that result from sequential presentation have higher probative value than those that result from simultaneous presentation for that reason.[126] While it has been suggested that making people more reluctant to choose will result in too many of the guilty going free, concern for those who may be wrongfully accused, arrested, and convicted is just as valid in this context.

Second, although the claim that sequential lineups undermine recognition warrants serious consideration, it is worrying that some experiments have not compared simultaneous presentation to the "practitioner" version of sequential presentation that law enforcement agencies have adopted across the country. Under this version, eyewitnesses may view the people or photos in a lineup as many as two times before being asked to state whether they recognize someone or not. As noted in Chapter 1, psychologist sometimes use and test a more rigid version of sequential presentation, according to which an eyewitness must render a verdict as to each person or photo presented before moving on to consider the next photo or person.[127] There is reason to believe that the former, practitioner version of sequential presentation incorporates some of the argued benefits of simultaneous presentation, insofar as the eyewitness has the opportunity to see more faces and can use them to zero in on the features they need to make an accurate recognition judgment.[128] Notably, those studies finding decreased diagnostic accuracy for sequential lineups have noted that the effects are not as pronounced for

---

125. *2019 Third Circuit Task Force Report*, *supra* note 20, at 75.

126. *Id.*

127. *See, e.g.*, Ruth Horry et al., *"Only Your First Yes Will Count": The Impact of Pre-Lineup Instructions on Sequential Lineup Decisions*, 27 J. Experimental Psychol. 170 (2021), https://doi.org/10.1037/xap0000337; Nancy K. Steblay et al., *Sequential Lineup Laps and Eyewitness Accuracy*, 35 L. & Hum. Behav. 262 (2011), https://doi.org/10.1007/s10979-010-9236-2.

128. *See* Horry et al., *supra* note 127.

lineups where the suspect is placed third or later in the lineup.[129] In other words, seeing as few as two fillers may be enough to enhance recognition. For this reason, it may be that the practitioner version manages to capture what the two sides of this debate perceive to be the advantages of both methods. In any case, it is important that the policy debate over sequential and simultaneous presentation be informed by relevant apples-to-apples comparisons. For these purposes, testing should focus at least as much on how sequential lineups actually are conducted by police as how researchers believe they should occur.

G. Suggestive Postidentification Feedback

It is beyond reasonable dispute that the reliability of identification evidence depends on whether the eyewitness has received any positive feedback from law enforcement in the aftermath of an identification. As Wixted and Wells wrote, such positive feedback is "[p]erhaps the biggest threat to our ability to rely on" eyewitness confidence as an indicator of eyewitness accuracy.[130] "There is now a large body of eyewitness-identification studies showing that a simple comment to an eyewitness who has made a mistaken identification (e.g., 'Good, you identified the suspect') can lead to immediate strong inflation of the witness's confidence."[131] Recent meta-analysis indicates that the effect of such positive feedback on eyewitness confidence in mistaken identifications is particularly large. In such studies, where eyewitnesses received positive feedback on a mistaken identification, their confidence in that identifications went up on average "by approximately a full standard deviation."[132]

Moreover, "[f]eedback need not be explicit" to inflate an eyewitness's confidence, "as an eyewitness may also interpret as feedback 'vague positive comments.'"[133] "Feedback can even be as subtle as making eye contact or using certain intonation, and the officer and witness may not even be aware

---

129. Wixted & Mickes, *supra* note 120, at 271 ("A sequential lineup eventually provides the same diagnostically useful information that is immediately apparent to the eyewitness when a simultaneous lineup is used."); Thomas D. Albright & Brandon L. Garrett, *The Law and Science of Eyewitness Evidence*, 102 B.U. L. Rev. 511, 572 (2022) ("The differences between the procedures may be further reduced, however, where law enforcement agencies allow more than one 'lap' in which an eyewitness can view photos in a sequential procedure.").

130. Wixted & Wells, *supra* note 32, at 18.

131. *Id.*

132. *Id.*

133. *2019 Third Circuit Task Force Report*, *supra* note 20, at 53 & nn.265 (citing Wells et al., *supra* note 67).

that it occurred."[134] The nonverbal cues that can be used to communicate that a witness has picked the right person out of a lineup or photo-array are as many and varied as those that may be used to suggest the location of that person in the first place. Studies have shown that "post-identification nonverbal or paralinguistic behaviors" tend to differ "as a function of lineup administrators' expectations about which lineup member was the perpetrator."[135]

"[P]ost-identification feedback not only affects current confidence but also distorts eyewitnesses' recall for how confident they were at an earlier time."[136] It tends to "enhance[] eyewitnesses' beliefs about their memory for a crime, including how well they could see a suspect's face and how much attention they paid."[137] "Researchers have consistently found, in both laboratory and field studies, that," in addition to "inflat[ing] a witness's level of confidence," "positive post-identification feedback can [also] impact the witness's memory of the conditions surrounding his or her viewing of the perpetrator, including how much attention he or she paid to the perpetrator, and how good a view he or she had of the perpetrator."[138]

Most importantly, eyewitnesses and administrators often have little awareness of how suggestive feedback has affected eyewitness confidence and thus cannot be expected to reliably self-report its effects. A 1998 study by Wells and Douglass (née Bradfield) found that "when witnesses were asked if post-identification feedback might have influenced how they answered the confidence question, most said 'no,' yet those who said 'no' were no less influenced than were those who said 'yes.'"[139] Likewise, in Garrioch and Brimacombe's 2001 study, where nonblind administrators were demonstrably more likely to have provided suggestive feedback, resulting in significant differences in eyewitness confidence levels, "100% of the lineup administrators indicated that they believed they did not provide any post-identification feedback, and 95% of the witnesses believed they did not

134. *Id.* at 53 & n.266 (citing Wixted & Wells, *supra* note 32, at 18; Garrioch & Brimacombe, *supra* note 32).

135. Wixted & Wells, *supra* note 32, at 18 (citing Garrioch & Brimacombe, *supra* note 32).

136. *Id.*

137. Michael & Garry, *supra* note 52, at 608 (citing Gary L. Wells & Amy L. Bradfield, *"Good, You Identified the Suspect": Feedback to Eyewitnesses Distorts Their Reports of the Witnessing Experience*, 83 J. Appl. Psychol. 360, https://doi.org/10.1037/0021-9010.83.3.360).

138. *2019 Third Circuit Task Force Report*, *supra* note 20, at 53 & nn.265 (citing Wells et al., *supra* note 67).

139. Wixted & Wells, *supra* note 32, at 18 (citing Wells & Bradfield, *supra* note 137).

receive any post-identification feedback."[140] Thus, the possibility of suggestive feedback is a vitally important factor for judges and juries to consider in evaluating the reliability of identification evidence.

H. Inherently Suggestive Identification Procedures

There is widespread agreement that the following procedures are inherently suggestive and therefore should not be used as a matter of course but rather only in limited circumstances where it is necessary. Scientific research confirms that each undermines the reliability of an identification or a witness's statement of confidence in their identification.

1. *Presenting the Same Suspect to the Same Witness Multiple Times*

Scientists agree that "[a] witness should have only one opportunity to make an identification of a suspect" because repeat identification attempts increase the likelihood of source monitoring error and transference.[141] As noted previously, transference happens when a witness recognizes the suspect from a prior identification procedure, but mistakenly attributes that familiarity to the witnessed crime, rather than the prior identification procedure.[142] Such repeat exposure to the suspect further has the tendency to induce overconfidence in subsequent identifications. The potential for transference and overconfidence that arise once a witness has been exposed to the suspect is one of many reasons to be skeptical of first-time in-court identifications, as they tend to follow multiple suggestive encounters with the defendant—during a previous, unsuccessful identification attempt, or while the suspect is sitting in the courtroom.

The risk of transference and overconfidence is exacerbated where a witness has not only been exposed to a suspect through a prior identification procedure but has also already indicated that the suspect might be the perpetrator during that prior procedure. This "commitment effect" helps explain why it is not reasonable to expect a lineup or photo-array to purge the taint of a prior suggestive identification procedure, such as a show-up or a mugshot search, as well as why an eyewitness's confidence in their identification on the witness stand is not a reliable indicator of the accuracy of their identification.[143]

---

140. *Id.* (citing Garrioch & Brimacombe, *supra* note 32).
141. *2019 Third Circuit Task Force Report*, *supra* note 20, at 60.
142. *See* Chapter 2 § II.B.2.a.ii.
143. *2019 Third Circuit Task Force Report*, *supra* note 20, at 60–61.

2. *Show-ups*

Show-ups involve the presentation of a single suspect to an eyewitness in the aftermath of a reported crime, for the purpose of allowing the eyewitness to say whether the police have apprehended the right person or not. Since the Supreme Court decided *Stovall v. Denno* in 1967 and well before, it has been "widely" agreed that show-ups are, by their very nature, "inherently suggestive" (that is, inherently more suggestive than a lineup or photo-array) and accordingly should be disfavored.[144] Consistent with this widespread condemnation, studies tend to confirm that show-ups produce a larger number of false identifications of innocent suspects than lineups or photo-arrays.[145]

a. Why Are Show-ups so Suggestive?

Conventional wisdom has long held that show-ups are inherently suggestive because they lack fillers to obscure the identity of the suspect and to "siphon" off guesswork by witnesses with poor memories of the perpetrator. First, unlike in a lineup or a photo-array, where even if the witness assumes the perpetrator is present, the witness still does not know who that person is (barring suggestion by the administrator), the person viewing a show-up cannot help but know that the person on display has been presented precisely because the police suspect him of being the perpetrator.[146] This knowledge may be enough to entice certain eyewitnesses into "guessing" or making an identification, despite having very low confidence

144. *Stovall v. Denno*, 388 U.S. 293, 302 & n.6 (1967) (citing Patrick Wall, EYE-WITNESS IDENTIFICATION IN CRIMINAL CASES 26–40 (1965); William Paul, *Identification of Accused Persons*, 12 AUSTL. L. J. 42, 44 (1938); Williams & Hammelmann, *Identification Parades*, Part I [1963] CRIM. L. REV. 479, 480–81; Frankfurter, THE CASE OF SACCO AND VANZETTI 31–32 (1927)); *2019 Third Circuit Task Force Report*, *supra* note 20, at 41 & n.197 ("There is general agreement in the scientific community that show-ups are, by their very nature, suggestive[.]").

145. *2019 Third Circuit Task Force Report*, *supra* note 20, at 41 & n.197 (noting "general agreement in the scientific community that show-ups result in a higher rate of false identifications of innocent suspects than lineups"; collecting authorities).

146. *See United States v. Brownlee*, 454 F.3d 131, 138 (3d Cir. 2006) ("As the Supreme Court has acknowledged, a show-up procedure is inherently suggestive because, by its very nature, it suggests that police think they have caught the perpetrator of the crime." (citation omitted)); *State v. Lawson*, 291 P.3d 673, 686 (Or. 2012) ("Police showups are generally regarded as inherently suggestive and therefore less reliable than properly administered lineup identifications because the witness is always aware of whom police officers have targeted as a suspect."); Nancy Steblay et al., *Eyewitness Accuracy Rates in Police Showup and Lineup Presentations: A Meta-Analytic Comparison*, 27 L. & HUM. BEHAV. 523, 525 (2003), https://doi.org/10.1023/A:1025438223608 ("The showup reveals police suspicions about the single suspect, and the witness is aware that only one person will be shown. Thus the procedure may be considered an 'inherently suggestive one.'").

in their selection. Second, because there are no fillers, innocent suspects are unprotected against an eyewitness's inclination to "guess."[147] On this view, there need not be anything particularly suggestive about the show-up itself. It is enough that the structure allows an eyewitness's natural predisposition toward guessing to impact the outcome more than it could in a lineup or a photo-array. In an unbiased lineup or photo-array, a predisposition toward guessing promises only a $1/(n+1)$ chance of selecting the suspect where "n" is the number of fillers.[148] In the show-up, it *guarantees* identification of the suspect.[149]

These explanations persist in part because they are easy to understand.[150] Yet, for all their intuitive appeal, it is possible they overlook certain layers of suggestivity imbedded in the show-up, thus understating how unreliable the results of a show-up may truly be. Research inspired by signal detection theory suggests that show-ups may also be suggestive because, in addition to making clear who the suspect is, the absence of fillers tends to increase the pressure to choose rather than indicate uncertainty and undermine "diagnostic accuracy"—that is, the witness's ability to tell innocent suspects apart from the perpetrator. In addition, the lack of blind administration inherent in the show-up is a factor that deserves independent consideration.

i. ***Pressure to Choose and Rates of Choosing*** To begin with, according to signal detection theory, it is not just that the absence of fillers in a show-up leaves the innocent unprotected against guessing. Rather, the absence of fillers in a show-up tends to *promote* guessing, insofar as witnesses are more inclined to make a selection (rather than declaring their uncertainty) when they are presented with fewer choices. Studies show that we tend to be less careful about choosing during a recognition task when we have

---

147. *Young v. State*, 374 P.3d 395, 421 (Alaska 2016) ("[I]n contrast to lineups and photo arrays, which allow a witness with a faulty memory to pick someone other than the suspect, every positive identification in a showup implicates the suspect." Thus, "[s]howups seemingly provide little protection against witnesses who are inclined to guess."); *2019 Third Circuit Task Force Report*, *supra* note 20, at 41-42 & n.198 ("In a lineup or photo array, by contrast, a witness's mistaken identification may fall on the innocent suspect but may also fall on one of the known-innocent fillers, who will not be charged with a crime."); Wells et al., *supra* note 67, at 7 (suggesting that this account is not universally agreed-upon).

148. Jeffrey S. Neuschatz et al., *A Comprehensive Evaluation of Showups*, *in* 1 Advances in Pyschology and Law 45–46 (Monica K. Miller & Brian H. Bornstein eds., 2016).

149. *Id.*

150. *See, e.g.*, *Young*, 374 P.3d at 421 (describing the suggestiveness of the show-up as "apparent").

fewer options to choose from because our odds of "success" seem more favorable.[151] On the whole, laboratory experiments appear to confirm that show-ups are more conducive to choosing than lineups or photo-arrays for precisely this reason.[152]

These studies "probably underestimate the actual choosing [disparity] because researchers cannot simulate the social pressure that a real eyewitness feels."[153] Indeed, in an archival analysis of real-world cases, the choosing rate for show-ups was 76 percent compared to only 48 percent for lineups.[154] In this regard it may be significant that, whereas a lineup or photo-array may be administered by an officer with no prior involvement in the investigation, this almost never happens in the context of a show-up. Where the show-up is administered by someone whose involvement in the investigation is known to the witness, the pressure to identify or choose may be compounded by the witness's desire not to disappoint the administrator by being inconclusive.

Insofar as show-ups are more conducive to choosing than a lineup or an array, they also would be more likely to yield identification.[155] This means more correct identifications when the target is presented and more misidentification when the target is absent.[156] Notably, signal detection theory predicts that in the context of a show-up, being less careful about choosing will increase the chances of misidentifying someone innocent (provided they look enough like the perpetrator) even more than it increases the chances of correctly identifying the perpetrator.[157] As a result, we might expect show-ups to yield less accurate outcomes than either lineups or photo-arrays, even setting aside other differences between them. Studies seem to bear out this prediction.[158]

---

151. Christian A. Meissner et al., *Eyewitness Decisions in Simultaneous and Sequential Lineups: A Dual-Process Signal Detection Theory Analysis*, 33 MEMORY & COGNITION 783, 787 (2005), https://doi.org/10.3758/BF03193074.

152. *Id.* at 788–89; Nancy Steblay et al., *Eyewitness Accuracy Rates in Police Showup and Lineup Presentations: A Meta-Analytic Comparison*, 27 L. & HUM. BEHAV. 523 (2003), https://doi.org/10.1023/A:1025438223608; *see also* Neuschatz et al., *supra* note 148, at 46 (noting the choosing disparity in Steblay's 2003 meta-analysis). Wells et al., *supra* note 67, at 26 (citing 1993 and 2001 studies that found otherwise).

153. Neuschatz et al., *supra* note 148, at 46.

154. *Id.*

155. *Id.*

156. *Id.*

157. Wixted & Mickes, *supra* note 120, at 264 ("[S]ignal-detection theory predicts that the diagnosticity ratio will increase as responding becomes more conservative.").

158. Neuschatz et al., *supra* note 148, at 65–66; *see also id.* at 49 ("Stated more simply, showups put innocent suspects at greater risk than lineups.").

ii. Loss of Diagnostic Accuracy The absence of fillers may further contribute to the suggestiveness of the show-up by undermining diagnostic accuracy—the eyewitness's ability to recognize the perpetrator and tell them apart from others. As already noted in the discussion of simultaneous and sequential lineups,[159] some scientists hypothesize that being able to compare features across distinct but similar faces enhances our ability to hone in on the ones that have diagnostic significance—in other words, those that enable us to recognize the perpetrator and distinguish them from others.[160] Like the prediction that show-ups increase the pressure to choose relative to lineups and photo-arrays, the notion that they also undermine diagnostic accuracy relative to lineups and photo-arrays appears to be borne out in the available data.[161]

iii. Lack of Blind Administration Although much of the suggestiveness of the show-up can be attributed to the absence of fillers, another structural deficiency involves the lack of blind administration. Although, as discussed above and below, police can and should attempt to counteract the impression that they "have their man" through the instructions that precede a show-up, to some degree, the conclusion that police consider the person they have presented a viable suspect is inescapable to both the eyewitness and the administrator, whoever that person may be. For this reason, and because it is harder to arrange for a separate administrator for a show-up conducted at the scene of a reported crime than it is to arrange one for a prearranged lineup or photo-array at the station house, show-ups are more likely to be administered by the same officers who took the initial report.

This lack of blind administration may exacerbate the suggestiveness of the show-up in a number of ways. As already noted, it may contribute to the pressure that someone feels to identify (especially when the show-up administrator is the officer to whom an initial report is given) or allow an officer to punctuate the message that the police "have their man," already inherent in the structure of the show-up, using verbal and nonverbal cues. Finally, as already noted, a nonblind administrator may, and is demonstrably more likely to, give positive feedback following the identification of a suspect that may inflate the witness's confidence in their identification.

159. *See supra* Section I.F.

160. Wixted & Mickes, *supra* note 120, at 269.

161. *See* Neuschatz et al., *supra* note 148, at 52–53. Not all psychologists find this data equally compelling. Wells et al., *supra* note 67, at 5.

iv. Lack of Redeeming Qualities Finally, recent research suggests that factors that were long thought to weigh in the show-up's favor—for example, the ability to use the suspect's clothing as a retrieval cue—do not bolster accuracy to the degree previously assumed. An oft-cited justification for using a show-up is the need for officers to resolve their suspicions quickly while the witness's memory is still "fresh" and before the suspect can alter their appearance. Along these lines, researchers have hypothesized that "the speed at which a showup can be conducted" may compensate for the suggestibility and loss of diagnostic accuracy that accompanies a show-up because the perpetrator is fresher in the eyewitness's mind and "may not have time to alter distinctive features noticed by the witness," such as clothing.[162] "According to the principle of encoding specificity, similar cues at study and test (same clothing) should enhance [recognition] relative to different cues (different clothing)."[163] Thus, it was widely believed that those who viewed a show-up might be able to make up for the decreased loss of diagnostic accuracy they suffer as a result of single-suspect presentation.

Recent research casts doubt on this hypothesis. Reviewing previous studies conducted in this area, Neuschatz et al. compared the diagnostic accuracy of eyewitnesses during "immediate showups in which the clothing was the same . . . to [photo-arrays] that were conducted immediately or after a delay with no clothing match."[164] Notwithstanding the apparent disadvantage of seeing the suspect in different clothing, those who viewed the photo-array displayed better diagnostic accuracy than those who viewed the immediate show-up.[165] This was true even when the photo-array was viewed after a delay that did not accompany the show-up. [166]

The results of this experiment have two important implications for how we think about show-ups. The first is that neither the freshness of a person's memory nor the availability of clothing as a retrieval cue is sufficient to compensate for the loss of diagnostic accuracy and caution that accompanies a show-up. The second is that clothing may not be an effective retrieval cue

162. Neuschatz et al., *supra* note 148, at 45.

163. *Id.* at 53.

164. *Id.* at 54.

165. *Id.* at 54–55.

166. *Id.*; *see also id.* at 65 ("Even in situations in which showups should have, based on memory theory, a memorial advantage to lineups (e.g., clothing match and shorter retention interval), they still underperformed lineups.").

insofar as it may tend to distract from careful consideration of the suspect's facial features rather than to promote it. In this regard, identical clothing might trigger an expectation of repetition that dulls consideration of other more important distinguishing features.

b. A Reckoning on the Horizon?

In light of the foregoing, a compelling case can be made that show-ups warrant much stronger condemnation and stricter regulation than they have heretofore received in the American legal system. Under *Stovall* and its progeny, a show-up can be excluded from a subsequent criminal trial if the defense can prove as a threshold matter that it was unnecessary to conduct a show-up in the first place or that the manner of the show-up was unnecessarily suggestive. However, as LaFave has noted, the standard for finding that a show-up was "necessary" at a suppression hearing has never been particularly "demanding."[167] Given that the police have identified a suspect, judges are inclined to think that it is better to let them resolve their suspicions on the spot by detaining the suspect and arranging a viewing, even where this detention occurs several hours after the crime itself and somewhere far removed from the crime scene.[168]

The rationale for such determinations is that the witness's memory will be fresher whenever the show-up occurs than it would be later.[169] However, as noted above, even in the case of an immediate show-up, the advantage of having a fresher memory may not be enough to compensate for the loss of diagnostic accuracy that results from seeing a suspect without any fillers. Of course, the case for doing a show-up is only weaker when it would occur several hours after the reported crime, rather than immediately after. This is to say nothing of the many other ways in which show-ups are suggestive and lead to misidentification of innocent suspects. On top of everything, under *Manson*, even if the accused can somehow prove that the show-up was unnecessarily suggestive, a judge may nevertheless admit it at trial based largely on the over-confidence that the show-up itself has induced.[170]

---

167. 2 Wayne R. LaFave et al., Criminal Procedure § 7.4(g) (4th ed.).

168. *Id.*

169. *Id.*

170. *State v. Henderson*, 27 A.3d 872, 918 (N.J. 2011).

For all these reasons, some have argued that it is long past time to ban the show-up altogether, at least where the witness does not purport to be familiar with the perpetrator.[171] Those arguments have been spelled out effectively by others and will not be further rehashed here. However, it is worth noting that the case for banning or severely curtailing the show-up grows stronger by the day, as the availability of technology that would allow police to assemble and present photo-arrays at the scene of a crime becomes more widely available. Indeed, giving police the capability to administer on-scene photo-arrays through the laptops or tablets that many officers already carry would not seem to require much in the way of innovation. Computerized databases already play a significant role in the construction of photo-arrays across the country.

And yet, this technology does not appear to be any closer to implementation than it was in 2018 when Gary Wells noted the possibility in an academic article.[172] The failure to develop this technology may speak to a lack of interest among its would-be consumers: law enforcement agencies and the government bodies that fund them. As time progresses, and the feasibility of on-scene photo-arrays becomes more apparent, it will counsel even further in favor of abolishing the show-up and may also raise interesting questions about the constitutionality of continuing to subject those under investigation to an unnecessary risk of mistaken identification. As the Sixth Circuit held, "a custom or practice of conducting show-ups without consideration of the circumstances" may give rise to liability under 42 U.S.C. § 1983.[173] It follows that a custom or practice of doing so, while ignoring the availability of less suggestive alternatives, may as well.

c. Circumstances Relevant to a Show-up's Admissibility and Weight

For however long show-ups remain a method by which police obtain the identification of a suspect unfamiliar to the eyewitness, there is widespread agreement about the circumstances that should dictate their weight and admissibility. In determining the admissibility of an identification derived from a show-up, courts should consider both whether the show-up itself

171. *See* Stephen P. Bertelsman, Note, *Defending Due Process: The Case for Abolishing the Show-Up Line-Up*, 68 WASH. U. J. L. & POL'Y 245, 269 (2022) (noting various proposals).

172. *See* Gary L. Wells, *Eyewitness Identification*, in 2 REFORMING CRIMINAL JUSTICE (Erik Luna ed., 2018); *see also* Mitchell L. Eisen et al., *Testing a Modified Procedure for Conducting Showups with Eyewitnesses*, POLICE CHIEF MAGAZINE, 2019, https://www.policechiefmagazine.org/testing-modified-procedure-showups-eyewitnesses/ (noting a pilot study).

173. *Gregory v. City of Louisville*, 444 F.3d 725, 755–57 (6th Cir. 2006).

was genuinely necessary and whether the police took reasonable steps to minimize its suggestiveness. A jury should likewise be instructed to consider the suggestiveness of show-ups in general, as well as any circumstance that exacerbates the suggestiveness of the show-up, as they bear on the probative value of the identification and any evidence introduced as to the eyewitness's level of confidence in that identification.

Circumstances relevant to whether a show-up was necessary in the first place include whether it was conducted more than two hours after the crime itself, as memory decay thereafter could undermine any potential memory-related advantages that the show-up could have over a lineup or a photo-array. Moreover, courts should consider whether a show-up is needed to establish probable cause to make an arrest insofar as an arrest is warranted in the first place. Regarding this factor, there is widespread agreement that after one witness has identified the suspect in a show-up, police should use more reliable methods (a lineup or photo-array) with any remaining witness whose identification they seek.[174]

Circumstances relevant to whether police took reasonable steps to minimize the suggestiveness of the show-up include whether, before the procedure, the police administered an unbiased instruction that "the person he or she is about to see may or may not be the perpetrator . . . [that] it is equally important to clear an innocent person[] [and] that the investigation will continue regardless of the outcome of the showup."[175] Other relevant circumstances include aspects of the suspect appearance that reinforce the impression, inherent in the structure of a show-up, that police "have their man." These include whether during the show-up, the suspect is held in handcuffs, surrounded by police, or in the back of a police car, and whether the suspect has apparent injuries from their encounter with the police.[176] All of these factors serve as further indicia of guilt that can influence the eyewitness consciously or subconsciously to make an identification. Finally, courts should consider whether the suspect appeared in clothing that the witness described, as research indicates that it is more of a distractor that impedes careful consideration of the suspect's face than a retrieval cue that facilitates it.[177]

---

174. *2019 Third Circuit Task Force Report*, *supra* note 20, at 45–46 & n.225.
175. *Id.* at 43–44 & n.209.
176. *Id.* at 45.
177. Neuschatz et al., *supra* note 148, at 53–55, 65.

3. *Mugshot Searches*

In a mugshot search, a witness peruses the routine booking photos of "known offenders" to see whether the perpetrator of the witnessed crime is among them.[178] Researchers agree that mugshot searches are inherently suggestive and therefore undesirable.[179] Nevertheless, mugshot searches remain one of the ways that police in major cities respond to "difficult-to-solve crimes," when "other evidence is scarce."[180] By a 2010 estimate, this technique was used by more than a quarter of the departments in the country, including 44 percent of those with 500 or more sworn officers.[181] Defenders of the mugshot search insist that it is a sound method of generating leads because any mistaken identifications can be ferreted out by placing the suspect in a lineup for confirmation of identification, after the witness recognizes the person's mugshot.[182] However, these claims do not hold up under even modest scrutiny.

Notably, a 2006 meta-analysis by Deffenbacher et al. found that mere exposure to a person's mugshots after witnessing a crime significantly increased the chances of misidentifying that person in a subsequent lineup procedure.[183] Such a misidentification is a form of "transference" because it involves misidentification of a familiar but innocent person. As noted in the previous chapter, researchers have been able to induce transference errors by including bystanders who moderately resemble the perpetrator in the lineup or photo-array.[184] However, mugshot exposure resulted in twice as much transference as researchers observed in the bystander experiments discussed in Chapter 3.

This transference effect was even worse for those who not only saw a person's mugshot before viewing a lineup, but also identified one of the mugshots as the perpetrator. Such prior commitment decreased a person's likelihood of selecting the true perpetrator from a lineup, even where the witness only indicated that the person mugshot "is or maybe" the perpetrator. For all these reasons there is widespread agreement that showing random photographs should be avoided. If such a procedure is used, the photographs presented should be documented.

---

178. PERF Survey, *supra* note 26, at 104.

179. *2019 Third Circuit Task Force Report*, *supra* note 20, at 68.

180. Joseph Goldstein, *Jailing the Wrong Man: Mug Shot Searches Persist in New York, Despite Serious Risks*, N.Y. Times (Jan. 5, 2019), https://www.nytimes.com/2019/01/05/nyregion/nypd-mug-shots-false-identification.html.

181. PERF Survey, *supra* note 26, at 67.

182. Goldstein, *supra* note 180.

183. Kenneth A. Deffenbacher et al., *Mugshot Exposure Effects: Retroactive Interference, Mugshot Commitment, Source Confusion, and Unconscious Transference*, 30 L. & Hum. Behav. 287, 287–307 (2006).

184. *Id.* at 289.

4. *Composite Images*

As noted in Chapter 1, when police want to enlist the help of others in identifying or apprehending a suspect, they may ask an eyewitness to assist in the creation of an image of the perpetrator's face that can be posted in a public space, circulated to other law enforcement agencies, and broadcast on media or social media.[185] The image itself can be drawn by a sketch artist or created using a computer or a set of acetate transparencies with facial features printed on them.

There is some agreement that police "should only use [composite images] rarely and with great caution" because they have potential to "taint an eyewitness's memory" and undermine the reliability of subsequent identifications.[186] The concerns underlying this assessment are threefold:

- First, a number of studies have shown that, as a general matter, we are not very good at capturing other people's likenesses using the kind of feature-based composite technology that is most often used in the United States.[187] We may be prone to inaccuracy in this activity because it requires us to relay specific information about a person's facial features—size, shape, and spacing—when we generally do not process faces in this way.[188] Rather, our facial processing tends to be holistic[189] and uneven, insofar as we do not take in the same amount of information about every part of a face when we look at it.[190] Attempting to

---

185. PERF Survey, *supra* note 26, at 66.

186. *2019 Third Circuit Task Force Report*, *supra* note 20, at 70.

187. *See, e.g.*, Graham M. Davies & Tim Valentine, *Facial Composites: Forensic Utility and Psychological Research*, in 2 Handbook of Eyewitness Psychology (Michael P. Toglia et al., eds 2007); C.D. Frowd et al., *An Evaluation of US Systems for Facial Composite Production*, 50 Ergonomics 1987 (2008), https://doi.org/10.1080/00140130701523611.

188. *2019 Third Circuit Task Force Report*, *supra* note 20, at 69 & n.378. Notably, our verbal descriptions tend to facilitate better identifications than the composites we create. Specifically, in experimental settings, when subjects are given a set of photos and another person's verbal description of someone in the photos, they tend to be better at selecting the person described than those who attempt the same task with another person's composite image. Annelies Vredeveldt & Colin Getty Tredoux, *Composite Communication: How Dissemination of Facial Composites in the Media Affects Police Investigations*, 1 Memory, Mind & Media 1, 8 (2022), available at https://doi.org/10.1017/mem.2022.4. Moreover, when people create feature-based composite images of celebrities with whom they are unfamiliar, these composites tend to be very poorly recognized by those familiar with that celebrity. C.D. Frowd et al., *An Evaluation of US Systems for Facial Composite Production*, 50 Ergonomics 1987 (2008), https://doi.org/10.1080/00140130701523611. Both outcomes suggest that something may be lost in translation when we try to make a feature-based composite of someone we do not know very well. *See* Vredeveldt & Tredoux, *supra*, at 8.

189. *Id.*

190. *See, e.g.*, Meissner et al., *supra* note 151, at 17.

retrieve information about specific features can hinder retrieval in a way that leaves us open to distortions, especially as to those features that are not as well remembered.

- Second, there is reason to believe that inaccurate composite images might "overshadow" the memory of their preparers,[191] just as an inaccurate verbal description or feature checklist can "overshadow" the memory of its source. Such overshadowing may impair the preparer's ability to recognize the true perpetrator but may also foster misidentification, insofar as anyone who becomes a suspect based on their resemblance to the image may end up resembling the image more than any filler in a lineup.[192]
- Third, exposure to an inaccurate or distorted composite image can contaminate the memory of other eyewitnesses, especially when viewed close in time to an identification procedure.[193] Such findings are particularly disconcerting given that composite images are sometimes generated for the exact purpose of being broadcast indiscriminately to the general public to generate leads.

When combined with the fact that composite sketch preparation was involved in 25 percent) of all DNA exonerations,[194] including the case of Ronald Cotton, as summarized in Chapter 2 of this book,[195] these factors suggest that composite images should, at the very least, be subject to certain procedural safeguards and limitations, if not categorically discouraged.

When considering whether to have a witness work on a composite image, police must vet that witness's memory carefully to ensure it is strong enough to have a reasonable chance of yielding an accurate image. Police should not allow witnesses to work together on a composite, should not expose one witness to another witness's composite, and should consider having only one witness create a composite instead of allowing multiple witnesses to create composites in the same case or for the same suspect.

---

191. *2019 Third Circuit Task Force Report*, *supra* note 20, at 69 & n.379.

192. *See People v. Maldonado*, 769 N.E.2d 1281, 1285–86 (N.Y. 2002) (noting that where a sketch "forms the basis for an arrest, one thing is certain . . . it will resemble the person accused," regardless of whether that person is actually the perpetrator).

193. Siegfried L. Sporer et al., *Does Exposure to Facial Composites Damage Eyewitness Memory? A Comprehensive Review*, 34 Appl. Cognitive Psychol. 1166, 1171–72 (2020), https://doi.org/10.1002/acp.3705; Vredeveldt & Tredoux, *supra* note 188, at 11.

194. *2019 Third Circuit Task Force Report*, *supra* note 20, at 70.

195. *See* Chapter 2, § III.B.

III. Estimator Variables

Estimator variables are circumstances that can affect the accuracy of an eyewitness identification but which are (for the most part) outside of law enforcement control.[196] Some of these variables (weapon focus effect, exposure duration, distance, and lighting conditions) relate to the circumstances of the event. Some (cross-race effect, age, stress, and intoxication) relate to the condition of the observer and/or the observed. These variables should always be assessed holistically, rather than in a piecemeal fashion.[197] Although, by definition, they lie outside of law enforcement control, it is nevertheless incumbent upon police to carefully document these variables when a crime is reported, as they may be important to determining the weight or admissibility of identification evidence.

A common objection to the use of estimator variables in jury instructions is that a jury may misconstrue them as *necessarily* indicative of inaccuracy, when they only suggest greater *potential* for inaccuracy.[198] There may be individual differences in how each variable affects different witnesses. Likewise, their effects may be mitigated or exacerbated by other circumstances. However, these same observations could be made about most of the original *Manson* factors—opportunity to view the perpetrator, degree of attention, and time between the incident and identification—that continue to dictate jury consideration of eyewitness reliability in jurisdictions across the country. Each of these factors (some of which are incorporated into the estimator variables listed below) suggests only a *potential* for inaccuracy that can be undermined or enhanced by other variables. The risk that a juror would give too much weight to an estimator variable can be effectively managed, as courts have always managed such risks: that is, by allowing parties to put on evidence and make arguments regarding the significance of each variable; and by instructing jurors to consider these variables holistically and based on the evidence presented.

---

196. *2019 Third Circuit Task Force Report*, *supra* note 20, at 77. Retention interval may be the most notable counterexample. Although police do not exercise absolute control over how long it takes to arrange an identification procedure, they can affect the timing.

197. *Id.*

198. *Cf. id.* at 77–92 (noting the minority view on the validity of various estimator variables).

A. (Why) Do Estimator Variables Still Matter, Given the Pristine Conditions Hypothesis?

As a historical matter, the development and embrace of estimator variables as a framework for assessing the reliability of eyewitness identifications can be traced back to the realization that eyewitness certainty can be manufactured easily by investigators both before and after an identification.[199] Numerous studies have shown that eyewitness confidence tends to bear little if any relationship to the accuracy of an identification by the time an eyewitness can testify in front of a judge or a jury.[200] Moreover, studies show that eyewitness overconfidence induced by suggestive police practices has played an outsized role in convicting the innocent.[201] Seventy-six percent of known DNA exonerees were identified by an eyewitness at trial,[202] and in every one of these trials, at least one eyewitness expressed "high confidence" in their identification.[203] Against this backdrop, researchers and advocates have urged judges and juries to determine the reliability of identification evidence using system and estimator variables, which are by definition less susceptible to manipulation. Some courts have further been inspired to eschew reliance on eyewitness certainty as a reliability factor in evaluating pretrial admissibility and to caution juries against uncritically relying on eyewitness certainty as a measure of accuracy.

As already noted, recent research indicates that some indications of eyewitness confidence, that is, those recorded in the immediate aftermath of an identification, may in fact be trustworthy. Recent attempts to probe the relationship between eyewitness confidence and accuracy suggest that statements of high initial confidence are extremely probative of accuracy when recorded by a blind administrator immediately after a lineup or photo-array that was administered under "pristine" conditions, that is, that was unbiased and double blind.[204] Some refer to this relationship as the pristine conditions hypothesis. Likewise, research tends to confirm something suggested by the many DNA exonerees who were confidently identified in court by witnesses who either lacked confidence or were unable to identify them at all during the initial identification procedure: identifications made with low

199. Wixted & Wells, *supra* note 32.
200. *2019 Third Circuit Task Force Report*, *supra* note 20, at 57–58 & nn.299–300.
201. Brandon L. Garrett, Convicting the Innocent 63 (2011).
202. *Id.* at 48.
203. Wixted & Wells, *supra* note 32, at 11.
204. *Id.*

initial confidence tend to be error prone, regardless of the circumstances under which the eyewitnesses made them.[205]

The foregoing research has inspired a variety of recommendations. Some are fairly uncontroversial. For instance, it seems inarguable that police should record contemporaneous statements of confidence and that judges and juries should not be discouraged from using them to assess the reliability of an identification at trial. As many others have observed, video recording these confidence statements (as well as the underlying identification procedure itself) would add highly probative information to assessments of eyewitness reliability.[206] Likewise, there appears to be expert consensus that identifications made with low initial confidence or that follow prior unsuccessful identification attempts warrant greater scrutiny and skepticism than they have previously received by judges or juries.[207]

Other recommendations inspired by the pristine conditions hypothesis have been controversial, to say the least. In particular, some have argued that the system/estimator variable paradigm is inherently flawed in that it allows judges and juries to disregard the high level of confidence that a witness has contemporaneously expressed in a "pristine" identification in favor of estimator variables that, under the circumstances, should carry only negligible weight.[208] Thus, some have argued that it may be time to dispense with estimator variables altogether, at least where some high-confidence identifications (those obtained under pristine conditions) and all low-confidence identifications are concerned.[209] However, there are several reasons why estimator variables should remain part of reliability assessments for the foreseeable future, even where there is a contemporaneous statement of high confidence.

To begin with, the methodologies underlying the pristine conditions hypothesis are the subject of ongoing scientific debate. Pristine conditions research has relied on laboratory testing and field studies involving real police departments.[210] A flaw inherent in field studies is that there is no "ground truth" regarding the guilt or innocence of any suspect who is

---

205. *2019 Third Circuit Task Force Report*, *supra* note 20, at 57.
206. *Id.* at 72; Wells et al., *supra* note 67, at 23.
207. *2019 Third Circuit Task Force Report*, *supra* note 20, at 57.
208. Wixted & Wells, *supra* note 32, at 13–14.
209. *Id.*
210. *Id.* at 40–41.

identified.[211] Thus, researchers must estimate the rate of misidentification for innocent suspects using the baseline probability that the real perpetrator is in the lineup. The problem is that nobody knows what this probability is (how could they?); that rate is likely to fluctuate by department and crime type (because it depends on the quality of the underlying investigation),[212] and research has shown that using different baseline probabilities can alter the predictive power of high initial confidence relative to certain estimator variables.[213]

At the same time, "many of the published tests of the pristine conditions hypothesis have not used especially strong manipulations of the estimator variables under consideration," either because ethical rules forbid it or because strong manipulations make gathering a large amount of data on identifications difficult.[214] In this regard, consider weapon focus and stress. Arguably, the only way to test for the maximum impact of these variables is to put a gun in someone's face and then put them through a mock identification procedure. However, an internal review board would never authorize that experiment, and it may be harder to gather a critical mass of identifications. Thus, the applicability of the pristine conditions hypothesis to conditions that have not been replicated in a laboratory setting remains subject to debate.

Another problem with the proposal to partially eliminate estimator variables in favor of confidence statements is that scientists have yet to agree on the "boundary conditions" for the pristine conditions hypothesis.[215] What does it mean for an identification to be made with high or low confidence such that (other) estimator variables lose their predictive power? How should officers measure that variable? Is a highly confident identification

211. Shari R. Berkowitz & Steven J. Frenda, *Rethinking the Confident Eyewitness: A Reply to Wixted, Mickes, and Fisher*, 13 PERSPECTIVES PSYCHOL. SCI. 336, 338 (2018), https://doi.org/10.1177/1745691617751883 ("As the authors acknowledge, however, accuracy cannot be directly measured in a field study of real-world lineup identifications.").

212. Wixted & Wells, *supra* note 32, at 41.

213. Andrew M. Smith et al., *Evaluating the Claim that High Confidence Implies High Accuracy in Eyewitness Identification*, 27 PSYCHOL. PUB. POL'Y & L. 479 (2021), https://doi.org/10.1037/law0000324; Amber Giacona et al., *Estimator Variables Can Matter Even for High Confidence Lineup Identifications Made Under Pristine Conditions*, 45 L. & HUM. BEHAV. 256 (2021), https://doi.org/10.1037/lhb0000381; *2019 Third Circuit Task Force Report*, *supra* note 20, at 55 n.282 ("[E]ven under pristine conditions, very high-confidence initial identifications are *not* related to accuracy where the 'base rate'—the likelihood that the lineup actually contains the perpetrator—is low.").

214. Giacona et al., *supra* note 213.

215. *Id.*; Smith et al., *supra* note 213.

rendered by an eyewitness during a "pristine" lineup sufficient to wash away the taint of being exposed to a suspect during a previous identification procedure? There is already disagreement among experts as to these important questions.[216]

Even if these outstanding disagreements are resolved in favor of accepting the pristine conditions hypothesis, estimator variables will still be needed (1) to illuminate the chances that a eyewitness's high-confidence identification is the product of a memory error that was not induced or suggested by law enforcement and (2) to help juries decide whether to take an eyewitness's initial statement of high confidence at face value. As discussed in the previous chapter, memory errors can happen organically, and unconscious transference need not be induced by exposure to a suspect in an identification procedure.[217] A witness laboring under such a delusion may nevertheless be very confident in their identification. Moreover, barring video-recorded documentation of an eyewitness identification, it is reasonable to expect the defense and prosecution in a criminal case to take different positions on whether the identification procedure was truly pristine and whether an officer's recording of a confidence statement should be deemed trustworthy beyond a reasonable doubt. Regarding the former, researchers have demonstrated that many lineups end up biased in favor of suspect identification despite good faith efforts to implement best practice recommendations.[218] Thus, "understanding how [estimator] variables affect the accuracy of eyewitness identifications" remains a "necessary" step "to assess[ing] the reliability of an identification."[219]

B. Weapon Focus

The presence of a weapon during a witnessed crime can reduce the accuracy of witness recall and subsequent identifications.[220] Researchers refer to this effect as "weapon focus," and there is also judicial consensus as to its potential impact on eyewitnesses.[221] It can potentially impair witness mem-

---

216. Berkowitz & Frenda, *supra* note 211.

217. Shari R. Berkowitz et al., *Convicting with Confidence? Why We Should Not Over-Rely on Eyewitness Confidence*, 30 Memory 10, 13 (2020), https://doi.org/10.1080/09658211.2020.1849308.

218. James D. Sauer et al., *Pitfalls in Using Eyewitness Confidence to Diagnose the Accuracy of an Individual Identification Decision*, 25 Psychol. Pub. Pol'y & L. 147 (2019), https://doi.org/10.1037/law0000203.

219. *2019 Third Circuit Task Force Report*, *supra* note 20, at 77.

220. *Id.*, at 78.

221. *Id.* at 78 & n.435 (collecting cases).

ory by directing attention toward the weapon and away from the person's appearance.[222] The weapon focus effect may also be related to the stress and arousal that one experiences as a result of seeing a weapon.[223] As noted in Chapter 3, both stress and attentional hijacking from a novel and unusual item have the potential to impact perception, encoding, and/or retrieval. That a weapon's presence tends to negatively impact eyewitness accuracy has been suggested by distinct meta-analyses authored by Steblay et al. and Fawcett et al., respectively.[224]

Those who argue otherwise point to a different meta-analysis by Kocab and Sporer that found no sound basis for concluding that weapon focus undermines the accuracy of identifications (as opposed to suspect descriptions, which did seem to be impaired).[225] However, this particular meta-analysis excludes archival data that are potentially highly relevant, as they tend to provide the most direct (and perhaps best) method of testing how eyewitnesses react when confronted with an actual weapon.[226] To comply with ethical standards, researchers must refrain from placing eyewitnesses in the kind of mortal danger that may accompany an actual criminal encounter.[227] As a result there seems to be consensus that weapon focus exercises at least a small effect on the accuracy of an identification and an even greater impact on the accuracy of a witness's verbal description of the perpetrator.[228]

C. Stress and Fear

"Highly stressful situations have been demonstrated to interfere with eyewitness memory."[229] "Under conditions of high stress, a witness' ability to identify key characteristics of an individual's face (e.g., hair length, hair

222. *Id.* at 78.

223. *But see* Jonathan M. Fawcett, *Looking Down the Barrel of a Gun: What Do We Know About the Weapon Focus Effect?*, 5 J. Appl. Res. Memory & Cognition 257, 259 (2016), https://doi.org/10.1016/j.jarmac.2016.07.005 (finding little empirical support for the threat/arousal explanation).

224. Jonathan M. Fawcett et al., *Of Guns and Geese: A Meta-Analytic Review of the Weapon Focus Literature*, 19 Psychol. Crime & L. 35 (2013), https://doi.org/10.1080/1068316X.2011.599325; Nancy Steblay, *A Meta-Analytic Review of the Weapon Focus Effect*, 16 L. & Hum. Behav. 413 (1992), https://doi.org/10.1007/BF02352267.

225. *2019 Third Circuit Task Force Report*, *supra* note 20, at 79 & n.483 (citing Kerstin Kocab & Siegreid L. Sporer, *The Weapon Focus Effect for Person Identifications and Descriptions: A Meta-Analysis*, *in* 1 Adv. Psychol. & L. 71 (Monica K. Miller & Brian H. Bornstein eds., 2016)).

226. *See, e.g.*, Fawcett, *supra* note 223, at 260–61.

227. *Id.*

228. *Id.*

229. *2019 Third Circuit Task Force Report*, *supra* note 20, at 79.

color, eye color, shape of face, presence of facial hair) may be significantly impaired."[230] Likewise, "meta analysis of 27 independent studies conducted on the effects of stress on identification accuracy showed that, while 59 percent of the 1,727 participants correctly identified the target individual in a target-present lineup after a low-stress encounter, only 39 percent did so after high-stress encounters."[231] Based on these findings, the authors of this study found that it was "safe" to conclude, inter alia, "that heightened stress debilitates eyewitness recall."[232]

In a 2004 study conducted by Morgan et al.:

> Military survival school participants were subjected to two 40–minute interrogations, each by different interrogators, following a 12–hour period of confinement without food and sleep in a mock prisoner of war camp. One interrogation was conducted under high-stress conditions, involving physical confrontation, while the other was conducted under low-stress conditions, involving only deceptive questioning. When asked the next day to identify their interrogators, only 30 percent of the participants correctly identified their high-stress interrogator, while 60 percent correctly identified their low-stress interrogator. The study also noted an associated increase in false identifications—56 percent of the participants falsely identified another person as their high-stress interrogator, compared to 38 percent who did so with regard to their low-stress interrogator.[233]

Scientists believe that stress may undermine eyewitness memory for the perpetrator by exacerbating the attentional trade-offs between those aspects of the event that tend to naturally command eyewitness attention, such as a weapon if one is present, and those that do not, such as details of the perpetrator's appearance. "In general, arousal should increase the effects of competition between different representations, leading to winner-take-more and

---

230. NAT'L RSCH. COUNCIL, *supra* note 2, at 94 (citing Charles A. Morgan et al., *Misinformation Can Influence Memory for Recently Experienced, Highly Stressful Events*, 36 INT'L J.L. & PSYCHIATRY 11 (2013)).

231. SUPREME JUDICIAL COURT STUDY GRP. ON EYEWITNESS EVIDENCE, REPORT AND RECOMMENDATIONS TO THE JUSTICES 59–60 (2013), http://www.mass.gov/files/documents/2016/08/ql/eyewitness-evidence-report-2013.pdf [https://perma.cc/22MF-7SUR] (citing Kenneth A. Deffenbacher et al., *A Meta-Analytic Review of the Effects of High Stress on Eyewitness Memory*, 28 L. & HUM. BEHAV. 687, 699 (2004)).

232. *Id.*

233. *Lawson*, 291 P.3d at 700–01 (citing Morgan et al., *supra* note 221).

loser-take-less effects, regardless of whether the 'winner' (the highest priority aspect of the experience) is spatially central or not."[234] As many courts and commentators have noted, clarification regarding the negative impact of high levels of stress on memory is paramount where identifications are concerned because lay jurors (and even some lawyers and judges) are likely to be operating under the mistaken impression that stress enhances an eyewitness's memory for details.[235] As Morgan wrote regarding the results of his 2004 study on military survival school subjects: "[c]ontrary to popular conception that most people would never forget the face of a clearly seen individual who had physically confronted them and threatened them for more than 30 min[utes], a large number of subjects in this study were unable to correctly identify their perpetrator."[236]

D. Cross-Race Effect/Own-Race Bias

"[W]itnesses may be less accurate when identifying members of another race or ethnicity compared to when they identify members of their own race or ethnicity."[237] Researchers have confirmed the existence of this cross-race effect, also known as own-race or other-race bias, over the course of 159 laboratory experiments and multiple meta-analyses.[238] Studies show that this effect is not limited to those who profess overtly discriminatory views toward members of other races.[239] Two recent meta-analyses have found that cross-race effect

---

234. Mara Mather & Matthew R. Sutherland, *Arousal-Biased Competition in Perception and Memory*, 6 PERSPECTIVES PSYCHOL. SCI. 114 (2011), https://doi.org/10.1177/1745691611400234.

235. *Minor v. United States*, 57 A.3d 406, 413–14 (D.C. 2012) (noting that the "average juror is likely to believe that witnesses remember the details of violent events better than nonviolent ones"); *People v. Campbell*, 847 P.2d 228, 233 (Col. Ct. App. 1992)("[C]ontrary to average juror expectations, stress actually decreases rather than increases accuracy of perception. . . ."), *United States v. Burton*, 1998 U.S. Dist. LEXIS 18730 at *1, *34 (E.D. Tenn. Oct. 8, 1998) ("The results of the psychological research [on stress and accuracy] could well be counter intuitive to a juror, *i.e.*, 'common sense' might tell one that if a weapon is present, the recollection of the event, and the face of the perpetrator, would somehow be forever etched in the mind of the witness (known as the 'flashbulb effect').")

236. *2019 Third Circuit Task Force Report*, *supra* note 20, at 81 (citing Charles A. Morgan III et al., *Accuracy of Eyewitness Memory for Persons Encountered During Exposure to Highly Intense Stress*, 27 INT'L J.L. & PSYCHIATRY 265, 265–79 (2004), https://doi.org/10.1016/j.ijlp.2004.03.004).

237. *Id.* at 82.

238. Jungwon Lee & Steven D. Penrod, *Three-Level Meta-Analysis of the Other-Race Bias in Facial Identification*, 36 APPL. COGNITIVE PSYCHOL. 1106 (2022), https://doi.org/10.1002/acp.3997; Christian A. Meissner & John C. Brigham, *Thirty Years of Investigating the Own-Race Bias in Memory for Faces: A Meta-Analytic Review*, 7 PSYCHOL. PUB. POL'Y. & L. 3 (2001), https://doi.org/10.1037/1076-8971.7.1.3.

239. Lee & Penrod, *supra* note 238; Meissner & Brigham, *supra* note 238.

tends to hinder accuracy more as an eyewitness's viewing opportunity or exposure duration gets shorter and the retention interval gets longer.[240] These meta-analyses further indicate that on average the effects of own-race bias are larger for white observers than for members of other races.[241]

Scientists have offered a few explanations for this phenomenon, some of which are mentioned in the previous chapter. One theory holds that we develop additional expertise in recognizing faces of our own race because of disproportionate contact with them in our own families and beyond.[242] Thus, we become more sensitive to subtle differences between and among the faces of members of our own race. Consistent with this explanation, there is some evidence that prolonged contact with members of a particular race reduces the cross-race effect vis-à-vis members of that race.[243] Another explanation supposes that we hold members of other races to a lower standard of "matching" before we decide that they are someone familiar.[244]

Some have suggested that the cross-race effect varies depending on the emotions of the observer and the observed. A few studies purport to show that people are less susceptible to the cross-race effect when they view someone who is displaying an expression of anger or power, on the theory that the perception of threat inspires greater motivation to encode the person's face.[245] Proponents of this research suggest that "anger expressed by an out-group member may be perceived as more threatening than anger expressed by an in-group member" because of the frequently "competitive" nature of intergroup interactions.[246] However, the methodology of these studies have been called into question by researchers who point out that the angry faces used in the experiment were not just angry but distinctive and unusual in other ways.[247] When researchers repeated the experiment using participants

---

240. Lee & Penrod, *supra* note 238; Meissner & Brigham, *supra* note 238.

241. Lee & Penrod, *supra* note 238; Meissner & Brigham, *supra* note 238.

242. NAT'L RSCH. COUNCIL, *supra* note 2, at 96.

243. *2019 Third Circuit Task Force Report*, *supra* note 20, at 85 & n.469.

244. *Id.*

245. *See, e.g.*, Steven G. Young & Kurt Hugenberg, *Individuation Motivation and Face Experience Can Operate Jointly to Produce the Own-Race Bias*, 3 SOC. PSYCHOL. & PERSONALITY SCI. 80 (2012), https://doi.org/10.1177/1948550611409759; Joshua M Ackerman et al., *They All Look the Same to Me (Unless They're Angry): From Out-Group Homogeneity to Out-Group Heterogeneity*, 17 PSYCHOL. SCI. 836–40 (2006), https://doi.org/10.1111/j.1467-9280.2006.01790.x.

246. Ackerman et al., *supra* note 245.

247. Jason D. Gwinn et al., *Face Recognition in the Presence of Angry Expressions: A Target-Race Effect Rather Than a Cross-Race Effect*, 58 J. EXPERIMENTAL SOC. PSYCHOL. 1, https://doi.org/10.1016/j.jesp.2014.12.001.

of multiple races, and less distinctive but equally angry pictures, they found evidence for the cross-race effect.[248] This result was consistent with another study that found that feelings of joy tended to mitigate the cross-race effect more than neutrality or negative emotion.[249]

E. Age

Eyewitness age can impact the accuracy of an identification. "[C]hildren . . . are generally less likely to make accurate identifications than adults, especially in target absent conditions."[250] One meta-analysis found a significant disparity between adults and children of all ages in terms of the ability to correctly reject a lineup where the target is absent.[251] Specifically, although children five and older were able to recognize mock perpetrators in target present lineups about as well as their adult counterparts, children of all ages were less likely to correctly reject a lineup in which the perpetrator was absent.[252] Even adolescents as old as thirteen misidentified innocent suspects more often than their adult counterparts, and the use of sequential rather than simultaneous lineups seemed to exacerbate this disparity.[253] A more recent meta-analysis using the signal detection framework has replicated this finding, suggesting that children are less capable than young adults of discriminating between innocent suspects and perpetrators.[254]

In addition, a significant body of research suggests that eyewitness accuracy starts to decline in middle age.[255] "A meta-analysis examining eyewitness accuracy throughout the lifespan found that young adults made more accurate identification decisions than either older adults (ages forty-five and older) or children (ages seventeen or under)."[256] This body of research sug-

---

248. *Id.*

249. Kareem J. Johnson & Barbara L. Fredrickson, "*We All Look the Same to Me*": *Positive Emotions Eliminate the Own-Race Bias in Face Recognition*, 16 PSYCHOL. SCI. 875 (2001), https://www.jstor.org/stable/40064333.

250. *Lawson*, 291 P.3d at 703 (citing Gary L. Wells & Elizabeth A. Olson, *Eyewitness Testimony*, 54 ANNU. REV. PSYCHOL. 277, 280 (2003)).

251. *2019 Third Circuit Task Force Report*, *supra* note 20, at 86 (citing Joanna D. Pozzulo & R.C.L. Lindsay, *Identification Accuracy of Children Versus Adults: A Meta-Analysis*, 22 L. & HUM. BEHAV. 549, 549–70 (1998), https://doi.org/10.1023/a:1025739514042).

252. *Id.*

253. Pozzulo & Lindsay, *supra* note 251.

254. Ryan J. Fitzgerald & Heather L. Price, *Eyewitness Identification Across the Life Span: A Meta-Analysis of Age Differences*, 141 PSYCHOL. BULL. 1228, 1228–65 (2015), https://doi.org/10.1037/bul0000013.

255. *Lawson*, 291 P.3d at 703 (citation omitted).

256. *2019 Third Circuit Task Force Report*, *supra* note 20, at 86 (citing Fitzgerald & Price, *supra* note 254).

gests that much like children, older adults are not as good at discriminating between innocent suspects and perpetrators as younger adults.[257]

There is reason to believe that children and the elderly will not be as good at recognizing a young adult perpetrator because of "own-age bias." A person's "ability to remember faces of his or her own age group is often superior to his or her ability to remember faces of another age group."[258]

Studies also suggest that children and the elderly are more susceptible to false memory than young adults.[259] For this reason, the various system variables that promote false memory—for example, suggestive questioning, verbal overshadowing from being led into an inaccurate description, participation in multiple identification procedures—may pose a heightened risk where children and the elderly are concerned. For all these reasons, judges and juries should consider age in deciding whether to admit or credit identification evidence.

F. Exposure Duration

"There is substantial agreement among eyewitness researchers that exposure duration—the length of time that the witness has to view the event perpetrator—can impact the accuracy of memory for an event. . . ."[260] Limited time of exposure can undermine the quality of eyewitness descriptions.[261] "Meta-analyses on the effects of exposure time have found that relatively long exposure durations produce greater accuracy[.]"[262] Although "[r]esearch has not established . . . a specific amount of time for optimal identification accuracy,"[263] one meta-analysis "shows that the beneficial

257. Fitzgerald & Price, *supra* note 254; Scott H. Fraundorf et al., *Aging and Recognition Memory: A Meta-Analysis*, 154 Psychol. Bull. 339, 339–71 (2019), https://doi.org/10.1037/bul0000185; Stephen Rhodes et al., *Age-Related Differences in Recall and Recognition: A Meta-Analysis*, 26 Psychonomic Bull. Rev. 1529, 1529–47 (2019), https://doi.org/10.3758/s13423-019-01649-y.

258. Nat'l Rsch. Council, *supra* note 2, at 93 & n.66 (citation omitted); Jeffery S. Anastasi & Matthew G. Rhodes, *The Own-Age Bias in Face Recognition: A Meta-Analytic and Theoretical Review*, 138 Psychol. Bull. 136 (2012), https://doi.org.10.1037/a0025750.

259. Deborah Davis & Elizabeth F. Loftus, *Age and Functioning in the Legal System: Perception Memory and Judgment in Victims, Witnesses and Jurors*, *in* Handbook of Human Factors in Litigation (Y. Ian Noy & Waldemar Karwowski eds. 2005); Jennifer K. Ackil & Maria S. Zaragoza, *Memorial Consequences of Forced Confabulation: Age Differences in Susceptibility to False Memories*, 34 Dev. Psychol. 1358 (1998), http://dx.doi.org/10.1037/0012-1649.34.6.1358.

260. *2019 Third Circuit Task Force Report*, *supra* note 20, at 86.

261. *Id.* (quoting Wells et al., *supra* note 67) (internal quotation marks omitted).

262. Nat'l Rsch. Council, *supra* note 2, at 114 (citing Brian Bornstein et al., *Effects of Exposure Time and Cognitive Operations on Facial Identification Accuracy: A Meta-Analysis of Two Variables Associated with Initial Memory Strength*, 18 Psychol. Crime & L. 473 (2012)).

263. *2019 Third Circuit Task Force Report*, *supra* note 20, at 86.

effect of longer exposure time on accuracy is greatest between the shortest durations, up to approximately 30 seconds. In contrast, for durations over 30 seconds, only substantial increases in exposure time produced marked improvement in witness performance."[264] Complicating matters further, witnesses are often inaccurate in their estimates of the length of encounters.[265] "[P]eople tend to overestimate the length of brief viewing experiences."[266]

G. Distance and Lighting

"[T]he physical distance between the witness and the perpetrator is an important estimator variable, as it directly affects the ability of the eyewitness to discern visual details, including features of the perpetrator."[267] As Nyman et al. noted in a recent publication, "[t]he negative impact of distance on identification accuracy is due to the fact that as distance increases the image projected on the retina becomes smaller," decreasing visual acuity and the ability to distinguish facial features and other identifying characteristics.[268] Just as "a large enough distance" may make "two separate lines" appear as "only one line or even just a dot," so too will it diminish the details that we rely on to ascertain identity.[269]

While some studies suggest that the relationship between distance and accuracy is linear,[270] others have suggested that there is a precipitous decline at fifteen meters/fifty feet.[271] A recent study found a 50 percent loss of accuracy when subjects initially observed a target at a distance of forty meters.[272] Judges and juries may be unaware that such upper limits exist or that the

264. *Lawson*, 291 P.3d at 702 (internal citations omitted).

265. Elizabeth Loftus et al., *Time Went by so Slowly: Overestimation of Event Duration by Males and Females*, 1 Appl. Cognitive Psychol. 3–13 (1987); *Lawson*, 291 P.3d at 702 ("Studies also show that witnesses consistently and significantly overestimate short durations of time (generally, durations of 20 minutes or less), especially during highly stimulating, stressful, or unfamiliar events."); *Henderson*, 27 A.3d at 905 ("studies have shown, and the Special Master found, 'that witnesses consistently tend to overestimate short durations, particularly where much was going on or the event was particularly stressful.'").

266. *2019 Third Circuit Task Force Report*, *supra* note 20, at 86.

267. Nat'l Rsch. Council, *supra* note 2, at 92 (citing Carla L. Maclean et al., *Post-Identification Feedback Effects: Investigators and Evaluators*, 25 Appl. Cognitive Psychol. 739–52 (2011)).

268. Thomas J. Nyman et al., *A Stab in the Dark: The Distance Threshold of Target Identification in Low Light*, Cogent Psychol. (2019), https://doi.org/10.1080/23311908.2019.1632047.

269. *Id.*

270. *2019 Third Circuit Task Force Report*, *supra* note 20, at 88.

271. *See, e.g.*, James Michael Lampinen et al., *Effects of Distance on Face Recognition: Implications for Eyewitness Identification*, 21 Psychonomics Bull. Rev. 1489, 1489–90 (2014), https://doi.org/10.3758/s13423-014-0641-2.

272. Thomas J. Nyman et al., *The Distance Threshold of Reliable Eyewitness Identification*, 43 L. & Hum. Behav. 527 (2019), https://doi.org/10.1037/lhb0000342.

effects of distance can be exacerbated by age, with young children and the elderly experiencing greater difficulties over long distances.[273] Moreover, recent research suggests that at large enough distances (forty meters or more) the relationship between eyewitness confidence and accuracy begins to break down.[274]

"Research has also shown that people have difficulty estimating distances."[275] In one study, participants were asked to view targets at various distances and then to estimate their proximity to those targets, before attempting to identify those targets in a lineup.[276] When attempting to estimate their proximity to the targets, participants "often" made "errors in judgement" which were "substantial."[277] Moreover, the "[a]ccuracy of [their] identification decisions was significantly influenced by the [objective] distance between the witness and the target at the time of exposure," even when participants mistakenly believed that they had been relatively close to their targets.[278]

Much like distance, poor lighting can also undermine visual acuity. It has been reported that for someone with 20/20 vision, "adjusting lighting conditions from daylight to starlight" can result in a loss of visual acuity to nearly 20/300, the visual acuity associated with legal blindness in the United States.[279] Research suggests that poor lighting can exacerbate the effects of longer viewing distance and vice versa.[280] Likewise, as noted in the preceding chapter, facial recognition processes can be compromised when a suspect is viewed under lighting conditions that are unusual or do not correspond with those present at the time of the witnessed crime.[281]

H. Disguises and Other Clothing

Disguises and distracting accessories and clothing articles have demonstrated capacity to impair future recognition. "[T]he hair and hairline have

273. *Id.*

274. *Id.*

275. *Henderson*, 27 A.3d at 906 (citing R.C.L. Lindsay et al., *How Variations in Distance Affect Eyewitness Reports and Identification Accuracy,* 32 Law & Hum. Behav. 526 (2008)).

276. Lindsay et al., *supra* note 275, at 526.

277. *Id.* at 528.

278. *Id.* at 533.

279. Nyman et al., *supra* note 268.

280. *Id.*

281. Wendy L. Braje et al., *Illumination Effects in Face Recognition*, 26 Psychobiology 371 (1998), https://link.springer.com/content/pdf/10.3758/BF03330623.pdf; *accord* Simone Favelle et al., *About Face: Matching Unfamiliar Faces Across Rotations of View and Lighting*, i-Perception 1, Nov. 29, 2017, https://journals.sagepub.com/doi/full/10.1177/2041669517744221.

been found to be important cues for identification accuracy."[282] A recent analysis based on "data from over 1300 eyewitnesses" suggests that eyewitness accuracy is "lower among eyewitnesses who viewed perpetrators wearing hats (44%) than among eyewitnesses who viewed perpetrators whose hair and hairlines were visible (57%)."[283] This trend was "present in each study" and "not qualified by type of lineup[.]"[284] Likewise, a recent exploration of the impact of disguises on identification accuracy concludes that disguises, such as a stocking worn over the face, reduce identification accuracy, and surprisingly, that wearing sunglasses can have an even greater effect than wearing a stocking over the face.[285] Precise jury instruction regarding the consideration of this factor is critical because, as the *Henderson* court noted, jurors are unaware of the effect of a disguise on the ability to make an identification.[286]

I. Retention Interval

Although common sense dictates that identifications will be more accurate when they occur closer in time to a witnessed event, considerable psychological research suggests, unintuitively, that "[t]he rate of forgetting for an unfamiliar face is greatest soon after the initial observation and tends to level off over time."[287] A meta-analysis of fifty-three studies by Deffenbacher et al. found that "increased delay of a test for recognition memory for the once-seen face portends decreased probability of correct recognition judgments."[288] These results "confirm that there is indeed a statistically reliable association between longer retention intervals and decreased face recognition memory. . . . That is, there is an increase in positive forgetting as the delay increases between encoding of a face and test of one's memory for it."[289]

---

282. Brian L. Cutler, *A Sample of Witness, Crime, and Perpetrator Characteristics Affecting Eyewitness Identification Accuracy*, 4 CARDOZO PUB. L. POL'Y & ETHICS J. 327, 332 (2006).

283. *Id.*

284. *Id.*

285. *2019 Third Circuit Task Force Report*, *supra* note 20, at 89 & n.504 (citing Jamal K. Mansour et al., *Impact of Disguise on Identification Decisions and Confidence with Simultaneous and Sequential Lineups*, 36 L. & HUM. BEHAV. 513, 513–26 (2012)).

286. *Henderson* , 27 A.3d. at 911 (Citing Brian Cutler, *Juror Sensitivity to Eyewitness Identification Evidence*, 14 L. & HUM. BEHAV. 185, 186–87 (1990)).

287. NAT'L RSCH. COUNCIL, *supra* note 2, at 99.

288. Kenneth A. Deffenbacher et al., *Forgetting the Once-Seen Face: Estimating the Strength of an Eyewitness's Memory Representation,* 14 J. EXPERIMENTAL PSYCHOL.: APPL. 139, 148 (2008).

289. *Id.* at 148.

7
Reform Possibilities

To meaningfully deter suggestive police practices that increase the risk of wrongful conviction—a risk that is disproportionately borne by poor people of color in this country[1]—the law should empower and obligate judges to exclude from trial those eyewitness identifications that have been obtained by suggestive police practices. In addition, to meaningfully promote the reliability of both identifications and convictions, judges should have the duty and authority to exclude those identifications whose probative value is eclipsed by the unfair prejudice that might arise from their consideration by the jury. Finally, judges and juries should determine the weight and admissibility of eyewitness identification using system and estimator variables that have proven capacity to affect the reliability of an identification.

As discussed at the end of Chapter 2, the exclusionary remedy provided in *Manson* cannot accommodate these goals because it is unmoored from any evidence-based understanding of eyewitness perception and memory, because is untethered from any evidence-based understanding of the jury, and because it fails to deter and may even encourage suggestive police practices. The *Manson* test's deficiencies throw into stark relief the need for cautionary instructions

1. *See, e.g.*, Margaret Bull Kovera, *The Role of Suspect Development Practices in Eyewitness Identification Accuracy and Racial Disparities in Wrongful Conviction*, 17 Soc. Issues Pol'y Rev. 125 (2024), https://doi.org/10.1111/sipr.12102.

on eyewitness identification and expert testimony to minimize the likelihood of wrongful conviction. However, these tools have been compromised by the absence of a right to receive them in anything but the most compelling and identification-dependent cases. In addition, the most popular jury instruction on this topic—the *Telfaire* instruction—lacks the specificity needed to enable the jury to meaningfully scrutinize an identification. The result is a situation where mistaken identifications are "responsible for more wrongful convictions than all other causes combined,"[2] unless these issues are addressed.

So, what can we do? What follows are a list of suggestions to improve the *Manson* test and the *Telfaire* instruction and, further, to rein in judicial discretion regarding the availability of cautionary instructions and expert witnesses.

I. Improving the Manson Test

A. Legislation

In the 1960s many commentators considered statutory reform to be the most promising means of reining in suggestive police practices.[3] In the last twenty or so years, nineteen states have adopted legislation regarding eyewitness identification procedures. Of these, eighteen (California, Connecticut, Florida, Georgia, Illinois, Kansas, Louisiana, Maryland, Nebraska, New Mexico, North Carolina, Ohio, Texas, Utah, Vermont, Virginia, West Virginia, and Wisconsin) have enacted statutes directly requiring that law enforcement officials adopt written procedures for eyewitness identifications.[4] These statutes "typically assert that a trial judge may consider the failure to follow the prescribed procedures as a factor in assessing admissibility and informing the jury" but "rarely require that a trial judge exclude such identification evidence from consideration by the jury."[5]

2. *2019 Report of the United States Court of Appeals for the Third Circuit Task Force on Eyewitness Identifications*, 92 Temp. L. Rev. 1, 10–11 (2019) [hereinafter *2019 Third Circuit Task Force Report*].

3. *United States v. Wade*, 388 U.S. 218, 239 n.30 (1967) (citing Wigmore, The Science of Judicial Proof 541 (3d ed. 1937)); 3 Wigmore, Evidence § 786a, at 210 (Chadbourn rev. 1970).

4. *See* Cal. Pen. Code 10 § 859.7 (2018); Conn. Gen. Stat. § 54-1p (West 2012); Fla. Code Ann. § 92.70 (West 2017); 11 Ga. Code Ann. § 17-20-2 (West 2016); 725 Ill. Comp. Stat. § 5/107A-5 (West 2003); Kansas 12 SB 428 (2016); La. Code Crim. Pro. 251-253 (2018); Md. Code Ann., Pub. Safety § 3-506 13 (West 2007); N.C. Gen. Stat. § 15A-284.52 (West 2007); Neb. R.S. § 81-1455 (2016); N.M. Stat. Ann. 1978, §§ 29-3B-1 To -4 (2019); Ohio Rev. 14 Code Ann. § 2933.83 (West 2010); Tex. Code Crim. Proc. Ann. Art. 38.20 (West 2011); Utah 15 Code Ann. § 77-8-4 (West 1980); Va. Code Ann. § 19.2-390.02 (West 2005); Va. Code Ann. 16 § 9.1-102.54; 13 V.S.A. § 5581; W. Va. Code Ann. § 62-1E-1 (West 2013); Wis. Stat. § 175.50 17 (West 2005).

5. Nat'l Rsch. Council of the Nat'l Acads., Identifying the Culprit: Assessing Eyewitness Identification 37 (2014) [hereinafter Nat'l Rsch. Council].

B. Attempts to Redeem the *Manson* Factors

"Some jurisdictions, though adhering to *Manson's* reliability-based framework, have taken modest measures to refine or expand upon Manson's reliability criteria to be more closely aligned with modern empirical realities."[6] In the "refinement" camp, Vermont, Kansas, and Utah have abandoned eyewitness certainty as a factor in evaluating the reliability of eyewitness identifications, while pointing to post-*Manson* scientific evidence "concerning the fallibility of eyewitness identification, and specifically the effect of suggestive circumstances on the degree of certainty the witness expresses in an identification."[7]

The "expansion" camp includes New Jersey, Alaska, Oregon, and Connecticut, each of which has incorporated an expansive list of system and estimator variables into their determinations regarding pretrial admissibility.[8] The New Jersey Supreme Court's opinion in *Henderson* represents the first effort to comprehensively reform eyewitness identification admissibility determinations, in light of recent research on eyewitness reliability. On appeal following Henderson's conviction, the Innocence Project and the Association of Criminal Defense Lawyers of New Jersey argued as *amici* that in light of this research, the *Manson* factors were generally insufficient to test the reliability of an identification in Henderson's case.[9] Citing the lack of a trial court record on this issue, the New Jersey Supreme Court remanded the case and appointed a Special Master to determine whether *Manson* "remained valid and appropriate in light of recent scientific and other evidence."[10] The Special Master presided over a ten-day hearing and issued an "extensive" report, based on testimony from seven experts and two hundred scientific studies.[11] Adopting the Special Master's recommendations almost entirely, the *Henderson* court held that the *Manson* test needed to be revised to reflect recent research on memory.[12] Specifically, the court held that more thorough and holistic consideration of "system variables" within

6. *State v. Martinez*, 478 P.3d 880, 898 (N.M. 2021).

7. *State v. Discola*, 184 A.3d 1177 (Vt. 2018).

8. *State v. Harris*, 191 A.3d 119, 134 (Conn. 2018); *Young v. State*, 374 P.3d 395, 427 (Alaska 2016); *State v. Henderson*, 27 A.3d 872 (N.J. 2011); *State v. Lawson*, 291 P.3d 673 (Or. 2012).

9. *Henderson*, 27 A.3d at 884.

10. *Id.*

11. *Id.* at 877; *see also id.* at 884–85 (naming experts).

12. *Id.* at 877. The *Henderson* court disagreed with the Special Master's recommendation that pretrial suppression hearings be available, even where there was no indication that the procedure was suggestive. *Id.* at 922–23; *see also State v. Chen*, 27 A.3d 930 (N.J. 2011) (holding that "highly suggestive" circumstances are required to warrant a hearing absent an indication of suggestive state action).

law enforcement control and "estimator variables" beyond law enforcement control was needed to deter suggestive practices and evaluate the risk of irreparable misidentification.[13] Thereafter, Oregon, Alaska, and Connecticut adopted similar reforms based on the findings of the Special Master.

Under the New Jersey, Alaska, and Connecticut approaches:

> [T]he defendant bears the burden of adducing evidence indicating that the identification procedure undermined the reliability of the identification [using system variables]; if the defendant makes such a showing, the state must offer evidence to demonstrate that the identification nevertheless was reliable under the totality of the circumstances; if the state adduces such evidence, the defendant assumes the burden of proving a very substantial likelihood of misidentification.[14]

By contrast, in Oregon:

> [W]hen a defendant has filed a motion to exclude eyewitness identification evidence, the state must establish that the evidence is admissible under the ordinary rules of evidence. If the state meets that burden, the burden shifts to the defendant to establish that, "although the eyewitness evidence is otherwise admissible, the probative value of the evidence is substantially outweighed by the danger of unfair prejudice, confusion of the issues, misleading the jury, or by considerations of undue delay or needless presentation of cumulative evidence." In determining the probative value of eyewitness evidence, "trial courts must examine the relative reliability of [the] evidence produced by the parties . . . The more factors—the presence of system variables alone or in combination with estimator variables—that weigh against reliability of the identification, the less persuasive the identification evidence will be to prove the fact of identification, and correspondingly, the less probative value that identification will have."[15]

Nevertheless, a common thread through all these approaches is a deliberate rejection of a rule of *per se* exclusion, akin to the *Manson* Court's.[16]

13. *Henderson*, 27 A.3d at 919–22.

14. *State v. Harris*, 191 A.3d 119, 134 n.18 (2018).

15. *Id.* at 141 (citations omitted).

16. *Henderson*, 27 A.3d at 922 (declined to adopt a *per se* rule because "[a]lthough that approach might yield greater deterrence, it could also lead to the loss of a substantial amount of evidence").

C. *Per Se* Approaches

On the other hand, New Mexico, New York, and Massachusetts have embraced the *per se* formulation that the *Manson* Court rejected.[17] In Massachusetts, "an out-of-court eyewitness identification made during a police identification procedure is not admissible 'where the defendant proves by a preponderance of the evidence, considering the totality of the circumstances, that the identification is so unnecessarily suggestive and conducive to irreparable misidentification that its admission would deprive the defendant of his right to due process.'"[18] "Under this per se formulation, 'a defendant must prove not only that the out-of-court identification procedure administered by the police was suggestive, but that it was *unnecessarily* suggestive,' an inquiry which focuses on whether police have 'good reason' to engage in a suggestive identification procedure in the first instance."[19]

New York has adopted a rule whereby a "pretrial identification procedure that is unduly suggestive violates a defendant's due process rights and is 'not admissible to determine the guilt or innocence of an accused.'"[20] In so doing, it expressly rejected the *Manson* test, finding that any allowance for the admission of identifications that were suggestively obtained pretrial would only "increase the risks of convicting the innocent in cases where it has the desired effect of contributing to a conviction."[21]

Finally, in New Mexico:

> [I]f a witness makes an identification of a defendant as a result of a police identification procedure that is unnecessarily suggestive and conducive to misidentification, the identification and any subsequent identification by the same witness must be suppressed. The question of whether the identification is "unnecessarily suggestive" focuses not only on the identification procedure itself but also on whether the police have a "good reason" to use a suggestive identification procedure in the first place.
>
> . . .
>
> [W]hen the defendant files a pretrial motion to suppress identification evidence, the initial burden is on the defendant to show some indication of suggestiveness in law enforcement's administration of the

17. *Martinez*, 478 P.3d at 889.
18. *Id.* (citations omitted).
19. *Id.* (citations omitted).
20. *People v. Marshall*, 45 N.E.3d 954, 960 (N.Y. 2015).
21. *People v. Adams*, 423 N.E.2d 379, 384 (NY. 1981).

> eyewitness identification procedure. Upon making this showing, the burden shifts to the state to prove by clear and convincing evidence that either (1) the procedure employed was not so suggestive as to materially taint the identification made by the eyewitness, which is to say that any departure from proper procedure could not have increased the risk of misidentification, or (2) good reason existed for the police to employ the suggestive procedure in the first instance. If the state fails to carry its responsive burden, the identification and any subsequent identification by the same witness must be suppressed.[22]

A significant feature of both the New Mexico and Massachusetts jurisprudence is the existence of protocols for conducting identification procedures that are binding on police.[23]

* * *

On paper, any of the aforementioned reforms would seem a marked improvement over the *Manson* test given its many shortcomings. However, there is reason to question whether expanding the reliability inquiry to include more factors will actually result in greater deterrence or accountability for suggestive police practices. In adding factors, courts may simply be giving the trial court more outlets for the exercise of unchecked and uncheckable discretion. From this perspective, the *per se* approach would seem to be vastly preferable.

II. Reining in the Discretion to Bar Eyewitness Research from the Courtroom

Although, as discussed in Chapters 2 and 3, cautionary instructions and expert testimony regarding the pitfalls of eyewitness identification are vital to minimizing the risk of wrongful conviction due to mistaken identification, both are all too frequently denied by judges who declare them unnecessary, based on the judge's impression that the jury does not need help to appreciate the risks inherent in eyewitness identification evidence and to weigh them intelligently in a specific case. Such decisions have been rendered effectively unreviewable by the application of the highly deferential abuse of discretion standard.

---

22. *Martinez*, 478 P.3d at 907.
23. *Id.* at 899, 907 (citations omitted).

As the First Circuit cautioned in 1979, "a trial court can, in its discretion, conclude that scientific evaluation either has not reached, or perhaps cannot reach a level of reliability such that scientific analysis of a question of fact surpasses the quality of common-sense evaluation inherent in jury deliberations."[24] Judges in the Eleventh Circuit may exclude eyewitness identification expert testimony with impunity, even as to those topics that lie "demonstra[bly]" beyond the jury's "common sense" comprehension, based on settled precedent holding that "the jury can adequately weigh the[] problems [of perception and memory] through common-sense evaluation."[25] Judges across the country retain "broad discretion" to decide whether to instruct on any specific risk factor with respect to an eyewitness identification, notwithstanding how strongly that factor may be implicated by the evidence.[26]

Courts of final resort should reconsider the wide latitude that the lower courts have been permitted to exercise with respect to foundational questions of expert admissibility and jury instructions. Such seemingly boundless discretion should be disfavored in all matters because it is antithetical to the role of the courts in a well-ordered democracy. As Justice Frankfurter wrote:

> Discretion without a criterion for its exercise is authorization of arbitrariness. [Appellate judges] ought to be able to do better than to tell the [judges in the trial court] . . . that they may do as they please—that they are not to be bound, nor to be guided, by considerations capable of rational formulation.[27]

Moreover, the question whether the contents of a jury instruction or an expert's testimony are sufficiently probative to warrant the jury's attention is one that strongly calls for authoritative appellate resolution for a number of reasons. Questions regarding the validity and helpfulness of an entire methodology or set of scientific conclusions necessarily transcend individual

---

24. *United States v. Fosher*, 590 F.2d 381, 383 (1st Cir. 1979).

25. *United States v. (Charles) Smith*, 148 F. App'x 867, 872 n.8 (11th Cir. 2005) (citing *United States v. (Fred) Smith*, 122 F.3d 1355, 1358 (11th Cir. 1997)).

26. *Corbin v. United States*, 120 A.3d 588, 606 (D.C. 2015) (The "trial court has broad discretion in formulating jury instructions." (internal quotations and citations omitted)); *Janey v. State*, 891 A.2d 355, 356 (Md. Ct. Spec. App. 2006) ("We shall hold that the decision of whether to give [an instruction on the cross-race effect], when requested, remains committed to the sound discretion of the trial judge.").

27. *Daniels v. Allen*, 344 U.S. 443, 496–97 (1953).

cases and require a policy judgment regarding whether the "law's need" for such evidence outweighs the risk of relying on it.[28] As such when disputes regarding these issues "are removed from appellate scrutiny, contradictory results are sure to follow, but with no mechanism to cure them."[29] Moreover, "appellate courts have more 'time and distance to become familiar with . . . complex science' and . . . 'appellate judges sit on panels and thus have the benefit of shared experience and expertise.'"[30] Finally, a sound determination of these questions "simply does not depend on the credibility of individual witness."[31] Nor should it. For all these reasons, a more rigorous standard of appellate review than the abuse of discretion should apply, whenever the decision to exclude an expert or refuse to give an instruction is based on judicial hesitation regarding the state of the science.

III. Improving the Telfaire *Instruction*

In the fifty years since *Telfaire*, many courts have either ordered or recommended changes to instructions based on the *Telfaire* instruction, based on a growing body of empirical research about the reliability of eyewitness identifications and jury understanding of that subject. Early modifications "tended to address only certain subjects, or to repeat the problematic *Manson v. Braithwaite* language, which was not intended as instructions for jurors."[32] However, as research in this area has matured, courts have increasingly embraced comprehensive reform.

---

28. David L. Faigman, *Appellate Review of Scientific Evidence Under Daubert and Joiner*, 48 Hastings L.J. 969, 977 (1997).

29. *Id.* at 978.

30. *State v. Olenowski*, 304 A.3d 598, 580 (N.J. 2023) (quoting Faigman, *supra* note 28, at 979; citing Christopher B. *Mueller*, *Daubert Asks the Right Questions: Now Appellate Courts Should Help Find the Right Answers*, 33 Seton Hall L. Rev. 987, 1021 (2003) (agreeing that appellate courts are better situated for determining reliability because they generally have more time, more judges assigned to individual cases, and more thorough briefing)).

31. *Id.* (quoting Faigman, *supra* note 28, at 979).

32. Nat'l Rsch. Council, *supra* note 5, at 112; *see, e.g.*, *Brodes v. State*, 614 S.E.2d 766, 770–71 (Ga. 2005) ("harmful error" to instruct, in accordance with *Manson*, that witness certainty is a factor to consider in assessing the reliability of an identification, because the "lack of correlation between a witness's certainty in his or her identification . . . and the accuracy of that identification" is well documented in scientific publications and judicial opinions); *State v. Ledbetter*, 881 A.2d 290, 301, 318 (Conn. 2005) (holding that "research on the perils of eyewitness identification" required that the jury be instructed to take into account whether the identifying witness was told that the suspect may not be present in the array or lineup, which decreases the risk of misidentification); *State v. Cromedy*, 727 A.2d 457, 461 (N.J. 1999) (holding that in light of "forty years [of] empirical studies concerning the psychological factors affecting eyewitness cross-racial or cross-ethnic identification," instruction on the cross-race effect was required where the issue was raised); *People v. Wright*,

Citing the Special Master's report on the degree to which juries understand the science of memory that controls eyewitness identification reliability,[33] the *Henderson* court further asked the Criminal Practice Committee and the Model Criminal Jury Charge Committee to draft revisions to the charges on eyewitness identification to address potential juror misunderstanding.[34] The court deemed such instructions necessary, notwithstanding the admissibility of expert testimony and even though the underlying science was likely to evolve.[35] The revised charges instruct the jury to consider the system and estimator variables noted in the Special Master's report and provide explanation for why each is relevant.[36] The model charge further advises that eyewitness confidence at the time of trial may not be an indication of reliability.[37]

After *Henderson*, high courts in Massachusetts, Connecticut, and Oregon called for similar reform without additional adversarial fact-finding. The Massachusetts Supreme Court convened a Study Group consisting of judges, prosecutors, defenders, law enforcement personnel, and academics "to consider," *inter alia*, "whether existing model jury instructions provide adequate guidance to juries in evaluating eyewitness testimony."[38] After reviewing the Special Master's Report from *Henderson* and the available research,[39] the Study Group issued a Report with proposed instructions that

45 Cal. 3d 1126, 1141, 755 P.2d 1049 (1988) (endorsing a model instruction that directed juries to consider "the stress under which the witness made the observations, the cross-racial nature of the identification, and whether the witness had an uncorrected vision deficiency."); *State v. Long*, 721 P.2d 483, 493–94 & n.8 (Utah 1986) (holding that "the *Telfaire* instruction, proposed in 1972, . . . d[id] not cover several factors which more recent empirical research have shown to be important, such as the limitations in our ability to perceive, store and retrieve information"; expanding the *Telfaire* instruction to reflect the risk of diminished capacity to observe given stress, bias, fatigue, and intoxication, and the risk of diminished reliability given the cross-race effect, exposure to pretrial publicity, and the use of a show-up instead of a lineup or photo-array).

33. *Id.* at 910–11.

34. *Id.* at 877–78.

35. *Id.* at 878.

36. *See, e.g.*, Report of the Supreme Court Committee on Model Criminal Jury Charges on the Revisions to the Identification Model Charges app. A, https://njcourts.gov/courts/assets/criminal/modelcrimjurychargereport.pdf.

37. *Id.*

38. *Commonwealth v. Walker*, 953 N.E.2d 195, 208 n.16 (Mass. 2011); *see also* Supreme Judicial Court Study Group on Eyewitness Evidence, Report & Recommendations to the Justices, at 1 (July 25, 2013), http://www.mass.gov/courts/docs/sjc/docs/eyewitness-evidence-report-2013.pdf [hereinafter Study Group Report] (noting the composition of the Study Group).

39. *Id.* at iii–xii.

the Massachusetts Supreme Court later adopted.[40] The final version of these instructions includes discussion of memory storage and retrieval, identification procedures, and several supplemental charges on the *Henderson* factors, like weapon focus and cross-race effect.[41]

Based on *Henderson* and its own review of the research, the Supreme Court of Connecticut held that criminal juries must be informed, either through jury instructions or expert testimony, of eight "widely accepted" facts about eyewitness identification, including stress, weapon focus, the cross-race effect, the, at best, weak correlation between confidence and accuracy, and the risk of unconscious transference.[42] Similarly, the Supreme Court of Oregon followed New Jersey's example in crafting a new test for the admissibility of eyewitness identifications based on scientifically tested system and estimator variables, relying on the Special Master's Report from *Henderson* and its own review of the available research.[43] The court "anticipate[d]" that the defense would be entitled to use "case-specific jury instructions" "to educate the factfinder about the potential effects of relevant estimator variables on the accuracy of eyewitness identification."[44]

In its landmark 2014 report, an ad hoc committee appointed by the National Academy of Sciences (NAS) recommended "the use of clear and concise jury instructions," like the *Henderson* instructions, to convey "information regarding the factors the jury should consider."[45] The committee consisted of federal judges (including multiple judges from the U.S. Court of Appeals for the District of Columbia), state court judges, prominent law and social science professors, members of the NAS, a police chief, a federal defender, and a district attorney, and "analyzed relevant published and unpublished research, external submissions, and presentations made by various experts and interested parties."[46] The committee noted the inaccuracy and inadequacy of model eyewitness identification instructions apart from the one in use in New Jersey—Massachusetts's proposal had not yet

40. *See Commonwealth v. Gomes*, 22 N.E.3d 897, 900–01 (Mass. 2015).

41. *See* Statement of the Supreme Judicial Court Model, Model Jury Instructions on Eyewitness Identification 1–3, 6 (Nov. 16, 2015), http://www.mass.gov/courts/docs/sjc/docs/model-jury-instructions-on-eyewitness-identification-november-2015.pdf.

42. *State v. Guilbert*, 49 A.3d 705, 721–23 & n.10, 733–35 (Conn. 2012); *see id.* at 727 n.27 (noting that "generalized instruction" on the *Telfaire* factors is "inadequate").

43. *State v. Lawson*, 291 P.3d 673, 685 & n.3 (Or. 2012) (en banc).

44. *Id.* at 697.

45. Nat'l Rsch. Council, *supra* note 5, at 112.

46. *Id.* at xiii.

passed—and recommended the convening of "a body to establish model jury instructions regarding eyewitness identifications."[47]

Since the NAS Report was issued, Alaska has heeded this recommendation, while relying on *Henderson* and the cases and studies that have come since.[48] In embracing such reform, the Alaska Supreme Court held that it was "unnecessary to retest the validity of the scientific evidence on which" *Henderson* and the cases that came after it relied.[49]

A. Specific Inadequacies of the *Telfaire* Instruction

As discussed in Chapter 3, the *Telfaire* instruction is both underinclusive, insofar as it fails to mention many factors that bear on the reliability of eyewitness identification, and vague, insofar as it fails to explain the relevance of those factors that it does mention.[50] In a nutshell, after explaining the government's burden to prove identity beyond a reasonable doubt and defining "[i]dentification testimony" as an "expression of belief or impression by the witness" the value of which "depends on the opportunity . . . to observe the offender at the time of the offense and to make a reliable identification later," the *Telfaire* instruction directs the jury to consider four issues in determining the reliability of an identification:

1. Whether "the witness had the capacity and an adequate opportunity to observe the offender," based on
    a. "[H]ow long or short a time" the witness had to observe that person.
    b. "[H]ow far or close the witness was" during that period of observation.
    c. "[H]ow good were lighting conditions" during that period of observation.
    d. "[W]hether the witness had had occasion to see or know the person in the past."

47. *Id.* at 112.

48. *See Young v. State*, 374 P.3d 395 (Alaska 2016) (announcing "a new test for the admissibility of eyewitness identification" based on scientifically tested "system" and "estimator" variables and ordering the Criminal Pattern Jury Instructions Committee to draft a model instruction for future cases consistent with the principles set forth in the opinion).

49. *Id.* at 414.

50. Fiona Leverick, *Jury Instructions on Eyewitness Identification Evidence: A Re-Evaluation*, 49 Creighton L. Rev. 555, 564 (2016); *accord, e.g.*, Study Group Report, *supra* note 38, at 54.

2. Whether "the identification made by the witness subsequent to the offense was the product of his own recollection," based on
   a. "[T]he strength of the identification."
   b. [W]hether "the witness [was] influenced by the circumstances under which the defendant was presented . . . for identification"—a circumstance that should prompt "scrutiny . . . with great care."
   c. "[T]he length of time that lapsed between the occurrence of the crime and the next opportunity of the witness to see [the] defendant."
   d. [W]hether the defendant "was pick[ed] . . . out of a group of similar individuals," which "is generally more reliable than" identification based on "the presentation of the defendant alone to the witness."
3. Whether "the witness [previously] failed to make an identification of defendant, or made an identification that was inconsistent with his identification at trial."
4. Whether the "identification witness . . . is truthful, and . . . had the capacity and opportunity to make a reliable observation on the matter covered in his testimony."[51]

In reconsidering Massachusetts' own *Telfaire*-based instruction in 2015,[52] the Massachusetts Study Group found that, though it "enumerate[d] several factors that jurors should consider in assessing identification testimony," it had three basic deficiencies: first, it omitted some factors that had proven potential to "influence the accuracy of an identification"; second, it "fail[ed] to explain the nexus between identification and memory," that is, "that certain . . . variables influence memory at its different stages, and therefore affect the reliability of an identification"; and third, it failed to instruct the jury on the ways in which these "variables can affect a witness's memory and confidence"—which is important because research shows that jurors rely heavily on a witness's expressed confidence.[53] What follows is a set of recommendations for addressing these deficiencies that are drawn from recent examples.

---

51. *United States v. Telfaire*, 469 F.2d 552, 558-59 (D.C. Cir. 1972) (per curiam).

52. *See Commonwealth v. Rodriguez*, 391 N.E.2d 889, 897 (Mass. 1979) (adopting the *Telfaire* instruction).

53. Study Group Report, *supra* note 38, at 54.

1. *Memory*

First, noticeably absent from the *Telfaire* instruction is any discussion of memory or how it works. In failing to impart even the most cursory information on this topic, the instruction does the accused and the jury a disservice—one that may undermine the jury's understanding of how system and estimator variables tend to affect the accuracy of an identification. To rectify this omission, the Alaska Criminal Pattern Instructions Committee has recommended the following:

> Eyewitness identifications should be examined with care. As with any witness, you must first determine the witness's credibility—that is, do you believe the witness is being honest? In making this determination, you should consider the factors listed in Instruction No. 1.10 (witness credibility).
>
> Even if you are convinced the witness honestly believes his or her identification of the defendant is accurate, you still must consider the possibility that the witness made a mistake in the identification. A witness may honestly believe he or she saw a particular person but perceive or remember the event incorrectly. You must decide whether the witness's identification is not only truthful but accurate.
>
> Scientific research has shown that human memory is not foolproof and that there are risks of making mistaken identifications. Memory does not function like a video recording where events are stored in a linear fashion; it is far more complex. The process of remembering consists of three stages: (1) the perception of the event; (2) the time that passes between the perception of the event and the recollection of the event; and (3) the moment when the witness recalls the event. At each of these stages, memory can be affected by a variety of factors. The witness may be unaware of these effects.[54]

2. *Stress*

"Under conditions of high stress, a witness' ability to identify key characteristics of an individual's face (e.g., hair length, hair color, eye color, shape

---

54. Alaska Crim. Pattern Jury Instructions § 1.24 (Crim. Pattern Jury Instructions Comm. 2020).

of face, presence of facial hair) may be significantly impaired."[55] The Massachusetts Study Group recommended addressing this inadequacy by adding the following sentence after directing the jury to consider the eyewitness's physical and mental characteristics: "High levels of stress may reduce a person's ability to make an accurate identification."[56]

3. *Exposure Duration/Length of Encounter*

The *Telfaire* instruction directs the jury to consider the length or brevity of the witness's opportunity to observe the person they are trying to identify. However, it does not explain that brief or fleeting contact is less likely to produce an accurate identification. Nor does it explain that witnesses tend to overestimate the duration of exciting or highly stressful encounters. The Massachusetts Supreme Judicial Court Study Group Report concluded, based on scientific consensus, that such an instruction on these topics is warranted.[57] New Jersey uses the following language to accomplish this goal:

> The amount of time an eyewitness has to observe an event may affect the reliability of an identification. Although there is no minimum time required to make an accurate identification, a brief or fleeting contact is less likely to produce an accurate identification than a more prolonged exposure to the perpetrator. In addition, time estimates given by witnesses may not always be accurate because witnesses tend to think events lasted longer than they actually did.[58]

4. *Weapon Focus*

The NAS Report explained that when an eyewitness's attention is "compellingly drawn to emotionally laden stimuli, such as a gun or a knife," it is "at the expense of acquiring greater visual information about the face of the perpetrator," and therefore increases the chances of a misidentification.[59] The Massachusetts Study Group concluded that jurors should be instructed

55. NAT'L RSCH. COUNCIL, *supra* note 5, at 94; STUDY GROUP REPORT, *supra* note 38, at 59 ("High levels of stress or fear can have a negative impact on a witness's ability to make accurate identifications.").

56. STUDY GROUP REPORT, *supra* note 38, at 120.

57. *Id.* at 119–20.

58. REPORT OF THE SUPREME COURT COMMITTEE ON MODEL CRIMINAL JURY CHARGES, *supra* note 36, at 19.

59. NAT'L RSCH. COUNCIL, *supra* note 5, at 55.

on this issue when weapons were involved and proposed the following language:

> You should consider whether the witness saw a weapon during the event. If the event is of short duration, the visible presence of a weapon may distract the witness's attention away from the person's face. But the longer the event, the more time the witness may have to get used to the presence of a weapon and focus on the person's face.[60]

5. *Distance*

The *Telfaire* instruction recommends that the jury consider "how far or close the witness was" to the culprit but does not explain how distance interacts with the risk of mistaken identification. Although a jury might think that this factor deserves little attention (because, surely, a witness who was not close enough to make a reliable identification will know that and say so), research suggests that this may not be true in all cases. "[P]hysical distance between the witness and the perpetrator is an important estimator variable, as it directly affects the ability of the eyewitness to discern visual details, including features of the perpetrator."[61] Nor does it explain that witnesses tend to have difficulty estimating distances.[62] New Jersey uses the following alternative language:

> A person is easier to recognize when close by. The greater the distance between an eyewitness and a perpetrator, the higher the risk of a mistaken identification. In addition, a witness's estimate of how far he or she was from the perpetrator may not always be accurate because people tend to have difficulty estimating distances.[63]

---

60. Study Group Report, *supra* note 38, at 120, 130.
61. Nat'l Rsch. Council, *supra* note 5, at 92.
62. *Henderson*, 27 A.3d at 906 ("Research has also shown that people have difficulty estimating distances."); Study Group Report, *supra* note 38, at 27 (same).
63. Report of the Supreme Court Committee on Model Criminal Jury Charges, *supra* note 36, at 21.

6. *Disguise*

The Massachusetts Study Group concluded that studies demonstrate that the use of a disguise negatively affects later identification accuracy, and recommended informing jurors about this factor when disguises are involved.[64] "Disguises" include not just masks, but common items such as hats, hoods, and sunglasses. *Gomes*, *Lawson*, and *Henderson* all recognized the impact of disguises on the ability to make an identification.[65] The *Henderson* court further recognized research that found that jurors are unaware of the effect of a disguise on the ability to make an identification.[66] To address this gap in the knowledge of the average juror, New Jersey has adopted the following instruction: "If the perpetrator wears items that obscure part of his or her appearance, the wearing of those items can affect a witness's ability both to remember and identify the perpetrator. Items like hats, sunglasses, or masks can reduce the accuracy of an identification."[67]

7. *Cross-Racial Identification*

It is well settled that people are better at identifying members of their own race than members of other races. This concept is referred to as the "cross-race effect" or "own-race bias." As noted at the end of Chapter 3, the *Telfaire* instruction would have included language addressing it, but for the fact that Judge Leventhal did not believe that the time was right to do so.[68] Judge Leventhal's objections were twofold and lack merit insofar as they had any to begin with.

Leventhal's first objection was that more research was needed to ascertain whether the cross-race effect had any basis in reality or was merely a shared delusion by its many proponents.[69] Leventhal wrote that the existence of a

---

64. STUDY GROUP REPORT, *supra* note 38, at 30, 66, 120, 132.

65. *See Gomes*, 22 N.E. at 920, n. 5; *Lawson*, 291 P.3d at 703 ("studies show that hats, hoods, and other items that conceal a perpetrator's hair or hairline also impair a witness's ability to make an accurate identification."); *Henderson*, 27 A.3d at 907 ("Disguises and changes in facial features can affect a witness' ability to remember and identify a perpetrator.").

66. *Henderson*, 27 A.3d. at 911.

67. *Telfaire*, 469 F.2d at 563 (Leventhal J., concurring).

68. *Id.* Presumably, the third judge on the panel, Judge Arlin Adams (sitting by designation from the Third Circuit) shared some of Judge Leventhal's reservations or else he would have broken the stalemate between his colleagues by supporting Judge Bazelon's call for an instruction on this issue. Two years after *Telfaire* was decided Judge Adams seemed to suggest that his views ultimately came down to "the data." *See United States v. Wilford*, 493 F.2d 730, 739 n.18 (3rd Cir. 1974).

69. *Telfaire*, 469 F.2d at 561 (Leventhal J., concurring) ("The issue of inter-racial identifications is not ripe for this kind of distillation of wisdom[.]").

cross-race effect was "a matter on which there [was] only 'meager data' and an assertion of 'common sense' views that merit further consideration."[70] However, whatever the state of the science in 1972, the existence of a cross-race effect is now the subject of "near consensus in the relevant scientific community."[71] As further detailed in Chapter 6, "research has shown that people of all races may have greater difficulty in accurately identifying members of a different race than they do in identifying members of their own race."[72] "Own-race bias occurs in both visual discrimination and memory tasks, in laboratory and field studies, and across a range of races, ethnicities, and ages."[73] Cross-racial identification has been a factor in roughly "42 percent of the cases in which an erroneous eyewitness identification was made."[74] It is for all these reasons that the Massachusetts Supreme Judicial Court has held that instruction on the cross-race effect "must be given in trials . . . where there is a cross-racial identification . . . unless all parties agree that there was no cross-racial identification."

Nor is Leventhal's second objection any more compelling, as he claimed that instructing a jury on the cross-race effect should be disfavored because it would inject race into the case in a manner that would be "divisive."[75] To paraphrase Judge Bazelon's original response to this argument, an instruction does not trespass the sacred norms requiring fair administration of justice merely because it alerts the jury that cross-racial identifications have a tendency to be less accurate.[76] Nor does it demean the court or any witness to suggest that the witness, like all other human beings, may have been influenced by this effect, albeit unconsciously.[77] On the other hand, it would demean the court to pretend as if the problem of cross-racial misidentification did not exist, thereby undermining the integrity of the jury's factfinding process, in the hopes of maintaining a façade of color blindness.[78]

---

70. *Id.*
71. *Com. v. Bastaldo*, 32 N.E.3d 873, 880 (Mass. 2015).
72. *Id.*
73. Nat'l Rsch. Council, *supra* note 5, at 96.
74. *Bastaldo*, 32 N.E.3d at 880, 883.
75. *Telfaire*, 469 F.2d at 562 & n.6; *see also Janey v. State*, 891 A.2d 355 (Md. Ct. Spec. App. 2006) (citing Judge Leventhal's concurrence with approval).
76. *Telfaire*, 469 F.2d at 560 (Bazelon, J., concurring).
77. *Id.*
78. *Id.*

In addition, it should be noted that although Judge Leventhal put great stock in a pair of New York cases for his divisiveness argument,[79] New York is now among several jurisdictions that provide for juries to be instructed regarding the existence of the cross-race effect.[80] In light of the foregoing, the following instruction from the Massachusetts Supreme Judicial Court is warranted: "If the witness and the person identified appear to be of different races, you should consider that people may have greater difficulty in accurately identifying someone of a different race than someone of their own race."[81]

8. *Passage of Time*

While the *Telfaire* instruction lists "the length of time that lapsed between the occurrence of the crime and the next opportunity of the witness to see [the] defendant" as a factor for the jury to consider, it does not explain that "[t]he rate of forgetting for an unfamiliar face is greatest soon after the initial observation and tends to level off over time."[82] Nor does it explain that the passage of time can lead not only to forgetting but also to increased susceptibility to memory distortion through events that take place after the witnessed event.[83] Nor does it explain that "[t]he amount of time between viewing a crime and the subsequent identification procedure can be expected to similarly affect the accuracy of the eyewitness identification, either independently or in combination with other variables."[84] For these reasons, the Massachusetts Study Group recommended the following alternative language: "You should consider how much time passed between the event observed and the identification. Generally, memory is most accurate immediately after the event and begins to fade soon thereafter."[85]

---

79. *Id.* at 562 n.6 (citing *People v. Burris*, 19 A.D.2d 557–58, 241 N.Y.S.2d 75, 76 (2d Dept. 1963); *People v. Hearns*, 18 A.D.2d 922, 923, 238 N.Y.S.2d 173, 174–75 (2d Dept. 1963)).

80. *People v. Boone*, 91 N.E.3d 1194, 1196, 1198–99 (N.Y. 2017); *State v. Guilbert*, 49 A.3d 705, 722, 732 (Conn. 2012); Florida Standard Jury Instructions For Crim. Cases § 3.9(c); *State v. Mahmoud*, 147 A.3d 833, 838–39 (Me. 2016); Missouri Approved Jury Instructions (MAI) § 310.02 (2016); *State v. Henderson*, 27 A.3d 872, 907, 917, 921 (N.J. 2011); Model Utah Jury Instructions, Second Edition § CR404 (2014); Virginia Model Jury Instructions-Crim., No. 2.800 (2019) (discussing state court's treatment of issue of jury instruction regarding eyewitness testimony).

81. *Bastaldo*, 32 N.E.3d at 883.

82. Nat'l Rsch. Council, *supra* note 5, at 99.

83. *Id.*

84. *Id.*

85. Mass. Continuing Legal Education, Criminal Model Jury Instructions for Use in the District Court, Instruction 9.160 (2015); *accord Com. v. Gomes*, 22 N.E.3d 897, 922 (Mass. 2015).

9. *Confidence*

The *Telfaire* instruction directs the jury to consider "the strength of the identification" but does not explain that an eyewitness's certainty on the witness stand is not a reliable indicator of accuracy, especially when the witness did not describe that level of certainty when the witness first made the identification. For these reasons, the *Telfaire* instruction "appears (erroneously) to associate confidence with identification accuracy."[86] Though the scientific research has established, and the courts have acknowledged, that "a witness's level of confidence at trial, standing alone, may not be an indication of the reliability of the identification,"[87] eyewitness confidence at trial has an extremely powerful effect on jurors.[88] For these reasons, the Massachusetts Study Group recommended that jurors be instructed: "You should consider that a witness's statement of how certain he/she is in an identification, standing alone, is generally not a reliable indicator of the accuracy of the identification, especially where the witness did not describe that level of certainty when the witness first made the identification.[89]

10. *Postevent Suggestion*

The instruction does not provide an explanation of the concept of postevent suggestion. Nor does it explain the types of postevent circumstances that could make the identification less reliable, such as exposure to information about other witnesses' identifications, physical descriptions, media accounts, or postidentification confirmatory feedback. One of the reasons that a witness's level of confidence may not be a reliable indicator of accuracy is that postidentification feedback—or confirmatory feedback that signals to

86. Leverick, *supra* note 50, at 564; *accord, e.g.*, Study Group Report, *supra* note 38, at 54.

87. *Henderson*, 27 A.3d at 899.

88. *Id.* at 911 (citing research that shows that eyewitness confidence is "the most powerful predictor of verdicts regardless of other variables."); *Gomes*, 22 N.E.3d at 913 ("there is a near consensus that jurors tend to give more weight to a witness's certainty in evaluating the accuracy of an identification than is warranted by the research."); *Lawson*, 291 P.3d at 704 ("Despite widespread reliance by judges and juries on the certainty of an eyewitness's identification, studies show that, under most circumstances, witness confidence or certainty is not a good indicator of identification accuracy."); *see Perry v. New Hampshire*, 565 U.S. 228, 264 (2012) (Sotomayor, S. dissenting) ("Study after study demonstrates that . . . jurors place the greatest weight on eyewitness confidence in assessing identifications even though confidence is a poor gauge of accuracy; and that suggestiveness can stem from sources beyond police-orchestrated procedures.").

89. Study Group Report *supra* note 38, at 128; *see also United States v. Jones*, 689 F.3d 12 (1st Cir. 2012); *State v. Mahmoud*, 147 A.3d 833 (Me. 2016); Pattern Criminal Jury Instructions for the First Circuit, 2.22 Eyewitness Identification Instruction, http://www.med.uscourts.gov/pdf/crpjilinks.pdf; Maine Jury Instructions Manual § 6-22A.

the witness that their identification is correct—can "increase confidence in an identification, regardless of whether the identification is correct."[90] The *Henderson* court wrote that postidentification confirmatory feedback can "reduce doubt and engender a false sense of confidence." The Massachusetts Study Group described the findings of a "more recent meta-analysis examining the results of 20 experiments involving over 2,400 participants confirmed that studies on this factor have produced 'remarkably consistent' effects and 'provide dramatic evidence that post identification feedback can compromise the integrity of a witness's memory.'"[91]

The Massachusetts Study Group recommended that jurors be instructed on the potential impact of pre-identification exposure to outside information, including identifications by other witnesses and news accounts.[92] The Massachusetts Study Group also recommended that jurors be instructed that a witness's confidence in the identification may have been affected by external factors between the encounter and the identification.[93]

> You should consider that the accuracy of identification testimony may be affected by information that the witness received between the event and the identification, or received after the identification. Such information may include identifications made by other witnesses, physical descriptions given by other witnesses, photographs or media accounts, or any other information that may affect the independence or accuracy of a witness's identification. Exposure to such information before or after the witness makes an identification not only may affect the accuracy of an identification, but also may affect the witness's certainty in the identification and the witness's memory about the quality of his or her opportunity to view the event. The witness may not realize that his or her memory has been affected by this information.
>
> An identification made after suggestive conduct by the police or others should be scrutinized with great care. Suggestive conduct may include anything that a person says or does prior to, during, or after an identification procedure that might influence the witness to identify a particular individual. Suggestive conduct need not be intentional, and the person doing the "suggesting" may not realize that he or she is doing anything suggestive.

90. Nat'l Rsch. Council, *supra* note 5, at 92.
91. Study Group Report, *supra* note 38, at 83.
92. *Id.* at 122.
93. *Id.* at 122, 125, 126, 129.

11. *Identification Procedures*

The *Telfaire* instruction recommends that jurors consider whether "the witness [was] influenced by the circumstances under which the defendant was presented . . . for identification," noting that such circumstances should prompt "scrutiny . . . with great care." However, the instruction does not contain any specific information about what types of circumstances can lead to misidentification or overconfidence in an identification. The Massachusetts Study Group recommended instructions regarding identification procedures, including how such procedures should—and should not—be conducted to ensure accuracy.[94]

> An identification may occur through an identification procedure conducted by police, which involves showing the witness a (set of photographs) (lineup of individuals).
>
> Where a witness identified the defendant from a (set of photographs) (lineup), you should consider all of the factors I have already described about a witness's perception and memory.
>
> You also should consider whether anything about the defendant's (photograph) (physical appearance in the lineup) made the defendant stand out from the others. A suspect should not stand out from other members of the lineup. The reason is simple: an array of look-alike faces forces witnesses to examine their memory. In addition, a lineup in which the defendant stands out may inflate a witness's confidence in the identification because the selection process seemed so easy to the witness. It is, of course, for you to determine whether the composition of the lineup had any effect on the reliability of the identification.
>
> You should consider whether the person (showing the photographs) (presenting the lineup) knew who was the suspect and could have, even inadvertently, influenced the identification, and whether anything was said to the witness that may have influenced the identification. You should consider that an identification made by picking a defendant out of a group of similar individuals is generally less suggestive than one that results from the presentation of a defendant alone to a witness.
>
> [b.] You have heard that the police showed the witness a number of photographs. The police have photographs of people from a variety of sources, including the Registry of Motor Vehicles. You should not

---

94. Study Group Report, *supra* note 38, at 122–29.

make any negative inference from the fact that the police had a photograph of the defendant.

[c. *If there was evidence of a showup*] In this case, the witness identified the defendant during a "showup," that is, the defendant was the [only] person shown to the witness at that time. Even though such a procedure is suggestive in nature, it is sometimes necessary for the police to conduct a "showup" or one-on-one identification procedure. Although the benefits of a fresh memory may balance the risk of undue suggestion, showups conducted a longer time after an event present a heightened risk of misidentification. Also, police officers must instruct witnesses that the person they are about to view may or may not be the person who committed the crime and that they should not feel compelled to make an identification. In determining whether the identification is reliable or the result of an unduly suggestive procedure, you should consider how much time elapsed after the witness last saw the perpetrator, whether the appropriate instructions were given to the witness, and all other circumstances surrounding the showup.[95]

B. Do More Comprehensive Instructions Make Better Juries?

It has been argued that lengthy cautionary instructions should be avoided in the context of eyewitness identification because juries tend either to disregard them or to be so overwhelmed by them that they will reject any identification offered, no matter how reliable it seems.[96] According to this argument, stronger cautionary instructions serve only to make jurors more skeptical about eyewitness testimony *across the board*, rather than enhancing their ability to rigorously evaluate identifications based on the factors that have demonstrated tendency to influence their reliability.[97] However, the evidence

95. Prof. Nina Chernoff, *Model Motion Requesting a Jury Instruction on Eyewitness Identification Testimony*, H2O, https://opencasebook.org/casebooks/4536-advanced-evidence-spring-2023-4-credit/resources/3.1.3.3-model-motion-requesting-a-jury-instruction-on-eyewitness-identification-testimony/.

96. *2019 Third Circuit Task Force Report*, *supra* note 2, at 97 & n.543 (citing Angela M. Jones et al., *Comparing the Effectiveness of Henderson Instructions and Expert Testimony: Which Safeguard Improves Jurors' Evaluations of Eyewitness Evidence?*, 13 J. Experimental Criminology 20–21 (2017); Athan P. Papailiou et al., *The Novel New Jersey Eyewitness Instruction Induces Skepticism But Not Sensitivity*, 10 PLoS One 9 (2015)).

97. *See, e.g.*, *2019 Third Circuit Task Force Report*, *supra* note 2, at 97; *see also, e.g.*, Brandon L. Garrett et al., *Factoring the Role of Eyewitness Evidence in the Courtroom*, 17 J. Empirical L. Stud. 556, 559–60 (2020), https://doi.org/10.1111/jels.12259 (summarizing

that has been offered to justify this exceedingly pessimistic view of the jury is inconclusive at best.

Experiments that purport to find that more comprehensive instructions on eyewitness identification do not promote better comprehension of the factors that tend to influence reliability suffer from significant design limitations, including, most notably, that they do not incorporate actual deliberations into their experimental designs.[98] As one researcher wrote, "the attempt to draw inferences [about the efficacy of jury instructions] from decisions rendered by nondeliberating mock *jurors* rather than deliberating mock *juries*" is "perhaps the greatest" shortcoming of this body of research "because deliberation is an essential part of the trial process—one that may influence comprehension of and compliance with laws and other legally relevant pronouncements."[99] Indeed, the very purpose of deliberation is to allow jurors the time and space to process their instructions and resolve any misunderstandings collectively.[100] Deliberation facilitates better comprehension and sounder application of jury instructions in two distinct ways. First, because deliberating jurors know that they will have to "justify their opinions to their fellow jury members," they have a strong incentive to pay closer attention to the instructions they receive and "to think more deeply and critically about" how to apply them.[101] By contrast, without deliberation, jurors have precious little to incentivize to listen to or read the instructions carefully or to reconsider "cognitively simplistic or 'lazy'" interpretations.[102] This is especially true where, as in mock juror experiments, participants are "aware[] that they are role playing and that their decision has no real life consequences."[103] Second, listening to and participating in the discussions

research); Kristy A. Martire & Richard I. Kemp, *The Impact of Eyewitness Expert Evidence and Judicial Instruction on Juror Ability to Evaluate Eyewitness Testimony*, 33 L. & HUM. BEHAV. 225 (2009), https://doi.org/10.1007/s10979-008-9134-z.

98. Leverick, *supra* note 50, at 566 & n.72 (citing Wayne Weiten & Shari S. Diamond, *A Critical Review of the Jury Simulation Paradigm: The Case of Defendant Characteristics*, 3 L. & HUM. BEHAV. 71 (1979)); *see, e.g.*, *id.* at 567–72 (summarizing research).

99. David R. Shaffer & Shannon R. Wheatman, *Does Personality Influence Reactions to Judicial Instructions? Some Preliminary Findings and Possible Implications*, 6 PSYCHOL. PUB. POL'Y & L. 655, 657–58 (2000).

100. *Id.* at 657.

101. *Id.*

102. *Id.*; *see also Ballew v. Georgia*, 435 U.S. 223, 233 (1978) ("When individual and group decisionmaking were compared, it was seen that groups performed better because prejudices of individuals were frequently counterbalanced, and objectivity resulted. Groups also exhibited increased motivation and self-criticism.").

103. Leverick, *supra* note 50, at 56.

that take place during a deliberation gives jurors an opportunity to question their own comprehension and to obtain clarification from their fellow jurors, written copies of the instructions (if one has been provided), or the judge.

That deliberation facilitates better adherence to jury instructions has been suggested by numerous studies that have found that deliberating juries tend to be more willing than nondeliberating jurors to set aside evidence they have been instructed to disregard.[104] Moreover, one of the more comprehensive jury deliberation studies to date found that deliberating "[j]uries worked hard to understand the law" and "spent an average of 21 percent of their time discussing the judge's instructions, primarily during the latter half of the[ir] hour[-long deliberation]."[105] Although the author of this study found no basis to conclude that these discussions actually improved overall understanding of the instructions, the external validity/applicability of this finding is significantly undercut by two design limitations that are characteristic of research in this area. First, while deliberations are supposed to enhance comprehension by creating space for jurors to seek clarification from judges and written copies of their instructions, in this experiment, jurors did not have access to either.[106] Second, comprehension of the instructions was tested by having jurors answer a series of true/false questions at the end of a mock deliberation that the jurors knew would last for precisely one hour, regardless of whether they reached a verdict or not.[107] Arguably, had they been put to the task of reaching a single, unanimous verdict, and

104. Shaffer & Wheatman, *supra* note 99, at 658.

105. Phoebe C. Ellsworth, *Are Twelve Heads Better Than One?*, 52 L. & CONTEMP. PROBS. 205, 218 (1989).

106. *Id.* at 224. The importance of judicial clarification of jury instructions is confirmed by just how often appellate courts are called upon to decide whether a judge has appropriately responded to a question posed by the jury. Over the course of the last decade, the D.C. Court of Appeals has addressed such an issue in at least seventeen published cases. *See Young v. United States*, 305 A.3d 402 (D.C. 2023); *Evans v. United States*, 304 A.3d 211 (D.C. 2023); *Johnson v. United States*, 290 A.3d 500 (D.C. 2023); *Gordon v. United States*, 285 A.3d 199 (D.C. 2022); *Parker v. United States*, 249 A.3d 388 (D.C. 2021); *Lucas v. United States*, 240 A.3d 328 (D.C. 2020); *Fitzgerald v. United States*, 228 A.3d 429 (D.C. 2020); *White v. United States*, 207 A.3d 580 (D.C. 2019); *Cheeks v. United States*, 168 A.3d 691 (D.C. 2017); *Buskey v. United States*, 148 A.3d 1193 (D.C. 2016); *Thomas v. United States*, 137 A.3d 166 (D.C. 2016); *Colbert v. United States*, 125 A.3d 326 (D.C. 2015); *Sanders v. United States*, 118 A.3d 782 (D.C. 2015); *Foreman v. United States*, 114 A.3d 631 (D.C. 2015); *Washington v. United States*, 111 A.3d 16 (D.C. 2015); *Shuler v. United States*, 98 A.3d 200 (D.C. 2014); *see also, e.g., Bost v. United States*, 178 A.3d 1156 (D.C. 2018).

107. Ellsworth, *supra* note 105, at 212 ("We did not ask them to vote at the end of the hour, and we did not expect them to reach a verdict.").

given indefinite time in which to do so, they would have felt more pressure to come to a common understanding of the applicable law, and thus would have tried harder to resolve disagreements about what the instructions required. It is for this reason that researchers have criticized "data collection techniques that do not reflect the reality of the juror's task at trial."[108]

Studies purporting to establish a generalized "skepticism effect" from instructions that explain the potential pitfalls of eyewitness identification are equally limited. Notably, in two of these studies, the research design was "hampered by the fact that the evidence against the defendant was weak even in the version of the experiment where it was supposed to be strong."[109] Thus, while both of these studies reported a skepticism effect based on the administration of a more comprehensive instruction, "*skepticism was an entirely appropriate attitude*."[110] Significantly, "both studies found that rewritten instructions improved juror comprehension of the relevant issues when compared to no instruction at all, or the *Telfaire* instruction."[111] Against this backdrop, "all that can really be said on the basis of the experimental studies on the effectiveness of jury instructions about eyewitness identification evidence is that they are inconclusive" because "[t]he studies are . . . 'few in number [and] plagued with methodological problems. . .'"[112]

---

108. Leverick, *supra* note 50, at 566 & n.72 (citing Wayne Weiten & Shari S. Diamond, *A Critical Review of the Jury Simulation Paradigm: The Case of Defendant Characteristics*, 3 L. & HUM. BEHAV. 71 (1979)). By contrast, there appears to be some basis to conclude that using college students as mock jurors does not necessarily undermine the validity of an experiment. *See* Brian H. Borstein et al., *Mock Juror Sampling Issues in Jury Simulation Research: A Meta-Analysis*, 41 L. & HUM. BEHAV. 13 (2017), https://doi.org/10.1037/lhb0000223.

109. Leverick, *supra* note 50, at 566.

110. *Id.*

111. *Id.*

112. *Id.* at 573 & n.72 (citing Lisa D. Dufraimont, *Regulating Unreliable Evidence: Can Evidence Rules Guide Juries and Prevent Wrongful Convictions?*, 33 QUEEN'S L.J. 261, 301 (2008)).

Epilogue: On the Importance of Persistence and Vigilance

Lest the preceding chapters leave you with the false impression that the past few decades have been a continuous string of eyewitness identification reform victories, I offer the following cautionary tale. In *Dennis v. Secretary, Pennsylvania Department of Corrections*,[1] a habeas case in which the underlying conviction relied primarily on eyewitness testimony, Chief Judge McKee "wr[o]te separately to underscore the problems inherent in eyewitness testimony and the inadequacies of our standard jury instructions relating to that evidence."[2] "Jury instructions," the chief judge continued, "must educate jurors on the relevant scientific findings regarding eyewitness reliability in order to mitigate the dangers associated with inaccurate eyewitness identifications."[3] For this reason, he believed that "the standard instructions" used in Dennis's case, which were based on *Telfaire*, were "not only insufficient, they [were] misleading."[4]

1. 834 F.3d 263 (3d Cir. 2016)
2. *See id.* 313 (McKee, C.J., concurring).
3. *Id.*
4. *Id.* Although Dennis went to trial in 1991, before the Third Circuit adopted model jury instructions (in 2004), the instruction given in his case nevertheless approximated the

The chief judge went on to note that "[s]ince *Manson*, more than 2,000 scientific studies have been conducted on the reliability of eyewitness identifications" and that those studies had revealed "that even seemingly neutral identification procedures can lead to unreliable results due to a myriad of subtle variables" and "that a witness' subjective confidence in the accuracy of her identification has limited correlation to the reliability of her identification."[5] Based on those studies, studies on jury understanding of memory, *Henderson*, and *Lawson*, Chief Judge McKee condemned the "plain vanilla" instruction that Dennis received, noting the need for the jury "to be informed of the applicable [system and estimator] variables before they [could] be in a position to exercise [due] caution" in their verdict.[6]

Telfaire instruction, which would serve as the basis for the Third Circuit's pattern instruction. Dennis's jury was instructed:

> There have been several Commonwealth identification witnesses. . . . However, a mistake can be made in identifying a person even by a witness attempting to be truthful.
>
> Where the opportunity for positive identification is good and the witness is positive in his or her identification and his or her identification is not weakened by prior failure to identify but remains, even after cross-examination, positive and unqualified, the testimony as to identification need not be received with caution and can be treated as a statement of fact.
>
> On the other hand, where a witness is not in a position to clearly observe the assailant or is not positive, as to identity, or his or her positive statements as to identity are weakened by qualification or by inconsistencies or by failure to identify the defendant on one or more prior occasions, then the testimony as to identification must be received with caution. You have heard the testimony in this case to the effect, and I leave it to your judgment and for your determination, but my recollection is that there were some prior identifications that were less than unqualified or positive. I think that's been gone over at length by counsel. Under those circumstances, you should receive the testimony with caution. But it's for you to determine whether or not this is so, you decide whether the testimony was weakened and what the evidence was.
>
> If, according to these rules, you decide that caution is required in determining whether or not to accept the testimony of the identifying witnesses, then you must take into consideration the following matters: A, whether the testimony of the identification witness is generally believable; B, whether his or her opportunity to observe was sufficient to allow him or her to make an accurate identification; C, how the identification was arrived at; D, all of the circumstances indicating whether or not the identification was accurate; and E, whether the identification testimony is supported by other evidence. And you must conclude that it is so supported before you can accept it as being accurate.
>
> My advice to you is this. In this case, my recollection, that's why I'm not being so emphatic, my recollection is that one of the witnesses said, "I think[,]" [] another witness, for example, said, at a certain time, "I can't be sure." Witnesses who testified that way, their testimony as to identification should be received with caution and you should follow the rules that I've given you.

Id. at 342.

5. *Id.* at 335.
6. *Id.* at 342.

Judge Ambro joined in the concurrence, and Judge Rendell, the author of the majority opinion, described it as "masterful."[7]

Following *Dennis*, the Third Circuit convened a Task Force on Eyewitness Identifications to "make recommendations regarding jury instructions, use of expert testimony, and other procedures and policies intended to promote reliable practices for eyewitness identification and to effectively deter unnecessarily suggestive identification procedures, which raise the risk of a wrongful conviction."[8] The Task Force, in turn, produced a 120–page, single-spaced report, which made best practice recommendations in a number of areas related to eyewitness identification. Although the Task Force declined to recommend any changes to the Third Circuit's model jury instruction on identification out of deference to the Committee on Model Criminal Jury Instructions, which was ultimately responsible for drafting the Circuit's model jury instructions, Judge McKee and Professor Jules Epstein recommended six changes to improve the model instruction:

1. "[A]dd language regarding system variables, including lineups, photo arrays, and show-up, which are not addressed in [the instruction]."
2. Add an instruction that "an honest and sincere witness may be mistaken."
3. "Remov[e] existing language directing jurors to consider whether the witness was certain on the stand or shaken-by cross-examination."
4. Add "weapon focus" and changes in appearance to the list of estimator variables covered in the instruction.
5. Add a note that identifications should be received by the jury with "caution" when certain estimator variables (such as cross-racial identification) were present.
6. Add an instruction that memory may be affected by suggestive influences, such as seeing the same suspect in multiple identification procedures.

Even so, the Committee on Model Criminal Jury Instructions rejected all but the third recommendation.[9] This vignette stands as a testament to the fact that there is nothing inevitable about progress. Persist.

---

7. *Id.* at 270 n.3.

8. United States Courts for the Third Judicial Circuit, Order, *available at* http://www.ca3.uscourts.gov/sites/ca3/files/TFEyewitnessIdOrder_11042016.pdf.

9. Third Circuit Model Jury Instructions—Criminal 4.15 (2022).

Index

Figures have an italicized *f* after the page number (123*f*).

Beck, misidentification and imprisonment of Adolf, 60–61, 61*f*
behaviorism, lack of credibility of forensic psychology and rise of, 126–127

D

E

G

M

O

P

S